Religion and Law in Spain

Religion and Law in Spain

Second Edition

Javier Martínez-Torrón

This book was originally published as a monograph in the International Encyclopaedia of Laws/Religion.

Founding Editor: Roger Blanpain
General Editor: Frank Hendrickx
Volume Editor: Rik Torfs

Wolters Kluwer

Published by:
Kluwer Law International B.V.
PO Box 316
2400 AH Alphen aan den Rijn
The Netherlands
E-mail: international-sales@wolterskluwer.com
Website: lrus.wolterskluwer.com

Sold and distributed in North, Central and South America by:
Wolters Kluwer Legal & Regulatory U.S.
7201 McKinney Circle
Frederick, MD 21704
United States of America
Email: customer.service@wolterskluwer.com

Sold and distributed in all other countries by:
Air Business Subscriptions
Rockwood House
Haywards Heath
West Sussex
RH16 3DH
United Kingdom
Email: international-customerservice@wolterskluwer.com

Printed on acid-free paper

ISBN 978-94-035-0043-0

e-Book: ISBN 978-94-035-0044-7
web-PDF: ISBN 978-94-035-0045-4

Printed in the United Kingdom.

The Author

Javier Martínez-Torrón is Professor of Law at Complutense University (Madrid) and doctor *utroque iure* (of Law and of Canon Law). Born in 1955, he studied Law and Canon Law at the Universities of Seville, Granada and Navarra. He joined the Law School of Complutense University in 1984 as associate professor. He obtained his first chair as *catedrático* at the University of Granada, in 1993, where he was director of the area of Law and Religion (1993–2000) and founded the seminar of comparative law in 1997. In 2000, he returned to Complutense University, where he has been director of the Department of Law and Religion (2009–2017). He has taught, lectured or been visiting scholar at more than eighty universities of the five continents, among them Cambridge, Oxford, Harvard, Chicago, Berkeley, Columbia, Stanford, Ottawa, Freiburg (Germany), Turin, UNAM (National Autonomous University of Mexico), Haifa, and Catholic University of Chile. Since 2001, he has been teaching Comparative Law at the Summer Law Courses of Saint Louis University (Madrid campus).

He is Vice-President of the Department of Canon Law and Church-State Relations of the Spanish Royal Academy of Jurisprudence and Legislation (1994). He has been a member of the Advisory Commission on Religious Freedom in the Spanish Ministry of Justice (2002–2014) and of the OSCE/ODIHR Advisory Council on Freedom of Religion of Belief (2005–2013).

He was a member of the founding directive board of the first Spanish legal periodical specifically focused on law and religion studies (*Anuario de Derecho Eclesiástico del Estado*, 1985). He is the founder and co-editor of the *Revista General de Derecho Canónico y Derecho Eclesiástico del Estado* (2003), the first electronic legal periodical in Spain specialized on law and religions issues and canon law. He is also a member of the editorial boards of the *Ecclesiastical Law Journal* (2006) and the *Oxford Journal of Law and Religion* (2011), as well as of the International Advisory Board of the *Revista Latinoamericana de Derecho y Religión* (Chile, 2015).

He is the author of numerous books and articles, published in 23 countries – 22 books as author or editor and more than 120 essays in legal periodicals or book chapters. His

writings have been published in Spanish, English, Italian, French, Russian, Polish, Lithuanian, Slovakian, Turkish, Indonesian, Chinese, Vietnamese and Catalan. His research is characterized by a predominant interest in comparative and international law issues relating to the treatment of freedom of religion and belief, and to the evolution of Western legal traditions. In 1998 he received the Arturo Carlo Jemolo Award (University of Turin) for his book *Le obiezioni di coscienza. Profili di diritto comparato* (co-authored with Rafael Navarro-Valls, 1995).
His other books include: *Separatismo y cooperación en los acuerdos del Estado con las minorías religiosas* (1994); *Anglo-American Law and Canon Law. Canonical Roots of the Common Law Tradition* (1998); *Religión, derecho y sociedad* (1999); *Conflictos entre conciencia y ley. Las objeciones de conciencia*, with Rafael Navarro-Valls (2nd ed., 2012); *Tensiones entre libertad de expresión y libertad religiosa* (editor with Santiago Cañamares, 2014); *Religion and the Secular State* (editor with W. Cole Durham Jr, 2015); and *Great Christian Jurists in Spanish History* (editor with Rafael Domingo, forthcoming in April 2018).

Table of Contents

The Author 3

List of Abbreviations 13

Preface 15

General Introduction 17

§1. General Background of the Country 17

I. Basic Information 17
II. Political and Legal Structure 19

§2. Social Facts about Religion 20

§3. Historical Background: Religion in the History of Spain 23

I. First to Fifteenth Centuries 23
II. Fifteenth to Twentieth Centuries 25
III. From the Second Republic to General Franco's Regime 28

Part I. Legal Framework and Sources 31

Chapter 1. Constitutional Position of Religion 31

Chapter 2. Other Legislations with Regard to Religion 35

§1. The Organic Law on Religious Freedom 35

§2. Agreements with the Holy See (the Concordat) 40

§3. Cooperation Agreements with Other Religious Communities 41

§4. Other Laws and Regulations 42

Chapter 3. Typology of the System 44

§1. Religious Freedom 44

§2. Equality 45

§3. State Neutrality 47

§4. State Cooperation with Religion 47

§5. Bilateral Sources of Law 49

§6. Case Law of the Constitutional Court with Respect to the 'Informing' Principles 49

Part II. Religious Freedom in General 53

Chapter 1. Individual Religious Freedom 53

§1. Normative Framework 53

§2. Protected Aspects of Religious Freedom 55

I. Internal and External Dimension of Religious Freedom 55
II. Freedom to Choose 56
III. Freedom to Manifest or Not to Manifest 57
IV. Freedom of Worship 58
V. Right to Religious Assistance 60
VI. Freedom of Teaching 60
VII. Right to Non-discrimination 61
VIII. Freedom of Conscience 62
IX. Compliance with Religious Dietary Rules 63

§3. Judicial Protection of Religious Freedom 64

§4. Protection of Religious Freedom by Criminal Law 66

§5. Limitations on Religious Freedom 66

§6. Parental Custody and the Religious Freedom of Minors 69

Chapter 2. Freedom of Conscience and Legal Obligations: Conscientious Objections 73

§1. Concept of Conscientious Objection 73

§2. Some Basic Criteria for the Legal Analysis of Conscientious Objections 74

§3. The General Position of the Constitutional Court 76

§4. Conscientious Objection to Military Service 78

§5. Conscientious Objection to Abortion 80

§6. Conscientious Objections of Pharmacists 80

§7. Conscientious Objection to Medical Treatments 80

§8. Conscientious Objection to Educational Contents or Practices 81

I. School Activities and Religious Observance of Holy Days 81
II. Freedom of Conscience and Homeschooling 82
III. Objection to Specific School Subjects 83
IV. The Case of Conscientious Objection to Education for Citizenship 84

§9. Freedom of Conscience and Religious Symbols 88

I. The Use of Personal Religious Symbols in the School Environment 89
II. The Use of Personal Religious Symbols in Public Spaces 90
III. The Use of Personal Religious Symbols at Work 93
IV. 'Secular' Objections to the Use of Religious Symbols in Public Institutions 94

§10. Conscientious Objections in Labour Relations 97

I. European and Spanish Normative Framework 97
II. The Restrictive Approach of 1992 Agreements to the Observance of Sabbath 98
III. The Case Law on Sabbath Rest 100
IV. Other Claims of Indirect Religious Discrimination in Employment 101

§11. Conscientious Objection in the Public Service 101

I. Conscientious Objection to Promissory Oaths 101
II. Conscientious Objection to Be Part of a Jury 103
III. Conscientious Objection to Be Part of a Polling Station 105
IV. Conscientious Objection to Perform a Ceremony of Same-Sex Marriage 106

Chapter 3. Collective Religious Freedom 108

Chapter 4. Organizational Religious Freedom 113

Table of Contents

§1. LEGAL PERSONALITY, RELIGIOUS FREEDOM AND STATE COOPERATION WITH RELIGIOUS COMMUNITIES 113

§2. THE REGISTRY OF RELIGIOUS ENTITIES 116

I. Basic Notions and Structure 116
II. Process and Effects of Registration 117
III. The RER and the Legal Concept of Religion 119
IV. Registration of Internal Associations and Foundations of Religious Communities 121

§3. THE ADVISORY COMMISSION ON RELIGIOUS FREEDOM 123

Part III. Legal Status of Religious Communities 127

Chapter 1. Formal Status of Religious Communities 127

Chapter 2. Autonomy of Religious Communities 132

Chapter 3. Places of Worship and Meeting 134

§1. A BROAD CONCEPT OF PLACE OF WORSHIP 134

§2. THE INVIOLABILITY OF PLACES OF WORSHIP 135

§3. PLACES OF WORSHIP AND URBAN PLANNING 136

§4. PRIVILEGES CONCERNING EXPROPRIATION, DEMOLITION, IMMUNITY FROM SEIZURE AND TAXES 139

Chapter 4. Fundamental Rights and Religious Communities 140

§1. THE PROTECTION OF FUNDAMENTAL RIGHTS OF RELIGIOUS COMMUNITIES 140

§2. THE PROTECTION OF FUNDAMENTAL RIGHTS BY RELIGIOUS COMMUNITIES 141

Chapter 5. Contractual Religious Freedom 144

§1. THE CONCORDAT WITH THE CATHOLIC CHURCH 144

§2. COOPERATION AGREEMENTS WITH OTHER RELIGIOUS COMMUNITIES 148

Chapter 6. Religious Assistance in Public Institutions 152

Part IV. International, Transnational, Regional Effects on Religious Communities 157

Chapter 1. International Law Effects on Religious Communities 157

Chapter 2. Transnational Law Effects on Religious Communities 162

Chapter 3. Regional Law Effects on Religious Communities 164

Part V. Religion and Politics 165

Chapter 1. Religion Influence in Politics 165

Chapter 2. Political Influence in Religion 168

Chapter 3. Interaction Between Religion and State on a Political and Legal Level 170

Part VI. Labour Law Within Religious Communities 173

Chapter 1. Scope of Application of Labour Law 173

Chapter 2. Religious Ministers and Labour Law 174

Chapter 3. Other Church Employees and Labour Law 177

Part VII. Religious Communities and Protections of the Individual 181

Chapter 1. Protection of Privacy 181

Chapter 2. Freedom to Marry 184

Chapter 3. Freedom of Expression 186

Chapter 4. Due Process Norms and Religious Groups 187

Chapter 5. Professional Secrecy 189

Chapter 6. Medical Deontology 191

§1. Conscientious Objection to Abortion 191

§2. Conscientious Objections of Pharmacists 193

§3. Conscientious Objection to Medical Treatments 195

Table of Contents

I. The Law on the Patient's Autonomy 195
II. Objection to Medical Treatment of Adults 196
III. Objection to Medical Treatment of Minors 197
IV. Objection to Medical Treatment and Criminal Liability 198
V. Objection to Medical Treatment and Reimbursement of Hospital Expenses 199

Chapter 7. Non-discrimination 201

Chapter 8. Penal Law and Religion 203

Part VIII. Church Financing 209

Chapter 1. Direct Financing of Religious Communities 210

§1. Direct Financing of the Catholic Church 210

§2. Direct Financing of Other Religious Communities 211

Chapter 2. Indirect Financing of Religious Communities 214

§1. Non-taxation and Tax Exemptions 214

§2. Tax-Deductible Donations 216

§3. Other Economic Contributions 217

Part IX. Education 219

Chapter 1. Religious Education in Public and Private Schools 220

§1. Teaching of Catholic Religion 221

I. The Normative Framework 221
II. The Case Law of the Constitutional Court 224
A. Courses on Catholic Religion 224
B. Religion Teachers 225

§2. Teaching of Religious Doctrines Other than Catholic 225

§3. The Possibility of Neutral Teaching on Religions and Beliefs 227

§4. Religious Symbols in Public Schools 229

Chapter 2. Religious Schools 230

Part X. Matrimonial and Family Law 233

Chapter 1. Legal Position of Religious Marriage 233

§1. The Right to a Religious Marriage 233

§2. The Civil Effects of Catholic Marriages 235

§3. The Civil Effects of Religious Marriages Other than Catholic 241

Chapter 2. Legal Position of Religious Family Law 244

Part XI. Religion and Culture 247

Chapter 1. Religion and Art 247

Chapter 2. Religion and Media 250

Chapter 3. Religion and Civil Society 253

Chapter 4. Religion and Public Debate 254

Selected Bibliography 257

Index 271

List of Abbreviations

AAP	Admissibility decision of a Provincial Court (*Auto de Audiencia Provincial*)
ATC	Admissibility decision of the Constitutional Court (*Auto del Tribunal Constitucional*)
ATS	Admissibility decision of the Supreme Court (*Auto del Tribunal Supremo*)
ATSJ	Admissibility decision of a Superior Court of Justice (*Auto de Tribunal Superior de Justicia*)
CALR	Advisory Commission on Religious Freedom (*Comisión Asesora de Libertad Religiosa*)
CC	Civil Code (*Código Civil*)
CE	Spanish Constitution (*Constitución Española*)
	Charter of Fundamental Rights of the European Union
CP	Criminal Code (*Código Penal*)
ECHR	European Convention on Human Rights
ECtHR	European Court of Human Rights
EU	European Union
FJ	As to the law (*Fundamento Jurídico*, in judicial decisions)
JPI	First Instance Court (*Juzgado de Primera Instancia*)
LO	Organic Law (*Ley Orgánica*)
LOLR	Organic Law on Religious Freedom (*Ley Orgánica de Libertad Religiosa*)
RD	Royal Decree (*Real Decreto*)
RER	Registry of Religious Entities (*Registro de Entidades Religiosas*)
SAN	Judgment of the National Court (*Sentencia de la Audiencia Nacional*)
SAP	Judgment of a Provincial Court (*Sentencia de Audiencia Provincial*)
STC	Judgment of the Constitutional Court (*Sentencia del Tribunal Constitucional*)
STS	Judgment of the Supreme Court (*Sentencia del Tribunal Supremo*)
STSJ	Judgment of a Superior Court of Justice (*Sentencia de Tribunal Superior de Justicia*)
UDHR	Universal Declaration of Human Rights
VAT	Value Added Tax

List of Abbreviations

Preface

Law and religion studies have a long tradition in Spain. For centuries, as a result of the conception of Spain as a confessional Catholic state, these studies focused on the relations between the Catholic Church and the Spanish state, as well as on the effects of canon law provisions and institutions in Spanish law. When in the mid-1970s the Spanish transition to democracy began, the academic study of law and religion – inspired by Italian scholarship, which had already experienced an analogous process long before – gradually shifted to the analysis of the state law on religious issues from the perspective of religious freedom and state neutrality vis-à-vis religion, in accordance with international standards. This has been the predominant view since then, giving rise to a specific area of legal studies that was called *derecho eclesiástico del estado* – which literally means ecclesiastical law of the state – following the German and Italian terminology.

The last decades have witnessed a clear evolution of Spanish law and society towards the acceptance of religious pluralism as an indicator of freedom and democracy rather than as a source of problems, as had often occurred in the past. In this respect, it is fair to say that Spanish scholarship on law and religion issues has been, in the recent history of Spain, a powerful influence that helped democratization in this particular area of public law. The legislator has frequently looked for advice among Spanish law and religion scholars. The specific office in charge of religious issues in the Ministry of Justice has very often been trusted to a professor of law and religion. Key decisions of the Constitutional Court in this area have been influenced by scholarly writings (although these are not cited, in accordance with the praxis of the Court).

The teaching of *derecho eclesiástico del estado* is common in Spanish universities and has inherited the academic position formerly held by the teaching of canon law. Not long ago, courses on law and religion were mandatory in the curriculum of all law schools across the country. After the decentralization of law curricula, most law schools have retained such courses, either with mandatory or with optional character. There are many legal scholars in Spain – around 200 – with a primary specialization in law and religion. This fact has produced, over the years, an immense bibliography, of which only a small selection is offered here. While taking into account such scholarly contributions and pointing out problematic or difficult issues, this monograph leaves aside sophisticated doctrinal discussions and concentrates on an explanation – as clear as possible – of the current Spanish law on religious issues. Such explanation has been conceived thinking of the information that could be of special interest from a comparative perspective and for a foreign reader.

By and large, we can affirm that this area of Spanish law works reasonably well. Indeed it has been often presented as an example to many other countries and has influenced – in a positive way – legal developments in Latin America in the late twentieth and the early twenty-first centuries. It is, however, far from perfection, especially from two perspectives: the application of the principle of equality with regard to religious minorities and the protection of individual rights of conscience in cases of conflict with 'neutral' state laws. For this reason, although description tends to prevail over analysis in the pages of this monograph, many critical remarks have been included, in order to highlight which aspects of Spanish law have proved to be until now unsatisfactory – at least in the author's view.

General Introduction

§1. General Background of the Country

I. Basic Information

1. Spain is located at the southwestern corner of Europe and, together with Portugal, forms the Iberian Peninsula (Spain comprises approximately 80% of the Peninsula). Part of the Spanish territory, however, is extra-peninsular – namely the Balearic Islands, the Canary Islands and the autonomous cities of Ceuta and Melilla, on the north coast of Africa. The total extension of the country is approximately 505,000 km^2. The capital city is Madrid, at the centre of the Peninsula; it is also the largest city in the country and, together with Barcelona, the most important nucleus of economic and industrial life in Spain. The Spanish geography is as diverse as the people of its different regions. Climate is equally diverse and includes various climatic zones: Mediterranean, continental, oceanic, semi-arid and subtropical.

2. According to official statistics of 2016, the population of Spain is estimated in more than 46 million, of which approximately 10% (4.6 million) are foreign residents.[1] The largest part of foreigners are from Europe (more than 2 million); together with a large population of immigrants from Eastern European countries who mainly came to Spain to work (1.2 million), there is another large number of citizens from Western European countries (850,000) many of which are retired people that have settled in some of the nice coastal places in Spain. Citizens of American origin still constitute the largest non-European community of immigrants (almost 1.1 million), most of them from Latin America, but the figures have been decreasing in the last years (not long ago they were almost 2 million). The population of African extraction is over 1 million, most of them from Morocco (750,000). Asian population is on the rise (around 420,000, half of which are from China).[2] About one-third of the population is concentrated in Madrid, Barcelona and four other large cities. Ethnically Spain has been traditionally quite uniform (white Caucasian, if we follow the usual North-American terminology), with the exception of the Gipsy minority, which is especially abundant in the South, in Madrid, in Barcelona, and in Valencia, with a total estimated population of about

---

1. National Institute of Statistics (*Instituto Nacional de Estadística*). *See* http://www.ine.es/dyngs/INEbase/es/operacion.htm?c=Estadistica_C&cid=1254736177012&menu=ultiDatos&idp=1254734710990 (accessed 9 Dec. 2017).
2. *See* http://www.ine.es/dynt3/inebase/index.htm?type=pcaxis&path=/t20/e245/p04/provi&file=pcaxis&dh=0&capsel=0 (accessed 9 Dec. 2017).

650,000.[3] Although white predominance still clearly subsists, the panorama has changed in the last decades with immigration, which has introduced a relatively large population of Arabic, Andean, Afro-American (above all from Dominican Republic), Chinese and Indian ethnic origin. The change is particularly visible in large cities.

3. The main official language is Spanish, one of the tongues that developed from Latin. Spanish is also the dominant language, spoken by the virtual entirety of the native population and legal aliens. There is bilingualism in some regions that possess a historical autochthonous language, especially Catalonia, Basque Country, Galicia, Balearic Islands and Valencia. Those are considered also official languages within their respective regions or *comunidades autónomas*. In 2016 it was reported that there were more than 650,000 people in a state of functional illiteracy, most of them aged over 50.[4] The net enrolment ratio in university studies is more than 30%.[5]

4. Spanish culture, of very ancient origins, is rich and diversified. It has produced masterpieces and has had a broad influence in other cultures, in virtually all branches – most remarkably in literature, painting, sculpture, architecture and theatre. Also in the area of law Spain has made significant contributions; it has provided many notable jurists over the centuries, most of them profoundly influenced by their Christian faith.[6] The cultural heritage of Spain is enormous, widespread across the country and very valuable; a large part of it is of ecclesiastical origin. The ancient Iberian peoples were unified under Roman rule; Rome gradually occupied the Peninsula beginning in 218 BC. The first time Spain became an independent kingdom was with the Visigoths, in the fifth century AD. In 711, however, the Muslim invasion of the Peninsula broke political unity and led to the presence of the Islamic rule in the territory, in continuous tension and war with Christian kingdoms, until the end of the fifteenth century. The contemporary political unity of Spain dates back to 1492, when the united crowns of Castile and Aragon conquered the last Muslim bastion – the Nasrid kingdom of Granada.

5. Spanish currency is Euro since 2002. Spain is economically a well-developed country and the fourteenth-largest economy in the world (the fifth-largest one in Europe). Its estimated GDP in 2016 was USD 1,232 million with a growth ratio of 3.2% and a GDP per capita of USD 36,290. It has modern infrastructures and communications, and possesses a diversified economy in the three sectors. Tourism is a major source of income for the country – it represents about 10% of the GDP and, with respect to international tourism receipts, Spain is ranked number two in the world, after the USA. In the last years, the country is overcoming the financial difficulties it experienced after the crisis of the mid-2000s. After some years of the unemployment rate dramatically increasing (by the end of 2012, according to the official figures, it

---

3. The numbers of Gipsy population in Spain are not certain. The figure of 650,000 is provided by studies published by the Foundation *Secretariado Gitano*, the main non-profit organization working with Gipsy people in Spain. Cf. http://www.gitanos.org/publicaciones/guiasalud/cultura_02.pdf (accessed 9 Dec. 2017).
4. *See* https://www.efe.com/efe/espana/sociedad/en-espana-hay-casi-700-000-personas-analfabetas/10004-3034673 (accessed 9 Dec. 2017).
5. Cf. https://sede.educacion.gob.es/publiventa/descarga.action?f_codigo_agc=18170 (accessed 9 Dec. 2017).
6. *See Great Christian Jurists in Spanish History* (R. Domingo & J. Martínez-Torrón eds, Cambridge U. Press, forthcoming in 2018).

reached 26%, with almost 6 million unemployed people), it has been steadily decreasing for four years; in October 2017 it was less than 17%, with 3.46 million unemployed people.[7] The public perception of these problems is that they are the result of bad governmental management – and sometimes corruption – at all levels (national, regional, local).

II. Political and Legal Structure

6. Since the Constitution was enacted in December 1978, Spain is a parliamentary monarchy with a hereditary constitutional monarch as head of state. Article 1 of the Constitution proclaims the rule of law and the supreme values that inspire the legal system, namely freedom, justice, equality and political pluralism. Articles 10–55 of the Constitution are devoted to the protection of fundamental rights and must be interpreted in accordance with the Universal Declaration of Human Rights and the international treaties signed by Spain (Article 10.2 CE). This provision is normally understood as implicitly recognizing the interpretive supremacy of the Court of Strasbourg with respect to the freedoms guaranteed by the European Convention on Human Rights (ECHR). Taking into account this nuance, the interpretation of the Constitution is the competence of the Constitutional Court, composed by twelve judges appointed for a non-renewable nine-year term. The Court is competent to adjudicate both on the compatibility of legislation with the Constitution in the abstract and on possible violations of fundamental rights in specific cases. In this and other matters, the Spanish Constitution was inspired by the precedent German, Italian and Portuguese models.

7. The Constitution is based upon the notion that the Spanish people are sovereign and the source of political power. It is also based upon the principle of separation of powers. The King is the head of state and, as such, promulgates legislation and assumes the highest representation of the state in international relations, but he has no direct political power (although he has the supreme command of the Armed Forces).

8. As in most other countries belonging to the civil law tradition, the term 'law' in Spain is often understood as almost synonymous with legislation or statutory law. This means that the legislative power has a predominant position vis-à-vis the executive and judicial powers. The legislative power is exercised by a bicameral legislature (*Cortes*), composed by the Congress, which is the most significant legislative house, and the Senate. Members of the Congress (350) are elected by universal suffrage every four years. Members of the Senate (currently 266) are partly elected by universal suffrage (208) and partly appointed by regional legislatures (58). Spain has a multiparty system, with two main parties until recently: liberal-conservative (*Partido Popular*, PP) and socialist (*Partido Socialista Obrero Español*, PSOE). Since 2014, two other parties of national range have forcefully emerged in the political arena with increasing popularity: a new party of communist and populist orientation (*Podemos*) and a new centre party with liberal and social-democratic elements (*Ciudadanos*). There are also

7. For precise data, see the official information provided by the Ministry of Employment and Social Services: https://www.sepe.es/contenidos/que_es_el_sepe/observatorio/observatorio.html (accessed 11 Dec. 2017).

some regional parties with a minority but significant representation in the national legislature, especially some Catalan and Basque parties with separatist tendencies. In June 2016, the Popular Party (PP) won the last general election but lost the absolute majority that it previously had in the Congress, while keeping it in the Senate.

9. The executive power is exercised by the Council of Ministers, which is presided, and elected, by the President of the Government. The President is voted by the Congress and, once he has obtained absolute or relative majority, is formally appointed by the King. The minister with most direct competence on religious issues is the Minister of Justice but other ministries have competences with indirect influence in religious matters (e.g., Foreign Affairs, Education, Finance or Defence).

10. The judiciary is independent and is bound only by the rule of law. Judges are mostly professional and recruited by a specific selection process through state national examinations, which are highly competitive. Once selected, their appointment is for life. The administration of justice is divided into four main branches: civil, criminal, administrative and labour. Special jurisdictions are forbidden by the Constitution, with the exception of military courts. The Supreme Court, with its five chambers (civil, criminal, administrative, labour and military) is the highest judicial body in all branches of justice – the Constitutional Court is considered to be out of the ordinary system of justice. The court system is hierarchically structured in parallel with the administrative territorial structure of the country, each region having its own superior court (whose decisions can be appealed, with certain conditions, to the Supreme Court).[8]

11. Spain is organized as a regional state, not equivalent to but in practice not very dissimilar from a federal state. There are seventeen autonomous regions (*comunidades autónomas*) with their respective legislatures and governments, as well as with their respective capital cities. Each region is divided into provinces (with a total of fifty). Ceuta and Melilla, located in the north coast of Africa, have the special status of 'autonomous cities', with lesser competences than ordinary regions. Regions do not have their own judicial institutions – the judicial power is unitary in Spain – and their superior courts are just the result of an administrative judicial demarcation. Articles 137–158 of the Constitution regulate the distribution of competences between the central state and the autonomous regions. This distribution was not closed in 1978 and indeed the Constitution envisaged a gradual increase of the regions' competences, specified in the basic law (*estatuto de autonomía*) that governs each region. Spain is at present a very decentralized state, as the political process in the last decades has led to a progressive growth of regional competences and structures at the expense of those of the central state.

§2. Social Facts about Religion

12. There are no official statistics about religion in Spain, for Article 16.2 CE ('nobody shall be obliged to declare about his ideology, religion or belief') has been

8. For a better understanding of the judicial structure of Spain and the jurisdiction of the courts cited in different parts of this monograph, *see* the monograph published within the International Encyclopaedia of Laws by L. Bachmaier & A. del Moral García, *Criminal Law in Spain* Part II, Ch. I § 1 (2nd ed., Wolters Kluwer 2012; 3d ed. forthcoming in 2018).

traditionally interpreted as preventing the elaboration of religious statistics or censuses. Nevertheless, questions about religion or belief are included in the monthly surveys (*barómetros*) performed by the Centre of Sociological Research (*Centro de Investigaciones Sociológicas*), which is a public agency.[9] It is undisputed that the Catholic Church is the religion of the vast majority of Spanish population. The last months' surveys show that approximately 70% of the Spanish people recognize themselves as Catholic (although the percentage of people that declare a regular practice of religion is much lower). Around 15% declare to be non-believer, 10% atheist and 2.5%–3% believer in other religions.

13. The Spanish extra-peninsular cities of Ceuta and Melilla constitute a particular case because of the clearly more visible presence of Islamic population. In these enclaves, a systematic calculation was done in 1986 by the National Institute of Statistics, with the result that the percentage of Muslims was 18% in Ceuta and 32% in Melilla (12,000 and 17,000 people, respectively – these are small cities). In 2014, a study of the Royal Institute Elcano provided a percentage of nearly 50% of adults and 70% of minors in school age.[10]

14. The overall figures about the percentage of Catholics in Spain correspond, by and large, to other data concerning the religious choices of citizens. Thus, close to 70% of parents request Catholic instruction for their children during primary school.[11] Significantly, the percentage of Catholic marriages, still high, has been experiencing a trend to decline in the last years: from 76% of the total number of marriages is Spain in 2000 to 63% in 2004, 55% in 2007, 38% in 2011 and 28% in 2016.[12] These data concerning marriage, however, must be interpreted in the light of the secularization of Spanish society but also in the light the indissolubility of Catholic marriage. After a civil divorce, a Catholic cannot remarry with a third person before the Church unless an ecclesiastical court has declared his previous canonical marriage null and void according to canon law (which recognizes only a limited list of causes of nullity). Therefore, it is not infrequent the situation of people that consider themselves Catholic but, after a civil divorce of their first canonical marriage, celebrate a second – and necessarily civil – marriage.

15. Despite the fact that since the 1978 Constitution there is no longer an official religion in Spain,[13] the Catholic Church retains an enormous influence in Spanish social, cultural and political life. In many regards, Spain can be considered a country predominantly Catholic. Many Catholic traditions, rites and festivities remain popular and permeate multiple aspects of private and public life – this is especially noticeable

9. The results of the surveys can be found in: http://www.cis.es/cis/opencm/ES/11_barometros/depositados.jsp (accessed 1 Aug. 2017).
10. *See Informe Elcano 18. España mirando al Sur: del Mediterráneo al Sahel*, pp. 156 et seq. Available in: http://www.realinstitutoelcano.org/wps/portal/web/rielcano_es/publicacion?WCM_GLOBAL_CONTEXT=/elcano/elcano_es/publicaciones/informe-elcano-18-espana-mirando-al-sur-mediterraneo-sahel (accessed 9 Dec. 2017).
11. *See infra*, para. 518.
12. The percentage of marriages of other religions in 2016 was approximately 0.6%. Source: Natl. Inst. Statistics, http://www.ine.es/jaxi/Tabla.htm?path=/t20/e301/provi/l0/&file=03008.px (accessed 9 Dec. 2017).
13. *See infra*, Part I, Ch. 1 and Ch. 3.

in specific times of the year, such as Christmas, the Holy Week or Corpus Christi. A high percentage of parents have their children baptized shortly after birth – including those parents that view themselves as not practising religion. However, the presence of other religions is more and more visible every day in social life, and there is an increasing social perception of religious minorities as a positive reality in the country, although not all religious minorities receive the same consideration by the general public. In particular, there is a certain tendency to distrust new or atypical religious groups and also to view the growth of Islamic communities with some suspicion.

16. The predominance of Catholicism coexists with many people's progressive distancing from regular ritual practice and from ecclesiastical structures or hierarchies, i.e., with a certain *deinstitutionalization* of religious beliefs, which is spreading in many Western countries. In addition, public morals are now much less rooted in the Catholic doctrine than in the past. The last decades have witnessed how some significant and traditional Christian values have been fading in Spanish society, especially in the areas of sexual morals, the protection of unborn children and in general human life, integrity in personal and professional relationships, and personal compromise to help people in need (although there is a remarkable number of charitable institutions and NGOs of Catholic inspiration, with numerous young volunteers). This phenomenon is particularly visible in the youth, which, in the eyes of an external observer, seem to experience a process of polarization into two opposite attitudes: almost complete disinterest in religion and serious religious compromise. The statistics about Catholic clergymen and members of religious orders also reflect the general situation. The overall number of clergymen is close to 19,000, but many of them are of old age and the annual number of ordinations has been than two hundred in the last years (162 in 2010, 117 in 2014 and 150 in 2015). There are more than 55,000 members of religious orders or institutes.[14]

17. If we look at the number of faithful of other religions, there is no doubt that religious pluralism has been increasing in Spain in the last decades. According to the data provided by the Ministry of Justice's 2015 report on religious freedom,[15] which largely rely on data provided by the relevant religious communities, there are approximately 1.5 million Protestants in Spain (many of them are permanent residents that came from other European countries after retirement), 1.5 million Christian Orthodox, 1.9 million Muslims, 45,000 Jews, 54,000 Mormons, 190,000 Jehovah's Witnesses, and 85,000 Buddhists. At a large extent, the high number of Christian Orthodox and Muslims is due to immigration, respectively, from Eastern Europe, and from African (especially Morocco) and Asian countries. However, these data do not correspond to the numbers provided by sociological surveys,[16] and this suggests that either the figures provided by the Ministry of Justice are higher than the real ones, or the surveys conducted by the Centre of Sociological Research are not sufficiently

14. Source: Spanish Bishops Conference. *See* : http://www.conferenciaepiscopal.es/datos-generales-la-iglesia-espana/ (accessed 9 Dec. 2017).
15. *Informe anual sobre la situación de la libertad religiosa en España 2016* (there is an English version). Available in: http://www.mjusticia.gob.es/cs/Satellite/Portal/es/areas-tematicas/libertad-religiosa/informe-anual-sobre-situacion (accessed 21 Nov. 2017).
16. *See supra* , para. 12.

precise, or members of religions other than Catholic feel reluctant to give true answers in officially conducted surveys.

§3. Historical Background: Religion in the History of Spain

I. First to Fifteenth Centuries

18. When Christianity began, the Iberian Peninsula was already part of the Roman Empire (*Hispania*); with the exception of some northern territories, Spanish people had been deeply Romanized. According to an old tradition, the Peninsula was evangelized by Apostle St James the Greater (this tradition was the base for the development of the Way of St James, or *Camino de Santiago*, in the Middle Ages). Although historical research has cast serious doubts on the reliability of this tradition, it is certain that conversion to Christianity was a relatively rapid process in the Roman Hispania notwithstanding the persecutions of Christians ordered by different Roman emperors. By the late third century, Christianity was deeply rooted in the population and Spain was producing mature theologians.[17]

19. Since 409 AD, Spain was invaded by different barbarian peoples from central and northern Europe. By the fall of the Western Roman Empire, in 476, the Visigoths constituted the dominant people in the Peninsula; the Visigoths were a minority in comparison with Hispano-Roman population but they were the rulers of the territory.[18] The kingdom's religion was a matter strongly controlled by the king. In the late sixth century, the Visigoths converted from Arianism – a Christian heresy – to Roman Catholicism. The initiative was taken by King Reccared, and the Third Council of Toledo (589) was the instrument for the conversion of Arian bishops and the integration of both ecclesiastical hierarchies. The Councils of Toledo, convoked by the king but presided by an archbishop, dealt both with religious and political issues, and were an important means to organize the coexistence between Visigoths and Hispano Romans. During the seventh century, the Catholic Church gave political cohesion to the Visigothic monarchy and made significant contributions to the Spanish cultural development, with St Isidore of Seville as the central figure of that period.

20. In 711, the Visigothic kingdom of Spain fell under the Muslims' invasion. The Muslims conquered almost the whole Iberian Peninsula – which they called Al-Andalus – in an astonishingly rapid military campaign. The Islamic rulers substituted for the Christian rulers. In the 750s, an Umayyad emirate, independent of Damascus, was established in Cordoba. The golden age of Islam in Spain came when the Cordoba emirate was transformed into a caliphate in 929. From the early eighth century, the Spanish political history is, up to a great extent, the history of the struggles and alliances between the emirate/caliphate – and later the various Islamic kingdoms that succeeded it – and Christian kingdoms. The latter finally took over the entire Peninsula in the

17. For a documented history of the evolution of Christianity in Spain, *see* *Historia de la Iglesia en España* (R. García Villoslada ed., BAC 1979–1982).
18. On the religious situation under the Visigoths, *see* J. Orlandis, *La Iglesia en la España visigótica y medieval* (Eunsa 1976).

late fifteenth century; this was the end of the eighth-century period called the Reconquest (*Reconquista*).

21. In those centuries, the degrees of religious tolerance, or intolerance, in Christian and Islamic territories, respectively, varied according to political and cultural circumstances. Overt persecution of faithful of the other religion was not the rule but rather an exception. However, despite some recent idealization of the coexistence of the three monotheistic religions in Islamic territories, there was nothing comparable with a contemporary notion of religious freedom. To be Christian in a territory governed by Muslims (*mozárabe*), and vice versa (*mudéjar*), usually entailed discrimination with regard to the people's legal, social and economic status. This fact often stimulated conversions on both sides, although coerced conversion was rare.[19]

22. There were important settlements of Jewish people in Spain at least since the late first century, after the great Diaspora following the destruction of the Temple of Jerusalem by Tito in 70 AD. Significantly, the Hebrew name of Spain, Sepharad, gives name to the Jewish branch of Sephardim. Their relationships with the Catholic Church were tense and difficult, as demonstrated by some anti-Jewish provisions of the Council of Iliberis (Granada) in the early fourth century. The Arian period of the Visigothic monarchy opened a period of tolerance and ameliorated the situation of Jews. However, shortly after the kingdom's conversion to Roman Catholicism in 589, new persecutions and measures against Jews came. During the first period of the Islamic domination in Spain (eighth to eleventh centuries) Jewish people could live and develop peacefully, particularly in southern Spain.

23. After the fall of the Caliphate of Cordoba, which disintegrated into independent *taifas* or petty kingdoms at the end of the 1020s, and especially after northern African peoples (the Almoravids and the Almohads) took control of the Muslim territories in Spain in the late eleventh century, there was a massive emigration of Jewish population to the Christian kingdoms, where they could find better life conditions. Some Jews fled out of Spain, as Maimonides, who was one of the leading philosophical figures of the twelfth century.

24. In Christian territories, until the late fifteenth century, the situation of Jews oscillated between tolerance and persecution. More often than not they were subject to discriminatory measures, but it was frequent to find Jewish people occupying important positions in the world of culture, finance and sometimes politics, as had occurred in the Cordoba Caliphate. They played a central role in the School of Translators of Toledo, which constituted, throughout the twelfth century, a unique environment of exchange between Christian, Islamic and Jewish cultures, and contributed substantially to the rediscovery of ancient Greek philosophy in medieval Europe. However, the ecclesiastical pressure determined that, in the long run, anti-Semitic policies prevailed in Spain. The paradox is that the Catholic Church that urged the persecution of Jews was the same Church that promoted the mendicant orders; built the magnificent Romanic and Gothic cathedrals, so full of spirituality; and impelled the foundation of the great European universities in the Lower Middle Ages, which paved the way for the

---

19. *See* generally *Christians, Muslims, and Jews in Medieval and Early Modern Spain: Interaction and Cultural Change* (M.D. Meyerson & E.D. English eds, U. Notre Dame 1999); J. Martos Quesada, *El mundo jurídico en Al-Andalus* (Delta 2005).

Renaissance (among the fifteenth first European universities, there were five Spanish universities, including Salamanca).

II. Fifteenth to Twentieth Centuries

25. It is usually assumed that the constitution of Spain as a modern state and nation began in the late fifteenth century. Queen Isabella of Castile and King Ferdinand of Aragon, married in 1469, united the two main Spanish crowns. In 1492, they conquered the Nasrid kingdom of Granada and constituted the unified kingdom of Spain (in reality it was a plurality of kingdoms with a common monarch until the Decree of *Nueva Planta* in 1716). Significantly, Isabella and Ferdinand are known as the 'Catholic Monarchs' (*Reyes Católicos*), because the spreading and strengthening of Catholicism was one of their main goals in politics, both within the territory of the Spanish Peninsula and in the subsequent Spanish expansion in America. With them, the idea that Catholicism is part of the Spanish national identity became firmly established and remained – with manifold consequences and only a few breaks – until the late twentieth century.

26. The year 1492 was also a decisive year because of two other reasons. One is the first expedition of Christopher Columbus to America, which marked the beginning of the Spanish expansion in the New World and permitted the spreading of Christianity throughout an immense continent. The other is the expulsion of Spanish Jews, shortly followed by the expulsion of Muslims, in 1502. Jews, like Muslims, had to choose between conversion to Catholicism or exile. This led to a new Diaspora of Sephardim Jews, who spread mostly over various Mediterranean countries (the precise number of Jewish people that left the kingdom is controversial, and different sources provide figures between 40,000 and 200,000). Most Muslims remained in Spain and converted – sincerely or just formally – to Catholicism.

27. For Queen Isabella, like for the Emperor-King Charles I (1516–1556) and for his son Philip II (1556–1598), religious unity was an essential element of political unity in Spain. In their foreign policy, as well as in their domestic policy, they endeavoured to build a great Catholic empire. This idea led them to fight for the purity of Catholic doctrine in the Iberian Peninsula, to urge an intense and prompt evangelization of indigenous peoples in America, and to fight against the advance of Protestantism in Europe. Significantly, the support of Charles I and Philip II, as well as the contribution of a considerable number of Spanish bishops and theologians, were essential for the development of the Council of Trent – the council of the Catholic Counter Reformation against Protestant Reformation.

28. The main instrument utilized by the Spanish monarchy to guarantee the kingdom's religious unity was the Spanish Inquisition, founded in 1478 by Queen Isabella and King Ferdinand with papal approval.[20] Since its very beginning, the institution was controlled almost entirely by the Spanish monarchy, which put the Inquisition in the hands of the Dominican Order. Initially, the Spanish Inquisition's

20. On the Spanish Inquisition, from a comparative perspective, *see Intolerancia e Inquisición* (J.A. Escudero ed., Sociedad Estatal de Conmemoraciones Culturales 2006); *see also* J.A. Escudero, *Estudios sobre la Inquisición* (Marcial Pons 2005).

main goal was to discover and punish insincere converts from Judaism (contemptuously called *marranos*) or from Islam. After the Lutheran Reformation, the extirpation of the first Protestant cells in Spain was also a main objective.

29. The Spanish Inquisition was particularly active during the fifteenth and sixteenth centuries (although it was formally abolished only in 1848). It conducted its procedures against heresy often with extreme harshness and sometimes cruelty, although seemingly with no more cruelty than the similar Anglican and Calvinist institutions. Spanish Inquisition's procedures followed always the same pattern and were carefully recorded. They frequently ended with an *auto de fe* – a public ceremony, presided by ecclesiastical and secular authorities, in which humiliated repentant sinners acknowledged their mistakes and pertinacious heretics were severely punished, sometimes publicly burnt to death at the stake. The purpose of *autos de fe* was to show the power of the Inquisition (also called the Holy Office) and to deter people from incurring heretical beliefs.

30. The Inquisition's activity impeded the development of Protestantism in Spain. In the mid sixteenth century, there were Lutheran communities of some significance in Seville and in Valladolid (the former gained a certain momentum among popular classes, the latter involved rather the social and intellectual elites). The nobility of the Kingdom of Navarre received the influence of Calvinism – with some episodes of intolerance towards Catholic practices – especially during the second half of the sixteenth century. However, the Inquisition repressed steadily and efficiently their activities and proselytism; the *autos de fe* celebrated in Seville and Valladolid in 1559 were particularly famous and important, but there were many others throughout the rest of the century. This fact determined that Protestantism was virtually inexistent in Spain from the late sixteenth century or the early seventeenth century until the nineteenth century. It is important to keep in mind that the Inquisition was an instrument of the monarchy and was not necessarily representative of the Spanish Church's attitude as a whole. On the contrary, there were frequent conflicts and tension between the Spanish Inquisition, run by the Dominicans, and the rest of ecclesiastical institutions – including the Popes.

31. A similar inquisitorial policy was applied in the viceroyalties of America. However, these policies must be counterbalanced by the fact that, due to the influence of the Catholic Church, the Spanish colonization of America was probably – in comparative terms and despite the many abuses against the natives – the most humane of all the enterprises of that kind developed by European kingdoms in those times (the so-called *black legend* has emphasized the negative aspects of Spanish intervention in the New World; but the fact is that no other colonization in history has produced such interracial societies as the ones existing in Latin America).

32. The Church and often the Spanish Crown were sincerely interested in the evangelization of the new continent. Most of the evangelists were members of religious orders and many of them – as, e.g., Bartolomé de las Casas – defended vigorously the indigenous peoples' rights. In particular, the 'reductions' established by Jesuits reached the very heart of numerous indigenous civilizations and, along with evangelization, performed a cultural and educational work of extraordinary efficiency. Indeed, the expulsion of Jesuits from Spanish territories, decreed in 1767 by King Charles III, did a serious harm to the indigenous cause. The school of Salamanca – and particularly

Francisco de Vitoria, a Dominican himself, who is considered the founder of international law – provided philosophical and theological support for the Indians' rights, and consequently for the spiritual and cultural work of religious orders in America. As an American historian has written, 'Spain was the only colonial power in which questions of just titles, ownership of human beings, and just sovereignty arose'.[21]

33. The evolution of Christianity in Spain and Spanish America was, therefore, fundamentally Catholic. The religious unity of Spain received an additional impulse in 1609 with the expulsion of *Moriscos* – i.e., Moors apparently converted to Catholicism but who, in a considerable percentage, had preserved their tradition, culture and beliefs. Around 400,000 people left the country. This fact, like the expulsion of Jews in 1492 (and probably like the prohibition and persecution of Protestantism) caused an irreparable damage to the Spanish economy and culture.

34. Since the late fifteenth century until 1978, Catholicism was the official religion of the Spanish state, with only two ephemeral interruptions. The Catholic Church was never a state church in the technical sense, but Spain was a confessional state. Throughout the nineteenth and twentieth centuries, almost all the numerous Spanish constitutions proclaimed Catholicism as the official religion of the country – including the Constitution of 1812, which introduced the principles of liberalism in Spain. There were two exceptions: the Constitution of 1869 (abolished in 1876) and the Republican Constitution of 1931 (abolished in 1939).

35. As in other European Catholic nations, Spain's consolidation as a modern state and as an absolute monarchy was accompanied by the typical characteristics of regalism.[22] There was a reciprocal support and concession of privileges between church and state. Essentially, the state guaranteed the Catholicism of the country and granted certain economic privileges to the Church, which enjoyed an enormous social and cultural influence in the kingdom and in the American territories. In turn, the monarchy obtained political support from the ecclesiastical authorities and benefited from certain prerogatives on ecclesiastical matters (*iura maiestatica circa sacra*), especially the power to control the appointment of bishops as well as the ecclesiastical laws that would be applied in its territory. In any event, we must not lose sight that in Spain, until the second half of the twentieth century, the ecclesiastical institutions took care, up to a great extent, of some assignments that are considered today part of the welfare state's typical competences, in particular education, charity and hospitals. The cooperation between church and state was materialized in the concordats of 1717, 1737, 1753, 1851 and 1953.

36. In the long run, the state became the strongest part of this bilateral relationship, as occurred in other European regalist states and in other analogous regimes in Protestant areas. This produced an increasing tension between secular and ecclesiastical authorities. The penetration of Enlightenment ideas in Spain reinforced the position of the monarchy, and led to the expulsion of Jesuits under Charles III in 1767 (supported by most Spanish bishops). A similar attitude, together with obvious economic interests, inspired the state's massive confiscation of a great part of the immense ecclesiastical properties in

21. K. Pennington, *Bartolomé de Las Casas*, in *Great Christian Jurists in Spanish History*, cited *supra* , note 6.
22. On Spanish regalism, *see* A. de la Hera, *El regalismo borbónico en su proyección indiana* (Eunsa 1963).

Spain through the nineteenth century (*desamortización* or confiscation of mortmain property), which was particularly intense between 1834 and 1855.[23] In addition, ecclesiastical taxes – another important source of income for the Catholic Church – were suppressed in 1841. As a consequence, the Church became economically dependent on the state, a fact that substantially modified their relationship in the future.

III. From the Second Republic to General Franco's Regime

37. The status quo experienced a dramatic change in 1931, when the Second Republic was declared in Spain. The 1931 Constitution proclaimed formally the freedom of religion and conscience, but the Constitution itself and the subsequent legislation adopted a markedly hostile regulation of religious institutions, which severely restricted the Catholic Church's freedom without actually creating an environment of freedom for other religious denominations.[24] Hostility replaced cooperation. The Republican Constitution proclaimed that the Spanish state had no official religion (Article 3) and the general principle of freedom of religion and conscience (Article 27) but imposed severe restrictions on the actual freedom of ecclesiastical institutions. Thus, the same Article 27 permitted only private worship, and public acts of worship were subject to a specific governmental authorization. Article 26 considered all religious denominations as 'associations subjected to a special law', and dissolved the Order of Jesuits[25] as well as all other religious orders whose activities 'constitute a danger for the state security'. Further controls and restrictions were imposed on religious orders, in particular with regard to their capacity to acquire and administer property and their obligation to render annually their internal accounts to the state. The same Article 26 eliminated tax benefits for religious congregations and prohibited them from engaging in teaching or educational activities; the latter provision was particularly severe and in addition unrealistic, considering that most schools in Spain were in the hands of the Catholic Church at that time. These provisions did not mention specifically the Catholic Church but must be understood within the social context of the time – in Spain there were virtually no other church, no other clergy, no other religious institutions.

38. The dominant sentiment in some Republican governments – particularly at the beginning and at the end of the Republic – was not desire for freedom but rather revenge, with the explicit intention of terminating the Catholic Church's mighty social

23. On the issue of *desamortización, see* F. Tomás y Valiente, *El marco político de la desamortización en España* (Ariel 1989).

24. *See* , among others, and from different perspectives, F. de Meer, *La cuestión religiosa en las Cortes Constituyentes de la II República española* (Eunsa 1975); F. Martí Gilabert, *Política religiosa de la Segunda República española* (Eunsa 1998); *Estado y religión. Proceso de secularización y laicidad* (D. Llamazares ed., Boletín Oficial del Estado 2001).

25. This was done with under the expression: 'There shall be dissolved those religious orders whose statutes impose, in addition to the three canonical vows, an special vow of obedience to an authority different from the legitimate state authority.' As is well known, in addition to the three traditional vows of poverty, chastity and obedience, the Jesuits have a fourth vow of obedience to the Pope. The same constitutional provision decreed the confiscation of Jesuits' properties.

and cultural influence in Spanish life, which they considered excessive and incompatible with a democratic and secular state. They failed to accept the incontrovertible fact that the Church had an enormous weight in Spain's social structure. Consequently, they refused to enact moderate legislation that could reconcile the ecclesiastical influence with a democratic system and, at the same time, attract the ecclesiastical hierarchy towards the Republican cause. Although it is certainly difficult to judge the protagonists of history from a contemporary perspective, it is significant that neither the Republican Constitution's provisions on religious issues nor the legislation later enacted to implement them would pass a test based on the standards set by international documents for the protection of human rights.

39. The excessive anti-ecclesiastical reaction led to opposite reactions on the other side. Spanish society became divided into two halves from a religious perspective. This fact seriously disturbed social peace – above all when the radical leftist parties formed government in 1936 – and was one of the main causes of the Civil War 1936–1939. Thus, the effects of the Second Republic experience were not limited to merely constituting a parenthesis in the Catholic tradition of the Spanish state. The intransigence of the main political forces and their inability to agree on a common project paved the way for a three-year civil war, which led to the dictatorship of General Franco, who ruled the country until his death in 1975.

40. Franco's regime returned to the confessional state – in a 'hard' version – and was supported by most Spanish bishops until the 1960s.[26] This new age of church-state close collaboration, expressed in the 1953 Concordat with the Holy See, has been often called 'National-Catholicism', for the identification between nation and religion was again a substantial part of public policies, especially inside the country. Of course, Catholicism was not the only element of ideological cohesion in Franco's regime, but religion provided a sort of historical legitimacy to the dictator. The natural consequence was intolerance of other religions, stimulated or consented by the Catholic Church, whose official doctrine still proposed the confessional state as the ideal regime. Religious non-Catholic worship was permitted only in private. In practice, the effects of this religious intolerance were particularly detrimental for other Christian churches. Spaniards of Islamic and Jewish religion resided mainly in the Spanish territories in Northern Africa (*Protectorado Español de Marruecos*), where they enjoyed a specific legal status, more favourable than the one recognized to the non-Catholics living in the Peninsula.

41. The first manifestation of religious tolerance by Franco's regime – the 1967 Law of Religious Freedom – was prompted by the Catholic Church, which had changed some of its basic views on church-state relations in the Second Vatican Council.[27] In addition, in the late 1960s some influential Spanish bishops were overtly willing to create a new framework for the relationships of the Catholic Church with Franco's dictatorship, which was noticeably in its final stage. The 1967 Law put an end to religious intolerance in Spain and provided a better legal status to non-Catholic religious

26. On the relationships between Franco and the Catholic Church, *see* A. de la Hera, *Actitud del Franquismo ante la Iglesia*, and P. Lombardía, *Actitud de la Iglesia ante el franquismo*, both in *Iglesia Católica y regímenes autoritarios y democráticos* 43–70 and 81–102 (I.C. Ibán ed., Edersa 1987).
27. *See* especially the Council's Declaration *Dignitatis Humanæ*.

denominations. It was certainly based upon a restrictive notion of religious freedom, but probably no more restrictive – and perhaps less – than the concept of other fundamental rights and public liberties in the Spanish political context of the time.[28]

42. In the last years of Franco's government, efforts were made to update the 1953 Concordat to make it more compatible with the new legal status of religious freedom and in a way that both the state and the Catholic Church would renounce some of their respective privileges.[29] Although the negotiations reached an agreement on same basic issues, the Holy See, realizing that Franco's life and regime were close to an end, decided to wait and not to conclude any agreement with a dictatorship, fearing that it could diminish the Catholic Church's legitimacy when the democratic period began, with the consequence that it could preclude further possibilities of negotiations of a new concordat in the next future.

43. Franco died in November 1975. In July 1976, the Spanish state and the Holy See signed an agreement in which they renounced their most significant respective privileges – the *benefit of clergy* on the part of the Catholic Church and the right of *presentation of bishops* on the part of the state – and formally announced the negotiation process of a new concordat that would be more appropriate to the new political situation and replace the 1953 Concordat signed with Franco. The new concordat was composed indeed of four independent agreements on specific issues, which were signed in January 1979, a few days after the 1978 Constitution was promulgated.[30] The text of the new concordat was ready before the Constitution was in force but its signature was deliberately postponed, as a way to emphasize that it was already part of the new constitutional order that constituted the fundamentals of the emerging Spanish democracy.

---

28. On the 1967 Law, *see* M. Blanco, *La primera ley española de libertad religiosa: la génesis de la Ley de 1967* (Eunsa 1999); J. Tusell, *El impacto del Concilio Vaticano II en la política y en la sociedad española*, in *El posconcilio en España* 377–390 (J.M. Laboa ed., Encuentro 1988).
29. *See* M. Sánchez-Lasheras, *Las negociaciones concordatarias y la transición política española* (1972-1976). *El Acuerdo de 28 de julio de 1976* (Comares 2012).
30. The 1979 Concordat is explained *infra* , in Part III, Ch. 5 §1.

Part I. Legal Framework and Sources

Chapter 1. Constitutional Position of Religion

44. The current legal and political framework of religion in Spain was designed by the Constitution promulgated on 27 December 1978,[31] which transformed the precedent regime in a democratic state that meets entirely the standards of freedom characteristic of Western democracies and international law. In the years that followed, the Spanish state signed the most relevant international documents regarding human rights, including the ECHR (in force in Spain since 1979) and the International Covenant on Civil and Political Rights (in force in Spain since 1977). Spanish society, in its largest part, accepted rapidly and enthusiastically the new model of political life. The increasing religious and ideological pluralism of society was soon no longer seen by Spaniards as a negative reality, or as contrary to the Spanish traditional identity, but rather as a normal effect of freedom.

45. The 1978 Constitution, inspired by the experience of other European countries, designed a system of relations between state and religion that contrasted sharply with the record of religious and anti-religious extremism described above. In this, as in other aspects of Spain's political development, the Constitution was aimed at three fundamental objectives, which were absent in Spain's previous constitutional experience: a high degree of freedom, a broad consensus among the Spanish population and political parties, and a reasonable chance of stability.[32]

46. The 1978 Constitution is the first Spanish constitution that has provided an adequate solution to the social and political conflicts that religious ideas have traditionally caused in Spain. With the constitutional change operated in 1978, religion ceased to be, for the first time in centuries, a major divisive factor in Spanish society. The reason for this success was the transformation of the confessional state into a regime based on religious freedom, but without breaking abruptly with the nation's historical tradition. The Constitution abandoned the customary Catholic confessionality of the state – there is no more an official religion in Spain – but looked at religion as a positive social phenomenon and adopted a system of state cooperation with religion instead of a separationist model. This secured the support of the Catholic Church, of vital importance in those times of political transition to democracy, which were still full of uncertainties after thirty-six years of dictatorship (especially considering that the army's highest

31. The Constitution was officially published and entered into force on 29 Dec. 1978.
32. *See* M. López Alarcón, *La superación de la 'cuestión religiosa' como tema clave de la transición: su expresión jurídica*, 23 *Anales de Derecho* 303–314 (2005).

officers – who had been appointed by Franco – held very conservative ideas and were not particularly friendly to the political change that was taking place in Spain).[33]

47. The constitutional framework of religion is presently based upon four fundamental principles, which will be discussed below: religious freedom, equality, neutrality and cooperation.[34] Two articles of the 1978 Constitution (CE) deal directly with religion. Article 14 CE guarantees that no one can be subject to discrimination on the ground of religion (among others), and Article 16 CE recognizes the right to religious freedom and establishes the main principles that define the constitutional status of religion in Spain:

Article 14 CE:

The Spanish are equal before the law and shall not be subjected to any discrimination on the ground of birth, race, sex, religion, opinion or any other condition or circumstance, personal or social.[35]

Article 16 CE:

1. Freedom of ideology, religion and worship of individuals and communities is guaranteed with no other limitations, in their manifestations, than those necessary for the maintenance of the public order protected by law.
2. Nobody shall be obliged to declare about his ideology, religion or beliefs.
3. There shall be no state religion. Public authorities shall take into account the religious beliefs of Spanish society and shall maintain the consequent relationships of cooperation with the Catholic Church and the other denominations.

48. The terminology employed by both articles – especially Article 16 CE – is explained in the light of the Spanish historical tensions with regard to religion. Thus, 'worship' is explicitly mentioned because the past repression of this religious manifestation in moments of hostility against religion (Catholic or others). 'Ideology' was the word chosen to indicate that all beliefs are protected by the Constitution, and not only religious beliefs. Article 16.2 CE reflects the deeply felt need to prevent that any religious test could be used, once again, to discriminate people in public and social life. Article 16.3 CE put an end to the traditional Catholic confessionality of the state and at the same time made clear that public authorities, at any level, cannot ignore religion as a social phenomenon – on the contrary, when organizing public life within the limits of their respective competences, they are obliged to take into account the religious choices of citizens. The specific mention of the Catholic Church should not be interpreted as a sign of *sociological confessionality* of the state (as for example in

---

33. *See* J. Martínez-Torrón, *Religious Freedom and Democratic Change in Spain*, 2006 BYU L. Rev. 777–809 (2006).
34. *See infra* , Part I, Ch. 3.
35. Author's translation from the Spanish original into English. Unless otherwise indicated, the author is responsible for all translations included in this monograph.

Greece), but rather as an indication of the fact that Catholicism was part of 'the religious beliefs of the Spanish society'. And this, in turn, was explained by the need to avoid – when the Constitution was being drafted – any suspicion on the part of the Catholic Church that the democratic change in Spain could degenerate into the anti-religious direction that characterized the Second Republic Constitution of 1931.

49. According to Article 10.2 CE, the constitutional rules on fundamental rights and freedoms shall be interpreted in accordance with the Universal Declaration of Human Rights and the international treaties ratified by Spain. As far as religious freedom is concerned, this implies a reference to the interpretation of Articles 14 and 16 CE in the light of Articles 2 and 18 UDHR, as well as Articles 9 and 14 of the ECHR (ratified by the Spanish state in 1979) and Articles 18 and 26 of the International Covenant on Civil and Political Rights (ratified by Spain in 1977).

50. Other constitutional provisions are relevant for the legal status of religion. In addition to articles relating to other public freedoms such as the right to privacy and family life (Article 18 CE), freedom of expression (Article 20 CE), freedom of assembly (Article 21 CE) and freedom of association (Article 22 CE), the most significant provisions are those concerning education and teaching, conscientious objection to military service, and the right to marriage.

51. Article 27 CE, when recognizing the right to education, enshrines the rights of parents to guarantee that their children will receive moral and religious teaching in accordance with their own convictions. This provision is similar but not exactly equivalent to Article 2 of the Protocol to the ECHR, according to which, '[i]n the exercise of any functions which it assumes in relation to education and to teaching, the State shall respect the right of parents to ensure such education and teaching in conformity with their own religious and philosophical convictions'. The scope of the latter provision seems broader and, according to Article 10.2 CE, this is a necessary criterion of interpretation of Article 27 CE. Another important provision contained in Article 27 CE recognizes all natural and legal persons the freedom to create educational centres, which is of utmost importance for a number of churches and religious organizations:

Article 27 CE:

1. Everyone has the right to education. Freedom of teaching is recognized.
2. The purpose of education is the full development of human personality, within the respect for the democratic principles of social life and for fundamental rights and freedoms.
3. Public authorities shall guarantee the right of parents to ensure that their children will receive moral and religious instruction in accordance with their own convictions.

…

– Every natural and legal person is recognized the freedom to create educational centres, with respect for constitutional principles.

52. Article 30.2 CE recognized the right to conscientious objection to military service and referred to a subsequent statutory regulation: 'The law shall determine the military obligations of Spaniards and shall regulate, with the appropriate guarantees, conscientious objection and other causes for exemption from military service, and can impose a substitutive social service.' Five years took to implement this constitutional provision, for legislation on conscientious objection to military service would not be enacted until 1984.[36]

53. Article 32.2 CE, after recognizing the right of men and women to marry 'with full legal equality', remitted to future statutory law to regulate 'the forms of marriage, the age and legal capacity to contract marriage, the rights and duties of spouses, the causes for separation and dissolution as well as their effects'. In the years immediately following the promulgation of the Constitution, this article generated a lively academic and legislative debate on the future of the matrimonial system in Spain, and in particular about how and to what extent the state law should recognize the civil effects of religious marriages. The modifications of the Civil Code in 1981, as well as the subsequent case law of the Supreme Court, the 1979 Concordat with the Holy See, and the cooperation agreements signed by the state with some religious minorities in 1992, have clarified how religious marriages interact with the civil marriage in Spain.[37]

54. Being religious freedom a fundamental constitutional right, Articles 53.1 and 81.1 CE have also an influence on the legal regulation of religion. According to these articles, fundamental rights can only be regulated and developed by organic laws, i.e., statutory laws that require the approval of the absolute majority of the Congress.

36. *See infra*, Part II, Ch. 2 §4.
37. *See infra*, Part X.

Chapter 2. Other Legislations with Regard to Religion

§1. The Organic Law on Religious Freedom

55. The most important statute on freedom of religion, and more generally on the relations between state and religion, is the Organic Law on Religious Freedom (*Ley Orgánica de Libertad Religiosa*, hereinafter 'LOLR'), enacted on 5 July 1980 with the aim of providing the framework for all future laws and regulations dealing with religious issues.[38] This was the first organic law enacted to develop some of the fundamental rights recognized by the 1978 Constitution, which reveals that there was a sense of urgency to pass a new law that settled the legal status of religion and replaced the law promulgated by Franco in 1967. Interestingly, the LOLR kept the spirit of consensus that prevailed in the political forces during the elaboration of the Constitution and was approved by an overwhelming majority of the Congress, indeed almost by unanimous vote.[39] This fact was indicative of the acceptance of the new constitutional system of church-state relations.

56. Considering that, at the time, Spain virtually had no experience in the protection of religious freedom and that religious pluralism in the country was very limited, the LOLR was a great step forward and contributed immensely to the normalization of religious freedom in Spain and to secure the constitutional design of relations between state and religion.[40] It is true that, if we judge it from our contemporary perspective, the LOLR contains some deficiencies, mainly due to its lack of anticipation of future problems that were then difficult to predict. However, by and large it has been widely accepted and only in recent years there have been voices calling for its modification or even for its substitution by a new law.

57. The debate on the possible substitution of the LOLR arose, above all, during the socialist legislature that began in 2008 and led to the public presentation of a project for a new law that was supposed to be one of the star governmental initiatives for that legislature. However, the difficulties to reach the degree of political consensus that accompanied the parliamentary approval of the LOLR in 1980, together with many other political and economic problems that appeared with higher priority, discouraged

38. *Ley Orgánica* 7/1980, 5 Jul. 1980, *de Libertad Religiosa*. The so-called organic laws require an absolute majority in Congress to be approved, modified or abrogated. The laws governing fundamental rights and public freedoms must be organic. Cf. Art. 81 CE.

39. More precisely by 294 votes in favour, with only 5 abstentions and no votes against it. *See* , for a detailed description of the parliamentary itinerary of the LOLR, M.J. Ciáurriz, *La libertad religiosa en el derecho español. La Ley Orgánica de Libertad Religiosa* 31–91 (Tecnos 1984).

40. The essential characteristics of the new constitutional system are explained in more detail *infra* , in Part I, Ch. 3

the government from pursuing this initiative.[41] By the last months of 2011, the project for a new law on religious freedom became discretely but completely abandoned and its precise details have never been revealed to the public.

58. The 1980 LOLR is a short law, with only eight articles. Roughly speaking, it is possible to distinguish two parts in the text. The first half (Articles 1–4) refers strictly to freedom of religion or belief, while the second half (Articles 5–8) deals with the basic legal status of religious denominations in Spain.

59. The first article of the LOLR essentially reiterates the constitutional provisions of Articles 16 and 14 CE, with some specifications about the application of the equality principle to the civil service and labour relations:

Article 1 LOLR:

1. The state guarantees the fundamental right to freedom of religion and worship recognized by the Constitution, in accordance with the provisions of this organic law.
2. Religious beliefs shall not constitute ground for inequality or discrimination before the law. No religious reasons can be alleged to prevent anyone from exercising any job or activity, or from occupying public offices or positions.
3. There shall be no state religion.

60. Article 2 LOLR is of the utmost importance, for it makes explicit the essential aspects of religious freedom that are protected by law, from an individual as well as from an institutional or collective perspective (paragraphs 1–2), and it clearly states that legal protection extends also to non-religious beliefs. It is commonly agreed that the enumeration of Article 2 is not exhaustive but merely indicative. This article also emphasizes (paragraph 3) that the state's role in the protection of religious freedom is not purely passive or negative but active and positive. In other words, the state must adopt appropriate measures to ensure that the right to religious freedom can actually be exercised by every individual and group, which is consistent with Article 9.2 CE, where the same role is assigned to the state with respect to fundamental rights in general:

Article 2 LOLR:

1. The freedom of religion and worship guaranteed by the Constitution comprises the right of every person, with immunity from coercion, to:

   a. Profess the religious beliefs of his free choice or not to profess any; to change or abandon his religion; to freely manifest his religious beliefs

41. *See* , for a deep and plural discussion of the opportunity to modify the LOLR and the challenges it implies, *La libertad religiosa y su regulación legal. La Ley Orgánica de Libertad Religiosa* (R. Navarro-Valls, J. Mantecón & J. Martínez-Torrón eds, Iustel 2009). For an explanation and comment on the articles of the LOLR, *see La libertad religiosa en España. XXV años de vigencia de la Ley Orgánica 7/1980, de 5 de julio (comentarios a su articulado)* (A.C. Álvarez Cortina & M. Rodríguez Blanco eds, Comares 2006).

or his absence of religious beliefs, or to abstain from declaring about his beliefs.

b. Practice acts of worship and receive religious assistance of his own denomination; to commemorate his festivities and celebrate his matrimonial rites; to receive a proper burial, without discrimination on religious grounds; and not to be compelled to practice acts of worship or to receive religious assistance that are contrary to his personal convictions.

c. Receive and provide religious instruction and information of all types, either orally, in writing or through any other means; to choose, for himself and for the minors or legally incompetent persons under his custody, in and out of the school environment, a moral and religious instruction in accordance with his own convictions.

d. Meet or assemble publicly for religious purposes and to form associations to develop religious activities in community, in conformity with the general legal order and with the provisions of this law.

2. It [freedom of religion and worship] also includes the right of churches, religious denominations and communities to establish places of worship or meeting for religious purposes; to appoint and train their ministers; to spread and propagate their own creed; and to maintain relations with their own organizations or with other religious denominations, in national or in foreign territory.

3. To ensure the real and effective application of these rights, public authorities shall adopt the necessary measures to facilitate religious assistance in hospitals, penitentiaries, public, military and charitable establishments, and other establishments under the public authorities' aegis, as well as religious instruction in public educational centres.

61. Article 3 LOLR defines the legitimate limitations on religious freedom (paragraph 1), with a text clearly inspired by Article 9 ECHR, which extends the meaning of the limit of public order mentioned by Article 16 CE. It also states unequivocally that the LOLR is of application only to religious institutions and endeavours to distinguish them from other types of non-religious entities or activities, using a peculiar – and not completely clear – wording (paragraph 2):

Article 3 LOLR:

1. The only limitations on the rights stemming from freedom of religion and worship are the protection of the right of others to the exercise of their public freedoms and fundamental rights, as well as the safeguard of public safety, health or morals, which are the constitutive elements of the public order protected by law in a democratic society.

2. The protection provided by this law shall not apply to those activities, purposes and entities relating to the study of and experimentation with psychic and parapsychological phenomena, to the dissemination of humanistic or spiritualistic values, or to other similar non-religious aims.

62. Article 4 LOLR reiterates, with specific reference to religious freedom, the guarantee of judicial protection already offered by Article 53.2 CE:

Article 4 LOLR:

The rights recognized by this law, when exercised within the limitations stipulated by the same law, shall enjoy the judicial protection of ordinary courts and the constitutional protection of the Constitutional Court, on the terms set up by its [the Constitutional Court's] organic law.

63. Article 5 LOLR has had a great practical impact in the Spanish law on religion. This article created a specific and comprehensive registry for religious institutions, the Registry of Religious Entities (*Registro de Entidades Religiosas*, RER). The aim of this registry does not seem to be controlling the life of religious bodies in Spain – note that the registry is within the Ministry of Justice and not the Ministry of Interior – but rather providing an easy channel for religious institutions to obtain legal personality in civil law.[42] This seems to be based on the assumption that legal personality is a necessary instrument for the actual exercise of religious freedom from a collective perspective, and also a way to facilitate state cooperation with religion, as mandated by Article 16.3 CE:

Article 5 LOLR:

1. Churches, religious denominations and communities, as well as their respective federations, shall have legal personality once they have registered in the appropriate public registry that is created, for that purpose, in the Ministry of Justice.
2. Registration shall be performed after the relevant application has been filed, accompanied by authentic document stating the applicant's foundation or establishment in Spain, its religious purposes, denomination and other identification data, internal rules and representative bodies, including such bodies' representation powers and the requisites for their appointment.
3. The entries relating to a given religious entity can only be cancelled upon request of the relevant representative bodies or in execution of a final judicial order.

64. Article 6 LOLR makes explicit one of the most significant aspects of collective religious freedom: the internal autonomy of religious institutions. The law refers religious autonomy specifically to those institutions that have registered in the RER but, being an intrinsic aspect of religious freedom, analogous rights should be recognized to those religious communities that choose not to register – registration is an option, not an obligation, under Spanish law:

Article 6 LOLR:

42. *See infra*, Part II, Ch. 4 §2.

1. Registered churches, religious denominations and communities shall have full autonomy and may establish their own organization rules, internal regime and personnel regime. These rules, as well as the rules governing the institutions created by churches, religious denominations and communities for the fulfilment of their religious purposes, can include clauses aimed at safeguarding their ethos and religious identity, as well as the due respect for their beliefs, without prejudice to the respect for the rights and freedoms recognized by the Constitution and in particular freedom, equality and non-discrimination.
2. Churches, religious denominations and communities may create and promote associations, foundations and institutions for the fulfilment of their purposes, in accordance with the general provisions of the law.

65. Article 7 LOLR created an important novelty without precedents in Spanish legislation: the cooperation agreements between state and religious communities, inspired by the renovation of the Concordat with the Catholic Church in 1979. The communities entitled to these agreements are those registered in the RER and with 'well-known roots' in Spain. The latter requisite is rather vague, and its more precise definition has created unending debates among Spanish scholars and in the Ministry of Justice until 2105, when a royal decree regulated the procedure and criteria to be recognized 'well-known roots'.[43] Once a denomination has been recognized as well-known roots the cooperation agreement appears as a mere possibility and not as an automatic consequence, which means that the government has unlimited discretion to decide if and when to negotiate an agreement with a given religious denomination. Indeed – leaving aside the 1979 Catholic Concordat, which was signed long before the LOLR was enacted and followed a different procedure – only three of these cooperation agreements have been signed and approved to date, all of them at the same time, in 1992.[44] Once negotiated and signed by the government, these agreements must be approved by a specific Act of parliament. Article 7 LOLR provides little guidance about the possible content of cooperation agreements:

Article 7 LOLR.

1. The state, taking into account the religious beliefs existing in Spanish society, shall establish, when appropriate, cooperation agreements or conventions with those registered churches, religious denominations and communities which, by their extension or number of adherents, have acquired well-knows roots in Spain. In all cases these agreements shall be approved by an Act of parliament [Cortes Generales].
2. These agreements or conventions, keeping due respect for the principle of equality, may grant to the relevant churches, religious denominations and communities the tax benefits specified in the general legal order for non-profit or other charitable entities.

43. *See* RD 593/2015, 3 Jul. 2015.
44. *See* , for a further explanation and analysis, *infra* , Part III, Ch. 5 §2.

66. Finally, Article 8 LOLR created a specific consultative body, the Advisory Commission on Religious Freedom (*Comisión Asesora de Libertad Religiosa*, CALR), which is supposed to be consulted by the government with regard to all issues relating to the application of the law. This Commission was designed as having a tripartite composition, which made of it also an interesting body from the perspective of the dialogue between government and religious denominations. Of the three-thirds of the Commission, one is reserved to representatives of different departments of the government, other to representatives of the main religions existing in Spain and other to experts of renowned authority:[45]

Article 8 LOLR:

1. It is hereby created, in the Ministry of Justice, a stable Advisory Commission on Religious Freedom, composed on equal parts by representatives of the central government; by representatives of the churches, religious denominations and communities, or their federations, among which must be in any event those with well-known roots; and by persons of recognized expertise whose counselling is deemed of interest with regard to the matters related to this law. Within this Commission there may be a permanent commission, whose members shall be also equally apportioned.
2. The functions of this Commission are studying, reporting and making proposals with respect to all issues related to the application of this law; in particular its intervention shall be mandatory with respect to the preparation of and report on the cooperation agreements or conventions mentioned in the preceding article.

§2. Agreements with the Holy See (the Concordat)

67. As explained below in more detail,[46] at the beginning of the democratic transition in Spain, in 1976, the government decided to renew and modify the 1953 Concordat signed with the Holy See in the times of Franco's regime, with two purposes: reaffirming the tradition of bilateral relations between Spain and the Catholic Church, and adapting those relations to the newborn democratic Spanish state.

68. A few days after the 1978 Constitution was enacted, in January 1979, a new concordat, composed by four partial agreements, was signed with the Holy See and came into force in December of the same year. Those four agreements deal, respectively, with juridical affairs, economic affairs, education and cultural affairs, and religious assistance to the army and military service of the clergy and members of religious orders. The 1979 Concordat is recognized as having a nature similar to international treaties, and indeed it was negotiated and ratified in accordance with the rules applicable to international treaties.

45. *See* , for a further explanation and analysis, *infra* , Part II, Ch. 4 §3.
46. *See infra* , Part III, Ch. 5 §1.

69. The Concordat confers to the Catholic Church in Spain a legal status superior to the status of other religions in aspects relating to state cooperation with religion.[47] However, not every provision of the Concordat contains a privilege granted to the Catholic Church. Sometimes, Concordat provisions merely make explicit some consequences of the autonomy of religious communities, which is part of their collective right to religious freedom, and apply them to the specific circumstances of the Catholic Church. This is the case, for example, of those articles of the 1979 Agreement on Juridical Affairs that recognize the Church's right 'to exercise its apostolic mission'; to publicly engage in worship and teaching activities; to provide spiritual assistance to persons staying in military establishments, hospitals, penitentiaries, orphanages or alike centres; to carry out charitable activities; to freely design and modify its internal administrative organization around dioceses or parishes; and the Holy See's and bishops' right to enact and publish provisions related to the Church's government, and to freely communicate between them as well as with the clergy and the faithful.[48]

§3. Cooperation Agreements with Other Religious Communities

70. As has been already mentioned and is explained below in more detail,[49] the 1980 Organic Law on Religious Freedom, inspired by the constitutional principle of equality, gave other churches or religious communities the possibility to sign a cooperation agreement with the state in terms similar to those of the Concordat with the Catholic Church (Article 7 LOLR). Such legislative choice implies a positive assessment of bilateral norms as an adequate instrument to regulate the legal status of religion – otherwise, the political evolution would have naturally led to the denunciation of the Concordat instead of creating an analogous institution for other religious denominations. The agreements envisaged by Article 7 LOLR do not have the nature of international treaties and must be approved by a specific parliamentary statute. This means that, within the system of sources of law, they are *formally* statutory laws and not treaties.

71. Cooperation agreements are accessible only to religious communities that have obtained legal personality through registration in the RER and have been recognized well-known roots (*notorio arraigo*) in Spain by the Ministry of Justice on account of their extension and number of adherents. Compliance with those two conditions, however, does not open automatically the door to a negotiation process that may eventually lead to a cooperation agreement. The commencement of that process depends exclusively on the government's discretion. This fact has caused patent and unjustified inequalities among the legal status, respectively, of religious communities with a cooperation agreement and those others that, having been recognized well-known roots, have not been given the opportunity to reach such agreement.[50]

72. So far, only three cooperation agreements have been concluded, in 1992, with the Evangelical, Jewish, and Islamic Federations, respectively, which are the

47. *See infra*, paras 298–299.
48. *See* Agreement on Juridical Affairs, Arts I, II, IV and V.
49. *See infra*, Part III, Ch. 5 §2.
50. *See infra*, paras 357–358 and 300–303.

institutions representing Protestantism, Judaism and Islam vis-à-vis the Spanish state. After them, no subsequent negotiation process has been initiated by the government – and no negotiation is foreseeable in the next future. Those three agreements followed a parallel itinerary – their signature, and later its legislative approval, took place in the same day.[51] Also, the three agreements have a very similar normative content, which was inspired by the 1979 Catholic Concordat. As in the case of the Concordat, not every provision of the 1992 Agreements contains a manifestation of state cooperation. Some provisions merely make explicit some consequences of individual religious freedom or of religious communities' autonomy – for example, the articles on religious assistance in public institutions, on the clergy-communicant privilege, or on the right to observe the sabbath.

§4. Other Laws and Regulations

73. The laws of different nature described in the preceding sections of this chapter constitute the essential legal framework of religion in the Spanish legal system. Many of their provisions have been developed by subsequent laws and regulations, or sometimes by specific agreements between the government and religious denominations – in particular with those denominations that have a cooperation agreement, i.e., the Catholic Church and the Evangelical, Jewish and Islamic Federations. Thus, for instance, a reform of the Civil Code in 1981 modified the legal regulation of the civil effects of religious marriage (which was modified again in 2015).[52] Shortly after the LOLR, in 1981, the government approved two royal decrees with detailed provisions on the structure and functioning of the Registry of Religious Entities and the Advisory Commission on Religious Freedom, respectively.[53] Different laws on education have addressed, since the early 1980s, the issue of religious instruction in public schools as well as the legal status of private schools with a religious (or non-religious) ethos. Several articles of the Criminal Code are aimed at the protection of freedom of conscience and religious feelings of citizens. Various statutes and regulations contain particular rules on religious assistance in the army, public hospitals and penitentiaries. Other laws have added significant nuances to the economic state cooperation with religion, especially through tax benefits, normally on equal conditions in comparison with non-religious charities or non-profit activities, etc. The most important of these laws will be mentioned in due course in the relevant parts of this monograph.

74. The Charter or Fundamental Rights of the European Union, as well as international treaties and conventions on human rights with binding force in Spain, are also part of the juridical framework of religion. In addition to being sources of

51. The three agreements were signed on 28 Apr. 1992, and approved, respectively, by the Laws 24/1992, 25/1992 and 26/1992, all of them promulgated on 10 Nov. 1992.
52. *See infra*, Part X.
53. The 1981 royal decree on the Registry was replaced by another royal decree of 2015. The 1981 royal decree on the Advisory Commission was replaced by a new royal decree in 2001, which was in turn replaced in 2013. *See infra*, Part II, Ch. 4, §§ 2 and 3.

law, they are mandatory criteria for the interpretation of fundamental rights, according to Article 10.2 CE.[54]

---

54. *See infra*, paras 102 et seq. and paras 369 et seq.

Chapter 3. Typology of the System

75. There have been numerous academic discussions about which principles define the typology of the system of relations between state and religion in Spain.[55] While there is partial disagreement about the existence of some of these principles, almost all legal scholars agree that four basic constitutional principles constitute the fundamentals of Spanish law on religious affairs – although authors disagree about their precise meaning and reach. These four principles, which are often called 'informing' or 'inspiring' principles, are: *religious freedom*, *state neutrality*, *equality* and *state cooperation with religion*. These four principles can be found in the Constitution of 1978 and were developed by the 1980 Organic Law on Religious Freedom. No strict hierarchical order governs the relationship between these principles, and they altogether establish a system of coordinates that define the plane of constitutional legitimacy to which legislator and government must limit their activity.[56]

76. As indicated above, the system of church-state relations established by the 1978 Constitution lacked precedent in Spain's constitutional history and represented a true Copernican revolution in the Spanish state's attitude towards the role of religion in law and in society. The novelty of the system consisted in rejecting a monochrome orientation (religious or secularist), while at the same time setting down a complex plane that had the principle of religious freedom as its main coordinate and specifically included the need for cooperative institutional relations between the state and religious denominations. In that way, the 1978 constitutional framework endeavoured to reconcile tradition with realism, considering the new social and political developments in Spain, and sought for full compatibility with international standards, particularly with the standard that is usually deemed most strict: the ECHR, as interpreted by its own jurisdiction, the European Court of Strasbourg.

§1. Religious Freedom

77. The first constitutional principle is religious freedom. According to it, all state law on religious issues must aim at guaranteeing this fundamental right, which Article 16 CE names 'freedom of ideology, religion and worship' (*libertad ideológica, religiosa y de culto*) and many international documents call 'freedom of thought,

55. The first, and still suggestive, comprehensive scholarly analysis of the constitutional principles on the relations between state and religion was written by P.J. Viladrich, *Los principios informadores del Derecho eclesiástico español*, in VV.AA., *Derecho eclesiástico del estado español*, 211–317 (1st ed., Eunsa 1980).

56. *See* J. Ferrer Ortiz, *Los principios constitucionales del derecho eclesiástico como sistema*, in VV.AA., *Las relaciones entre la Iglesia y el Estado: estudios en memoria del Profesor Pedro Lombardía* 309–322 (Edersa 1989).

conscience and religion',[57] or 'freedom of religion or belief'.[58] Although this principle is not, strictly speaking, in a position of hierarchical pre-eminence with respect to the other three principles, religious freedom certainly constitutes the primary objective that should define the state policies in this realm. It is conceived as a sort of lodestar that gives sense to and delineates the true dimension of the other constitutional principles. Protection of religious freedom is not only a limit to the legislative or governmental activity – in the sense that unjustified restrictions on freedom of religion or belief are unconstitutional – but it serves also a positive teleological function with regard to public policies. In other words, the higher the degree of guarantee of religious liberty provided by public policies the better they comply with the constitutional mandate.

78. The other three principles, however, cannot be regarded simply as mere developments of the principle of religious freedom. On the contrary, those other principles define and cement the functional efficiency of religious liberty in Spanish legal order. And, at the same time, the right to freedom of religion or belief acquires a particular meaning when understood in the light of neutrality, equality and cooperation. For instance, the principle of religious freedom is incompatible with any aim of indoctrination (religious or anti-religious) on the part of public authorities, or with the unjustified privileged treatment of some religious denominations in comparison with others. Instead, public policies oriented to provide or facilitate financing of religious organizations or activities – on equal terms – are perfectly permissible, for they are aimed at rendering 'real and effective' a public freedom of individuals and groups, as required by Article 9.2 CE.

§2. Equality

79. The principle of equality requires that all citizens and groups are equal before the law with respect to the exercise of religion or belief. The immediate consequence is that the same degree of freedom must be recognized to all, but equality also acts as a limit to the general rules governing the legal position of churches in Spain. Thus, differences between the legal statuses of various religious denominations are legitimate only if they are not discriminatory. Such differences are allowed when a specific legal treatment is deemed necessary to provide adequate guarantee of the freedom of a certain group or individual in accordance with their particular circumstances. In other words, according to the case law of the European Court of Human Rights (ECtHR)[59] and the Spanish Constitutional Court,[60] differences in legal treatment are

57. For instance, the Universal Declaration of Human Rights (Art. 18), the European Convention on Human Rights (Art. 9), or the International Covenant on Civil and Political Rights (Art. 18).
58. This terminology has been gaining ground since the 1981 UN Declaration on the Elimination of All Forms of Intolerance and of Discrimination Based on Religion or Belief, and is widespread within the OSCE environment.
59. The ECtHR enunciated its basic doctrine on the principle of equality for the first time in the *Belgian linguistic case*, 23 Jul. 1968 (*see* in particular 'As to the law' I.B. para. 10), and has reiterated it innumerable times since then.
60. Cf. STC 49/1982, FJ 2; STC 144/1988, FJ 1; STC 45/1989, FJ 4, and many others. *See* some applications of this doctrine to the realm of religious freedom *infra* , in this same chapter, §6.

legitimate when they are grounded on a reasonable and objective justification, when they pursue a legitimate aim, and when there is an adequate relationship of proportionality between the aim pursued and the means employed. What is more, differential legal treatment is sometimes not just legitimate but also obliged when freedom of conscience is involved.[61]

80. Equality is perhaps the principle most difficult to apply in practice in this as in other areas of constitutional law, for there is not always a clear dividing line marking the end of what is open to the discretion of public authorities and the beginning of what is obliged by the Constitution. Indeed, the biggest challenges of the current Spanish system of relation between state and religion refer to the implementation of the equality principle. As indicated in various sections of this monograph, apparent – and unjustified – inequalities exist in the Spanish law on religious denominations and the Constitutional Court has not taken a clear stance against them. These inequalities refer to a variety of issues, most often to expressions of state cooperation with religion rather than to aspects of strict guarantee of religious freedom – for instance, in areas such as state's economic cooperation with religion, recognition of religious marriages or religious teaching in public schools.

81. In the last two decades, there have been numerous claims on the part of religious minorities alleging that they are subject to discriminatory treatment in comparison with the Catholic Church or with the three religious federations (Evangelical, Jewish and Muslim, respectively) that have a cooperation agreement with the state. Almost none of these claims have succeeded, but many scholars have the clear perception that religious equality is still underachieved in the Spanish law, especially with regard to minority religions without cooperation agreement with the state. Although there are many of these minority religions, they represent only a residual percentage of the country's population, but still several hundred thousand people. Many scholars are of the opinion that, since 1992, no government, either socialist or conservative, have taken seriously the need to put an end to these *residual* inequalities of the Spanish law on religion.[62]

---

61. An interesting case in this regard is the ECtHR's decision *Thlimmenos v. Greece*, 6 Apr. 2000, in which the Court held that sometimes the different legal treatment of individuals is necessary in the light of Art. 14 ECHR. In particular, the Court declared that a behaviour inspired by personal beliefs constitutes a relevant differentiating factor when determining the consequences deriving from a criminal conviction. The applicant in the *Thlimmenos* case was a Jehovah's Witness who had been convicted of insubordination for refusing to perform unarmed military service, at a time of general mobilization, on account of his religious beliefs. He was sentenced to four years' imprisonment, and was released on parole after two years. In 1988, he passed a public examination to become chartered accountant and, in spite of his successful examination, the Executive Board of the Institute of Chartered Accountants refused to appoint him because, according to the law, conviction of felony constituted a disqualification for the civil service. The ECtHR held that there had been a violation of Art. 14 ECHR taken in conjunction with Art. 9.
62. *See* for further references J. Martínez-Torrón, *El estatuto jurídico de las minorías religiosas sin acuerdo de cooperación en España*, in *Constitución, leyes de libertad religiosa, acuerdos, Derecho común* 165–176 (P. Pardo Prieto ed., Servicio de Publicaciones de la Universidad de León 2010).

§3. State Neutrality

82. The third constitutional principle is state neutrality on religious matters, which appears to be the main instrument chosen by the Constitution to protect the religious liberty of all citizens and groups in equal conditions. Some authors, and some case law of the Constitutional Court and other Spanish courts, often call this principle *aconfesionalidad* (aconfessionality) or *laicidad* (i.e., secularity, which is not exactly equivalent to the French understanding of *laïcité*). The deep meaning of neutrality goes beyond mere formal impartiality. A neutral state, and its legal system, is *incompetent* with regard to purely religious questions and therefore unable to make value judgments on them.

83. Such notion of neutrality does not imply that public authorities must be indifferent towards the results of the exercise of freedom of religion or belief, or that they ignore completely the content of personal choices in this particular area of human rationality. Neutrality means that public authorities cannot judge the truth or falsity of the dogmas or tenets of the diverse religions. However, state action with respect to religion may be based on other judgments. In particular, it may take into account the social effects of the religious activity, or the predictable effects of religious moral doctrines, including the cases in which those effects conflict with the law or with values that the legal system considers essential.

84. Two important consequences derive from the foregoing. First, state action with regard to religion must be, for the most part, a legal action – i.e., an action defined by law, with narrow margin for public authorities' discretion that could lead in practice to value judgments on religious doctrines or customs. Second, neutrality implies recognition of the reciprocal autonomy of state and religion and, therefore, state's interference with religious autonomy must be reduced to a minimum and its necessity must be clearly justified.[63] We must keep in mind that, as indicated above, neutrality – or *laicidad* – is conceived not as an aim in itself but as a means to guarantee and facilitate the exercise of freedom of religion or belief by all individuals and groups on equal terms.

§4. State Cooperation with Religion

85. Finally, the principle of state cooperation with churches or religious communities provides an additional and specific profile to neutrality. The reciprocal autonomy of state and churches is not understood in terms of strict separation but rather in terms of friendly relations and mutual cooperation – at least, cooperation of

63. The ECtHR has often emphasized this idea since the late 1990s. *See* , for instance, *Serif v. Greece*, 14 Dec. 1999; *Hasan and Chaush v. Bulgaria*, 26 Oct. 2000; *Metropolitan Church of Bessarabia v. Moldavia*, 13 Dec. 2001; or *Agga v. Greece*, 17 Oct. 2002. However, some recent cases concerning the labour relations between churches and their employees demonstrate that defining the limits of religious autonomy is far from easy. *See* , for example, *Obst v. Germany* and *Schüth v. Germany*, both of 23 Sep. 2010; *Siebenhaar v. Germany*, 3 Feb. 2011; *Fernández Martínez v. Spain* (GC), 12 Jun. 2014; *Károly Nagy v. Hungary*, 1 Dec. 2015 and (GC) 14 Sep. 2017; and *Travaš v. Croatia*, 4 Oct. 2016.

the state with religious denominations. In the words of Article 16.3 CE, 'public authorities shall take into account the religious beliefs of Spanish society and shall maintain the consequent relationships of cooperation with the Catholic Church and the other denominations'. This is consistent with Article 9.2 CE, which requires public authorities to create the conditions to make 'real and effective' the freedom and equality of individuals and groups.

86. In the years after the Constitution was enacted, Spanish scholars widely discussed the potential legal effects of the specific mention of the Catholic Church by Article 16.3 CE.[64] The passage of time has demonstrated that the specific mention of the Catholic Church should not be interpreted as a sign of 'sociological confessionality' of the state, but rather as recognition of the fact that Catholicism was part of 'the religious beliefs of the Spanish society'. The *mens legislatoris* in that article seems to be explained by the need to achieve what could be described as a 'tranquilizing' effect. In brief, as the new regime of relations between state and religion implied a deep change in Spanish tradition, and opening the doors to religious freedom and state neutrality, the drafters of the Constitution did not want the Catholic Church to think that they were following the path of the Constitution of 1931, which, as indicated above,[65] replaced the long-established Catholic confessionality of the state with an anti-ecclesiastical stance. Including the name of the Catholic Church in Article 16.3 was a way to avoid the risk of a negative reaction on the part of conservative religious circles in Spain. It contributed to eliminate possible attacks against the extraordinary political change that was developing in Spain, which some influent social forces of Catholic pedigree regarded with diffidence at the time.[66]

87. The principle of cooperation poses some interesting questions with respect to the criteria that should determine state cooperation with churches. Two questions are particularly important: (a) how, when, and in which areas, is the state obliged to cooperate with religious denominations? and (b) which factors could, or should, be taken into account to justify differences in state cooperation with diverse religious denominations?

88. Scholars have endeavoured to answer the second question indicating that state cooperation should differ depending on three main elements.[67] First, the particular characteristics of each religious denomination (e.g., some religions keep a strict observance of sabbath and some others are more flexible; some religions have precise inhumation requirements while others do not, etc.). Second, the social utility of religious denominations, including their specific contributions to educational, humanitarian or charitable initiatives (this factor tends to be more and more used to define the state economic cooperation with religion, on equal grounds with other non-profit institutions without specific religious nature). And third, the social roots of each religious

---

64. *See* , for instance, P.J. Viladrich, *Los principios informadores*, 231–236.
65. *See supra* , paras 37–39.
66. This explains an apparent paradox, that the Spanish Communist Party – which traditionally had been, and was in 1978, an anticlerical party – did not oppose the specific mention of the Catholic Church in Art. 16.3. For a description of parliamentary debates on Art. 16 CE, *see* J.J. Amorós, *La libertad religiosa en la Constitución Española de 1978* 120–153 (Tecnos 1984).
67. *See* J. Martínez-Torrón, *Religión, derecho y sociedad. Antiguos y nuevos planteamientos en el derecho eclesiástico del Estado* 191–193 (Comares 1999).

denomination, which, as indicated above,[68] is one of the criteria used by the law to determine which religious communities can reach a formal cooperation agreement with the state.

89. With regard to the first question, it is commonly understood that Article 16.3 of the Constitution imposes on the state a general duty to cooperate with religion but does not specify when, in which areas or through which channels state cooperation must materialize. There is an implicit agreement that public authorities have a wide discretion to decide how to concretize state cooperation, which is limited only by the principles of neutrality and equality – for instance, an alleged aim of cooperation would not allow the government to invade the realm of religious autonomy; all differences in cooperation with religious denominations must have an objective and reasonable justification, etc.

§5. Bilateral Sources of Law

90. After the Constitution was promulgated, the governmental praxis has been to channel most of the state cooperation with religion through formal agreements with religious denominations. This first happened with the Catholic Church, when the 1979 Concordat was signed; and later, in 1992, with the most significant religions in the history of Spain – Protestantism, Judaism and Islam – in application of Article 7 LOLR, which extended, *mutatis mutandis*, the Concordat model to other religious denominations that had acquired 'well-known roots in Spain'.

91. Very little state cooperation, if any, is left to those religions not included in the agreements' system.[69] This is why we can affirm that the constitutional principle of cooperation has been complemented, by way of legal and political practice, with the principle of bilaterality of sources of law – i.e., the use of mixed sources that involve both the authority of the state and religious denominations.

§6. Case Law of the Constitutional Court with Respect to the 'Informing' Principles

92. The constitutional or *informing* principles have often been mentioned, directly or by obiter dicta, in the case law of the Spanish Constitutional Court, which has thus clarified their precise meaning and some of their practical consequences.

93. With respect to the principle of religious freedom, the Constitutional Court has distinguished a subjective and an objective perspective. Understood as a *subjective right*, the Constitutional Court has remarked – in parallel with the distinction between *forum internum* and *forum externum* drawn by the Strasbourg jurisprudence[70] – that religious freedom comprises two aspects, internal and external. The internal side of religious freedom 'guarantees an intimate cluster of beliefs and, therefore, a space of intellectual auto-determination regarding religion, in connection with one's own

68. *See supra*, para. 65.
69. *See infra*, Part II, Ch. 4 §1.
70. *See infra*, para. 108.

individual personality and dignity'. In addition, religious freedom 'includes an external aspect of *agere licere*, according to which citizens are entitled to act in conformity with their own convictions and to maintain their convictions in the face of others', with 'full immunity from coercion by the state or by any social groups'.[71]

94. There is also, according to the Court, an *objective dimension* of religious freedom, understood in the light of Article 16.3 CE, which implies for public authorities a duty of neutrality – intrinsic to the state's aconfessionality or secularity – and at the same time the maintenance of relations of cooperation with religion. The combination of neutrality and cooperation introduces in Spanish law a notion of 'positive aconfessionality or secularity' (*laicidad positiva*) that 'prohibits any sort of confusion between religious and state functions' in the development of the relations of cooperation with religious denominations.[72]

95. While the Court's case law has unequivocally emphasized the essential role that neutrality plays in the constitutional system of relations between state and religion, a number of decisions have held that state neutrality, and equality, are compatible with some traditional expressions of protection of religion, and in particular of the majority religion in Spain, namely Catholicism.

96. Thus, the Constitutional Court has held that the neutrality principle is compatible with the presence of Christian symbols in public corporations, as far as they are linked to the history of the institution and imply neither the adherence of the state to a particular creed nor any coercion on the religious freedom of individuals. For instance, it would have been legitimate for a public University to keep an image of the Holy Virgin that had been traditionally present in its coat of arms if its governing bodies had so decided;[73] and it was legitimate for a local bar association to keep the Immaculate Conception of the Holy Virgin as its honorary patron, provided that the bar association itself was aconfessional.[74] In a similar direction, the Court has found nothing unconstitutional in the fact that a military garrison organized a solemn parade in honour of a local advocation of the Holy Virgin,[75] or in the fact that a unit of the National Police participated in a religious procession during the celebration of the Catholic Holy Week (the National Police Corps was a member of the relevant religious fraternity),[76] as far as no officer was obliged to take part in those religious ceremonies against his personal convictions.

97. Following an analogous approach, the Constitutional Court has held the constitutionality of the Concordat's articles that provide that confessional teaching of Catholic religion has to be included, as an elective subject and under the same conditions as any other 'fundamental course', in the curricula of public schools and university

71. *See* STC 154/2002, FJ 6, citing STC 19/1985, FJ 2; STC 120/1990, FJ 10; STC 137/1990, FJ 8; STC 177/1996, FJ 9; STC 46/2001, FJ 4. *See also* STC 24/1982, FJ 1.
72. *See* STC 24/1982, FJ 1; STC 340/1993, FJ 3; STC 177/1996, FJ 5; STC 154/2002, FJ 6; STC 38/2007, FJ 5; STC 51/2011, FJ 3.
73. *See* STC 130/1991. In this case, the supreme governing body of the University had decided the opposite, i.e., to remove the image of the Virgin from the coat of arms.
74. *See* STC 34/2011.
75. *See* STC 177/1996.
76. *See* STC 101/2004.

schools for teacher training.[77] Therefore, it would be illegitimate to ignore the Concordat's provisions either by excluding Catholic instruction – as an optional course – from the curriculum[78] or by assigning Catholic instruction a reduced number of credits that is not in fair proportion with other fundamental courses.[79] According to the Court, it is likewise fully compatible with the state neutrality the system of appointment and payment of Catholic religion teachers established by the Concordat, which require that public authorities pay the salary of religion teachers and hire them among those that have been proposed by the competent ecclesiastical authority.[80] Indeed, both state neutrality and churches' right to their religious autonomy require guaranteeing that only ecclesiastical authorities are competent to determine the appropriate persons to teach Catholic religion and the contents of that teaching.[81]

98. Two other areas exemplify the Constitutional Court's approach when holding that neither state neutrality nor the principle of equality are violated by a specific treatment of the Catholic Church that is comparatively more favourable than the treatment of other religions. One is the system of the so-called organic integration (*integración orgánica*) of Catholic military chaplaincies. According to that system, spiritual assistance was provided by an ecclesiastical corps whose members were integrated into the hierarchical structure of the army. The Court affirmed that this system was one of the legitimate choices that the legislator could make, and added that providing Catholic religious assistance to the military was a way of facilitating the exercise of religious freedom to members of the Armed Forces. Such system did not violate the equality principle as long as followers of other religions had the opportunity to receive their own religious assistance through appropriate channels.[82] The second area is marriage law. The Constitutional Court has never questioned the constitutionality of the privileged treatment enjoyed by canonical marriage under Spanish law,[83] which recognizes not only the validity of the Catholic form of marriage but also grants civil effects to the decisions of ecclesiastical jurisdiction on the nullity of canonical marriages, in contrast with the treatment reserved other religious marriages – these are accepted only as valid forms of celebrating a marriage but the decisions of the relevant religious courts do not have any effect in civil law.[84]

99. A similar doctrine had been applied one year before with respect to a curious and very different issue, such as the mandatory study of canon law (Catholic) in law schools. At the time, all law schools in public universities had to offer a mandatory one-year course on canon law (all courses were then mandatory in the official curriculum of law schools). The Constitutional Court held that practice constitutional, emphasizing that the teaching of canon law had a secular and not a religious purpose, not only because it was a useful subject for legal practice (canonical marriage has civil effects

77. *See* for further details *infra* , Part IX, Ch. 1 §1.
78. *See* STC 187/1991.
79. *See* STC 155/1997.
80. *See* STC 38/2007 and STC 51/2011.
81. *See* STC 38/2007, FJ 9; and STC 51/2011, FJ 4.
82. *See* STC 34/1982.
83. *See* for further details *infra* , Part X.
84. *See* , for instance, STC 328/1993 and STC 6/1997.

in Spain) but also because canon law was an integral part of Spanish legal history – and indeed an essential element that has marked the entire Western legal culture.[85]

100. In other decisions relating to tax benefits for churches[86] the Constitutional Court performed a more arguable interpretation of the principle of equality, declaring that it was not discriminatory to reserve tax exemptions exclusively for those religious denominations with special social and historical significance – namely those that had signed a cooperation agreement with the state.[87] The Court failed to demonstrate that there was a 'reasonable justification' for granting tax exemptions to churches solely on the basis of history, bilateral institutional relationships or social influence, instead of granting those benefits taking on account of the religious and non-profit character of the relevant institutions, irrespective of their roots in the country or their number of adherents.[88]

85. *See* ATC 359/1985.
86. *See* ATC 480/1989.
87. At the time, only the Catholic Church; since 1992, also the Evangelical, Jewish and Islamic Federations.
88. The Constitutional Court took a similar stance in another case in which two members of a Baptist church requested the state economic cooperation through the tax assignment system, which was reserved to the Catholic Church. In this occasion, however, it seemed that those two members acted on their own individual capacity and not in representation of their church, which indeed had not requested formally such method of economic cooperation (decision of 13 May 1999, unreported; cited by the ECtHR in *Alujer Fernández and Caballero García v. Spain*, decision on the admissibility of Appl. Nr. 53072/99, 14 Jun. 2001).

Part II. Religious Freedom in General

Chapter 1. Individual Religious Freedom

§1. Normative Framework

101. Various types of sources delineate the essential normative framework of individual religious freedom in Spain. From a national perspective, as stated in Part I, the fundamental right to 'freedom of ideology, religion and worship' is protected by the Constitution (Articles 16 and 14) and by the 1980 Organic Law on Religious Freedom, which developed those constitutional provisions. Articles 1–4 LOLR are of special interest from the perspective of individual religious freedom.

102. From a supranational perspective, the Charter of Fundamental Rights of the European Union (CFREU) is legally binding in Spain. Its Article 10 guarantees freedom of thought, conscience and religion, as well as the right to conscientious objection. Article 14.3 CFREU guarantees parent's rights over the religious, philosophical and pedagogical orientation of their children's education. Articles 10.1 and 14.3 are almost literally inspired by the equivalent provisions of the ECHR:

Article 10 CFREU – Freedom of thought, conscience and religion.

1. Everyone has the right to freedom of thought, conscience and religion. This right includes freedom to change religion or belief and freedom, either alone or in community with others and in public or in private, to manifest religion or belief, in worship, teaching, practice and observance.
2. The right to conscientious objection is recognised, in accordance with the national laws governing the exercise of this right.

Article 14 CFREU – Right to education.

…

– The freedom to found educational establishments with due respect for democratic principles and the right of parents to ensure the education and teaching of their children in conformity with their religious, philosophical and pedagogical convictions shall be respected, in accordance with the national laws governing the exercise of such freedom and right.

103. From an international perspective, the essential normative framework of individual religious freedom is designed, within the United Nations' milieu, by the Universal Declaration of Human Rights (especially Article 18); the International Covenant on Civil and Political Rights (especially Article 18); the International Covenant on Economic, Social and Cultural Rights (especially Article 13.3). Within the domain of the Council of Europe, the basic normative reference is the ECHR (especially Article 9 and Article 2 of its First Protocol). It is worth quoting here the latter provisions, which are the most influential in Spanish law because of the subjection of Spain to the jurisdiction of the ECtHR:

Article 9 ECHR – Freedom of thought, conscience and religion:

1. Everyone has the right to freedom of thought, conscience and religion; this right includes freedom to change his religion or belief and freedom, either alone or in community with others and in public or private, to manifest his religion or belief, in worship, teaching, practice and observance.
2. Freedom to manifest one's religion or beliefs shall be subject only to such limitations as are prescribed by law and are necessary in a democratic society in the interests of public safety, for the protection of public order, health or morals, or for the protection of the rights and freedoms of others.

Article 2 of the Protocol to the ECHR – Right to education:

No person shall be denied the right to education. In the exercise of any functions which it assumes in relation to education and to teaching, the State shall respect the right of parents to ensure such education and teaching in conformity with their own religious and philosophical convictions.

104. These international sources not only entail the international responsibility of the Spanish state but also constitute, in accordance with Article 10.2 CE, compulsory criteria for the interpretation of the fundamental rights protected by the Constitution.[89] This is particularly important taking into account that the constitutional provisions on religious freedom are not very detailed and omit some aspects that are instead present in international documents. Moreover, Article 10.2 CE is normally understood as implicitly including the interpretive authority of the case law of the ECtHR.

105. There are other international documents that, though not legally binding, are normally regarded as authoritative sources that help interpret the constitutional and legislative provisions on religious freedom. For instance, the 1981 Declaration on

89. Article 10.2 CE provides: 'The provisions relating to the fundamental rights and freedoms recognized by the Constitution shall be interpreted in accordance with the Universal Declaration of Human Rights and with the international treaties and conventions on those matters ratified by Spain.'

the Elimination of All Forms of Intolerance and of Discrimination Based on Religion or Belief, or the documents containing the OSCE human dimension commitments.[90]

106. There are a number of other laws and regulations with specific provisions on individual freedom of religion and conscience, or against religious discrimination – e.g., the Concordat with the Holy See, the 1992 Agreements with the Evangelical, Jewish and Islamic Federations, the Criminal Code or the Statute of Workers. Appropriate references to these and other laws will be made in due course in the relevant sections of this monograph.

§2. Protected Aspects of Religious Freedom

I. Internal and External Dimension of Religious Freedom

107. As already mentioned, the Constitutional Court has remarked that we must distinguish two dimensions, internal and external, in the fundamental right to religious freedom. The internal side of religious freedom 'guarantees an intimate cluster of beliefs and, therefore, a space of intellectual auto-determination regarding religion, in connection with one's own individual personality and dignity'. In addition, religious freedom 'also includes an external aspect of *agere licere*, according to which citizens are entitled to act in conformity with their own convictions and to maintain their convictions in the face of others', with 'full immunity from coercion by the state or by any social groups'.[91]

108. We can see that this judicial doctrine runs parallel to and is likely inspired by the distinction between *forum internum* and *forum externum* drawn by the ECtHR,[92] which in turn is equivalent to the distinction between *freedom to believe* and *freedom to act* affirmed by the United States Supreme Court long ago.[93] While both the Strasbourg and US jurisdictions have been explicit about the fact that the internal dimension of religious freedom is absolute and not subject to legitimate limitations, the Spanish Constitutional Court has only implicitly accepted it. This absolute aspect of religious freedom is also implicit in Article 16.1 CE, which indicates that only limitations

90. These documents are available in: http://www.osce.org/odihr/76902 (accessed 9 Dec. 2017).
91. *See* STC 154/2002, FJ 6, citing STC 19/1985, FJ 2; STC 120/1990, FJ 10; STC 137/1990, FJ 8; STC 177/1996, FJ 9; STC 46/2001, FJ 4. *See also* STC 24/1982, FJ 1.
92. *See*, for instance, implicitly, *Kokkinakis v. Greece*, 25 May 1993, para. 33; and, explicitly, *Saniewski v. Poland*, ECtHR, decision on the admissibility of Appl. Nr. 40319/98, 26 Jun. 2001, The Law, para. 1). This doctrine had already been proposed by the formerly existing European Commission on Human Rights. Cf. its decisions on the admissibility of the following applications: Appl. Nr. 10358/83, *C. v. United Kingdom*; Appl. Nr. 10678/83, *V. v. the Netherlands*; and App. Nr. 14049/88, *Raoult v. France*. Cf. also the report of the Commission on Appl. Nr.11581/85, *Darby v. Sweden*, para. 44 (adopted on 9 May 1989). *See* M.D. Evans, *Religious Liberty and International Law in Europe* 298–314 (Cambridge U. Press 1997); and C. Evans, *Freedom of Religion under the European Convention on Human Rights* 68–79 (Oxford U. Press 2001); P.M. Taylor, *Freedom of Religion: UN and European Human Rights Law and Practice* 115–202 (Cambridge U. Press 2005).
93. *See* *Cantwell v. Connecticut*, 310 U.S. 296, 303–304 (1940).

necessary for the public order can be imposed on the *manifestations* of freedom of ideology, religion and worship.

109. The state has a double role vis-à-vis the protection of religious freedom. First, it must guarantee that citizens can exercise their freedom to believe and their freedom to act according to their beliefs without coercion from other individuals or groups – and, of course, from public authorities. Moreover, following the mandate of Article 9.2 CE, the state must also adopt a more active function and create the appropriate conditions to make 'real and effective' the religious freedom and equality of individuals and groups.

110. 'Every person', and not only Spanish citizens, is entitled to the guarantee of his religious freedom, in accordance to Article 2.1 LOLR and Article 13.1 CE. The following paragraphs examine in more detail the degree of protection of different aspects of religious freedom in Spanish legislation and case law.[94]

II. Freedom to Choose

111. The 1980 Organic Law on Religious Freedom unambiguously guarantees every person's right to free choice with regard to his beliefs. This individual right must be broadly interpreted and does not imply the need to choose a particular religion or church. Indeed, according to Article 2.1.a) LOLR, religious freedom 'comprises the right of every person, with immunity from coercion, to ... profess the religious beliefs of his free choice or not to profess any ... '. Thus, in Spanish law the term 'freedom of religion and worship' embraces the freedom to hold and profess any type of beliefs, be they religious or non-religious, as well as the right to abstain from professing any belief. Spanish scholars have maintained, since the Constitution was in force, that the constitutional right to freedom or ideology and religion refers both to religion and atheism, and therefore protects the atheistic convictions of individuals in the same conditions as religious beliefs.[95]

112. The Constitutional Court, in addition to emphasizing that ideological freedom 'always excludes violence as a means to impose one's own opinions',[96] has held that public authorities' acts are illegitimate and can be annulled when they 'perturb or prevent in any way the free adoption or maintenance of a particular ideology'.[97] The safeguard of the individual against undue state interferences with his freedom of choice can be of particular significance in the case of minors, especially in the public schools' environment, to protect students against indoctrination in a particular religion or morals against the wishes of their parents or legal guardians. This is the reason why

94. For a recent discussion of the types of manifestation of religion or belief in the Strasbourg jurisdiction, *see* J. Martínez-Torrón, *Manifestations of Religion or Belief in the Case Law of the European Court of Human Rights*, 12 Religion and Human Rights 112–127 (2017).

95. *See* , for instance, P.J. Viladrich, *Ateísmo y libertad religiosa en la Constitución española*, 22 Ius Canonicum 31–86 (1982); J.J. Amorós, *La libertad religiosa en la Constitución española de 1978* 176–186 (Tecnos 1984).

96. STC 20/1990, FJ 5.

97. STC 120/1990, FJ 10.

the ECtHR[98] and the Spanish Constitutional Court[99] have unequivocally affirmed the guarantee of minors against the possibility of state indoctrination through the system of public education.

113. As a corollary, individual's freedom to choose their beliefs includes the right 'to change or abandon his religion' (Article 2.1.a) LOLR). This aspect of religious freedom is indisputable and is also explicitly recognized by Article 9 ECHR, of binding force in Spain. The Strasbourg jurisdiction has added an interesting nuance to this aspect of freedom of choice by holding that individuals do not have the right to remain in a religious community in a position deemed heterodox by the relevant religious authority. The autonomy of religious communities guarantees their right to impose doctrinal uniformity and, consequently, to sanction or expel members that refuse to accept those doctrines, or to oust them from their positions in the community's organizational structure. In cases of doctrinal or disciplinary conflict between an individual and his community, only the religious authorities – and not the civil authorities – are legitimate to intervene. The Strasbourg jurisdiction has traditionally considered that individual religious freedom is sufficiently guaranteed by the individual's right to abandon his religion at any time.[100] The same criteria should apply to institutions or entities inspired in specific religious principles.[101]

114. Another significant question relating to conflicts between individuals' freedom to choose and religious autonomy is to what extent an individual can oblige his former church to formally recognize his withdrawal or apostasy. This issue has been raised in Spain by persons that, having apostatized their Catholic faith by a formal statement, demanded ecclesiastical authorities to remove all their data from baptism registries; later, having obtained a negative response, the same persons filed a suit before the civil courts alleging their rights under data protection laws. In 2008, the Supreme Court sustained the position of the Catholic Church's authorities but left unresolved the substantive issue of the conflict between religious autonomy and individual freedom.[102]

III. Freedom to Manifest or Not to Manifest

115. The Organic Law on Religious Freedom recognizes also the guarantee of every person's right to the free expression of his religious or non-religious beliefs. According to Article 2.1.a) LOLR, religious freedom 'comprises the right of every

98. This doctrine was first enunciated by the ECtHR in *Kjeldsen, Busk Madsen and Pedersen v. Denmark*, 7 Dec. 1976, and later reaffirmed in *Folgerø et al. v. Norway*, 29 Jun. 2007, *Zengin v. Turkey*, 9 Oct. 2007, and *Mansur Yalçin et al. v. Turkey*, 16 Sep. 2014.

99. Cf. STC 5/1981, FJ 9.

100. Cf., for example, the decisions of the European Commission on Human Rights on the admissibility of Appls Nr. 7274/76, 10901/84, 12356/86 and 11045/84 (*Knudsen v. Norway*).

101. Cf., for instance, the decisions of the European Commission on Human Rights on the admissibility of Appls Nr. 12242/86 (*Rommelfanger v. Germany*) and 11002/84 (*Van der Heijden v. The Netherlands*).

102. *See infra* , paras 425–426.

person, with immunity from coercion, to ... freely manifest his religious beliefs or his absence of religious beliefs or to abstain from declaring about his beliefs'.

116. Individuals' right not to declare about their religion or beliefs is of particular importance in a country as Spain, with a long history of religious discrimination. Indeed, this right was already explicitly guaranteed by the Constitution (Article 16.2)[103] and had at the time the effect of immediately modifying the Spanish matrimonial system before the 1981 reform of the Civil Code. Prior to that reform, Spain had a system called *subsidiary civil marriage*, according to which a Spanish citizen was allowed to celebrate civil marriage only after declaring that either he was not Catholic or that he did not profess the Catholic faith any more (in the context of a confessional state, it was assumed that the civil law could accept the canon law rule that provides that canonical marriage is the only valid marriage for a Catholic). While a broader modification of the matrimonial system was prepared, and in order to adapt the matrimonial legislation in force to the new Constitution, the Ministry of Justice ordered all public officials to authorize civil marriages without any inquiry about the religion or beliefs of the intending spouses.[104]

IV. Freedom of Worship

117. Article 2.1.b) LOLR recognizes freedom of worship in its double dimension, positive and negative – i.e., the right to 'practice acts of worship' and, in parallel, the right 'not to practice acts of worship'. Conceived as an individual right, the positive side of freedom of worship comprises the citizen's right to engage in both individual and collective worship, especially taking into account that collective prayers or ceremonies are often compulsory in institutional religions.

118. The fact that the LOLR explicitly mentioned the negative side of freedom of worship was important in a country with a past of religious monopoly – and often repression of dissidents – in which mandatory attendance to acts of Catholic prayer or worship in the school or in the military had been regular practices. In this respect, the Constitutional Court has affirmed the right of police and military officers to refuse to be present in religious acts or ceremonies in which there is an institutional involvement of their regiment, such as a military parade in honour of a local advocation of the Holy Virgin,[105] or the participation of a company of the National Police, attired in gala uniform, in a Holy Week Catholic procession.[106] In the view of the Court, it is acceptable to consider that, out of respect for tradition, the inveterate presence of the police or the Armed Forces in some religious ceremonies is compatible with the principle of state religious neutrality; but it is not acceptable to make participation in those events obligatory for officers that oppose to them on conscience grounds. The latter aspect is unmistakably forbidden by Article 2.1.b) LOLR.

---

103. It was also recognized, with a different wording, by Art. 27 of the 1931 Constitution of the Second Republic.

104. *Instrucción de la Dirección General de los Registros y del Notariado, sobre no manifestación de creencias religiosas en el expediente del matrimonio civil*, 26 Dec. 1978.

105. Cf. STC 177/1996.

106. Cf. STC 101/2004.

119. The same article of the LOLR provides a non-exhaustive list of some specific examples of acts of worship protected by law:

- *The commemoration of religious festivities*. One of the main questions raised by this aspect of worship is to what extent employees and civil servants are entitled to the protection of their religious days of rest – imposed by some religions on a certain day of the week or in specific holy days of the year – when there is a conflict or incompatibility with their labour obligations. As explained in other sections of this monograph, neither the Spanish legislation nor the case law of the Constitutional Court are particularly sensitive to this aspect of the individual's right to religious freedom.[107] More protection receives the right to the observance of religious rest in the case of students, according to the 1992 Agreements with the Evangelical, Jewish and Islamic Federations (Article 12). Upon request, students shall be excused from attending classes or passing examinations in the holy days of their respective religions. A similar right is recognized to candidates that must pass a public examination to enter the civil service; if their examination is fixed in one of the days of mandatory religious rest they can ask for an alternative date but their petition can be rejected with 'good cause'.
- *The celebration of religious matrimonial rites*. The LOLR only recognizes every person's right to a religious ceremony of marriage but does not explicitly state that such ceremony shall have civil effects – these were traditionally reserved to the canonical marriage of the Catholic Church. However, at the time that the LOLR was enacted, it was predictable that the Catholic marriage would not be any longer the only religious marriage recognized by civil law; this could be inferred from Article 32.1 CE, which implicitly envisioned the possibility of a plurality of religious forms of marriage in concurrence with the civil form.[108] In fact, one year later, in July 1981, a reform of the Civil Code opened the door to the future recognition of the civil effects of religious marriages other than Catholic. And, in 1992, such possibility was materialized when the cooperation agreements signed between the state and the Protestant, Jewish and Islamic federations granted civil effects to their respective religious celebrations of marriage. In 2015, a new modification of the Civil Code extended the same civil effects to the marriage of those religious communities that had been recognized 'well-known roots in Spain'.[109]
- *A proper religious burial, without discrimination on religious grounds*. In connection with inhumation rights, the 1992 Agreements with the Jewish and the Islamic Federations (Articles 2.6 and 2.5, respectively) recognize the right of Jewish and Islamic communities to have their own private religious cemeteries, as well as to reserve specific areas in municipal cemeteries for their religious burial needs. These religious cemeteries shall enjoy the same legal protection as places of worship. Cemeteries and burials are the competence of local and regional authorities, which in some places have developed the rules of the 1992 Agreements with the Jewish and Islamic communities, and normally have endeavoured to be as flexible

107. *See infra*, Part II, Ch. 2 §10.
108. *See supra*, para. 53.
109. This issue is discussed in more detail *infra*, in Part X.

as possible to make the religious rules on inhumation compatible with the administrative regulations aimed at the protection of public health.[110]

V. Right to Religious Assistance

120. Article 2.1.b) LOLR also guarantees every person's right to spiritual care, again in its positive and negative side; i.e., the right to 'receive religious assistance of his own denomination', as well as the right not to be compelled to receive religious assistance against his personal convictions. In normal conditions, no specific state action is required to ensure the exercise of this right, but in certain circumstances the state active cooperation is necessary. This occurs when people are confined in places, under the responsibility of public authorities, where they do not enjoy freedom of movement for a variety of reasons. As a consequence, Article 2.3 LOLR adds that, '[t] o ensure the real and effective application of these rights, public authorities shall adopt the necessary measures to facilitate religious assistance in hospitals, penitentiaries, public, military and charitable establishments, and other establishments under the public authorities' aegis'.

121. It is important to note, therefore, that the main purpose of state's intervention to guarantee religious assistance in the military, penitentiaries and hospitals is not to grant a particular status or privileges to well-established religious communities but to facilitate individuals the actual exercise of their right to religious assistance – it they so wish – in places where they are under the responsibility of public authorities and cannot easily obtain spiritual assistance by themselves. In practice, however, the mandate of Article 2.3 LOLR calls for a dialogue and cooperation with the main religious denominations operating in the country.[111]

VI. Freedom of Teaching

122. Article 2.1.c) LOLR guarantees the teaching dimension of religious freedom, i.e., the right to 'receive and provide religious instruction and information of all types, either orally, in writing or through any other means'. This includes the right to engage in religious propaganda and the right to proselytize, affirmed by the ECtHR long ago.[112] The recognition of these rights has not raised particular issues in Spain, except in cases of suspected abuse or 'brainwashing' by religious movements regarded as 'sects' by public authorities. Such was indeed the situation in the case *Riera Blume v. Spain*, judged in 1999 by the ECtHR,[113] which reached the conclusion that the allegedly

110. *See* M. Rodríguez Blanco, *Libertad religiosa y cementerios (primeras aproximaciones)*, in *La libertad religiosa y su regulación legal*, 824–846 (R. Navarro-Valls, J. Mantecón & J. Martínez-Torrón eds, Iustel 2009).

111. *See* , for further details on how state cooperation with religious assistance works in Spain, *infra* , Part III, Ch. 6.

112. Cf. *Kokkinakis v. Greece*, 25 May 1993. Interesting nuances on the guarantee of and limitations on the right to proselytism were added in *Larissis et al. v. Greece*, 24 Feb. 1998.

113. *Riera Blume v. Spain*, 14 Oct. 1999.

abused persons were actually competent and had acted on their free will. The applicants were members of an organization named 'Esoteric Centre of Investigations'. Following the issuance of a judicial order, the applicants' homes were searched, and the applicants themselves, all of whom were adults, were subsequently confined in a nearby hotel against their will for 'deprogramming'. The confinement of the applicants, however, was not supported by any judicial order but was carried out by a private 'anti-sect' association with the consent of the applicants' families and a limited cooperation of the Catalan police. The European Court avoided pronouncing any opinion under Article 9 ECHR (freedom of religion) and decided in favour of the applicants under Article 5.1 ECHR (right to liberty and security).

123. Article 2.1.c) LOLR reiterates the provision of Article 27.3 CE and declares every individual's right 'to choose, for himself and for the minors or legally incompetent persons under his custody, in and out of the school environment, a moral and religious instruction in accordance with his own convictions'. The reference to 'in and out of the school environment' is an interesting nuance added to the text of Article 27.3 CE, making explicit something that was implicit in the Constitution. These provisions are normally understood as constituting the basis both for the current system of religious instruction in public schools and – together with Article 6 LOLR (right to religious autonomy) – for the recognition of the private schools' right to preserve their own ethos, which are discussed in the relevant section of this monograph.[114] The same provisions have been alleged by parents to justify their conscientious objection to have their children instructed – in public schools – in some subjects, such as sex education or certain contents of the so-called civic education, which they considered to be inappropriate moral indoctrination of students. The relevant case law is discussed below, when analysing the different types of conscientious objection.[115]

VII. Right to Non-discrimination

124. In coherence with the constitutional principle of equality (Article 14 CE), Article 1.2 LOLR bans all kinds of discrimination on religious grounds: 'Religious beliefs shall not be ground for inequality or discrimination before the law. No religious reasons can be alleged to prevent anyone from exercising any job or activity, or from occupying public offices or positions.' According to the case law of the ECtHR[116] and the Spanish Constitutional Court,[117] unequal treatment is discriminatory when it is not grounded in a reasonable and objective justification, when it does not pursue a legitimate aim or when there is no adequate relation of proportionality between the aim pursued and the means employed.

125. While it is not difficult to find examples of legitimate differences in the legal treatment of religious denominations due to their diverse degree of social rooting

114. *See infra*, Part IX
115. *See infra*, Part II, Ch. 2 §8.
116. The ECtHR enunciated its basic doctrine on the principle of equality for the first time in the *Belgian linguistic case*, 23 Jul. 1968 (*see* in particular 'As to the law' I.B. para. 10), and has reiterated it innumerable times since then.
117. Cf. STC 49/1982, FJ 2; STC 144/1988, FJ 1; STC 45/1989, FJ 4, and many others.

– we have already seen some differences between the Catholic Church and other denominations – it is much more problematic to justify cases in which the law may treat individuals differently on the sole ground of their religion or beliefs. Indeed, the Constitutional Court has unambiguously affirmed that 'it is not possible to establish any type of discrimination or a dissimilar legal treatment of citizens depending on their ideology or beliefs'.[118] Blatant situations of direct discrimination of individuals on religious or belief grounds are normally easy to identify. Sometimes, however, the factual situations may offer some complexity because of the entanglement of religious and non-religious factors, as in administrative decisions refusing to grant Spanish citizenship to some individuals, often involving Muslims. Spanish courts try to keep a balanced position in this regard when assessing if the person applying for citizenship has 'a sufficient degree of integration into Spanish society', as required by Article 22.4 CC. Thus, the Supreme Court has been in favour of refusing Spanish citizenship when the applicant's membership to a fundamentalist Islamic group was substantiated[119] but has been in favour of granting it otherwise.[120] The National Court has adopted a similar position and, in the case of some Muslim applicants, has emphasized that the judgment about the applicants' lack of integration into Spanish society was not grounded on an evaluation of their religious beliefs but on their insufficient knowledge about Spanish culture, laws, history and constitutional freedoms,[121] or on their support and practice of polygamy.[122]

126. In practice, most cases of alleged discrimination are *indirect* and caused by prima facie *neutral* laws of general applicability that enter into conflict with the conscience of some individuals. In other words, even when state laws do not intend to differentiate between citizens of diverse beliefs and just pursue a legitimate secular goal, they may create serious moral scruples on people with certain beliefs. The crucial question in those cases, which we usually call conscientious objections, is to what extent there is discriminatory treatment of individuals in practice, even if it is an indirect and non-intended consequence of the law. Sometimes the Spanish legislator has been sensitive to this sort of situations and has provided a priori for the appropriate solutions. Not always, however, the legislator or the courts have been so sensitive towards the religious or moral needs of citizens, as explained in other parts of this monograph.[123]

VIII. Freedom of Conscience

127. An important aspect of freedom of religion or belief is freedom of conscience, which entails the individual's right not only to form his own opinion about what is moral and what is immoral, but also to conduct his life in accordance with his ethical convictions. Many people, irrespective of their attitude towards religious teaching,

118. STC 24/1982, FJ 1.
119. STS 2445/2015, 15 Jun. 2015; STS 3777/2015, 18 Sep. 2015.
120. STS 171/2014, 22 Jan. 2014.
121. SAN 4013/2015, 17 Nov. 2015; SAN 449/2015, 10 Feb. 2015.
122. SAN 3107/2015, 10 Sep. 2015.
123. Some cases of conscientious objection will be examined *infra* , in Part II, Ch. 2.

worship or prayer, have firm moral principles – religious or non-religious – about how they must behave in their daily lives, and consider that respect for those principles is an essential element of their human dignity.

128. Freedom of conscience is not explicitly mentioned by the Constitution or by the Organic Law on Religious Freedom. However, it is usually deemed as implicitly recognized and protected by the Constitution, taking into account that Article 10.2 CE remits, for the interpretation of fundamental freedoms, to the Universal Declaration of Human Rights and to international treaties signed by Spain. As is well known, 'freedom of thought, conscience and religion' is recognized by the UDHR (Article 18), and guaranteed by the ECHR (Article 9) and the International Covenant on Civil and Political Rights (Article 18).

129. Indeed, the Spanish Constitutional Court has unambiguously held that freedom of conscience is protected by Article 16 CE. Sometimes the Court has used not totally clear expressions, for instance when it declared that 'freedom of conscience is a concrete aspect of the freedom of ideology recognized by Article 16 of the Constitution'.[124] However, the Court has been more specific about the scope of protection of this freedom, which goes beyond the mere right to have moral principles and comprises the right to carry a life coherent with those principles. In the Court's words, freedom of conscience 'not only implies the right to form one's own conscience but also the right to act in accordance with its dictates'.[125] In other decisions, the Constitutional Court has emphasized that freedom of conscience consists in the fact that 'a person has the possibility, legally guaranteed, to accommodate his religious conduct and his way of life to his own convictions', with the consequence that the state is not only prohibited from interfering with the individual's decisions but is also obliged to protect 'the exercise of that freedom against interference from other persons or social groups'.[126]

130. As indicated in the previous subsection, the most frequent and significant problematic issues with respect to freedom of conscience refer to situations of conscientious objection, i.e., to conflicts between individual conscience and legal obligations, especially those derived from prima facie neutral laws of general applicability. They deserve a separate section in this monograph.[127]

IX. Compliance with Religious Dietary Rules

131. Although the Organic Law on Religious Freedom does mention it explicitly, freedom of conscience is commonly understood as embracing individuals' right to comply with the dietary rules that their respective religions may impose. To observe those rules, state cooperation is normally needed in the same cases as religious assistance,[128] and sometimes also in the case of students – especially in big cities, where it is customary that pupils do not return home for lunch and many schools provide a meal for them in a dining room. So far, some Spanish courts have been not

124. STC 15/1982, FJ 6.
125. *Ibid.*
126. *See* ATC 617/1984, FJ 4; and ATC 551/1985, FJ 3.
127. *See infra*, Part II, Ch. 2
128. *See supra*, paras 120–121.

very sensitive to non-discrimination issues in the concrete area of education and have held that public schools are not obliged to provide a specific menu to accommodate the religious needs of Muslim students.[129]

132. The general regulations of the army[130] do not contain specific provisions to protect this aspect of freedom of conscience. Instead, the general Regulation of Penitentiaries provides that meals provided to inmates must be adequate to their 'age, health, work, climate, customs and, as far as possible, personal and religious convictions'.[131] A certain trivialization of religious dietary requirements seems to be present in this provision. On the one hand, religious convictions are put on the same level as other 'personal' convictions (for instance vegetarianism or veganism, which are perfectly legitimate options but often not based on beliefs protected by a constitutional right). On the other hand, the fact that the proviso 'as far as possible' is referred only to personal and religious convictions indicates that they are put on an inferior level in comparison with other individuals' preferences stemming, for instance, from customs or climate.

133. State cooperation with individuals' compliance with religious dietary restrictions is envisaged in the particular case of Muslims. Article 14.4 of the 1992 Agreement with the Islamic Federation specifically provides:

> Meals for persons confined in public centres or military establishments, as well as for Muslim students of public schools and publicly funded private schools, when they so request, shall be adapted to Islamic religious rules. The same policy shall be applied to the schedule of meals during the fasting month of Ramadan.

134. Curiously, no parallel provision exists in the Agreement with the Jewish Federation, despite the fact that it was included – even in more protective terms – in the first proposal for an agreement that Jewish communities presented to the government in 1981. After that, it disappeared from all subsequent drafts.[132]

§3. Judicial Protection of Religious Freedom

135. Article 4 LOLR applies to freedom of religion or belief the general provision of Article 53.2 CE, which prescribes that every citizen is entitled to request the judicial protection of his fundamental rights by ordinary courts, 'according to a preferential and summary procedure', as well as by the Constitutional Court through a specific constitutional procedure.

136. The judicial protection of fundamental rights by ordinary courts follows a procedure that is given priority in the daily business of the courts. The rules applicable

129. *See* STSJ Madrid 388/2015 (*Sala de lo Contencioso-Administrativo, sección 8ª*), 16 Jun. 2015.
130. Cited *infra* , para. 364.
131. Article 226 of the *Real Decreto* 190/1996, 9 Feb. 1996, *por el que se aprueba el Reglamento Penitenciario*.
132. *See* J. Martínez-Torrón, *Separatismo y cooperación en los acuerdos del Estado con las minorías religiosas* 158–159 (Comares 1994).

to this procedure are contained in some specific laws as well as in the codes of civil procedure and criminal procedure.[133]

137. Article 161.1.b) CE, together with Article 53.2 CE, accords the Constitutional Court jurisdiction to judge alleged violations of fundamental rights and freedoms through the so-called appeal for protection (*recurso de amparo*), which is a remedy against concrete violations of constitutional rights with identifiable victims. The rules governing the constitutional *recurso de amparo* are in the 1979 Organic Law of the Constitutional Court.[134] This type of constitutional appeal is admissible only once the plaintiff has exhausted all available remedies before the ordinary courts. In addition to individuals claiming to be victims of a violation of their fundamental rights, the public prosecutor (*Ministerio Fiscal*, which represents the 'public interest') and the ombudsman (*Defensor del Pueblo*) have standing to file a *recurso de amparo*, but they very rarely have exercised this prerogative. Instead, it has been more usual that, when the ombudsman has perceived that a law was constitutive of infringement of fundamental rights, it has brought another type of constitutional challenge (*recurso de inconstitucionalidad*), which is aimed directly at declaring the law itself unconstitutional; only the president of the government, the ombudsman, and a group of at least fifty congressmen or senators have standing to present a *recurso de inconstitucionalidad.*[135] In the area of religious freedom this has occurred once, when the *Defensor del Pueblo* brought a constitutional challenge in 1985 to defend the rights of conscientious objectors to military service.[136]

138. Prompted by the increasing delays caused by overload of appeals, a legislative reform of Article 50 of the Organic Law of the Constitutional Court, in 2007,[137] requires that, to be admissible, *recursos de amparo* must show 'especial constitutional consequence'. In the literal words of the law, a constitutional appeal for protection shall be admissible only if that issue:

> justifies a decision on the merits by the Constitutional Court as a result of its especial constitutional consequence, which shall be evaluated in the light of its significance for the interpretation, the application or the general efficacy of the Constitution, as well as for the determination of the content and reach of fundamental rights.

---

133. See, for a detailed analysis and references, with special attention to the civil procedure, R. Garcimartín Montero, *El proceso civil de tutela de los derechos fundamentales* (Thomson Reuters–Aranzadi 2016).

134. *Ley Orgánica* 2/1979, 3 Oct. 1979, *del Tribunal Constitucional*, Arts 41–58 (some of them modified by the *Ley Orgánica* 6/2007, 24 May 2007).

135. In some cases, also the regional governments and legislatures. *See ibid.*, Art. 32 and Art. 162 CE.

136. The challenge, however, was not successful and the Constitutional Court rejected all the claims of the ombudsman in STC 160/1987. The challenge had been directed against two laws of 1984 that regulated the exercise of conscientious objection to military service and the characteristics of the alternative civil service.

137. *Ley Orgánica* 6/2007, 24 May 2007, which modified various articles of the Organic Law of the Constitutional Court.

This legal reform has made easier for the Court to reject the admissibility of the vast majority of appeals without the need to provide specific grounds of inadmissibility. The system thus established, in practical terms, is not very dissimilar from the *certiorari* used by the US Supreme Court or from the practice of the German *Bundesverfassungsgericht* – which seems to have been the direct source of inspiration for the Spanish legal reform.[138]

139. Spain being part of the Council of Europe, religious freedom enjoys also the judicial protection of European Court of Strasbourg. Not many applications alleging violation of religious freedom have been filed against Spain since it became signatory of the ECHR in 1979.[139]

§4. Protection of Religious Freedom by Criminal Law

140. In Spain, there is a tradition of protecting religion by means of criminal law. After the promulgation of the 1978 Constitution, criminal legislation was adapted to the new constitutional principles informing the relations between state and religion.[140] The Constitutional Court has held that using criminal law as a means to guarantee religious freedom is a legitimate choice for the legislator.[141]

141. The Criminal Code in force, enacted in 1995, contains some provisions aimed at the protection of religious freedom, both from an individual and collective perspective. Indeed, the Code has a specific section, composed by Articles 522–526, on 'crimes against freedom of conscience, religious feelings and respect for the deceased'. In addition, other articles out of that section have an influence on the protection of individual religious freedom. All these articles are inspired by the aim of preventing violence, coercion or discrimination associated, one way or other, with religious ideas or practices. They are explained in a different part of this monograph.[142]

§5. Limitations on Religious Freedom

142. According to Article 16.1 CE, 'manifestations' of freedom of ideology, religion and worship may be subject only to those limitations that are 'necessary for the maintenance of the public order protected by law'. As noted above,[143] the wording of this article implicitly recognizes that the internal dimension of religious freedom is absolute and not limitable, as has been affirmed by the Strasbourg jurisdiction and by the Spanish Constitutional Court. That is to say, *no limitation can be imposed legitimately on the internal freedom of choice in matters of religion or belief*, and only

138. *See* L. Bachmaier Winter, *La reforma de la LOTC y la ampliación del incidente de nulidad de actuaciones*, 13 Revista General de Derecho Procesal 1–23 (2007).
139. The main decisions are mentioned *infra* , in paras 373–379.
140. These principles have been explained *supra* , in Part I, Ch. 3.
141. *See* ATC 271/1984, and ATC 180/1986.
142. *See infra* , Part VII, Ch. 8.
143. *See supra* , paras 107–108.

the external expressions of religion or beliefs are susceptible of state interference, which must be at all events duly justified.

143. Article 16.1 CE mentions *public order* as the only legitimate cause for restricting religious freedom. Nevertheless, on the European level Article 9.2 ECHR conceives legitimate limitations on religious freedom more broadly. This is the reason why Article 3.1 LOLR, without altering the letter of the constitutional text, endeavoured to adapt it to the European Convention by defining the other concepts present in Article 9.2 ECHR (the protection of public safety, health and morals, as well as the rights and freedoms of others) as 'constitutive elements of the public order protected by law in a democratic society'. For the rest, taking into account the reference of Article 10.2 CE to international treaties as a necessary guide for the interpretation of fundamental rights, it is indisputable that both Article 16.1 CE and Article 3.1 LOLR must be understood in the light of Article 9.2 ECHR and of the relevant Strasbourg case law.

144. This implies that, following a general and commonly accepted doctrine in constitutional and international law, limitations on (the external aspect of) religious freedom must be construed *narrowly*, like limitations on any other freedom – which runs in parallel with the need for a *broad* construction of the scope of protection of fundamental rights. In addition, according to the ECHR and the ECtHR, limitations on religious freedom are acceptable only when they comply with three requirements. First, they must be *prescribed by law*. Second, the limitative measure must pursue one of the *legitimate aims* enunciated by Article 9.2 ECHR, namely the protection of public order, safety, health or morals, or the protection of the rights and freedoms of others. Third, the limitation must be *necessary in a democratic society*. This triple requirement is common to other fundamental rights recognized by the European Convention, in particular those guaranteed by Articles 8-11, although the legitimate aims justifying limitations vary depending on the right concerned. From the ECtHR's case law that has interpreted paragraph second of Articles 8-11 we can infer the following guiding criteria, which are also applicable to religions freedom.[144]

145. The expression 'prescribed by law' is aimed to prevent national authorities from acting with full discretion – or arbitrariness – against activities that they consider harmful to the public interest, but it does not prevent them from adopting concrete measures within a general framework of competences previously conferred by law, as far as the law does not grant uncontrolled power to administrative authorities. In this context, the term 'law' has to be interpreted in a broad sense, inclusive not only of legislation or statutory law but also of judge-made law. What is essential is that the principle of legal certainty is respected. Legal certainty requires that applicable law – be it legislation or case law – is formulated with sufficient precision and is adequately accessible to the citizens, so that they can foresee the legal consequences of their actions and can regulate their own conduct accordingly.

146. The expression 'democratic society' means, according to the case law of the ECtHR, a society based upon the guarantee of pluralism and upon the supremacy

144. The doctrine of the ECtHR has been elaborated mostly in relation to freedom of expression (Art. 10 ECHR) and freedom of association (Art. 11 ECHR), some of whose limitation clauses are coincident with those applicable to religious freedom. *See* , for further details and references, J. Martínez-Torrón, *Limitations on Religious Freedom in the Case Law of the European Court of Human Rights*, 19 Emory Intl. L. Rev. 587–636 (2005).

of law. In other words, a society whose legal and political values correspond to those inspiring the ECHR. With respect to the adjective 'necessary', the European Court has held that it is not equivalent to 'indispensable', 'absolutely necessary' or 'strictly necessary' as utilized in other articles of the ECHR.[145] But, at the same time, it cannot be attributed the flexibility of expressions such as 'admissible', 'ordinary', 'useful', 'reasonable' or 'desirable'.[146] In the interpretation of the Court, the word 'necessary' implies the existence of a 'pressing social need', which cannot be determined in the abstract but must be ascertained *ad casum*, after evaluating a variety of factors. Among those factors are: the nature of the right involved and the degree of interference in its exercise; the nature of the activities subjected to restriction; the nature of the public interest that allegedly justifies the limitation on freedoms; and the level of protection which that interest requires in the precise circumstances of the case. The restrictive measures adopted by national authorities, ultimately, can be deemed necessary when they are 'proportionate to the legitimate aim pursued'.[147]

147. With a different wording, the Spanish Constitutional Court has accepted the general doctrine of the ECtHR with respect to limitations on fundamental rights, emphasizing that they are subject only to the limits foreseen by the Constitution or by other legal interests protected by the Constitution;[148] that limitations must be necessary to reach the aim pursued;[149] that they must also be proportionate,[150] cannot interfere with the fundamental right in question 'beyond what is reasonable',[151] and must respect in any event the 'essential content' of the relevant right.[152] In addition, the Constitutional Court has held that limitations on fundamental rights must be rejected when there is a *less burdensome alternative* that can achieve the same goal[153] with the same efficacy.[154] In connection with religious freedom, this criterion has been applied – together with other arguments – to exonerate from criminal responsibility the parents of a minor that needed a blood transfusion in a situation of emergency. The minor – a Jehovah's Witness, like his parents – was so terrified by his understanding of the moral consequences of that medical procedure that, according to the medical team in charge, the transfusion was not safely practicable without his consent. The parents refused to try to persuade his son to accept the blood transfusion voluntarily and the minor died without the transfusion having been performed. Among other things, the Court noted that 'it was not proved either that the parents' persuasion would have been efficacious or that ...

145. Cf. Arts 2.2, 6.1 and 15.1 ECHR.
146. Cf. Arts 4.3, 5.3 and 6.1 ECHR.
147. *See* , precisely in relation to religious freedom, *Kokkinakis v. Greece*, 25 May 1993, para. 49, which reiterates words used by the ECtHR since the late 1960s.
148. *See* STC 11/1981, FJ 7; and STC 1/1982, FJ 5. With specific reference to religious freedom, *see* STC 154/2002, FJ 8.
149. *See* STC 69/1982, FJ 5; and STC 13/1985, FJ 2.
150. *See* STC 37/1989, FJ 7.
151. *See* STC 53/1986, FJ 3.
152. *See* STC 11/1981, FJ 10; STC 196/1987, FJ 4–6; STC 12/1990, FJ 8; and STC 137/1990, FJ 6.
153. *See* STC 178/1989, FJ 5; STC 66/1991, FJ 2.
154. *See* STC 66/1995, FJ 5.

there were not other alternatives less burdensome [for the parents' rights] that could have made the transfusion possible'.[155]

148. Some other decisions of the Constitutional Court have applied the limitation clauses of Article 3.1 LOLR specifically to manifestations of the freedom of ideology, religion and worship guaranteed by Article 16 CE. In 1982, the Court held that the limit of *public morals* is fully applicable.[156] The case in question referred to the criminal proceedings initiated against the publisher of a book oriented to the sex education of children, and the plaintiff argued on the basis of freedom of expression and freedom of ideology, among other grounds. The Court interpreted the Constitution – which does not mention public morals as a ground for limitations on freedom of expression or freedom of religion – in the light of the ECHR and the LOLR. In another decision relating to Jehovah's Witnesses and emergency medical procedures, the Court has utilized the notion of *public health* to declare legitimate the conduct of a judge that authorized a hospital to practise an urgent blood transfusion on a woman that suffered a haemorrhage after giving birth to a child.[157] Neither she nor her husband consented to the transfusion, which was performed with judicial authorization. After the woman died, the husband initiated criminal proceedings against the judge, who was absolved. The husband appealed to the Constitutional Court alleging that he had been deprived from his right to 'adequate judicial protection'. The Court rejected his claim on the ground – among others – that the LOLR includes the protection of health as a legitimate limitation on religious freedom and therefore the judge's action was legitimate. The notion of *respect for the rights and freedoms of others* has been implicitly used by the Constitutional Court in a case concerning the right to the observance of sabbath raised by an employee who, after her conversion to the Seventh-Day Adventist Church, refused to work on Saturdays and was consequently dismissed.[158] One of the grounds for the Court's rejection of her appeal was that one of the parties in a labour contract could not invoke her constitutional rights to impose unilaterally contractual modifications on the other party.

§6. Parental Custody and the Religious Freedom of Minors

149. The decisions concerning the exercise of religious freedom by minors are normally a responsibility of their parents or legal guardians.[159] There is no specific general provision of Spanish law in this respect but, in addition to being the logical solution, it is coherent with the provisions of the Civil Code that attach overall legal

155. STC 154/2002, FJ 12.
156. *See* STC 62/1982.
157. *See* ATC 369/1984.
158. *See* STC 19/1985.
159. *See* B. Rodrigo Lara, *Minoría de edad y libertad de conciencia* (Servicio de Publicaciones de la Facultad de Derecho de la Universidad Complutense 2005); M.A. Asensio Sánchez, *La patria potestad y la libertad de conciencia del menor. El interés del menor a la libre formación de su conciencia* (Tecnos 2006); M. Moreno Antón, *Minoría de edad y libertad religiosa: estudio jurisprudencial*, in *La libertad religiosa y su regulación legal*, 241–278 (R. Navarro-Valls, J. Mantecón & J. Martínez-Torrón eds, Iustel 2009).

representation of minors to parental authority, emphasizing that this 'shall always be exercised for the benefit of children, in accordance with their personality, and respecting their physical and psychological integrity'.[160]

150. There is one aspect of religious freedom whose exercise is specifically placed by the Spanish Constitution under parental responsibility: *decisions about receiving religious or moral instruction.*[161] More broadly, the ECHR has recognized the parents' rights to ensure that the education of their children is in conformity with their philosophical and religious convictions.[162] The CFREU recognizes the same right with almost identical wording, and includes a reference to the protection of 'pedagogical' convictions.[163] Such parental right includes agnostic and atheistic convictions. Indeed, some recent decisions of Spanish courts have recognized one of the parents' right to send the child to a state neutral school when the choice of the other parent for a religious school was not grounded on religious convictions but on geographical proximity;[164] and also the right of agnostic parents to have their child matriculated at a public neutral school even though the local educational authorities had sent him to a subsidized religious school because of lack of places available in public schools.[165] Parental rights over the education of their children have raised some conflictive issues before the Spanish courts when parents reject some teaching subjects on religious or moral grounds and declare themselves conscientious objectors on behalf of their children. These conflicts are examined in other sections of this monograph.[166]

151. The *notion of minor* is very broad and it seems sensible, as the child matures, to take into account his evolving capacities in order to give him more responsibility about decisions affecting his religious freedom. This is for the rest obliged under the 1989 UN Convention on the Rights of the Child.[167] Its Article 14.2, after guaranteeing the freedom of thought, conscience and religion of minors, recognizes the rights of parents or legal guardians 'to provide direction to the child in the exercise of his or her right in a manner consistent with the evolving capacities of the child'. The relevance of the child's maturity was specifically mentioned by the Constitutional Court with respect to the refusal of blood transfusions by a Jehovah's Witness; in that judgment, the Court considered uncertain that a 13-year old child could be deemed mature enough to adopt a life-or-death decision by rejecting an emergency medical treatment, and therefore such decision could not be binding for his parents.[168] Apart from this, there is no clear legal notion about the precise time when a minor can take his own autonomous legal decisions on diverse aspects of religious freedom or, at least, when his opinion must be taken into account. The Civil Code, however, provides some guidance when it indicates that children with 12 years of age must be heard in the proceedings for

---

160. *See* Civil Code, especially Arts 154 and 162.
161. *See* Art. 27.3 CE, quoted *supra* , in para. 51.
162. *See* Art. 2 of the Protocol to the ECHR.
163. *See* Art. 14.3 CFREU.
164. *See* decision of JPI N° 1 of Moncada (Aragón), 21 Jun. 2017, Proc. 1/2017.
165. *See* STSJ Aragón 60/2017 (*Sala de lo Contencioso-Administrativo, Sección 1ª*), 17 Feb. 2017.
166. *See infra* , Part II, Ch. 2 §8.
167. Spain signed and ratified this international convention in 1990.
168. *See* STC 154/2002, FJ 10, cited *supra* , in para. 147.

awarding custody in cases of separation or divorce of the parents;[169] and also when it determines the age of 16 years as the time from which a minor can emancipate.[170] In the area of medical treatments, according to current legislation, parents or legal representatives cannot replace the informed consent of minors after they have turned 16 unless the treatment in question is necessary to prevent a serious danger for the minor's life or health; in any event, the minor's opinion must be taken into account in those cases.[171]

152. If the responsibility about decisions affecting the religious freedom of minors is linked to parental authority and custody, it is to be expected that conflicts may arise when the capacity of parents is questioned and when parents divorce or separate. The first type of situation was examined by the Constitutional Court in a decision of 1994,[172] related to the children of several parents that belonged to a religious movement called 'The Children of God', characterized, among other things, by its tendency to establish models of communal life more or less detached from mainstream society. The regional Catalan government, considering that the children were in a situation of abandonment and negligence, expressed – among other things – in their lack of proper schooling, obtained judicial authorization to retire the custody from the parents and assume the legal guardianship of the children. Part of the court's reasoning when granting such authorization was grounded on the alleged nature of 'sect' of the Children of God, against which criminal proceedings had been initiated. On appeal, the parents had that judicial authorization revoked and the Catalan government appealed to the Constitutional Court. The Court did not make any judgment on the issue of the alleged negligence and abandonment of the children, or on the nature of 'dangerous sect' of the Children of God, but circumscribed its analysis to a concrete and rather formal question, namely the proportionality of the deprivation of parental custody vis-à-vis the need to provide an adequate schooling for the children. The Court reached the conclusion that the Catalan government had alternative means to enforce and guarantee the children's schooling and therefore denied that the dispossession of parental authority were a proportionate measure.

153. The Constitutional Court has also examined the issue of the influence of religious divergences between parents on the allocation of visitation rights after a divorce, following the doctrine of the ECtHR in the *Hoffmann* case.[173] In this judgment, the European Court held that a national court had incurred religious discrimination by taking into account, when deciding on the children's custody, that one of the parents was a Jehovah's Witness. The case decided by the Spanish Constitutional Court[174] related to a convert to the 'Universal Christian Gnostic Movement of Spain' who had separated from his wife. In the judicial proceedings, the mother was awarded the custody of their two children, aged 5 and 12 respectively; the judge granted the father the usual visitation rights, and at the same time explicitly prohibited him from

169. *See* Civil Code, Art. 159.
170. *See* Civil Code, Arts 314–321.
171. *See* *Ley* 26/2015, de 28 de julio, *de modificación del sistema de protección a la infancia y a la adolescencia*, 2nd final provision.
172. STC 260/1994.
173. *Hoffmann v. Austria*, 23 Jun. 1993.
174. STC 141/2000.

proselytizing his children or taking them to any religious meeting. The mother appealed the decision, arguing that all available information on the father's new religion suggested that it might be a 'destructive sect', and hence there was a serious risk to the children's psychological health and education, which required a single religious and moral orientation. The Court of Appeals substantially accepted the mother's reasoning and severely restricted the father's visitation rights. The Spanish Constitutional Court reversed the latter decision, holding that the noncustodial parent's visitation rights could not be arbitrarily reduced by the courts on account of his religious beliefs, regardless of how strange those ideas might appear in a certain social milieu, without proof that the children's health or education were endangered. The Court accepted that the judicial reduction of the father's visitation rights pursued a legitimate aim, namely the protection of the best interest of his children. Furthermore, it affirmed that the judicial order banning the father's proselytism was justifiable as far as it was aimed at safeguarding the 'moral integrity' of the children – it is normally accepted that the best interest of the child requires continuity in his moral and religious education also after the separation of his parents.[175] However, the Constitutional Court found that the drastic reduction in his visitation rights decreed by the Court of Appeals was a measure clearly disproportionate because there was no evidence suggesting that the father had tried to convert his children or take them to any religious meeting, or that the children had been negatively affected in any way by their father's belief. These factors led the Constitutional Court to conclude that the decision of the Court of Appeals rested only on the factually unsupported assumption that the Gnostic Movement was a dangerous sect, and therefore it held that the father had been the victim of discriminatory treatment on account of his beliefs.

175. There is a certain case law in Strasbourg following this line of thought. *See* J. Martínez-Torrón, *Derecho de familia y libertad de conciencia en el Convenio Europeo de Derechos Humanos*, in *Derecho de familia y libertad de conciencia en los países de la Unión Europea y el derecho comparado* 153–154 (A. Castro Jover ed., Servicio Editorial de la Universidad del País Vasco 2001).

Chapter 2. Freedom of Conscience and Legal Obligations: Conscientious Objections

154. As indicated above, the Constitutional Court has unambiguously stated that freedom of conscience is an integral part of the freedom of ideology, religion and worship guaranteed by Article 16 of the Constitution.[176] The most frequent and important issues with respect to freedom of conscience refer to situations that are normally called conscientious objections, i.e., conflicts between individual conscience and legal obligations, especially those obligations stemming from prima facie neutral laws of general applicability.[177] This chapter will analyse the most significant cases of conscientious objection in Spanish legislation and case law.

§1. Concept of Conscientious Objection

155. Understood in a broad sense, conscientious objection is the individual's refusal, on conscience grounds, to perform a conduct that in principle could be legally required from him as a direct or indirect consequence of a state legislative provision, a contract, or a judicial or administrative resolution. On many occasions, the required activity is not an absolute legal obligation but a condition to be entitled to a legal benefit or to keep a determined legal status; in these cases, rather than a direct violation of freedom of conscience, denying the right of conscientious objection might constitute indirect discrimination on the ground of religion or belief. Only reasons of moral or religious nature generate, strictly speaking, attitudes of conscientious objection, which cannot be assimilated to other kinds of refusals to comply with the law on political, psychological or other grounds. Sometimes conscientious objectors attempt to change the law for the entire community and engage in movements that are normally called 'civil disobedience', but very often the objectors' primary intention consists in being exempted from a general legal obligation.

156. In most cases, objectors face a serious internal conflict. He must choose between submitting to the state legal rule or to the moral rule that his own conscience invokes as supreme law. The immediate consequence is that objectors find themselves under an important moral burden, for they cannot obey the state law and their own conscience at the same time. Disobeying the former entails a material penalty and disobeying the latter a spiritual sanction.

157. In the juridical analysis of conscientious objection, it is important to avoid a frequent mistake, typical of positions suffering from a radical legalism. These positions tend to look at conscientious objections from a negative perspective and characterize

176. Cf. *supra*, paras 128–129.

177. *See*, for a detailed treatment of these issues, in Spanish, international and comparative law, R. Navarro-Valls & J. Martínez-Torrón, *Conflictos entre conciencia y ley. Las objeciones de conciencia* (2nd ed., Iustel 2012). *See also* J. Martínez-Torrón, *Conscientious objections: protecting freedom of conscience beyond prejudice*, in *Routledge Handbook on Law and Religion* 191–207 (S. Ferrari ed., Routledge 2015).

them as mere phenomena of legal disobedience or 'insubmission'. They lose sight of the fact that conscientious objectors are not primarily infractors of the law but persons that exercise a fundamental right, freedom of conscience, which is an integral part of the legal system. In addition, conscientious objectors are normally persons of high moral standards, a characteristic that is a condition to be a good citizen. Their elevated concept of morals is precisely the cause of their scruples of conscience and the origin of their personal drama.

§2. Some Basic Criteria for the Legal Analysis of Conscientious Objections

158. In essence there are two main approaches to the issue of how to deal with conscientious objections from a juridical perspective. One is *legalism* and the other is the *balance of interests*.

159. The *legalist approach* is based on a double assumption: the legislator is always right and the core of law can be reduced to legislation, i.e., statutory law. From this perspective, every conflict between law, which would represent public interest, and individual conscience, which is portrayed as a private interest – must be resolved in favour of the former. Any other solution would entail a risk of legal uncertainty and even of 'pulverization' of the legal system, for the efficacy of general rules would be ultimately determined by individual moral choices, which are unpredictable and not always reasonable. Freedom of thought, conscience and religion would protect individuals only against laws directly aimed at restricting a particular religion or belief (or religion in general). Instead, exemptions from compliance with 'neutral laws' – i.e., laws that pursue legitimate secular goals – may be granted only by legislation, and therefore conscientious objections would be legitimate and could be protected by the courts only when explicitly recognized by the legislator (*interpositio legislatoris*).

160. The *approach of the balance of interests*, inspired by the US and Canadian case laws, pivots on the search of the highest possible protection of the fundamental right to freedom of conscience and is less concerned about the intangibility of concrete legislative provisions. It rejects the notion that legislation has the monopoly of justice and that conscientious objection is at most a 'tolerated' exception from general legislative rules. On the contrary, being freedom of conscience a constitutional right, it is part of the law itself – a fundamental rule and not an exception from the rules. Conscientious objections are not watched with diffidence, as 'evasions' from the legal order, but are analysed as constitutive of fundamental legal interests that must be balanced with other legal interests at issue in a particular case.

161. Article 10.2 CFREU seems to support the balance of interests' approach when providing – in general terms and not with reference to a particular type of objection – that 'the right to conscientious objection is recognised, in accordance with the national laws governing the exercise of this right'. By this explicit recognition, and by implicit remarking its connection with 'freedom of thought, conscience and religion', guaranteed in the first paragraph of the same article (Article 10.1 CFREU), the EU Charter makes it impossible to understand conscientious objections as expressions of a purely private interest. It would be also inaccurate to interpret the Charter's reference to national laws as subjecting the guarantee of conscientious objection to the condition of its prior recognition by ad hoc legislation. On the one hand, it would be unreasonable to make the existence and protection of a fundamental right in Europe dependent on the autonomous will of each national legislator. And on the other hand, if that were the case, it would not make any sense to include conscientious objection as a fundamental right in the CFREU. The Charter's reference to national laws, in the author's view, should be construed as recognizing the national legislators' competence to regulate common types of conscientious objection, in order to facilitate their exercise and at the same time to make them compatible with the protection of other legal interests. In no case could it be understood as giving the legislator the prerogative of denying the existence of that fundamental right – and even less by its mere silence.

162. The analysis of the Spanish law in the following pages is inspired by the balance of interests' approach, whose analysis of facts is, in the author's opinion, more precise and realistic than the one underlying the legalist approach. Two main reasons move the author to assert this. In the first place, the so-called *neutral* laws are not so neutral. All laws rest on ethical foundations, more or less explicit, which normally depend on the majority values present in a given society. Often, neutral laws are aimed at realizing and preserving ethical values – sometimes with an identifiable religious origin – that are socially accepted as civic values by the largest part of society. This is the reason why the conflicts of conscience caused by neutral laws usually relate to people in minority positions. Ignoring, or persecuting, conscientious objections, is a way of discriminating minorities that do not share majority moral values. In the second place, protecting freedom of conscience is not a private interest but a public interest of the highest rank, which must be balanced with the specific public interest of the legal rule in question, taking into account that objectors normally do not attempt to have the law repealed but just to obtain an exemption from it. Therefore, the balancing process in these cases entails comparing two factors: on the one hand the potential harm that dismissing the objector's claim would cause to freedom of conscience, and on the other hand the potential harm that granting the particular exemption requested by the objector would cause to the public interest represented by a particular law.

163. Naturally, the foregoing observations imply that *defending an automatic predominance of conscientious objection over legislation is as inappropriate as defending an automatic predominance of legislation over conscientious objection.* The right approach is to perform a comparative analysis of both interests in order to decide which must prevail in the concrete case, keeping in mind that every restriction on freedom of conscience must be duly justified by the state as 'necessary in a democratic society' and not merely as convenient, useful or practical.[178] Ultimately, the approach of the balance of interests compels the state to demonstrate that, in situations of conscientious objection, it is 'necessary in a democratic society' to refuse all possible exemptions from the application of the law.

178. *See* the observations apropos of limitations on religious freedom in the case law of the ECtHR and the Constitutional Court, *supra* , Part II, Ch. 1 §5.

§3. The General Position of the Constitutional Court

164. We have already seen that the initial position of the Constitutional Court with regard to freedom of conscience was open and receptive.[179] Nevertheless, the application of its own doctrine to the particular issue of conscientious objection has been irregular and even, to all appearances, contradictory.

165. Through the mid-1980s, the Court based its decisions in this matter upon an expansive interpretation of freedom of conscience. Thus, in 1982, in one of its first decisions on conscientious objection to military service, the Court declared that there is a direct connection between conscientious objection and freedom of conscience, which is a particular aspect of the freedom of ideology enshrined in Article 16 CE. Conscientious objection was, therefore, 'a right recognized explicitly and implicitly in the Spanish constitutional order'.[180]

166. Even more clearly, in 1985 the Constitutional Court not only reaffirmed the link of conscientious objection with freedom of conscience but also unambiguously declared that it was a right that could be exercised without the *interpositio legislatoris*, i.e., without the support of an ad hoc legislative provision. The Court's statement referred to conscientious objection to abortion but at the same time was intentionally expressing a doctrine of general applicability. In particular, the Court had to decide whether a statute decriminalizing some cases of abortion could be deemed unconstitutional because it did not contain any specific provision protecting the conscientious objection of physicians and other healthcare personnel. The response of the Court was clear: strictly speaking a conscience clause was not needed because the Constitution itself protected conscientious objectors. These were the precise words of the Court:

> The right to conscientious objection…exists and can be exercised irrespective of the fact that it has been regulated by a statute or not. Conscientious objection is an integral part of the fundamental right to freedom of ideology and religion, recognized in Article 16.1 of the Constitution; and, as this Court has repeatedly indicated, the Constitution can be directly applied, especially when fundamental rights are concerned.[181]

167. However, beginning with a series of cases decided in the mid-to-late 1980s, the Constitutional Court has taken a more restrictive approach to the rights of individual conscience. And, most surprisingly, it has done so without overruling its previous decisions, which proposed an expansive interpretation of religious freedom. The most significant cases adopting this restrictive view are two 1987 decisions, delivered the same day, concerning conscientious objection to military service,[182] which is explicitly recognized as an individual right by the Constitution. Beyond the holdings directly related to objection to military service, the most noteworthy aspect of the 1987 decisions

179. *See supra* , paras 128–129.
180. *See* STC 15/1982, FJ 6.
181. STC 53/1985, FJ 14. For an analysis of this judicial doctrine in the light of comparative law, *see* R. Navarro-Valls, *La objeción de conciencia al aborto: derecho comparado y derecho español*, 2 Anuario de Derecho Eclesiástico del Estado 257–310 (1986).
182. STC 160/1987 and STC 161/1987.

is the restrictive concept of freedom of conscience employed by the Court in contradiction with applicable precedent. The Constitutional Court affirmed drastically that recognizing a general right to conscientious objection was unthinkable, for it 'would imply denying the very idea of state'. And the Court continued: 'What can occur is that [conscientious objection] is exceptionally admitted with regard to a particular duty.'[183] Thus, the Constitutional Court tried to break the obvious link existing between conscientious objection – in this case to military service – and freedom of religion and belief, with the consequence that, without specific statutory support, there would not be any right to be exempted from a legal obligation on moral or religious grounds, even under the umbrella of freedom of conscience.[184]

168. The contradictions inherent to this case law of the Constitutional Court can perhaps be explained, at least in part, by a contextualized interpretation. The judgment of 1985 would cover a broader spectrum of cases, as the Court unmistakably held that Article 16 CE is sufficient to guarantee the rights of conscientious objectors and that no additional legislative provision is needed in rigour. Certainly, the Court did not intend to say that conscientious objection is an absolute or unconditional right. On the contrary, in its mention of Article 16 CE there was an implicit reference to the constitutional limitations that can be legitimately imposed on freedom of conscience, as on any other fundamental right. Limitations on conscientious objection are precisely what the Constitutional Court seemed to have in mind in its 1987 decisions. The Court's extreme assertion that a general recognition of conscientious objection 'would imply denying the very idea of state' only makes sense if we understand it as related to a hypothetical recognition of that right in absolute terms, without any limitation whatsoever. We must keep in mind that the decisions of 1987 resolved numerous questions contained in several appeals of unconstitutionality against the 1984 laws that regulated, for the first time in Spain, conscientious objection to military service. The strong wording of the Court was likely caused by the fact that it was dealing with objection against a constitutional obligation – military service is mentioned in Article 30.1 CE as a 'right and duty' of Spanish citizens – and not just against an obligation derived from an ordinary statute. In other words, while the 1985 broad recognition of conscientious objection would refer to a variety of areas in which freedom of conscience can be exercised, the restrictive interpretation of conscientious objection operated by the 1987 decisions would refer in particular to military service. In this respect, it is not unrealistic to presume that the Constitutional Court was in 1987 under the pressure of the fear of opening the way to an uncontrolled spread of conscientious objection, in the context of a European debate about the desirable profiles of the legal recognition of objection to military service, and also in the context of a political debate about the role that the army should play in the evolution of the still incipient democracy in Spain.

169. In any event, as we will see in the following subsections, the doctrine of the Constitutional Court after 1987 has been far from uniform and clear on the issue of the relationship between conscientious objection and freedom of conscience, as well as on the issue of the need (or not) of specific legislative provisions to guarantee the rights of objectors in particular cases.

---

183. STC 161/1987, FJ 3.

184. *See also* STC 160/1987, FJ 3.

§4. Conscientious Objection to Military Service

170. The right to conscientious objection to military service is explicitly recognized by Article 30.2 CE, which remits to the legislature for its precise regulation. This article is located out of the section of the Constitution devoted to 'fundamental rights and public freedoms' and begins a new section entitled 'rights and obligations of citizens':

Article 30 CE:

1. Spanish citizens have the right and duty to defend Spain.
2. The law shall determine the military obligations of Spanish citizens and shall regulate, with adequate guarantees, conscientious objection as well as other causes for exemption from compulsory military service; the law may also, when appropriate, impose a substitutive social service.

171. For political reasons, which included the opposition of a military establishment that was still powerful and – in a high percentage – not particularly fond of the evolution of the new democracy in Spain, it took six years to develop this constitutional provision. In 1984, the national legislature (*Cortes Generales*) passed two statutes to regulate the procedure that a citizen should follow to be legally recognized as a conscientious objector and the conditions for performing alternative civil service.[185] These laws, inspired by the recommendations and resolutions of the Council of Europe on the subject, were complemented and modified by subsequent laws and regulations until 1998.[186] No specific exemption from military service was envisaged for religious ministers, but the Catholic Concordat, as well as the 1992 Agreements with the Evangelical, Jewish and Islamic Federations, provided that they should be assigned functions that were compatible with their religious status.[187]

172. The Constitutional Court has ruled on this subject several times prior to and since the 1984 statutes, but not always has followed a coherent approach. In 1982, the Court held that there was a direct connection between the right to conscientious objection recognized by Article 30.2 CE and the freedom of ideology and religion guaranteed by Article 16 CE. According to the Court, the enactment of a specific statute was not strictly necessary to exercise that right – it was already recognized by the Constitution and the function of statutory law was only to 'regulate' it 'in terms that make possible its full applicability and efficacy'.[188] Since 1987, however, the Constitutional Court has adopted a more restrictive interpretation of conscientious objection, denying

185. *Ley* 48/1984 and *Ley Orgánica* 8/1984, both of 26 Dec. 1984.
186. *See* , for more details and references, R. Navarro-Valls & J. Martínez-Torrón, *Conflictos entre conciencia y ley*, 88–94, 111–115.
187. Cf. Art. V of the 1979 Agreement on Religious Assistance to the Army and Military Service of the Clergy and Members of Religious Orders, between Spain and the Holy See; and Art. 4.1 of the 1992 Agreements with the Evangelical, Jewish and Islamic Federations.
188. STC 15/1982, FJ 6.

its character of fundamental right[189] and breaking its direct link with the freedom of ideology guaranteed by Article 16 CE. In the words of the Court, 'the right to be declared exempted from military service does not derive directly from the exercise of freedom of ideology but only from the fact that the Constitution has explicitly recognized the right to conscientious objection in Art. 30.2'.[190] The Court has also rejected all claims from objectors that refused to perform substitutive civil service on conscience grounds.[191]

173. The legal configuration of the right to conscientious objection to military service, in accordance with the 1984 statutes and the subsequent laws and regulations, can be summarized as follows. The person claiming to be recognized as objector could allege convictions of diverse nature: 'religious, ethical, moral, humanitarian, philosophical or others of analogous nature'. Significantly, political convictions were not mentioned. In practice, however, this omission was not important, for applications were treated favourably with increasing laxity. Applications could be presented before, but not during, effective incorporation to the military service and were decided by an administrative body, the National Council on Conscientious Objection. Once accepted as objector, the applicant became obliged to perform substitutive social service, consisting in 'activities of public utility that do not require use of weapons and do not entail being under the authority of military institutions'. Social service was performed in areas such as, for instance, civil or environmental protection, health programmes or international cooperation. The Ministry of Justice was in charge or organizing social substitutive service. In practice, a high – and obviously undetermined – percentage of applications came from people that were not real objectors at all but just preferred a social service instead of military service, which appeared more burdensome to them.

174. The legal regime succinctly described above became obsolete when the compulsory military service was 'suspended' in Spain on 31 December 2001.[192] Spain has now a professional army and it is not foreseeable, in the next future, a return to mandatory military service. This does not discard, of course, that a change in the convictions of professional soldiers or officers makes them develop a conscientious objection to being in the army, or that they have serious moral scruples to participate in a particular military conflict, but so far no conflict of this kind has been reported.

175. The professionalization of the army has not precluded the possibility of cases of conscientious objection to paying taxes in the percentage that the state budget allocates to defence expenses, although these cases have never been numerous or successful in Spain. In 2005, a left-wing minority Catalan party of republican orientation (*Esquerra Republicana de Catalunya*) presented a legislative proposal that would

189. *See* STC 160/1987 and STC 161/1987. *See supra*, paras 167–168. These two decisions responded, respectively, to an appeal of unconstitutionality presented by the Spanish Ombudsman (*Defensor del Pueblo*) and four questions of unconstitutionality posed by the National Court (*Audiencia Nacional*) against different provisions of the 1984 statutes.

190. STC 321/1994, FJ 4. Such formalist approach reminds of the one adopted by the European Court of Human Rights on the same issue until the Grand Chamber's judgment in the case *Bayatyan v. Armenia*, 7 Jul. 2011. *See* J. Martínez-Torrón, *Conscientious objections: protecting freedom of conscience beyond prejudice*, 196–197.

191. Cf., for instance, STC 321/1994; STC 55/1996; STC 88/1996.

192. By force of the *Real Decreto* 247/2001, 9 Mar. 2001.

allow citizens to make a choice with regard to a percentage of their income tax equivalent to the percentage of the Ministry of Defence within the state general budget. According to the proposal, taxpayers could decide that this percentage of their taxes was devoted to fund organizations aimed at fostering peace and solidarity. This initiative was rejected by an overwhelming majority in the Congress. Also, in the last years, several regional Supreme Courts have refused to protect conscientious objection to paying taxes in the proportion of the public expenditure on defence, arguing that conscientious objection to cooperate with the army must be strictly interpreted according to the Constitution, which refers only to objection to perform military service; all of them confirmed the sanctions imposed by the tax authorities on objectors for lack of due payment.[193]

§5. Conscientious Objection to Abortion

176. Conscientious objection to abortion has been an issue in Spain since abortion became partly decriminalized in 1985 (in 2010, abortion was more broadly recognized by a new statute). Since then abortion can be performed in a public hospital (or in a private hospital) in the circumstances established by law, thus raising the question whether the healthcare personnel is legally obliged to cooperate in that procedure. The details of Spanish law on this topic are explained in a different part of this monograph.[194]

§6. Conscientious Objections of Pharmacists

177. Conscientious objections of pharmacists have often been aimed at guaranteeing their right not to dispense contraceptive or abortive products. Their conscientious scruples not necessarily are grounded on religious beliefs. Sometimes they are based on pure deontological grounds. As pharmacists are deemed to provide as a public service, the question arises whether they are legally obliged to sell those products in their pharmacies. The details of Spanish law on this topic are explained in a different part of this monograph.[195]

§7. Conscientious Objection to Medical Treatments

178. Conscientious objection to medical treatment is a particularly delicate issue, for the protection of the right to life is often at stake, and for it entails the opposition of two different and opposing consciences: the conscience of the objector and the conscience of the healthcare professional, who normally thinks that trying to save the patient's life is a paramount deontological duty. Conscientious objection to

193. Cf. STSJ Cataluña 206/2006 (*Sala de lo Contencioso, Sección 1ª*), 24 Feb. 2006; STSJ País Vasco 571/2013 (*Sala de lo Contencioso, Sección 1ª*), 23 Oct. 2013; STSJ Valencia 708/2015 (*Sala de lo Contencioso-Administrativo, Sección 3ª*), 29 Jun. 2015.

194. *See infra*, Part VII, Ch. 6 §1.

195. *See infra*, Part VII, Ch. 6 §2.

medical treatment has usually a religious origin. The details of Spanish law on this topic are explained in a different part of this monograph.[196]

§8. Conscientious Objection to Educational Contents or Practices

179. In contemporary societies, education is subject to an intensive state regulation. The moral and religious orientation of the education of minors is undoubtedly a primary responsibility of their parents or legal guardians, as recognized by the international instruments for the protection of human rights as well as by some constitutions.[197] At the same time, it is universally acknowledged that public authorities are responsible for ensuring a minimum level of education to children, in defence of the interest of society in general and of minors in particular. The convergence of parental and state responsibilities in this sensitive area increases the possibilities of conflicts between law and individual conscience, among other reasons because both public authorities and families are obliged to pursue the 'best interest of the child' but they may have a different notion of which the best interest of the child is in particular cases. Often these conflicts relate to certain educational contents or practices, or even to the obligation of schooling the children out of the family environment.

180. In Spain, the basic normative framework is formed by two provisions. One is Article 27.3 of the Constitution: 'Public authorities shall guarantee the right of parents to ensure that their children will receive moral and religious instruction in accordance with their own convictions.' The other is Article 2 of the Protocol to the ECHR: 'In the exercise of any functions which it assumes in relation to education and to teaching, the State shall respect the right of parents to ensure such education and teaching in conformity with their own religious and philosophical convictions.' In addition, we should mention Article 12 of the 1992 Agreements with the Evangelical, Jewish and Islamic communities, on the particular issue of the students' right to religious rest in holy days.

I. School Activities and Religious Observance of Holy Days

181. Sometimes, conscientious objection to school activities is not caused by the activity as such but by the fact that it is scheduled to take place in sabbath or other day considered holy by the objector's religion. For some religions, there is a strict duty to abstain from work in those days. Religious rest is mandatory on Saturdays, according to some interpretations of Judaism as well as to Seventh-Day Adventists and other

196. *See infra*, Part VII, Ch. 6 §3.
197. Cf. Art. 26.3 of the Universal Declaration of Human Rights (1948); Art. 2 of the Protocol to the European Convention on Human Rights (1952); Art. 18.4 of the International Covenant on Civil and Political Rights (1966); Art. 13.3 of the International Covenant on Economic, Social and Cultural Rights (1966); Art. 14.2 of the Convention on the Rights of the Child (1989). Cf. also Art. 14.3 of the Charter of Fundamental Rights of the European Union. In Spain, *see* Art. 27.3 CE.

Evangelical churches. For Muslims there is no such obligation of religious rest, but they must attend collective prayer on Friday afternoon. In addition, they celebrate, like Jews, some religious festivities throughout the year.

182. Article 12 of the 1992 cooperation Agreements recognizes the students' right to the observance of sabbath, the attendance to collective prayer and the commemoration of some holy days of their religion. Upon request of their parents or legal guardians, Protestant, Jewish or Muslim students have the unconditional right to be excused from attending classes or passing examinations in those days. This rule applies to students of public schools and private schools funded by the state (*colegios privados concertados*).

183. It is interesting to note that the same article of the three Agreements contains a parallel rule for applicants to enter the civil service that have been summoned for examination in one of those holy days, but they are not entitled to an unconditional right. Their examination shall be transferred to an alternative date if they request it, except when there is a 'good cause' (*causa motivada*) to refuse their petition. In practice, public examinations to enter most branches of civil service often are held on Saturdays and it is not uncommon that public authorities make difficult the exercise of this right, insisting that these examinations are competitive and in writing, and require that all applicants pass an identical examination, in the same date and under the same conditions. In 2015, however, the Supreme Court recognized the right to a change of dates in the case of a Seventh-Day Adventist who had requested an alternative date for a language exam in the selection process to be accepted as teacher in public schools in the region of Galicia. The exam sitting was on Saturday and Galician authorities rejected the alternatives that the appellant had proposed to make compatible her religious duty of rest with fairness and equality of treatment of all candidates – for instance, to take the exam after sunset and remain isolated in the meantime in the facility where the exam was held, or to be subject to a similar exam in a different date, following the praxis of other public institutions. The Supreme Court's central argument pivoted around a restrictive interpretation of 'good cause'; after reminding that limitations on fundamental rights should be understood as the exception and not the rule, the Court held that Galician authorities had not justified that it was not possible to accept some of the alternative solutions proposed by the appellant, which were commonly used by other public institutions.[198]

II. Freedom of Conscience and Homeschooling

184. The expansion of mandatory schooling of children in Western countries since the late nineteenth century was based on two correlative duties: the state obligation to guarantee that children had the opportunity to be schooled and the parallel parents' obligation to send their children to school. This fact has raised the opposition of parents that demanded to be permitted to educate their children at home, for religious, moral, pedagogical, philosophical or just convenience reasons.

198. STS 3533/2015 (*Sala de lo Contencioso-Administrativo, Sección 7ª*), 6 Jul. 2015.

185. In Spain, demands of homeschooling are relatively recent but tend to spread rapidly.[199] There have been some isolated criminal proceedings against parents that had decided to assume – seemingly with seriousness – the responsibility to educate their children at home instead of sending it to a public or private school, but the courts have been reluctant to accept that homeschooling could qualify as a crime of 'abandonment of the family' (Articles 227 et seq. CP).[200]

186. The Constitutional Court has adjudicated twice on this issue. The first decision, in 1994, is not very relevant, for the key issue was, rather than the legality of homeschooling, to determine if members of an atypical religious movement (The Children of God) could be held criminally liable for neglecting their children – members of this movement tended to follow models of communal life and they not only deprived their children from ordinary schooling but also separated them from virtually all contact with the surrounding social environment.[201] The second decision, in 2010,[202] is much more significant and was influenced by the Strasbourg case law.[203] The Constitutional Court rejected the claim of some parents, homeschoolers, which had been judicially urged to send their children to school. Their objection to ordinary schooling was not based on religious grounds but on their profound disagreement with the pedagogical model that inspired Spanish compulsory education. The Court held that Article 27.3 CE did not prevent the legislator from imposing mandatory schooling for a specific range of ages. The Court also denied that parents had any right to homeschool their children in the absence of an explicit legislative provision permitting it, even in the hypothesis that their objection would have been grounded on religious or moral reasons.

III. Objection to Specific School Subjects

187. More often, parents object not to the schooling of the children in itself but to having them exposed to certain educational contents of the school curriculum, or to some teaching methodologies practised in the school. These are not easy cases, for the dividing line between the legitimate moral choices of parents and the best interest of the child is sometimes very thin. Except for the case of objection to 'education for citizenship', which is explained in more detail in the next subsection, there have been

199. *See* the main page of the homeschooling movement in Spain: http://www.homeschoolingspain.com (accessed 9 Dec. 2017).
200. *See* , for instance, SAP Teruel of 16 Dec. 2009. The press also informed that the public prosecutor ordered the closing of some criminal proceedings initiated in San Sebastián (*see Diario Vasco*, 17 Jul. 2008).
201. *See* STC 260/1994, mentioned in more detail *supra* , in para. 152.
202. STC 133/2010. For a critical view of this judgment, *see* M.J. Valero, *Homeschooling en España. Una reflexión acerca del artículo 27.3 de la Constitución y del derecho de los padres a elegir la educación de sus hijos*, 28 Revista General de Derecho Canónico y Derecho Eclesiástico del Estado 1–32 (2012).
203. *See Konrad and others v. Germany*, decision on the admissibility of Appl. Nr. 35504/03, 11 Sep. 2006. The applicants, on religious grounds, wanted to have their children educated through homeschooling, which is illegal in Germany. The application was declared manifestly ill-founded by the Court, following the criteria formerly held by the European Commission of Human Rights in *Leuffen v. Germany*, decision on the admissibility of Appl. Nr. 19844/92, 9 Jul. 1992.

few cases of conscientious objection to educational contents brought to the Spanish courts.

188. One of them, rather peculiar, related to university education and was decided by the Constitutional Court in 1985.[204] The plaintiff was not a parent but a law student that alleged conscientious objection to the study of canon law, which was a mandatory subject in the curriculum of all law schools in Spain at the time (indeed, there were not then elective courses in law schools), arguing that she should not be obliged to follow a course focused on the legal system of a religion – Catholicism – that she rejected. Although the plaintiff insisted that the study of the course on canon law violated her freedom of ideology and religion, her reasoning was based mainly on the religious neutrality of the state, which, in her view, should exclude imposing the study of a religious legal system in a secular law school. The Court declared the appeal inadmissible, holding that the reason of the study of canon law at public universities was not its religious character but the fact that it was a distinctive and essential part of the evolution of Western law. This – the Court added – was not exceptional, for 'many other legal subjects pivot on the study of juridical theories or texts of identifiable ideological substratum'.

189. In 1998, a regional superior court decided a very different case, such as the conscientious objection of a minor, and her parents, to receive sex education in a public school within a course devoted to the study of natural sciences.[205] Indeed, the student had ceased to attend the classes of that course with the consequence that she received a failing grade. The court denied that either the student or her parents had any right to be exempted from the school subject in question. Two aspects of the judgment seem surprising. First, the court declared that the parents' rights were sufficiently protected by the possibility of sending their daughter to a private school – in contradiction with the Strasbourg doctrine, which has held that the existence of funded private schools does not excuse states from their obligation to guarantee the parents' right over the religious or philosophical orientation of their children's education in the realm of public schools.[206] Second, the court emphasized that the parents could not impose their views on other people and their rights were limited by the rights of others, but it did not specify which rights of other members of the school community would have been infringed by the parents' request – which in fact was not aimed at imposing anything on anyone but only to have their daughter exempted from some teaching contents that they considered seriously offensive for their religious beliefs.

IV. The Case of Conscientious Objection to Education for Citizenship

190. In more recent times, there has been a massive case of conscientious objection to a specific school subject, called 'education for citizenship'. The introduction of these courses, a few years ago, gave rise to an unprecedented reaction of citizens,

204. *See* ATC 359/1985. *See* , on this issue, R. Navarro-Valls, *La enseñanza del derecho canónico en la jurisprudencia española*, 1 Anuario de Derecho Eclesiástico del Estado 49–92 (1985).
205. *See* STSJ Cantabria of 23 Mar. 1998, RJCA 1998/1686.
206. Cf. *Kjeldsen, Busk Madsen and Pedersen v. Denmark*, 7 Dec. 1976, para. 50; and *Folgerø and others v. Norway*, 29 Jun. 2007, para. 101.

with the support of the Catholic Church and numerous associations of parents and teachers, mostly of Catholic inspiration. They considered that a significant part of the new subject, as it had been designed, as well as many of the materials used in it, constituted state indoctrination in ethical questions in which only the parents are legitimated to tell their children which is the morally correct choice.

191. 'Education for citizenship' was the name given by the 2006 Organic Law on Education[207] to a new mandatory subject to be taught in all schools, private and public, on all levels of pre-university education – elementary, secondary and high school. The preamble of the law affirmed that the aim of these courses was to provide an occasion for the study of the fundamental principles of democracy, the rights and principles enshrined by the Constitution and international documents on human rights, as well as 'the common values that constitute the substratum of democratic citizenship in a global context'. This description corresponded to the alleged source of inspiration of the initiative, namely a 2002 recommendation of the Council of Europe aimed at promoting the 'education for democratic citizenship', which expressed the Council's concern about 'the growing levels of political and civic apathy and lack of confidence in democratic institutions', and about 'the increased cases of corruption, racism, xenophobia, aggressive nationalism, intolerance of minorities, discrimination and social exclusion'.[208]

192. Nevertheless, the announced profile of the new courses caused anxiety in a high number of families, which feared that, beyond the legitimate contents focused on human rights and constitutional values, the courses could be used as an instrument of moral indoctrination to students. Consequently they requested that their content was modified or that their children were exempted from them. The Spanish Bishops Conference explicitly seconded and encouraged those families.[209] The Ministry of Education reacted by drastically refusing to negotiate or change the design of the subject of education for citizenship and simply reaffirming that it did not have any indoctrinating character. The response of society was a massive use of conscientious objection on the part of parents, with an estimated number of 60,000–80,000 written objections all across the Spanish geography, many of which ended up in lawsuits. The irony is that a subject that was supposed to transmit – according to its promoters –

207. *Ley Orgánica* 2/2006, of 3 May 2006, *de Educación*. The criteria for the implementation of this course were provided in three royal decrees: RD 1513/2006, of 7 Dec. 2006 (primary school); RD 1631/2006, of 29 Dec. 2006 (secondary school); and RD 1467/2007, of 2 Nov. 2007 (high school). For a detailed (and critical) analysis of the law, *see* L. Ruano Espina, *Objeción de conciencia a la Educación para la Ciudadanía*, 17 Revista General de Derecho Canónico y Derecho Eclesiástico del Estado 1–61 (2008).

208. Recommendation Rec (2002)12 of the Committee of Ministers to Member States on education for democratic citizenship (Adopted by the Committee of Ministers on 16 Oct. 2002 at the 812th meeting of the Ministers' Deputies).

209. *See* the documents of the Permanent Commission of the Spanish Bishops Conference entitled *La Ley Orgánica de Educación (LOE), los Reales Decretos que la desarrollan y los derechos fundamentales de padres y escuelas*, 28 Feb. 2007, and *Nueva declaración sobre la LOE y sus desarrollos: profesores de Religión y Ciudadanía*, 20 Jun. 2007. The texts are available in the online archive of documents of the Bishops Conference: http://www.conferenciaepiscopal.nom.es/archivodoc/jsp/ (accessed 9 Dec. 2017).

commonly shared civic values created an unprecedented social divide and an awkward situation in the realm of Spanish education.

193. Two aspects of the design of the new courses raised particular concern in those families. In the first place, a substantial part of the subject's description made reference to the world of emotions and affectivity, personal feelings, human relationships, the need to build an autonomous and critical conscience, human sexuality and sexual orientations, reproductive health, diverse models of family, etc. Many families considered that the mere presence of these contents implied a risk, in practice, of transmitting moral views at school that were in contradiction with the moral convictions of the parents, and therefore with their right to guarantee the education of their children according to their religious or philosophical convictions. In other words, the subject called ‘education for citizenship’, as it was conceived, created the *danger of moral indoctrination* of young students in Spanish schools, against the parents' rights guaranteed by Article 27.3 CE and against the well-established case law of the ECtHR.[210] According to the people opposing the law, this risk would not be only a consequence of the door that the curriculum of the new subject opened for practical abuses. It was also the consequence of trivializing, under the guise of an alleged ‘objective and scientific treatment’, the study of topics that have an intrinsic and essential moral dimension. That is to say, studying in class themes as, for instance, ‘sexuality’ or ‘the world of emotions’ ignoring or prescinding from their moral dimension entails in itself a certain moral indoctrination.

194. In the second place, many parents deemed the description of some contents inappropriate in itself. It was pointed out that, for example, when the official curriculum mentioned human rights and democratic values as the ultimate and maximum source of morality, there was a confusion between the notions of private and public sphere and their reciprocal boundaries vis-à-vis the legitimate ethical choices of individuals. In other words, saying that, in the public sphere, we agree on certain common values that are our point of reference in organizing social or civic life is very different from teaching the students what the ultimate and maximum source of morality is for themselves as persons – not as citizens, but as persons. According to the objector parents, states can teach values that are valid for the public sphere but cannot teach what citizens must or must not believe. This is the realm of what the ECtHR has called the *forum internum*, free from any state's interference;[211] and also, in the case of minors, the area reserved to the parents' rights protected by Article 2 of the Protocol to the ECHR.

195. As the Ministry of Education was inflexible in keeping its project intact despite the conscientious objections formulated by thousands of parents, and as many of those requests for exemption from the new mandatory course were rejected at

210. *See* the decisions *Kjeldsen* and *Folgerø*, cited *supra* , in para. 189. Also *Zengin v. Turkey*, 9 Oct. 2007.
211. *See supra* , para. 108.

administrative level, a number of parents turned to the courts, giving rise to hundreds of judicial decisions of diverse orientation.[212]

196. In 2009, the Supreme Court delivered four judgments aimed at unifying the diverse jurisprudence of Spanish courts on this complex issue.[213] The Court rejected the objectors' claims with a reasoning that was contested in the dissenting opinions of ten of the twenty-nine judges that composed the chamber, and that has been also strongly criticized by some scholars.[214] In summary, the rationale of those decisions was based on the following points. First, the Court denies that there is any right to conscientious objection except when the legislator explicitly grants it. Second, as a consequence, the Court denies that there is any specific right to conscientious objection in the educational environment in spite of the parents' rights guaranteed by Article 2 of the Protocol to the ECHR. Curiously enough, the Court affirmed that the *Folgerø* and *Zengin* decisions of the ECtHR were 'of not much use in this case' because they adjudicated on claims against mandatory religious instruction. The Court seemed to forget that the religious instruction considered in those cases was allegedly neutral, precisely like 'education for citizenship'; and also that the ECtHR has emphasized, since *Kjeldsen*, that the parents' rights, and the correlative state obligations, are applicable to the entire organization of the school system and not only to religious teaching. Third, in the Court's view, there was nothing contrary to Article 16 or Article 27.3 CE in the aims and curriculum of 'education for citizenship', for the new courses were oriented to inculcate in the students the 'moral values subjacent' in the constitutional order. The Court found also legitimate, in order to foster a spirit of tolerance, to let the students know about diverse 'cultural, moral or ideological positions' that are 'beyond the common ethical space', but without indoctrinating in them.

197. Notwithstanding the latter remarks, the Supreme Court admitted that part of the terminology and notions included in the description of the new school subject could induce worry or uneasiness in families about its indoctrinating effect when implemented in practice. However, instead of declaring that the deficiencies of the regulations of 'education for citizenship' made it inadequate to comply with its announced purpose, the Court contented itself with warning public authorities about the need to be vigilant to prevent the occurrence of practical abuses of moral indoctrination to students, which would be certainly contrary to the ideological neutrality of the state.

---

212. For a detailed analysis of the Spanish case law in those years, *see* M.T. Areces, *Derecho a objetar en el ámbito educativo: educación para la ciudadanía. Resoluciones judiciales*, 25 Anuario de Derecho Eclesiástico del Estado 343–347 (2009); A. López-Sidro, *La objeción de conciencia a la educación para la ciudadanía ante los Tribunales Superiores de Justicia*, 17 Revista General de Derecho Canónico y Derecho Eclesiástico del Estado 1–26 (2008).

213. The three most important judgments are: STS 340/2009, STS 341/2009 and 342/2009 (*Sala de lo Contencioso-Administrativo*), all of them of 11 Feb. 2009.

214. *See* L. Ruano Espina, *Las sentencias del Tribunal Supremo de 11 febrero 2009 sobre objeción de conciencia a EpC*, 20 Revista General de Derecho Canónico y Derecho Eclesiástico del Estado 1–60 (2009); A. González-Varas, *La educación para la ciudadanía: entre la objeción de conciencia y recursos contencioso-administrativos*, 10 Anuario de Derechos Humanos 331–388 (2009); R. Navarro-Valls & J. Martínez-Torrón, *Conflictos entre conciencia y ley*, 303–309. In favour of the government's position, *see* D. Llamazares, *Educación para la ciudadanía democrática y objeción de conciencia* (Dykinson 2008) (the author was one of the persons responsible for the theoretical background of the government's initiative).

For the rest, the Court concluded that parents always had the possibility to go to the courts in case they thought that indoctrination was actually happening. This aspect of the judgment was particularly criticized by one of the dissenting judges, which remarked that the Court, when tipping the scales, had preferred to leave the regulations intact instead of ensuring a fundamental right of parents, even in such a sensitive realm as the moral education of minors. The same judge added that the solution reached by the Court was bound to prove unsatisfactory in practical terms, for it would leave the door open to a constant litigation.

198. Indeed, litigation has continued, beginning a few weeks after the Supreme Court's decisions.[215] After the general election of November 2011, the new government, shortly after taking office, announced its intention to modify the contents and methodology of 'education for citizenship', eliminating those of its aspects more related to issues of individual morals and focusing on human rights and democratic and constitutional values. This modification was operated by the 2013 Organic Law for the improvement of quality in education.[216] Courses on 'education for citizenship' have been substituted by an obligatory cross-disciplinary teaching of 'civic and constitutional education'. In addition, students can choose elective courses on 'social and civic values' (primary school) or 'ethical values' (secondary school) as a necessary alternative to denominational courses on religion.[217] Although this and other aspects of the 2013 statute have been criticized by opposition parties, the fact is that it seems to have solved the problem of parents' conscientious objection except in some regions governed by left-wing parties (as Andalusia, Aragon or Extremadura), whose educational authorities have kept courses on education for citizenship – in the line of the 2006 law – within the quota of specific subjects that each region can add to the national school curriculum.

199. The case of 'education for citizenship' in Spain demonstrates that, in order to reconcile the parents' rights with the legitimate state competences on education, it is important to keep an open and inclusive approach, based on dialogue and respect for pluralism, when facing the structuring and implementation of school subjects or practices that necessarily touch on moral and religious sensitivities. This has been indeed the continuous recommendation of international organizations in recent times.[218]

§9. Freedom of Conscience and Religious Symbols

200. In contemporary Western societies, there are increasing conflicts between freedom of conscience and legal obligations stemming from the fact that some people

215. *See* R. Navarro-Valls & J. Martínez-Torrón, *Conflictos entre conciencia y ley*, 309–312. For a more detailed and updated information about the case law after the 2009 Supreme Court's decision, *see* the jurisprudence section of *Revista General de Derecho Canónico y Derecho Eclesiástico del Estado*, in www.iustel.com (accessed 23 Aug. 2017).

216. *Ley Orgánica* 8/2013, of 9 Dec. 2013, *para la mejora de la calidad educativa* (LOMCE).

217. *See infra*, Part IX, Ch. 1.

218. *See*, for instance, the *Toledo Guiding Principles on Teaching about Religions and Beliefs in Public Schools*, prepared in 2007 by the OSCE/ODIHR Advisory Council of Experts on Freedom of Religion or Belief, in collaboration with an international group of experts in education. Its text is available in: http://www.osce.org/odihr/29154 (accessed 9 Dec. 2017).

consider a moral duty to wear symbols or garments that express their religion. The observance of this religious duty sometimes contravenes legal rules or contractual clauses. While normally conscientious objections are caused by incompatibility of moral duties with neutral laws, an interesting characteristic of the conflicts related to religious symbols is that, in occasions, the legal rules in question have been specifically designed to prohibit visible expressions of religiosity, as has occurred in Europe with female clothing attached to certain interpretations of Islam.[219]

I. The Use of Personal Religious Symbols in the School Environment

201. In recent times, there has been in Europe a significant number of clashes between students or teachers that wore a particular religious garment for considering it a moral duty, and state laws supposedly aimed at guaranteeing the neutrality of the public school environment, which was in turn deemed an indispensable element to guarantee the spirit of tolerance and respect in school. Most often these conflicts relate to Islamic symbols, especially the hijab or other female clothing, and in some cases the state laws in question were motivated by the public authorities' interest in reducing the visibility of Muslim students in public schools.[220]

202. In Spain, there is no national or regional legislation on the issue of religious clothing in public schools and therefore its regulation is in the hands of the school boards. Normally, the internal rules of schools refer to clothing in general rather than to religious garments in particular, and tend to be applied with flexibility. Until now, conflicts of this type have been significantly less numerous than in other European countries and, by and large, in public schools there is an atmosphere of tolerance for wearing religious symbols of any kind, including Islamic clothing. There have been only two known cases, both of them in the region of Madrid, which gathers a high percentage of the Muslim population of Spain.

203. The first one, in 2002, related to a 13-year old Moroccan student that remained several months without schooling because the (state funded) Catholic school in which she was registered prohibited the use of hijab, by reason both of its religious ethos and its rules on the students' uniform. As neither the student's parents nor the school would make their respective positions more flexible, regional public authorities found a practical solution consisting in transferring the student to a nearby public school where such prohibition did not exist.[221]

219. An example of it is the anti-burka French legislation of 2010 challenged in the case *S.A.S. v. France*, decided by the Grand Chamber of the European Court of Human Rights on 1 Jul. 2014.

220. *See* , for a comparative legal analysis of these issues, with bibliographic and legal references, R. Navarro-Valls & J. Martínez-Torrón, *Conflictos entre conciencia y ley*, 321–363.

221. *See* S. Cañamares Arribas, *Tratamiento de la simbología religiosa en el Derecho español: propuestas ante la reforma de la Ley Orgánica de Libertad Religiosa*, 19 Revista General de Derecho Canónico y Derecho Eclesiástico del Estado 7–9 (2009).

204. The second case occurred in 2010 and generated a more intense attention from the media as well as a judicial decision.[222] The problem arose when the board of a public school in the town of Pozuelo (near Madrid) forbade a young Muslim student to wear her hijab, in a strict interpretation of the internal regulations that vetoed the use of 'caps or any other head-covering garment' while in school. The student had begun to wear a hijab when she turned 16 and was sanctioned (with a written warning) for disobeying the school rules despite the fact that these rules also mentioned, among the students' rights, respect for their 'identity and moral integrity and dignity', as well as respect for their 'freedom of conscience, religious and moral convictions'. The student decided to stop attending classes and registered in other nearby public school shortly afterwards. In any event, her father initiated an administrative review procedure and later a judicial procedure against the school sanction. In 2012, a Court of First Instance rejected his claim[223] with a judgment – not particularly rich in nuances – that justified the school board's position by reference to the European Court's case law, indicating that the board was free to interpret the notion of public order as excluding the use of veils.[224]

205. It is worth noting that, when the sanctioned student was looking for a new educational centre to register, a nearby public school modified its internal rules, through an urgent procedure, to ban the use of head-covering garments. For those of us who think that limitations on religious freedom must be grounded on consistent and concrete arguments, and not just on vague references to general concepts, this fact reveals that a more accurate regulation of the wearing of religious symbols at school is needed at a national level.

II. The Use of Personal Religious Symbols in Public Spaces

206. The use of religious clothing in identification photographs has raised some questions with regard to the interests of public security in different countries. Spanish regulations on identification documents is sufficiently flexible as to permit providing personal photographs wearing a hijab and most common religious garments, but obviously not a burka or niqab, which cover the entire face of the woman.

207. The regulations on the issuing of passports, of 2003, simply require that the applicant provides a recent colour photograph taken from the front, without dark glasses or any other garment that may prevent or make difficult the identification of

222. In the Internet pages www.webislam.com (accessed 9 Dec. 2017), it is possible to find a dossier about Najwa Malha (the student's name) with information about the abundant media reactions to this case.

223. *See Juzgado Contencioso-Administrativo* Nr. 32 of Madrid, Judgment Nr. 35/2012, 25 Jan. 2012. Confirmed by STSJ Madrid 129/2013 (*Sala de lo Contencioso-Administrativo*), 8 Feb. 2013.

224. The decisions of the ECtHR cited by the judgment of the Madrid court are *Dogru*, *Kervanci* and *Dahlab*, which are not, in the view of many scholars, particularly good examples of interpretation of Art. 9 ECHR. *See* , for a critical analysis of those and other ECtHR's decisions concerning the wearing of hijab, J. Martínez-Torrón, *Islam in Strasbourg: Can Politics Substitute for Law?* in *Islam, Europe and Emerging Legal Issues* 49–59 (W.C. Durham Jr., D.M. Kirkham, C. Scott & R. Torfs eds, Ashgate 2012).

the person.[225] The subsequent regulations on the issuing of national ID cards and driving licences, of 2009, added the requirement that the photograph must show the applicant's head completely uncovered.[226] However, apparently upon request of the Islamic communities, the Ministry of Interior reminded the relevant public offices that an instruction of 11 April 2006 of the *Comisaría General de Extranjería y Documentación* is still in force.[227] According to this instruction, it is sufficient that the applicant provides identification photographs with a veil or cloth, when this is imposed by her religion, as far as the oval of the face is entirely visible. In fact, the information available in the official Internet pages that explain the application procedure for driving licences specify that photos with a headscarf are acceptable provided that the oval of the face appears totally uncovered.[228] The equivalent pages for national ID cards do not make any reference to the possibility of wearing a head-covering and just remarks the need to leave the oval of the face visible.[229]

208. The use of full veils that cover the entire face of women – such as burka or niqab – in public places has become a controversial question in some European countries in recent years. Some countries, as France and Belgium, have adopted strong legislative measures to prohibit wearing such garments in any public area. A similar debate has taken place in Spain at both national and local level.[230]

209. At a national level, the Spanish Senate approved in June 2010, by a narrow margin (131 to 129 votes), a motion requiring the government to promote legislative and administrative reforms aimed at banning full-face covering clothing in public spaces or events that do not have a specific religious purpose.[231] A few weeks later, the motion was rejected in the Congress. However, the Congress accepted the presentation,

---

225. Cf. Art. 4.1.c) of the *Real Decreto* 896/2003, of 11 Jul. 2003, *por el que se regula la expedición del pasaporte ordinario y se determinan sus características*.
226. Cf. Art. 5.1.b) of the *Real Decreto* 1553/2005, of 23 Dec. 2005, *por el que se regula la expedición del documento nacional de identidad y sus certificados de firma electrónica*, according to the modifications introduced by the *Real Decreto* 1586/2009, of 16 Oct. 2009; *Reglamento General de Conductores*, Anexo III, A.1.b), approved by the *Real Decreto* 818/2009, of 9 May 2009.
227. To the author's knowledge, this instruction has not been published and is not available to the public. *See* information about it in: http://www.webcciv.org/es/wp-content/uploads/2011/07/CARTAdointeriorsobreusovelo.pdf (accessed 24 Aug. 2017); http://www.webcciv.org/es/wp-content/uploads/2011/07/INFORMEDEFENSORdelPUEBLO_hiyab.pdf (accessed 9 Dec. 2017); and http://www.webislam.com/noticias/54684-el_dni_si_podra_hacerse_con_un_hiyab_o_panuelo_en_la_cabeza.html (accessed 24 Aug. 2017)
228. *See* https://sede.dgt.gob.es/es/tramites-y-multas/permiso-de-conduccion/obtencion-permiso-licencia-conduccion/ (accessed 9 Dec. 2017).
229. *See* http://www.interior.gob.es/web/servicios-al-ciudadano/dni/documentacion-necesaria-para-su-tramitacion (accessed 9 Dec. 2017).
230. This type of legislation has been considered also in The Netherlands. The issue of full veil in Spain, from a comparative perspective, has been analysed in detail by V. Camarero, *El velo integral y su respuesta en democracias europeas* (Tirant Lo Blanch 2012). *See also* R. Navarro-Valls & J. Martínez-Torrón, *Conflictos entre conciencia y ley*, 378–384.
231. Consider that some very popular religious processions during the Catholic Holy Week (*Semana Santa*) across Spain gather many thousands of 'penitents' that wear a robe – the official habit of their respective fraternities – that covers the entire body, including the face. The motion was tabled by the Popular Party, and the Socialist Party opposed to it. *See* the oral interventions in *Diario de Sesiones del Senado (Pleno), IX Legislatura*, Núm. 85, 23 Jun. 2010.

some days later, of a non-legislative proposal by another parliamentary group, which asked the government to 'request from the Council of State a study on the possibilities of regulation of the full veil within the legal order in force'.[232] No such study has been done to date.

210. At a local level, around the same years, several city councils in the region of Catalonia – including the provincial capitals Barcelona, Tarragona and Lérida[233] – enacted municipal ordinances prohibiting the use of full veil in municipal facilities.[234] A similar position was taken by two other city councils out of Catalonia,[235] although it is definitely in this region – likely because of the number of women wearing full veil – where the subject became more controversial and more debated by public institutions. A judicial appeal against the ordinance of Lérida, alleging that city councils did not have competences on fundamental rights, was decided by the Superior Court of Justice of Catalonia in 2011.[236] The ordinance forbade 'the access or permanence in places or facilities destined to the public use or service to those people wearing full veil, balaclava, full-face helmet or other clothing or items that prevent the identification and the visual communication of persons, when those items are prohibited or restricted by the specific rules' of the relevant public facility'. In addition, the city council modified accordingly the rules governing three different municipal services. The Court sustained the validity of the ordinance, holding that the city council had acted within its competences when it enacted a rule that was based on reasons of public order, even if that rule indirectly impinged on the religious choices of citizens. Such negative effect on a fundamental right was justified by the possibility of imposing legitimate limitations on religious freedom. The reasons of public order mentioned by the Court were: the connection between visual identification of people and public security in public facilities; and the fact that hiding one's face in daily life caused anxiety and worry in surrounding people, except when it was required by the weather or by the performance of certain jobs. The Court also indicated that the use of burka or similar garment, which is done exclusively by women, was not compatible with the principle of equality between men and women, even if the latter wear it voluntarily.

211. That decision was overruled by the Supreme Court in a judgment of 2013,[237] which declared the ordinance of Lérida null and void for violation of the freedom of religion protected by Article 16 CE. The Court's rationale focused on the lack of competence of city councils to regulate fundamental rights guaranteed by the Constitution, even in aspects that can be considered accessory or secondary. The Supreme Court held that municipal by-laws may impose limitations on religious freedom only on the bases of a prior ad hoc legislation, as required by Article 53.1 CE. In the absence of such legislation, Lérida's by-laws prohibiting the use of garments that constitute a

232. *See Boletín Oficial de las Cortes Generales, Congreso de los Diputados, IX Legislatura, Serie D,* Núm. 432, 27 Jul. 2010, 8.

233. To the author's knowledge, another eleven city councils have adopted similar ordinances: El Vendrell, Manresa, L'Hospitalet de Llobregat, Mollet del Vallès, Vic, Cunit, Santa Coloma, Figueres, Reus, Roses y Martorell.

234. References can be found in V. Camarero, *El velo integral.*

235. Galapagar (Madrid) and Coín (Andalusia).

236. STSJ Cataluña 489/2011 (*Sala de lo Contencioso-Administrativo, Sección 2ª*), 7 Jun. 2011.

237. STS 693/2013, 14 Feb. 2013.

manifestation of religion for some women must be considered invalid, with one exception, namely the regulation of the city public transportation service, which requires the identification of passengers with personal cards that permit the use of public transportation at a reduced price. The Supreme Court also rejected the argument of the inferior court based on the equality between men and women, and declared that there was no sufficient evidence to sustain that public peace was disturbed by people hiding their faces. In any event, the Court's judgment was essentially grounded on the lack of legal competences of city councils to regulate fundamental freedoms, according to Article 53.1 CE, and it explicitly made clear that the legislator was competent to impose limitations on the use of full veil, if it considered it appropriate. The judgment added some interesting precisions, in the light of the Strasbourg case law, about the requisites that limitations on religious freedom must meet, with especial emphasis on the notion of public order and the necessity of limitative measures. However, the Court carefully clarified that this judgment should not be interpreted as an attempt to condition the choices available to parliament – it would be an 'unacceptable interference' with the legislator's competences – but just as a counter-argument to the reasons provided by the overruled decision of the regional court.[238] In 2015, this same regional court followed the Supreme Court's doctrine and suspended the enforcement of an anti-burka municipal ordinance of another Catalan town.[239]

III. The Use of Personal Religious Symbols at Work

212. In the area of labour relations there have been, in various European countries, conflicts between the employer's rules and the use of garments of religious significance while at work. In Spain, one case of this kind was decided by the Superior Court of Justice of Baleares in 2002.[240] The case related to a Jewish bus driver that worked for the municipal transportation service (*Empresa Municipal de Transportes*) of Palma de Mallorca. After several years wearing a cap at work on religious grounds, as a sign of respect for God, he was sanctioned by the company for not complying with the rules on uniform. The Court decided in favour of the employee, noting that imposing a uniform on employees is part of the employer's right to control and manage his business, but is not an unlimited right, for it may collide with employee's fundamental rights, as religious freedom. In the Court's view, such conflicts are not susceptible of only one a priori solution and must be analysed taking into account the particular circumstances of each case, especially considering if the employee's religiously motivated behaviour caused any harm to the employer's legitimate interests. In this occasion, the Court concluded that there was no such harm – indeed, the employer had not even hinted at such possibility when arguing in court – and consequently sanctioning the employee denoted an attitude 'close to authoritarianism'. The Court also remarked that sanctioning an employee because of a harmless expression of religiosity was even less acceptable in the case of 'a municipal company that was part

238. *See ibid.*, FJ 10.
239. ATSJ Cataluña 1/2015 (*Sala de lo Contencioso-Administrativo, Sección 5ª*), 29 Jan. 2015.
240. STSJ Baleares 457/2002 (*Sala de lo Social, sección 1ª*), 9 Sep. 2002.

of the public sector and, therefore, more committed than private employers to the effective compliance with constitutional values'.

213. Another, more recent, case was decided by an employment court of first instance in Mallorca in 2017, also in favour of a broad protection of religious freedom.[241] A female Islamic employee of a handling company at the airport of Palma de Mallorca was prohibited from wearing her hijab at work – and sanctioned because of her refusal to comply with the prohibition. The company alleged the contractual rules on the employees' uniform, which in its opinion contained a closed list of wearable items. The Court decided in favour of the employee, arguing on the basis of the Spanish Constitution, the EU law (especially the Council Directive 2000/78/EC), the ECHR and the case law of the Strasbourg Court (especially in the *Eweida* case).[242] In the Court's view, the employer had treated the employee's hijab as a mere decorative garment and ignored its religious dimension, thus failing to make any effort to accommodate the general rules on uniform to the plaintiff's religious freedom. The Court noted also that the rules on uniform did not contain any prohibition of Islamic headscarves, that the company did not have any specific policy of religious neutrality, and that other employees were permitted to wear crosses, piercings or tattoos in apparent contraventions of uniform rules without any reaction from the company's management. Considering that the employee did not intend to substantially alter her employment contract but just to observe what she considered an important moral obligation in exercise of a constitutional freedom, the Court concluded that she had been discriminated on the ground of her religious beliefs.

IV. 'Secular' Objections to the Use of Religious Symbols in Public Institutions

214. As in other European countries, in recent years Spanish courts have adjudicated on claims against the visibility of Christian symbols present in some public institutions out of a long-standing tradition. Normally these claims have been presented formally as individual objections inspired by a 'secular conscience' (*conciencia laica*), arguing that the freedom of conscience of atheists was violated by having to bear the presence of a religious symbol that they considered 'offensive' for their convictions.[243] Actually, however, rather than being the result of an 'injured conscience', most of these judicial claims were apparently driven by the plaintiffs' interest in obtaining from the courts a particular interpretation of the consequences of the constitutional principle of state neutrality vis-à-vis certain popular and old expressions of Christian religiosity.

215. In the educational environment, we can mention a case that attracted considerable media attention and was resolved by a decision of the Superior Court of Castile and León in 2009.[244] The case originated in a complaint about the crucifixes

241. Juzgado de lo Social nº 1 of Palma de Mallorca, judgment 31/2017, 6 Feb. 2017.
242. *Eweida and others v. United Kingdom*, 15 Jan. 2013.
243. *See* for further details and references J. Martínez-Torrón, *Institutional religious symbols, state neutrality and protection of minorities in Europe*, 171 Law & Justice 21–51 (2013).
244. STSJ Castilla y León 3250/2009 (*Sala de lo Contencioso-Administrativo, Sección 3ª*), 14 Dec. 2009.

that hung on the classrooms of a public school in Valladolid. A cultural association, following the unsuccessful request of some students' parents to the school board, demanded that the crucifixes were removed from the classes and all common spaces of the school. The Court of First Instance decided in favour of the plaintiffs and ordered the immediate removal of all the crucifixes, on the ground that the display of religious symbols in an educational centre could generate in young students the 'feeling' that the state was 'closer' to the Christian religions than to other worldviews.[245] On appeal, the Superior Court overruled partially the first instance decision. On the one hand, the Court rejected – as contrary to Article 16 CE and to the case law of the Constitutional Court – any 'maximalist' or 'extreme' interpretation of the constitutional principle of secularity (*laicidad*) leading to erasing all traces of religion from public life. On the other hand, the Court held that state neutrality obliged to take away from school those religious symbols whose presence could be 'emotionally perturbing' for students and contrary to the parents' rights to have their children educated in accordance with their convictions. As a consequence, in a sort of Solomonic judgment, the Court decreed that crucifixes should be removed only from the school common areas and from those classrooms attended by students whose parents had specifically complained about their presence; they could remain in the rest of rooms if the school board so determined. It is perhaps interesting to note that the Superior Court's judgment was explicitly grounded on the first *Lautsi* decision of the ECtHR, which held that the display of the Catholic crucifix in a public school violated Article 9 ECHR. The second and final *Lautsi* decision, which held just the opposite and overruled the Chamber's decision, was still to arrive.[246]

216. In a different context, the display of religious symbols in a public school had already been declared constitutional by a judgment of the Superior Court of Justice of Murcia of 2008.[247] In that occasion, no student or student's parent was involved. The claim came from a teacher of a public school that demanded the removal of a Christmas crèche placed in the hall of the school, alleging safety reasons – difficulties for the centre's evacuation in an emergency – as well as incompatibility with the state's obligation of religious neutrality. The Court dismissed the appeal, noting that it could find no imposition of religious beliefs or practices on any person.

217. Out of the school environment, the presence of the crucifix in a public space, and more precisely in the city hall of Saragossa, originated another interesting case widely spread by the media. A group of left-wing councilmen demanded that the mayor ordered the removal of an old crucifix from the plenary hall, where the city council meetings were usually held. The mayor – of the Socialist Party – refused to remove the crucifix, making reference to its historical and artistic value as well as to the significance of respect for traditions – that crucifix was linked to the life of the Saragossa's city council since the seventeenth century. The issue was put to a vote and

245. *See Juzgado de lo Contencioso-Administrativo* Nr. 2 of Valladolid, Judgment Nr. 288/2008, 14 Nov. 2008, FJ 4.
246. The case of *Lautsi v. Italy*, 3 Nov. 2009 (Chamber's decision) and 18 Mar. 2011 (Grand Chamber's decision), originated in the application of the mother of two students of a public school in Italy, where the law provides that the crucifix must be displayed on the walls of the classrooms of all public schools.
247. STSJ Murcia 2269/2009 (*Sala de lo Contencioso-Administrativo, Sección 2ª*), 30 Sep. 2009.

the majority of the council decided in favour of keeping the crucifix. The case was taken to a Court of First Instance, which confirmed in 2010 the legitimacy of the council's decision.[248] Interestingly, the court analysed the issue from the perspective of judicial self-restraint. For the court, the right question was not how or if the council could justify the display of a historic crucifix in the plenary hall but, on the contrary, to elucidate if there was any reason why a court must prohibit the council from having that crucifix in its plenary hall. The court did not find any reason for the prohibition, considering that the principle of secularity does not entail erasing the visibility of religion from public life, and noting that the display of the crucifix was not aimed at imposing a particular religion over other religions or beliefs – it simply reflected the history of a city council more than nine centuries old. In addition, the court pointed out that this case was not comparable to the display of symbols in public schools, because neither the protection of minors nor the parents' rights over the education of their children were at issue.

218. An analogous position has been adopted by the Spanish Supreme Court in two cases regarding the presence of huge and very visible Christian crosses in public places, one on an old castle of Islamic origin in Murcia (*Cristo de Monteagudo*)[249] and the other on a mountain near Orihuela (*Cruz de la Muela*), where it has been placed since the fifteenth century and rebuilt several times by popular initiative.[250] In both cases the Supreme Court confirmed the decisions of two regional Supreme Courts of justice that had refused to decree the removal of those Christian symbols. The Court's rationale, with numerous references to the *Lautsi* judgment of the ECtHR's Grand Chamber,[251] was based on respect for religious tradition, deeply embedded in the culture of the country, as in many others of Christian heritage. For the Court, as far as religious symbols are expression of tradition and social consensus, they constitute identity signs of a community and their maintenance is just a manifestation of respect for historical tradition. Therefore – the Court concluded – their mere presence in public places cannot be understood either of a violation of state duty of neutrality (*laicidad*) or an imposition of particular religious beliefs and expression of intolerance of non-believers.[252]

219. The foregoing judgments of Spanish courts are consistent with the case law of the Constitutional Court, which has been very open to the maintenance of religious traditions in public places or institutions, and at the same time very firm in proclaiming that no person can be obliged to take an active part in those traditions.

220. Thus, the Court has found nothing unconstitutional in the fact that a military garrison organized a solemn parade in honour of the local advocation of the Holy Virgin,[253] or in the fact that a unit of the National Police participated in a religious procession during the celebration of the Catholic Holy Week – not to guarantee the safety of the event but in its quality of a member of the relevant religious fraternity,

248. *Juzgado de lo Contencioso-Administrativo* Nr. 3 of Saragossa, Judgment Nr. 156/10, 30 Apr. 2010.
249. STS 1798/2013 (*Sala de lo Contencioso, Sección 7ª*), 4 Mar. 2013.
250. STS 5166/2014 (*Sala de lo Contencioso, Sección 7ª*), 2 Dec. 2104.
251. *See supra* , note 246.
252. *Ibid.*, FJ 9.
253. *See* STC 177/1996.

with police officers wearing their gala uniforms.[254] However, the Court has made clear that no officer can be obliged to be present in those religious ceremonies against his personal convictions, for public events reflecting a religious tradition must be reconciled with the individuals' freedom of conscience.

221. For analogous reasons, the Constitutional Court held that it would have been legitimate for the University of Valencia – a public University – to keep an image of the Holy Virgin that had been traditionally present in its coat of arms, if the University governing bodies had so decided.[255] And, more recently, the Court has sustained the constitutionality of the statutes of the Bar Association of Seville, which have kept, as 'a secular tradition', the Immaculate Conception of the Holy Virgin as its honorary patron.[256] The Court noted that, being the bar association itself aconfessional, preserving this tradition does not infringe either the neutrality of public institutions or the religious freedom of non-Christians. The Court added that symbols reflect the history of institutions, and it is natural to find in the Spanish culture plenty of symbols, with religious connotations, that represent public institutions. Furthermore, the Court observed that in contemporary societies passive symbols have virtually no influence on the people's beliefs and, therefore, the religious freedom of individuals is safe, provided that no one is compelled to participate in rites or ceremonies in honour of those symbols. In the absence of such coercion – the Court concluded – the mere subjective perception of offence is not sufficient to appreciate that freedom of ideology or religion has been violated.

§10. Conscientious Objections in Labour Relations

I. European and Spanish Normative Framework

222. Conflicts between freedom of conscience and state law in the area of labour relationships sometimes result in situations of direct or indirect discrimination. This fact has moved the European Union to develop some initiatives aimed at promoting equal treatment of employees without discrimination – among other factors on religious or belief grounds. The main outcome of these initiatives has been, so far, the Council Directive 2000/78/EC,[257] whose purpose is to help fight against direct and indirect discrimination in employment and ensure that no person is treated in a less favourable fashion for his religion or convictions, among other reasons. In practice, the situations more problematic and more difficult to identify are those of *indirect discrimination*, which is defined by Article 2.2.(b) of the Directive with these words:

254. *See* STC 101/2004.
255. *See* STC 130/1991. In this case, the supreme governing body of the University had decided the opposite, i.e., to remove the image of the Virgin from the coat of arms.
256. *See* STC 34/2011.
257. Council Directive 2000/78/EC, of 27 Nov. 2000, establishing a general framework for equal treatment in employment and occupation.

> indirect discrimination shall be taken to occur where an apparently neutral provision, criterion or practice would put persons having a particular religion or belief, a particular disability, a particular age, or a particular sexual orientation at a particular disadvantage compared with other persons unless: (i) that provision, criterion or practice is objectively justified by a legitimate aim and the means of achieving that aim are appropriate and necessary

223. The same article of the Directive adds that 'the employer or any person or organisation to whom this Directive applies, is obliged, under national legislation, to take appropriate measures ... in order to eliminate disadvantages entailed by such provision, criterion or practice'. Unfortunately, this obligation of taking an active approach to implement the principle of equal treatment only refers to 'persons with a particular disability'.

224. In Spain, the basic normative framework for this type of issues is designed by the Organic Law on Religious Freedom, the 1992 Agreements with the Evangelical, Jewish and Islamic Federations (see next paragraph), and the Statute of Workers (*Estatuto de los Trabajadores*).[258] Article 2.1 LOLR provides that religious freedom includes every person's right to 'practice acts of worship' and 'to celebrate his festivities', but it does not add further details about the consequences of these rights in the area of employment. Article 37.1 of the Statute of Workers indicates that the employees' imperative weekly rest of one day and a half – without interruption – shall ordinarily comprehend the entire Sunday plus half Saturday or half Monday, but this general rule can easily be modified by the parties of the labour contract. Article 17.1 of the same law declare null and void any provision, agreement or unilateral employer's decision that cause 'direct or indirect discrimination' on the ground – among others – of religion or convictions.

II. The Restrictive Approach of 1992 Agreements to the Observance of Sabbath

225. Article 12 of the 1992 Agreements faces the issue of religious rest on Saturdays and other holy days for Jews, Seventh-Day Adventists and member of other Evangelical churches, as well as Muslims' obligation of observing the collective prayer on Fridays and the Ramadan fast. Strictly speaking, this article of the cooperation agreements does not recognize or grant any individual right at all on this aspect of religious observance. It just contains a sort of 'declaration of good intentions' with regard to the *possibility* of fixing the weekly rest of Jewish, Evangelical or Muslim employees in a way compatible with their religious duties. Such possibility is subject to an *agreement between the parties of the labour contract.*

226. More precisely, the Agreements with the Evangelical and Jewish federations provide that, for Jews, Seventh-Day Adventists and members of other Evangelical churches whose day of rest is Saturday, 'the weekly rest period might comprise the afternoon and evening of Friday as well as the entire Saturday, instead of what is

258. *Real Decreto Legislativo* 2/2015, 23 Oct. 2015, *por el que se aprueba el texto refundido de la Ley del Estatuto de los Trabajadores.*

provided by Article 37.1 of the Statute of Workers as a general rule, as far as there is an agreement between the parties [of the labour contract]'.[259] Likewise, the Agreement with the Islamic Federation provides that Muslim employees, 'if they so wish, can request the interruption of their work on Fridays, day of mandatory and solemn collective prayer for Muslims, from 13:30 to 16:30, as well as the end of their working day one hour before sunset during the fasting month (Ramadan). In both cases an agreement between the parties [of the labour contract] is required.'[260] Identical treatment is given to the observance of Jewish and Islamic religious festivities – the days therein described can replace the days established as a general rule by Article 37.2 of the Statute of Workers – provided, again, that there is an agreement between the parties.[261]

227. Thus, the text of Article 12 of the 1992 Agreements seems, to some extent, superfluous. The insistence on the need of an agreement between employee and employer gives the latter, in practice, unlimited discretion to accept or reject the requests of his employees for religious observance. No obligation to justify his denial of those requests, or to search for a reasonable accommodation of the employee's religious duties, is imposed on the employer. Moreover, the Agreements do not distinguish between labour relationships with private employers and with public agencies or companies. Not surprisingly, this article has been criticized by scholars,[262] which have pointed out that it is not only redundant but contains also a restrictive interpretation of the religious freedom protected by the Constitution, the Organic Law on Religious Freedom and the Statute of Workers, whose Article 17.1 specifically forbids indirect discrimination – a notion that should be interpreted in the light of the European Union's Council Directive 2000/78/EC.

228. The reason of this restrictive interpretation of the employee's religious freedom is to be found in an opinion of the Council of State of 31 January 1991 on the drafts of the three cooperation agreements. The version of the drafts submitted to the Council of State followed the example of the Italian cooperation agreements (*intese*), and recognized employees a proper right to religious observance, provided that it was compatible with the employer's organization and with the maintenance of minimum services. The Council of State, however, held the view that the drafts should be modified in accordance with a judgment of the Constitutional Court of 1985 and its opinion prevailed in the elaboration of the final text of the Agreements.[263]

---

259. Article 12.1 of the 1992 Agreements with the Evangelical and the Jewish Federations.

260. Article 12.1 of the Agreement with the Islamic Federation.

261. Cf. Art. 12.2 of the respective Agreements with the Jewish and the Islamic federations. These articles contain a detailed list of religious festivities.

262. *See* , for instance, J. Martínez-Torrón, *Separatismo y cooperación en los acuerdos del Estado con las minorías religiosas* 153–155 (Comares 1994); D. Llamazares, *Los acuerdos y el principio de igualdad: comparación con los acuerdos con la Iglesia católica y situación jurídica de las confesiones sin acuerdo*, in *Acuerdos del Estado español con confesiones religiosas minoritarias* 198–199 (V. Reyna & M.A. Félix eds, Marcial Pons 1996).

263. A. Fernández-Coronado, *Estado y confesiones religiosas: un nuevo modelo de relación (los pactos con las confesiones: leyes 24, 25 y 26 de 1992)* 61–77 (Civitas 1995).

III. The Case Law on Sabbath Rest

229. The 1985 judgment of the Constitutional Court that inspired the opinion of the Council of State decided the claim of a woman, converted to the Seventh-Day Adventist Church, that had been dismissed for refusing to work on Saturdays.[264] The employee had made different proposals to her company in order to reconcile her work and her religious duties; those proposals included a change of shift and a reduction in her salary as compensation for her absence on Saturdays but none of them was accepted. The Court rejected the employee's claim with a reasoning that revolved around the secular character of Sundays as a common day of rest in contemporary Spain – as in other countries of Christian tradition – despite its religious origins. On this basis, the Court held that changing that day of weekly rest for other was *a possibility but not a duty* that could be imposed unilaterally on the employer by the other party of the labour contract, not even for the protection of her freedom of conscience.

230. Remarkably, this judgment of the Constitutional Court focused almost completely on the analysis of the secular nature of Sundays as a common weekly day of rest in labour relationships instead of analysing the central issue, namely if the employee's fundamental right to religious freedom generated any obligation of reasonable accommodation for the employer as far as it was not detrimental to the organization of work. In this regard, the Court refused to recognize such an obligation; indeed, the employer was not even obliged to justify his refusal to accept the alternative solutions proposed by the employee. In other words, the Court allowed the employer to treat the employee's request to rest on Saturdays for religious reasons as if it were grounded in any personal, trivial or whimsical motivation. The implication is that, at least in the area of labour relationships, employees' choices grounded on serious religious duties – and therefore on the exercise of a fundamental right – are considered as purely personal matters, as irrelevant for the labour contract as in the case of ordinary private law contracts.

231. Subsequent decisions of the Central Labour Court and of superior courts of justice have followed this restrictive interpretation of the employees' freedom of conscience.[265] However, a judgment of the Supreme Court of 1988 gave priority to the employee's freedom of conscience, based upon some distinctive elements of the case.[266] The plaintiff was also a convert to the Seventh-Day Adventist Church that worked for a rental car company. After his conversion, he had been authorized by the local director to move to the Sunday shift, and he did so for three months. A new director revoked the authorization and sent him back to the Saturday shift, with the consequence that, after a few absences from work, the employee was dismissed. The Supreme Court decided in favour of the employee, understanding that the first authorization had the effect of a tacit modification of the labour contract clauses. As that modification had been adopted by mutual agreement and with good cause – the employee's right to religious observance – it could not be annulled later by the employer's unilateral

264. STC 19/1985. For a critique to this decision, *see* A. Castro Jover, *Libertad religiosa y descanso semanal*, 6 Anuario de Derecho Eclesiástico del Estado 299–312 (1990).

265. *See* Judgment of the *Tribunal Central de Trabajo* of 26 Sep. 1986, and STSJ Valencia of 24 Jun. 1997 (AS 1997, 2078).

266. STS (*Sala de lo Social*) of 20 Apr. 1988 (RJ 1988/2999).

decision, and even less in the actual context of the employer's organization of work, which made easy to assign a Sunday shift to the employee.

IV. Other Claims of Indirect Religious Discrimination in Employment

232. A different claim of indirect religious discrimination in employment was decided by the Superior Court of Justice of Madrid in 1997,[267] with notable lack of sensitivity to the exercise of employees' freedom of conscience and to the notion of indirect discrimination. The plaintiff was a Muslim female employee of the company that manages the duty free shops in the Madrid airport. After three weeks at work, she made a written request asking for some specific working conditions in order to reconcile her job with their religious beliefs. In particular, three were the conditions she asked for: to be exempted from the obligation to wear a short skirt (the company's rules on uniform prescribed a skirt above the knees); to be authorized to leave the working place for three hours on Fridays for the collective prayer; and to be excused from working at sections where she had to handle pork or alcoholic products. All her requests were rejected by the management. The Court confirmed the employer's position, emphasizing that the employee, as a manifestation of 'loyalty and good faith', should have declared her religious beliefs and explained her requests when applying for the job, in order to let the employer decide if they were compatible with its organizational needs. The Court made no reference to the notion of indirect discrimination or to any obligation of reasonable accommodation on the part of the employer.

§11. Conscientious Objection in the Public Service

233. Conflicts between individual duties of conscience and legal obligations can arise also in the area of public service. This may be the case of persons called to perform a civil service and also the case of public officials before or in the exercise of their functions. In addition to the case of people objecting to take an exam to enter the public service in a day that they consider holy and of mandatory rest, which was mentioned above,[268] the Spanish law has dealt mainly with four situations of this kind: conscientious objection to promissory oaths, to be part of a jury, to be part of a polling station, and, more recently, to officiate a ceremony of same-sex marriage.

I. Conscientious Objection to Promissory Oaths

234. In Spain, as in many other countries, it is mandatory to express formally and publicly a personal compromise of loyalty and obedience to the Constitution as a condition to take possession of a public office, at all levels. While in history this promise usually took the form of an oath, in the last decades the Spanish law has provided more flexible ways of satisfying this obligation, taking into account the

267. STSJ Madrid (*Sala de lo Social, sección 5ª*), 27 Oct. 1997 (AS 1997/3751).
268. *See supra*, para. 183.

principle of state's religious neutrality and also the fact that people may have conscientious scruples to swear their allegiance – sometimes because they do not believe in God, and some other times because their religious beliefs forbid them to swear on the name of God, on the basis of their interpretation of the Gospel.[269]

235. Currently, Article 1 of the Royal Decree 707/1979[270] permits a free choice between oath or pledge, without the need to provide a concrete reason to take one or the other:

> In the act of taking possession of public offices or positions in the public administration, the person in charge of giving possession shall ask the appointee the following question: "do you swear or promise on your conscience and honour to comply faithfully with the obligations of your office and, with loyalty to the King, to respect and make respect the Constitution as the fundamental law of the state"?
>
> This question shall be answered by the person taking possession with a plain affirmative.
>
> The foregoing formula can be replaced by the oath or pledge taken in person by the appointee, declaring that he will comply faithfully with the obligations of his office and, with loyalty to the King, will respect and make respect the Constitution as the fundamental law of the state.

236. Analogously, the standing orders of the Congress (Article 20) and the Senate (Article 12) impose on elected candidates the obligation to take oath or pledge to observe the Constitution as a requisite to fully acquire the status of congressman or senator, respectively.

237. The same free option between oath or promise on one's conscience and honour is recognized to military personnel in the mandatory ceremony of pledge of allegiance to the flag, in which they must accept the compromise of complying with their military obligations, observing the Constitution, keeping loyalty and obedience to the King and to their superiors, as well as defending Spain with their lives if necessary.[271]

238. By and large, the foregoing legal provisions have been very effective in protecting the freedom of conscience of public officials. There have been, however,

269. More precisely Matthew 5:33–37: 'Again, you have heard that it was said to the people long ago, "Do not break your oath, but fulfil to the Lord the vows you have made". But I tell you, do not swear an oath at all: either by heaven, for it is God's throne; or by the earth, for it is his footstool; or by Jerusalem, for it is the city of the Great King. And do not swear by your head, for you cannot make even one hair white or black. All you need to say is simply "Yes" or "No"; anything beyond this comes from the evil one.'

270. *Real Decreto* 707/1979, 8 Apr. 1979, *por el que se establece la fórmula de juramento en cargos y funciones públicas.*

271. Cf. Art. 3 of the *Ley* 17/1999, 18 May 1999, *de Régimen del Personal de las Fuerzas Armadas.*

some isolated problems raised by people that, on political grounds derived from their radical opposition to some provisions of the Constitution, have refused to accept the pledge of observing the constitutional order. More precisely, the problems were raised by elected members of parliament that represented extremist political parties with radical pro-independence ideas. The Constitutional Court has adjudicated on this type of issues several times. In 1983, the Court rendered two judgments apropos of constitutional appeals lodged, respectively, by elected members of the national Congress and of an autonomous regional parliament (Galicia).[272] In both of them, the Court held that is fully legitimate to impose a compromise of observance of the Constitution as a requisite for the exercise of the fundamental right of access to public offices on equal conditions (Article 23 CE). The reason – the Court explained – is that, by its very nature, holding a public office entails respect for the Constitution, although this does not imply an internal adhesion to its entire content.[273] What respect for Constitution implies – added the Court – is the compromise of accepting the democratic rules and not attempting to modify the juridical order through illegal means. Hence, the pledge of allegiance to the Constitution – the Court concluded – is not synonymous with renouncing free criticism or freedom of ideology.[274] Subsequent judgments of the Constitutional Court on similar claims have confirmed this doctrine.[275]

239. One of the plaintiffs of those constitutional appeals[276] filed an application before the Strasbourg jurisdiction. The (no longer existing) European Commission of Human Rights declared the application inadmissible as manifestly ill-founded and confirmed the ruling of the Spanish Constitutional Court.[277] The rationale of the Commission's decision focused on the legitimate limitations that could be imposed on the exercise of freedom of thought, conscience and religion according to Article 9.2 ECHR. The Commission held that, on the ground of public order, Spanish law could legitimately require an oath or pledge of allegiance to the Constitution, which was but a symbolic act by which an elected member of the legislature accepted that only legal means might be used to modify the constitutional order.

II. Conscientious Objection to Be Part of a Jury

240. Mandatory participation of citizens in a jury, when they have been summoned, has typically raised religious conscientious objection in two categories of persons: those who refuse to judge other human beings because of their interpretation of the Evangelical prohibition thereof,[278] as Jehovah's Witnesses and other minority Christian

272. STC 101/1983 (appeal lodged by two elected members of Herri Batasuna, a radical party, unofficially attached to the Basque terrorist group ETA), and STC 122/1983 (appeal lodged by three elected members of a radical party pro-independence of Galicia).
273. *See* STC 101/1983, FJ 3.
274. *See* STC 122/1983, FJ 5.
275. *See* STC 119/1990 and 74/1991, both of them related to appeals lodged by elected members of Herri Batasuna for the Congress and the Senate, respectively.
276. More precisely, the appeal decided by STC 122/1983.
277. Decision on the admissibility of Appl. Nr. 11321/85, 6 Oct. 1986.
278. Matthew 7:1: 'Do not judge, or you too will be judged.'

groups; and people with a canonical status that is considered incompatible with the exercise of civil authority, as members of the clergy and religious institutes in the Catholic Church.[279] The conflict of conscience is particularly important in countries as Spain, where the jury is foreseen only for criminal trials for serious offences.

241. In Spain the prospect of such conflicts properly commenced with the 1995 Organic Law on Jury,[280] which developed the constitutional provision that foresees the possibility that citizens 'participate in the administration of justice through the institution of jury' in criminal trials (Article 125 CE). In the 1995 Law, participation in jury is conceived as an inexcusable civic obligation, save for the exemptions specifically mentioned in Article 12. When a person has been summoned to be part of a jury, failure to appear is punished with an administrative economic sanction; and, if that person has accepted the appointment, administrative sanctions for not complying with jury duties may be accompanied by moderate criminal penalties.

242. Despite some proposals during the parliamentary procedure, Article 12 of the Law on Jury does not mention specifically conscientious objection as a legitimate cause for excuse. Nevertheless, scholars have maintained that conscientious objection can be operative through the 'open clause' of Article 12.7, which allows the competent judge to exonerate from the jury those persons who 'sufficiently allege and prove any other cause that creates for them a grave difficulty to perform as jurors'.[281] A serious conflict of conscience stemming from the exercise of a fundamental right, as freedom of religion, is definitely susceptible of being included in the category of 'grave difficulty'.

243. In practice, not many issues of conscientious objection to be a juror have been raised until now. The main reason is that jury trials are not numerous in Spain throughout the year. In addition, Spanish judges have normally been flexible to admit, in the light of Article 12.7, all kinds of reasonable excuses, among them conscientious objection. An interesting example of it is the pragmatic approach of a decision of a provincial court, in 1998, which accepted the conscience scruples of a woman, among other reasons, because forcing a person to participate in a jury against his will would most likely have a negative repercussion for the efficient functioning of the jury.[282]

244. This open attitude normally prevailing in Spanish judicature contrasts with the formalistic approach to the same issue taken by the Constitutional Court in a judgment of 1999.[283] The constitutional appeal was lodged by a person that had been included in the preliminary list of candidates apt to be drawn by lot in order to select the final members of a jury. Her pleading of conscientious objection had been rejected

279. The 1983 Code of Canon Law (canon 285.3) provides: 'Clerics are forbidden to assume public offices which entail a participation in the exercise of civil power.' The same rule applies to religious, by virtue of canon 672.

280. *Ley Orgánica* 5/1995, 22 May 1995, *del Tribunal del Jurado*. The institution of jury had existed intermittently in Spain since the nineteenth century but never lasted long.

281. *See* J. Martínez-Torrón, *Ley del jurado y objeción de conciencia*, 48 Revista Española de Derecho Constitucional 119–143 (1996); J. Ferrer Ortiz, *La objeción de conciencia a formar parte del jurado*. in VV.AA., *Estudios acerca de la reforma de la Justicia en España*, vol. 1, 613–622 (Real Academia de Jurisprudencia y Legislación-Ministerio de Justicia 2004); also in 2 Revista General de Derecho Canónico y Derecho Eclesiástico del Estado 1–30 (2003).

282. *Resolución de la Audiencia Provincial de Castellón*, 8 Oct. 1998, *Causa del Tribunal del Jurado* Nr. 4/97.

283. STC 216/1999.

by the competent local judge. The Constitutional Court did not make any judgment on the merits arguing that, as the plaintiff has been merely included in a preliminary list but not actually summoned, the alleged violation of a fundamental right was 'hypothetical', with the consequence that the plaintiff's claim was 'premature' and should be declared inadmissible. Thus, the Court lost an interesting occasion to clarify the criteria applicable in this type of conscientious objection.

III. Conscientious Objection to Be Part of a Polling Station

245. According to the 1985 General Law on Elections,[284] members of polling stations (*mesas electorales*) for national, regional or municipal elections are selected by drawing lots among citizens with right to vote, provided that they are literate and have not reached the age of 70 (Article 26). Once selected by lots, participation in a polling station is mandatory (Article 27). Failure to appear or abandonment of the polling station without good cause is considered an 'electoral offence', which can be punished with economic penalties or deprivation of liberty (Article 143). Causes of exemption from this civic obligation are mentioned by the Law in a very general way. A citizen selected to be part of a polling station has seven days to allege a 'good cause' (*causa justificada*) that prevents him from appearing and to provide evidence thereof. Applications for exemption are decided, without further appeal, by District Electoral Boards (*Juntas Electorales de Zona*), although the Central Electoral Board (*Junta Electoral Central*) is competent to provide general criteria for the unification of decisions (Article 27).

246. Over the last decades, on the ground of Article 16 CE, a number of Jehovah's Witnesses have requested to be excused from being part of a polling station, affirming that it is an act of political nature, forbidden by their religious beliefs. Sometimes the District Electoral Boards have not accepted their claims, with the consequence that, as objectors refused to appear, they were sentenced as guilty of electoral offence.

247. The case law of the Supreme Court is not entirely clear, but it has been often contrary to the protection of objectors. In a few occasions, the Court has exonerated an objector from criminal responsibility, with a rationale focused on the fact that he had not been completely aware of the illegality of his behaviour rather than on the protection of his freedom of conscience by Article 16 CE.[285] However, most judgments of the Supreme Court have confirmed the objectors' convictions for electoral offence. Some of those judgments were based on the lack of evidence about the objectors' claims, and it was not explicit what the Court would have decided if sufficient proof had been provided. In those cases, the Supreme Court highlighted that electoral rules should be strictly applied in order to prevent legal fraud on a civic duty that is so significant for the democratic system; and noted that the appellant had not proved his moral impossibility to be part of a polling station, either because he did not supply evidence of his membership of Jehovah's Witnesses or because the 'institutional'

284. *Ley Orgánica* 5/1985, 19 Jun. 1985, *de Régimen Electoral General.*
285. *See* STS 2174/1993, 29 Sep. 1993 (RJ 1993/7016); and STS of 30 Jan. 1979 (RJ 1979/277).

opposition of that church to observing this civic obligation was not proved.[286] Other judgments of the Supreme Court, instead, have been clearer about the fact that freedom of conscience did not constitute sufficient ground to be excused from the obligation of being part of a polling station, either because the public order is a legitimate limitation that can be imposed on fundamental freedoms[287] or because – in the Court's view – being part of a polling station was just a civic duty and not a political activity that could infringe on the objector's religious neutrality on political issues.[288] The latter statement certainly seems problematic, for it implies that the Court substituted the objector's moral judgment with its own opinion.

IV. Conscientious Objection to Perform a Ceremony of Same-Sex Marriage

248. After the Spanish Civil Code was modified in 2005 to eliminate heterosexuality as an intrinsic characteristic of marriage,[289] some public officials competent to celebrate civil marriages have alleged conscientious objection to perform civil ceremonies of same-sex marriages. When that legal reform was effected, the public officials competent to celebrate civil marriage, in ordinary situations and within national territory, were, alternatively, at the choice of the parties of the marriage, the judge in charge of the Civil Registry and the mayor of the town or person delegated by him – both referred to the place of celebration of the marriage (Article 51 CC).

249. The concrete reasons alleged for conscientious objection vary, but they normally had an element in common: the conviction that same-sex marriages, although permitted by positive law, are contrary to the natural law governing marriage. On that basis, objectors requested to be exempted from taking part in an act that they consider morally illegitimate. In practice, the conscientious objection of mayors did not raise problems, for the law specifically gave them freedom to delegate in the councilman they choose, without the need to provide any particular reason.[290] The conscientious objection of judges was more problematic, for the law did not grant them an analogous choice. In addition to practical solutions suggested to prevent moral conflicts in those cases, some scholars have supported the judges' right to conscientious objection arguing – among other things – that the authorization of marriages is not strictly a judicial function but a peripheral protocolary activity that the Civil Code happened to assign to judges in charge of the Civil Registry. From this perspective, excusing a judge from

286. *See* STS 753/1993, 30 Mar. 1993 (RJ 1993/2939); STS 2814/1992, 23 Dec. 1992 (RJ 1992/10325); STS 2856/1992, 30 Dec. 1992 (RJ 1992/10543); STS 1301/1998, 28 Oct. 1998 (RJ 1998/8947).

287. *See* STS 2317/1993, 15 Oct. 1993 (RJ 1993/7717). A similar approach was taken by a first instance criminal court, in 2016, in a case of an objection based on political conscience; the objector refused to cooperate with an electoral system which he abhorred (*Sentencia* 235/2016, *del Juzgado de lo Penal nº 2* of Elche, Alicante, 2 Jun. 2016).

288. *See* STS 1209/1994, 8 Jun. 1994 (RJ 1994/4548); STS 1868/1994, 18 Oct. 1994 (RJ 1994/8027); STS 2212/1994, 14 Dec. 1994 (RJ 1994/9810); STS 466/1995, 27 Mar. 1995 (RJ 1995/2238); STS 536/1995, 17 Apr. 1995 (RJ 1995/2891).

289. *See Ley* 13/2005, 1 Jul. 2005, *por la que se modifica el Código Civil en materia de derecho a contraer matrimonio.*

290. *See* Art. 51.1 CC, prior to the 2015 reform (*see infra*, para. 251).

performing such secondary administrative function when his freedom of conscience is at stake, while at the same time providing for adequate solutions that permit the intending spouses to celebrate their civil marriage, would not cause a serious disruption in his compliance with proper judicial duties, which focus on the application of the law to solve conflicts brought up in courts.[291]

250. In any event, the Supreme Court, in 2009, reaffirming once again its position not particularly protective of freedom of conscience in a variety of issues, declared that the judges' conscientious objection to celebrate same-sex marriages is not acceptable. The Court's rationale emphasized the necessary subjection of judges to the rule of law as a condition for the guarantee of the rights of all citizens.[292]

251. A reform of the Civil Code operated in 2015[293] has minimized the problem of this type of conscientious objection. The new Article 51.2 CC removed judges from the list of public officials competent to officiate a civil wedding and replaced them by justices of the peace – who are a figure of little significance in Spain – and by judicial secretaries of the place of celebration. In addition, it introduced the possibility of celebrating a civil marriage in the presence of a notary public freely chosen by the parties among those with jurisdiction in the place of celebration. This has been an important change, for notaries are well-known and respected legal figures in Spain, as in many others civil law countries. In practice most civil marriages are officiated either by a notary public or by the town's mayor (or a councilman delegated by him). No cases of conscientious objection to same-sex marriages have been reported since 2015.

291. *See* R. Navarro-Valls, *La objeción de conciencia a los matrimonios entre personas del mismo sexo*, 9 Revista General de Derecho Canónico y Derecho Eclesiástico del Estado 1–27 (2005).

292. STS 3059/2009 (*Sala de lo Contencioso-Administrativo, Sección 8ª*), 11 May 2009. For a critical analysis of this judgment, noting its grandiloquent language to explain general principles instead of facing the concrete issue of the conflict of laws present in the exercise of freedom of conscience by judges, *see* A. López-Sidro, *La objeción de conciencia de los jueces a los matrimonios entre personas del mismo sexo en la doctrina del Tribunal Supremo*, 21 Revista General de Derecho Canónico y Derecho Eclesiástico del Estado 1–18 (2009).

293. By the *Ley* 15/2015, *de la Jurisdicción Voluntaria*, 2 Jul. 2015.

Chapter 3. Collective Religious Freedom

252. Article 9 of the European Convention of Human Rights is even clearer than the Spanish Organic Law on Religious Freedom about the fact that freedom of thought, conscience and religion entails the right to manifest one's religion or belief through collective activities:

Article 9 ECHR – Freedom of thought, conscience and religion:

1. Everyone has the right to freedom of thought, conscience and religion; this right includes freedom to change his religion or belief and freedom, either alone or in community with others and in public or private, to manifest his religion or belief, in worship, teaching, practice and observance.
2. Freedom to manifest one's religion or beliefs shall be subject only to such limitations as are prescribed by law and are necessary in a democratic society in the interests of public safety, for the protection of public order, health or morals, or for the protection of the rights and freedoms of others.

253. Article 9 ECHR is in force in Spain, being the Spanish state part of the Council of Europe and a signatory to the Convention (since 1979). In addition, as indicated above,[294] according to Article 10.2 CE, all constitutional rules on fundamental rights and freedoms – and hence also Article 16 CE – shall be interpreted in the light of international treaties ratified by Spain.

254. As a consequence, the provisions of Article 2 LOLR for the protection of freedom of worship, religious teaching, religious meeting and religious assistance[295] are fully applicable to the collective exercise of religious freedom, i.e., to the interaction between individual and group in those expressions of freedom of religion. This implies that individuals are free, 'with immunity from coercion', to gather with other individuals to practice their religion. And it also implies that they are free to constitute religious groups or communities, with or without legal personality, and with the degree of institutionalization – higher or lower – they choose.

255. At the same time, according to the Strasbourg jurisdiction's interpretation of Article 9 ECHR, individuals do not have the right to remain in a religious community in a position considered heterodox by the relevant religious authority. When there is a conflict between individuals and their respective communities, the religious autonomy of the group prevails over the religious freedom of the individual, which is deemed sufficiently protected by the individual's right to abandon his church.[296] The situation, however, may become less certain when the conflictive issue is not the heterodox position of an individual within his church or religious community but the fact that an employee of a church or an institution permeated by a particular religious ethos holds

294. *See supra*, para. 49.
295. *See supra*, para. 60.
296. *See supra*, para. 113.

dissident doctrinal views or a conduct that is considered morally inappropriate by his employer.[297]

256. The Organic Law on Religious Freedom protects *the freedom of all religious groups*, irrespective of the fact that they have or have not obtained legal personality through registration at the Ministry of Justice. Under Spanish law, registration is not a legal obligation but an option, which – to some extent – grants a plus of legal protection and, above all, opens the door to some channels of state cooperation.[298] As the LOLR does not distinguish between registered and non-registered religious groups in this respect, all of them must be guaranteed the right to proselytize and to have places of worship and meeting, as well as essential rights attached to religious autonomy, such as the right to the free appointment of their ministers and the right to free communication within their organization and with other churches. These are the literal words of Article 2.2 LOLR:

> It [freedom of religion and worship] also includes the right of churches, religious denominations and communities to establish places of worship or meeting for religious purposes; to appoint and train their ministers; to spread and propagate their own creed; and to maintain relations with their own organizations or with other religious denominations, in national or in foreign territory.

257. For similar reasons, all churches and religious groups are entitled to the protection of their freedom through criminal law, although registered groups enjoy a slightly better position in this regard.[299] From the perspective of the protection of their freedoms, the main difference between registered and non-registered religious communities seems to be that the former can prove their religious nature much more easily. While registration in the Registry of Religious Entities constitutes per se an evidence of religious nature, non-registered communities should prove their religious character when they request from public authorities the guarantees of religious freedom envisaged by the legal system.

258. It is interesting to note that, from the collective perspective of freedom of ideology, religion and worship, the 1980 Organic Law on Religious Freedom is designed specifically for the protection of, and the cooperation with, churches and religious denominations but *not with groups of atheistic or humanistic orientation.*[300] Indeed, the latter are explicitly excluded from the scope of application of the Law by Article 3.2 LOLR:

> The protection provided by this law shall not apply to those activities, purposes and entities relating to the study of and experimentation with psychic and parapsychological phenomena, to the dissemination of humanistic or spiritualistic values, or to other similar non-religious aims.

---

297. *See* , e.g., in the recent Strasbourg jurisdiction, *Obst v. Germany* and *Schüth v. Germany*, both of 23 Sep. 2010; *Fernández Martínez v. Spain* (GC), 12 Jun. 2014; *Travaš v. Croatia*, 4 Oct. 2016. *See also infra* , Part VI, especially Ch. 3.

298. *See infra* , paras 265–270 and 273–280.

299. *See infra* , paras 318–321 and Part VII, Ch. 8

300. *See* J. Martínez-Torrón, *Religión, derecho y sociedad*, 141–145.

259. This characteristic of the LOLR has posed typically two questions. First, if there is an operational and distinguishable notion of religion in Spanish law – this question is analysed in another chapter.[301] Second, to what extent this position of the LOLR constitutes a breach of the equality principle. It is clear that individual freedom of ideology and religion receives the same degree of protection in the case of atheists or agnostics and in the case of religious believers, but the exclusion of atheistic groups from the scope of application of the LOLR might seem discriminatory at first glance. Leaving aside theoretical considerations about the notion of religion and its role in society vis-à-vis organizations based on atheistic beliefs, the question can be responded in the negative from a pragmatic point of view. On the one hand, state cooperation with religious communities – especially economic cooperation – tends to be more and more equalized with state cooperation with foundations or non-profit institutions in general. On the other hand, in Spain there is no possible comparison between the respective social weight of religions and institutionalized atheistic groups. The latter's social influence is minimal, and they are hardly representative of the attitudes of atheistic people in Spain. For the rest, they can benefit from the autonomy that corresponds to their registration as ordinary associations, which is less than the autonomy recognized to religious denominations but is normally sufficient to protect adequately their freedom to disseminate their ideas in society; and, moreover, makes them eligible for some ways of state economic cooperation when they meet the requirements of non-profit institutions. In addition, these groups do not usually request other types of state cooperation that Article 16.3 of the Constitution reserve for religious denominations. This would be contradictory with their principles, for they preach strict separation between state and religion. Rather than aspiring to receive the same cooperation as religions, they ask the state not to cooperate with religion at all. They tend to conceive themselves – at least in Spain – not as groups that desire to be compared to religions (traditional or new) but as a counter-influence of religion in society.[302]

260. The same *limitations* applicable to individual religious freedom are applicable to collective religious freedom. Therefore, in accordance with Article 16.1 CE, Article 3.1 LOLR and Article 9.2 ECHR, a limitative measure on collective religious freedom is justified only when it is prescribed by law and necessary in a democratic society for the protection of public order, safety, health and morals, as well as for ensuring the rights and freedoms of others.[303]

261. With regard to limitations on collective religious freedom, one of the interesting issues raised before the Spanish courts is to what extent it is legitimate to proceed to a *preventive application* of the public order clause when an allegedly religious group is deemed to be socially dangerous. The issue was raised by the Unification Church after it was refused registration in the Registry of Religious Entities on two grounds: (a) that it was not properly a religious group; and (b) that it developed

301. *See infra*, Part II, Ch. 4 §2 III.

302. Some characteristics of atheistic groups in Spain, in the light of the so-called atheist bus campaign, are discussed in J. Martínez-Torrón & S. Meseguer Velasco, *The atheist bus campaign and the uncertain future of organized atheism in Spain*, in *The Atheist Bus Campaign: Global Manifestations and Responses* 286–310(S. Tomlins & S.C. Bullivant eds, Brill 2016).

303. *See supra*, Part II, Ch. 1 §5.

activities that were contrary to the public order and morals, and it should therefore be considered 'dangerous'.

262. The case arrived on appeal to the Constitutional Court, which, in a judgment of 2001 concerning the refusal of registration of the Unification Church in the Registry of Religious Entities,[304] provided an unclear answer to the two main questions posed by the appeal, namely whether there was a legal notion of religion[305] and whether it was possible for an administrative authority to apply the public order clause to prevent future harm to the rights of other citizens. With respect to the second question, the Court initially discarded such a possibility and held that the danger for the public order had to be substantiated in a judicial process. In the words of the Court:

> being the "only limitation" on the exercise of a right, public order cannot be interpreted as a clause preventive of hypothetical risks, for in that case the clause itself would become the gravest sure danger for the exercise of that right. ... [A] s a general rule, only when the courts have certified the existence of a definite danger for "public safety, health and morals", as these concepts must be understood in a democratic society, it is appropriate to invoke public order as a restriction on the exercise of the right to freedom of religion and worship.[306]

263. Nevertheless, the Constitutional Court restricted the significance of the above statement when it immediately added that there are 'certain sects or groups' that use illegal 'recruitment methods that may impair the free development of their followers' personality'. In those concrete situations, the Court held that:

> it cannot be deemed contrary to the Constitution the exceptional preventive use of the public order clause, as far as it is directly aimed at safeguarding the public safety, health and morals in a democratic society, the danger is 'duly ascertained', and the restrictive measures against a group are proportionate and adequate to the aims pursued.[307]

264. In this particular case, the Court held that the Unification Church was entitled to register as a religious entity, for the evidence provided by the government with respect to its alleged dangerous activities was inconsistent and even, sometimes, contradictory. However, the Court did not indicate more precisely which factors can justify the exceptional recourse to the public order clause without the courts' intervention, nor did it explain how the dangerous character of a 'sect' can be 'duly ascertained' without a judicial procedure and a public hearing of those under suspicion. This fact

---

304. STC 46/2001.
305. The answer of the Constitutional Court to this question is explained *infra* , in paras 282–285.
306. *Ibid.*, FJ 11.
307. *Ibid.*

leaves the door open to the possible surveillance of some groups by police activities not backed by a judicial order or by any evidence other than mere suspicion.[308]

308. Activities of this type were indeed at issue in a case brought to the European Court of Human Rights: *Tsavachidis v. Greece*, 21 Jan. 1999. The case related to the surveillance of Jehovah's Witnesses by the National Intelligence Service. It ended in a friendly settlement in which the Greek government agreed to pay a sum of money for the costs and submitted a formal statement declaring that 'Jehovah's Witnesses are not, and will not in the future be, subject to any surveillance on account of their religious beliefs'. By then, the European Commission had already elaborated its report on the merits of the case, and expressed the opinion that there had been a violation of Art. 8 ECHR (by a vote of 13 to 4) and there had been no violation of Art. 9 ECHR (by a vote of 9 to 8). In Spain, long ago, criminal proceedings were initiated against the President of the Church of Scientology but the case was closed after a few years for lack of evidence.

Chapter 4. Organizational Religious Freedom

§1. Legal Personality, Religious Freedom and State Cooperation with Religious Communities

265. As indicated in the precedent chapter, all religious groups or communities enjoy the freedom of ideology, religion and worship recognized by Article 16 of the Constitution, irrespective of the fact that they have or have not obtained legal personality as religious entities, which is *an option and not a legal obligation*. In practice, most churches or religious communities are interested in obtaining legal personality specifically as groups of religious nature, which is normally achieved by registration in the RER – which is explained in a different section.[309]

266. The *Catholic Church* enjoys a privileged status with respect to legal personality. The Church as such did not need to register in the RER, for its specific mention by Article 16.3 CE implied recognition of its legal personality *ope legis*. In addition, by virtue of the 1979 Concordat, and in particular the Agreement on Juridical Affairs, the entities that compose the hierarchical organization of the Catholic Church are recognized legal personality in civil law without the need to register. The Concordat directly recognized the civil legal personality of the Spanish Bishops Conference.[310] Other ecclesiastical structures obtain legal personality through mere notification to the state; thus, dioceses, parishes and other entities that constitute the territorial organization of the Church 'shall enjoy civil legal personality as soon as they have canonical legal personality and this is notified to the competent state department'[311] (currently the Directorate General of Foreign Juridical Cooperation and Relations with Religious Communities in the Ministry of Justice). This rule does not apply, however, to other ecclesiastical juridical persons out of the public administrative structure of the Church. Religious orders and other types of canonical associations or foundations are subject to the ordinary rules on registration in the RER (although the Concordat automatically recognized the civil legal personality of those institutions that already existed when it came into force).[312]

267. The *rest of churches or religious communities*, as well as their federations and their internal entities, acquire legal personality by registration in the RER (Article 5 LOLR), which has a constitutive effect. If their application for registration in the RER is rejected, or if they just prefer not to be included in that specific registry, religious groups may choose between either not registering at all or registering as common associations in accordance with the provisions of the 2002 Organic Law on the Right of Association.[313] The latter option, however, imply some limitations on their autonomy,

309. *See infra* , in this same chapter, §2.
310. *See* Agreement on Juridical Affairs (*Acuerdo sobre Asuntos Jurídicos*), Art. I.3.
311. *Ibid.*, Art. I.2.
312. *Ibid.*, Art. I.5.
313. *Ley Orgánica* 1/2002, 22 Mar. 2002, *reguladora del derecho de asociación*.

such as, for instance, the requirement of democratic functioning,[314] the opening of their accountancy to the scrutiny of their members,[315] or the fact that public authorities shall not provide any kind of support to associations that, in the admission process of associates, discriminate persons on personal grounds, including religion.[316] In sum, although it is legally possible, registering as ordinary associations is not likely a convenient choice for religious groups that have been rejected by the Registry of Religious Entities. It must be noted that registering in the Registry of Associations has a mere declaratory, not constitutive, effect on legal personality; i.e., registration has only the effect of publicity *erga omnes*.[317] Registration in the Registry of Associations permits the relevant associations to apply for the status of 'association of public utility', which may make them eligible for some tax benefits but imply further limitations on the associations' autonomy and make them more accountable to public authorities.[318]

268. By contrast, registration in the Registry of Religious Entities has some direct advantages for religious communities, although some of them are more theoretical than real. One obvious advantage is the relative 'aura of respectability' that recognition as a religious community often implies in front of society. From a legal perspective, other advantages are the strengthening of their internal autonomy, provided by Article 6 LOLR,[319] the reinforced protection by criminal law in comparison with non-registered religious groups,[320] and the fact that their foreign ministers can obtain legal residence in Spain without having a working permit.[321] These are, however, not very significant benefits in practice, for those criminal law provisions are hardly ever applied, and the internal autonomy of religious communities is well protected by Article 2 LOLR and other international conventions or commitments accepted by Spain. Registration in the RER, however, could be important as evidence of the religious nature and purposes of a group, which is thus 'authenticated' by the Ministry of Justice. A community requesting from public authorities the protection of collective religious freedom granted by criminal law, or the protection of its internal religious autonomy, can easily prove its religious nature by its registration in the RER.

269. In addition to the foregoing, the main beneficial consequence of registration in the RER consists in opening the doors to future state cooperation with the relevant churches or religious communities in a variety of areas, for instance the recognition of civil effects of religious marriages (Article 59 CC) and the possibility to have their religious doctrines taught at public schools (Article 2.3 LOLR). However, these manifestations of state cooperation are conceived as legal *possibilities* in the literal sense and their realization is left to the public authorities' discretion. In practice, actual state cooperation begins only when a religious community is recognized to have 'well-known roots' (*notorio arraigo*) in Spain, according to criteria that are explained

314. *See ibid.*, Arts 7.1.g) and 12.
315. *See ibid.*, Art. 14.
316. *See ibid.*, Art. 4.5.
317. *See ibid.*, Art. 10.1.
318. *See ibid.*, Arts 32–34.
319. *See infra* , Part III, Ch. 2.
320. *See infra* , Part VII, Ch. 8.
321. *See infra* , para. 411.

below.[322] In that case, such community will have its religious marriages granted civil effects if it so wishes (Article 60 CC), is entitled to be represented in the Advisory Commission on Religious Freedom in the Ministry of Justice (Article 8 LOLR), and has the possibility to start a negotiation process eventually leading to sign a formal cooperation agreement with the state (Article 7.1. LOLR).

270. Cooperation agreements are precisely, until now, the cornerstone of state cooperation with religion in Spain. To reach a cooperation agreement with the state requires not only the recognition of 'well-known roots' (*notorio arraigo*) but also the political will of the government, which has unlimited discretion to that purpose; therefore, recognition of *notorio arraigo* does not imply, necessarily or automatically, the opening of a negotiation process with the government.[323] To put it in clearer words, the Spanish law foresees various types of state cooperation with religion in theory linked to registration in the Registry of Religious Entities or to the subsequent recognition of 'well-known roots', but the government have full – and virtually uncontrolled – power to decide when, how and with whom the state will cooperate.

271. In addition to churches and religious denominations and communities (*iglesias, confesiones y comunidades religiosas*), also federations of religious communities may obtain legal personality through registration in the RER, as well as internal entities, such as religious associations or foundations, created within the respective religious communities for specific purposes.[324]

272. Religious federations do not imply bringing into existence a new religious denomination. They gather a number of religious communities of common roots and beliefs for the purposes of managing issues of shared interest, including especially those attached to their relationship with the public authorities. Indeed, the most significant religious federations were created with the aim of negotiating cooperation agreements with the government, in the 1980s. They are the Protestant federation (FEREDE, *Federación de Entidades Evangélicas de España*);[325] the Jewish federation (FCJE, *Federación de Comunidades Judías de España*, formerly named FCI);[326] and an Islamic federation (CIE, *Comisión Islámica de España*),[327] which is, in reality, a federation of federations, for Muslims are organized in Spain around a variety of autonomous federations. Although these federations began for the sole purpose of unifying the voice of Protestantism, Judaism and Islam vis-à-vis the Spanish government, they have remained active after the 1992 Agreements, developing an internal life of their own and reinforcing the spiritual and organizational links between Protestant, Jewish and Islamic communities, respectively. There are also some federations of Catholic entities, which were born as well, to a large extent, with the aim of speaking with the government with a unified voice. Among them are a federation of members of religious orders (CONFER, *Confederación Española de Religiosos y Religiosas*),

322. *See infra*, para. 356.
323. *See infra*, paras 357–358.
324. *See* Art. 5.1 LOLR.
325. *See* information about it in: http://www.ferede.es (accessed 9 Dec. 2017).
326. *See* information about it in: http://www.fcje.org (accessed 9 Dec. 2017).
327. *See* information about it in: http://comisionislamicadeespana.org (accessed 9 Dec. 2017). The RD 1384/2011, 14 Oct. 2011, facilitates the integration of new Islamic communities into the Islamic Commission of Spain.

a federation of members of religious institutes devoted to teaching activities (FERE, *Federación Española de Religiosos de la Enseñanza*), a federation of members of religious institutes devoted to healthcare activities (FERS, *Federación Española de Religiosos Sanitarios*), and a federation of canonical secular institutes (CEDIS, *Confederación Española de Institutos Seculares*).

§2. The Registry of Religious Entities

I. Basic Notions and Structure

273. The RER was created by Article 5 of the 1980 Organic Law on Religious Freedom. It is a public registry in the Ministry of Justice, currently under the authority of the government's department with competence to deal with religious juridical persons and, in general, with competence on religious freedom issues: the Vice-Directorate General of Relations with Religious Communities, which is part of the Directorate General of Foreign Juridical Cooperation and Relations with Religious Communities. The provisions of Article 5 LOLR on the RER were developed by a specific royal decree of 1981,[328] which was replaced by a new regulation in 2015.[329]

274. As explained in the previous section, the RER is the instrument through which the state recognizes the legal personality of religious entities. *Registration is an option and not a legal obligation.* The diverse nature of entities eligible for registration has led scholars to distinguish between 'major' and 'minor' entities. The former are churches and religious denominations or communities (*iglesias, confesiones y comunidades religiosas*), as well as their federations; the latter are internal associations or foundations created by 'major' entities for the pursuance of their aims.[330] For instance, the Greek Orthodox Church in Spain or the Evangelical Federation (FEREDE) are considered 'major' entities; and religious orders, specific associations or foundations

328. *Real Decreto* 142/1981, 9 Jan. 1981, *sobre organización y funcionamiento del Registro de Entidades Religiosas*. For an analysis of this regulation, *see* I. Aldanondo, *El Registro de Entidades religiosas*, 7 Anuario de Derecho Eclesiástico del Estado 13–48 (1991); wish specific emphasis on the problems caused by the configuration of the RER prior to 2015, *see* M.E. Olmos, *Personalidad jurídica civil de las entidades religiosas y Registro de Entidades Religiosas*, and A. López-Sidro, *La cuestión de la reforma del Registro de Entidades Religiosas: examen de as propuestas reglamentarias de 2003 y 2004*, both in *La libertad religiosa y su regulación legal* 577–620 and 621–643 respectively (R. Navarro-Valls, J. Mantecón & J. Martínez-Torrón eds, Iustel 2009). *See also* the more comprehensive and systematic study by E. Herrera Ceballos, *El Registro de Entidades Religiosas. Estudio global y sistemático* (Eunsa 2012).

329. *Real Decreto* 594/2015, 3 Jul. 2015, *por el que se regula el Registro de Entidades Religiosas*. For an analysis of this new regulation *see* E. Herrera Ceballos, *Hacia la construcción de un Registro fiel reflejo de la realidad. La reforma del Registro de Entidades Religiosas*, 39 Revista General de Derecho Canónico y Derecho Eclesiástico del Estado 1–35 (2015).

330. *See* M. López Alarcón, *Confesiones y entidades religiosas*, in *Derecho eclesiástico del Estado español* 186–189 (J. Ferrer Ortiz ed., 6th ed., Eunsa 2007).

within a church – including the Catholic Church – are considered 'minor' entities, as well as seminars and theological centres.[331]

275. The RER has been traditionally divided into three sections that do not relate to the classification explained in the previous paragraph but rather to the formal status of the registered entities. There is, first, a 'special section' for the registration of those religious communities that have concluded a cooperation agreement with the state, as well as for the religious associations created by them. These include the canonical associations of the Catholic Church erected by the competent ecclesiastical authority. Second, there is a 'general section' of equivalent structure but for those religious communities that do not have a cooperation agreement with the state (i.e., the immense majority). Third, there is a 'section of foundations', in which the foundations of the Catholic Church are registered – while other religious foundations are registered in the general registry for foundations. According to the 2105 regulation, this section will be preserved until a law on religious foundations is passed.[332] The same royal decree of 2015 has added a new fourth section in the RER, called 'historical', which keeps a record of registrations that have been either rejected or cancelled.[333]

276. In addition to religious entities (major or minor), the new royal decree foresees the possibility to register specific acts of religious communities, such as their foundation or dissolution in Spain, modifications of their statutes, the integration of entities into a federation or their segregation thereof. Places of worship, religious ministers and representatives of religious communities can also be registered.[334] The RER is a public registry and consequently the information about the religious entities registered in it is freely accessible to the public, also online.[335] Indeed, the new royal decree of 2015 tries to reinforce and facilitate the publicity of the RER and contains a specific ad hoc section (Title IV, Articles 30–34), which did not exist in the previous regulation.

II. Process and Effects of Registration

277. The registration process is relatively simple and easy and can be done also via electronic channels. To register a church or a religious community, only limited evidence is required, and no minimum number of members or adherents is necessary. The process commences with a written application of the representatives of the relevant religious entity, accompanied by authenticated document (*escritura pública*) attesting its creation or establishment in Spain, which can be accompanied optionally by a list of twenty or more persons, all of them adults and legal residents in Spain, who endorse the establishment of the applicant entity. The application must contain also the following data:[336]

331. *See* RD 594/2015, Art. 2.
332. *See ibid.*, second transitional provision.
333. *See ibid.*, Art. 26.
334. *See ibid.*, Art. 3.
335. *See* http://www.mjusticia.gob.es/cs/Satellite/Portal/es/areas-tematicas/libertad-religiosa/registro-entidades-religiosas (accessed 9 Dec. 2017).
336. *See* Art. 5.2 LOLR and Art. 6 RD 594/2015.

a. Name of the applicant entity, which must not induce confusion about its religious nature and must also be adequate to distinguish it from other religious entities that are already registered. By and large, this requisite has raised only residual practical problems. In the 1980s, the RER rejected the registration of a church – the *Iglesia Cristiana Palmariana de los Carmelitas de la Santa Faz*, stemming from a schism from the Catholic Church – on the ground that its name could lead to confusion with other Christian churches. The Supreme Court overruled the administrative decision and authorized the registration, considering that the adjective *Palmariana* – taken from the town where the Church had its see – was distinctive enough to avoid misunderstandings.[337]
b. Institutional domicile of the applicant entity.
c. Territory in which the religious community will develop its activity.
d. Expression of the religious purposes of the applicant entity and any other indication that may attest to its religious nature. In the past, this requisite has raised important issues with respect to the registration of 'major' entities.[338] This is probably the reason why the 2015 regulation explicitly refers to some examples of indications of religious nature, such as doctrinal principles, activities or places related to worship and preaching, and religious assistance or education among others. The justification of the religious purposes of 'minor' entities raises less complex issues, for it mostly based on the certification of the relevant 'major' entity. The most frequent cases are Catholic entities, which must obtain a certification of canonical legal personality from the competent ecclesiastical authority; and Evangelical, Jewish or Islamic entities, which must obtain their certification of religious purposes from their respective federations, signatories of the 1992 Agreements.[339]
e. Organizational rules and governing bodies. With regard to the latter, the application must indicate explicitly their powers as well as the procedure for their appointment.
f. The names of the applicant entity's legal representatives and proof of their legal residence in Spain if they are foreigners.
g. If the application is submitted by religious entities that are a branch of a foreign entity, it must contain additional information about the statutes, recognition and legal representatives of that entity in the country of origin, as well as proof of their legal representatives in Spain.

278. If the Ministry of Justice – in practice the officials in charge of the RER[340] – consider that the applicant entity meets the legal requisites and provides the required evidence thereof, registration shall be accepted and immediately communicated to the applicant. In case of doubt – normally about the religious purposes of the applicant entity – it is possible to request the opinion of the Advisory Commission on Religious Freedom. If the applicant is not given an answer within six months, registration is tacitly accepted. If the Ministry of Justice rejects registration, the applicant entity can

337. STS of 2 Nov. 1987 (RJ 8764/1987).
338. These issues are analysed in paras 281–285.
339. *See* Art. 1.3 of the 1992 Agreements with the Evangelical, the Jewish and the Islamic Federations.
340. *See* para. 273.

challenge that decision in the courts. Any modification on the data provided in the application must be communicated to the RER.

279. Once a religious entity has been registered, registration can be cancelled only upon request of its legal representatives or in execution of a final judicial decision – for instance, a judgment ordering the dissolution of an entity for criminal or other illegal activities. To the author's knowledge, the latter way of cancellation has never occurred to date, and the former is very rare.

280. Together with the lack of substantial consequences that registration produces per se from the perspective of state cooperation with religion,[341] one of the factors that led to the reform of the RER was the fact that many data kept in it were outdated and therefore the Registry was deemed not to reflect adequately the social reality of religion in Spain. Indeed, it was well known that an undetermined number of registered religious communities were actually no longer existing (among other reasons because some of them were registered by immigrants that had returned to their countries of origin). However, it was not possible to cancel the registration of those communities unless they explicitly requested it (which was unlikely); as mentioned in the precedent paragraph, rules on cancellation are very strict and determined by an organic law (Article 5 LOLR), which cannot be modified by a royal decree. In order to minimize the negative impact of this circumstance on the accuracy of the data kept in the Ministry of Justice, the new regulation of 2015 has introduced a double obligation for all registered entities. They must keep their information in the RER updated and they must submit every second year a so-called *declaración de funcionamiento* (literally, 'statement of functioning'), confirming that they are active. If such statement is not submitted in time, the RER shall make a marginal note on their registration 'for informative purposes'.[342] This solution certainly does not solve the problem but at least contributes to presume the disappearance of those entities that do not present their statement of functioning in due course.

III. The RER and the Legal Concept of Religion

281. The fact that only entities with religious purposes can be registered in the RER has posed in the past some important questions about *the notion of religion* that pervades the Spanish law.[343] Article 3.2 LOLR is of no much help in this respect. Apart from indicating that the LOLR is not applicable to non-religious entities and activities, this provision only mentions a few examples of activities that must not be considered religious, such as the study of psychic and parapsychological phenomena or the

341. *See supra* , paras 268–270.

342. *See* Art. 29 RD 594/2015.

343. For a detailed analysis of the theoretical and practical challenges that a legal notion of religion implies for the protection of religious freedom in Spain, and generally in Western societies, *see* R. Palomino, *Religión y derecho comparado* (Iustel 2007). By the same author, with specific reference to the notion of religious community in Spanish law, *see* R. Palomino, *Iglesias, confesiones y comunidades religiosas: el concepto legal de confesión religiosa en la LOLR y la doctrina*, in, *La libertad religiosa y su regulación legal*, 556–575 (R. Navarro-Valls, J. Mantecón & J. Martínez-Torrón eds, Iustel 2009).

dissemination of spiritualistic or humanistic values. Apparently, the LOLR departed from the assumption that it was 'easy' to know what was religious and what was not. In this context, for many years the praxis of the RER, confirmed by the Spanish courts, was to perform a moderate filtering of applicant 'major' entities, based upon an explicit notion of religion elaborated for legal purposes and inspired in the Judaeo-Christian religious tradition of the West. More precisely, to be considered a 'major' religious entity, the RER required three main elements: (a) it had to be composed by a group of people that professed and shared a common and relatively homogeneous system of doctrines – dogmas and morals – derived from the belief in a supreme being; (b) they should have a collective worship expressed in external rites or practices; and (c) they must be structured around an organization relatively clear and stable.[344]

282. On this conceptual basis, the Spanish courts confirmed the denial of registration of, for example, the Church of Scientology,[345] the Monist Order of the Perfect Reflection[346] and the Unification Church,[347] holding that they did not meet the legal requirements to be deemed a religion in Spanish law. Nevertheless, in 2001 a judgment of the Constitutional Court changed completely this situation.[348]

283. As mentioned above,[349] this decision of the Constitutional Court addressed the issue of the refusal of registration of the Unification Church in the RER, on the grounds that it was not properly a religious group, and that it was a 'dangerous' sect that developed activities harmful to the public order and morals. The Court decided in favour of the plaintiff and ruled that the Unification Church was entitled to register as a religious entity. The Court's judgment, however, was not very illuminating. Instead of shedding light on the questions raised by the legal concept of religion in Spain, the Court opted for rendering this concept inoperative. According to the judgment, the authorities in charge of the RER do not have any discretion, or margin of appreciation, to examine the religious nature of any group that has applied to register; they must limit themselves to confirm that this group is not excluded from registration by Article 3.2 LOLR.[350] The problem is that this legal provision specifically excludes not only entities focused on 'the study of and experimentation with psychic and parapsychological phenomena, to the dissemination of humanistic or spiritualistic values', but also entities with 'similar non-religious aims'. Consequently, administrative authorities do of necessity have to make, implicitly or explicitly, a judgment about the religious nature and purposes of the applicant entity.

284. The contradictions inherent in the holding of the Constitutional Court could be explained, to some extent, by a certain confusion between two very different possible actions: on the one hand, the administrative judgment on the religious nature of an entity; and on the other hand, the administrative judgment on the legitimacy of the religious beliefs of an entity (the latter would be incompatible with the state's religious

344. *See* J. Martínez-Torrón, *Religión, derecho y sociedad. Antiguos y nuevos planteamientos en el derecho eclesiástico del Estado* 199–202 (Comares 1999).
345. *See* SAN of 23 Jun. 1988, confirmed by STS of 25 Jun. 1990 (RJ 5700/1990).
346. *See* SAN of 8 Nov. 1985.
347. *See* SAN of 30 Sep. 1993, confirmed by STS of 14 Jul. 1996.
348. STC 46/2001.
349. *See supra* , paras 261–264.
350. *See* STC 46/2001, FJ 10.

neutrality). In this regards, it is revealing that the Court, before asserting that administrative authorities cannot examine the religious nature of a group applying for registration, declared:

> [The existence of the RER] does not make the state competent to perform an activity of control on the legitimacy of the beliefs of religious entities or communities, or on the various ways of expressing them; it only gives the state competence to check, through mere statement and not assessment, that the applicant entity is not excluded by Article 3.2 LOLR.[351]

285. In any event, the Constitutional Court's decision of 2001 was sufficiently clear to be understood as prohibiting public authorities in charge of the RER from evaluating the religious nature of applicant entities. The consequence is that the Registry must accept, without further inquiries, all applications from entities that claim to be religious, except in the unlikely hypothesis that the applicant group explicitly presents itself as a non-religious organization, or as an organization for the study of psychic or parapsychological phenomena, or for the dissemination of humanistic or spiritualistic values. In application of these judicial doctrine and criteria, in 2007 the National Court held that the Church of Scientology in Spain was entitled to register in the RER (Scientology, under a new name, had applied again for registration in 2004, unsuccessfully).[352]

IV. Registration of Internal Associations and Foundations of Religious Communities

286. As indicated above, it is possible to register 'minor' religious entities in the RER, i.e., those internal associations or foundations created by churches or religious communities ('major' entities) for the pursuance of their aims. The requisites for registration are substantially the same for both types of entities, but minor entities must provide additionally a document of the church of religious community to which they belong authenticating their constitution.[353]

287. All internal *associations* of this kind abide by the same laws with respect to obtaining civil legal personality. To that purpose they must register in the RER – in the 'special section', in the case of the Catholic Church and the religious minorities signatories of a cooperation agreement with the state; or in the 'general section', in the case of registered religious communities without cooperation agreement.[354]

288. The case of *foundations* is different. Religious foundations canonically erected by the competent ecclesiastical authority of the Catholic Church have a specific regulation that dates back to a royal decree of 1984.[355] They can register in a specific section of the RER,[356] in principle after a mere formal examination of the required

351. *Ibid.*, FJ 8.
352. SAN 4394/2007, 11 Oct. 2007. *See supra*, para. 282.
353. *See supra*, para. 277 and Art. 7 RD 594/2015.
354. *See supra*, para. 275.
355. RD 589/1984, 8 Feb. 1984, *sobre fundaciones religiosas de la Iglesia Católica.*
356. *See supra*, para. 275.

documents. Instead, foundations of other churches or religious communities are subject to the common law on foundations and acquire legal personality by registration in the general registries of foundations, national or regional.[357] The three religious federations signatories of the 1992 Agreements have been requesting for years – unsuccessfully until now – that their foundations be granted the same legal treatment as the religious foundations of the Catholic Church. The 2015 regulations on the RER, in its second transitional provision, refer to a future general law on religious foundations, but to the author's knowledge no legislative initiative in this regard has been activated so far.

289. One of the main issues raised by registration of Catholic associations and foundations, as well as by registration of other religious associations, is the *degree of control of their religious aims* that can be exercised by the officials in charge of the RER. According to the Concordat[358] and to the 1992 Agreements with the Evangelical, Jewish and Islamic Federations,[359] the certification of religious aims issued by the respective religious structure should be sufficient to guarantee registration – i.e., a certificate issued by the competent ecclesiastical authority in the case of Catholic associations and foundations, and by the relevant federation in the case of Evangelical, Jewish or Islamic associations. Nevertheless, Spanish courts have sometimes asserted their competence to control the religious aims of applicant Catholic entities, without feeling bound by the relevant certification issued by ecclesiastical authorities; and, at the same time, they have interpreted the notion of religious aims in a restrictive manner, as synonymous with aims of worship and prayer.[360] This has occurred occasionally not with respect to institutes of consecrated life, whose religious aims are indubitable, but with regard to other types of canonical associations or foundations. Such judicial position certainly contrasts with the subsequent case law of the Constitutional Court in 2001, which substantially undercut the competence of public authorities to impose a definite notion of religion.[361]

290. Trying to solve these practical problems, in 1999, the Spanish Bishops Conference issued an instruction, which was accompanied by a letter of the Minister of Justice, confirming that: (a) the RER should merely effect a formal scrutiny of the applications for registration of foundations; and (b) the concept of religious aims should be construed broadly, as embracing all aims congruous with the functions and mission of the Catholic Church.[362] Among those aims the instruction included activities directly linked to worship, preaching, evangelization, preservation of sacred property, training and support of religious ministers, moral and religious teaching of the faithful, religious assistance, confessional teaching through the creation of schools, and charitable

357. The main statute on foundations is the *Ley* 50/2002, 26 Dec. 2002, *de Fundaciones*.

358. *See* Art. I.4 of the Agreement on Juridical Issues.

359. *See* Art. 1.3 of each agreement.

360. *See* , for instance, STS 1361/1994, 1 Mar. 1994. *See* M. López Alarcón, *La función calificadora en el Registro de Entidades Religiosas*, 14 Anuario de Derecho Eclesiástico del Estado 459 (1998).

361. *See supra* , paras 282–285.

362. The text of this instruction was published in 60 Boletín Oficial de la Conferencia Episcopal Española 36–40 (1999). For a comment on this document, *see* M.E. Olmos Ortega, *La instrucción de la Conferencia Episcopal Española sobre la inscripción de asociaciones y fundaciones de la Iglesia Católica en el Registro de Entidades Religiosas. Texto y comentario*, 148 Revista Española de Derecho Canónico 213–226 (2000).

activities. Although this instruction is an intra-ecclesiastical document and does not have binding character for the Spanish courts, no recent problems have been reported on this question. Indeed, this broad approach to the notion of religious aims seems to inspire Article 6.1.d) of the 2015 royal decree, which is applicable to the registration of all types of entities, major or minor, Catholic or else.

§3. THE ADVISORY COMMISSION ON RELIGIOUS FREEDOM

291. Article 8 of the 1980 Organic Law on Religious Freedom[363] created a consultative body in the Ministry of Justice, at a national level, called the Advisory Commission on Religious Freedom (*Comisión Asesora de Libertad Religiosa*, CALR), with the specific function of providing advice and expert opinion on all legislative and governmental initiatives that may have an influence on the protection of religious freedom and, generally, on the legal treatment of religion in Spain. The first regulation of the CALR dates back to 1981[364] and was replaced by another regulation in 2001.[365] After studying the experience of the past years, and taking into account some of the proposals formulated by the members of the CALR,[366] the government approved a new regulation in 2013, which introduced significant modifications on the composition and concrete competences of the Commission.[367]

292. The CALR is now presided by the Minister of Justice. There is also a vice-president, the Director General competent on religious affairs (currently named Director General of Foreign Juridical Cooperation and Relations with Religious Communities[368]), who often is substituted by the Vice-Director General of Relations with Religious Communities and who attends in an advisory capacity and without voting rights when the Minister is presiding. According to Article 8 LOLR, members of the CALR must be divided into three sections, in conditions of parity. One section is reserved for representatives of different departments of the government,[369] other for representatives of the most significant religions existing in Spain and other for independent experts. The government's representatives are selected by the respective

363. *See* its text *supra* , in para. 66.
364. *Real Decreto* 1890/1981, 19 Jun. 1981, *sobre constitución de la Comisión Asesora de Libertad Religiosa en el Ministerio de Justicia.*
365. *Real Decreto* 1159/2001, 26 Oct. 2001, *por el que se regula la Comisión Asesora de Libertad Religiosa*. Some months later, an order of the Ministry of Justice introduced more detailed provisions on the organization and competences of the CALR: *Orden* JUS 1375/2002, of 31 May 2002, *sobre organización y competencias de la Comisión Asesora de Libertad Religiosa.*
366. These proposals can be found in the volume VV.AA., *Comisión Asesora de Libertad Religiosa: realidad y futuro* (Ministerio de Justicia 2009), which gathers several reports by some members of the CALR commissioned by the Ministry of Justice, commented by the rest of the members of the CALR.
367. *Real Decreto* 932/2013, 29 Nov. 2013, *por el que se regula la Comisión Asesora de Libertad Religiosa.*
368. The former name was Director General of Religious Affairs. *See* *infra* , para. 396.
369. According to Art. 8 of the 2013 regulations, seven different ministries in charge of the following areas: foreign affairs, finance, interior, education, employment, presidency, and health and social services.

ministers and appointed by the Minister of Justice; the religious representatives are proposed by the respective churches or religious communities and appointed also by the Minister of Justice; and the experts are chosen by the Ministry of Justice and appointed by the Council of Ministers. In practice, since the creation of the CALR most of the experts have been professors of law with specialization in law and religion issues. Religious representatives must include representatives of those religions that have been recognized 'well-known roots' (*notorio arraigo*).[370] At present, there are representatives of the Catholic Church (four), Protestantism (two, proposed by the Evangelical Federation, FEREDE), Judaism (one, proposed by the Jewish Federation, FCJE), Islam (two, proposed by the Islamic Federation, CIE), the Mormon Church (one), Buddhism (one, proposed by the Buddhist Federation, FCBE), and Christian Orthodoxy (one, proposed by the Assembly of Orthodox Bishops in Spain and Portugal).[371] Members of the CALR are appointed for four years and can be reappointed for further terms without limitation.

293. The CALR functions in *plenary session* or in *permanent commission.* The plenary of the CALR must meet in ordinary sessions twice per year but can be convoked in additional extraordinary sessions at the president's initiative or upon request of the majority of its members. Traditionally, the provision of Article 8 LOLR about parity and equal representation of the three sections of the CALR was interpreted as requiring that each section had exactly the same number of members. However, the 2013 regulations addressed this issue in a different way, in an attempt to reconcile parity and functional efficiency, which demands a not too high number of members (it must be taken into account that, since 2003, four religions have been recognized 'well-known roots' in addition to the Catholic Church, Protestantism, Judaism and Islam, and this is not a closed list). To keep a reasonable dimension of the CALR while at the same time maintaining the equal representation and voting power of the three categories, the royal decree of 2013 has designed an original solution for the plenary of the CALR.[372] The total number of members with voting rights is 26: 8 members in the government section (the president plus 7 representatives of ministries), 12 in the religious communities section and 6 in the experts section. To equalize the voting rights of all sections, each of the government representatives is given 3 votes in the plenary, each of the religious representatives is given 2 votes, and each of the experts is given 4 votes. Thus, although the number of members is different in the three sections, their respective number of votes in plenary sessions is the same (24). The permanent commission is composed of nine members plus the president, with a structure and distribution of voting rights that reproduces the same notion of equality and parity between the three sections that governs the functioning of the plenary.[373] The permanent commission meets more often and takes care of the urgent business as well as of those tasks delegated by the plenary.

294. The 2013 regulation endeavours to involve regional governments (*comunidades autónomas*) with competence on religious affairs in the activity of the CALR. When

370. *See infra*, para. 356.

371. The Church of Jehovah's Witnesses, which is recognized well-known roots in Spain since 2006, explicitly renounced its right to have a representative in the CALR.

372. Cf. Art. 15 RD 932/2013.

373. Cf. Art. 17 RD 932/2013.

the agenda of the session includes issues of their interest, those regional governments shall be given the opportunity to send a representative to the plenary and the permanent commission, who can attend the meeting without voting rights. In addition to those representatives and the ordinary members of the CALR, the president may invite, both to the meetings of the plenary and the permanent commission, and without voting rights, persons that may provide information of interest about specific issues included in the agenda; in practice they are usually external experts or members of religious minorities without representation in the CALR. An interesting novelty of the 2013 rules with regard to the structure of the CALR, and with the aim of making the Commission more operative and dynamic, is the possibility of creating temporary working groups for the study of specific issues, which may include experts outside the CALR. The reports and proposals they produce shall be remitted to the permanent commission for approval and, when appropriate, for the further consideration by the plenary.[374]

295. The most important *functions* of the CALR are exercised by the plenary. Article 8.2 LOLR describes quite generally those functions and refers to the study, report and proposals with respect to all issues relating to the application of the LOLR. It mentions, however, a concrete function. It is mandatory to request the opinion of the CALR on the preparation of the cooperation agreements between the state and religious communities mentioned in Article 7 LOLR – but the CALR's opinion is not binding for the government. It is normally understood that concordats with the Holy See, which are conceived as international treaties, are not included in this provision. In any event, this function of the CALR, while significant in theory, has been unimportant in practice, for the Concordat was signed in 1979 and other cooperation agreements between state and religious minorities have been signed only once, in 1992.[375] The royal decree of 2013 contains a more detailed list of the CALR's functions than the precedent regulations.[376] These include, among others, elaborating reports on various types of draft legislation or regulations (of national and also, upon request of the Minister of Justice, of regional application), on the registration of religious entities (this only occurs occasionally, when a difficult case is submitted to the CALR), and on religious communities' applications for recognition of 'well-known roots' (*notorio arraigo*). The latter has been traditionally one of the clear competences recognized to the CALR and so far the government has always followed its opinion on this matter, be it affirmative or negative. The 2013 regulations also give the CALR autonomy to present to the government any proposal or initiative it deems appropriate in the area of religious freedom. The CALR is also tasked with elaborating and sending to the government an annual report on the situation of freedom of religion in Spain, which is made public.

296. Looking at the experience of the CALR in the past years, it is possible to find lights and shadows. In the positive side, we can mention that the CALR has been a useful forum for dialogue, in which representatives of the main religions existing in

---

374. Cf. Art. 20 RD 932/2013. Currently there are five working groups: on the report about the situation of religious freedom in Spain, opening of worship places, cemeteries of minority religions, public examinations in holy days, and religious dietary rules.

375. *See infra*, Part III, Ch. 5.

376. *See* Art. 3 RD 932/2013.

Spain have been able to explain their position and interact with the government in relation to a variety of issues. It has effectively intervened in some new regulations, especially in the area of religious assistance in public institutions. The Commission has also asserted its undisputed competence with regard to the applications for recognition of 'well-known roots' (*notorio arraigo*). In addition, the CALR has elaborated interesting and detailed studies, published by the Ministry of Justice, with proposals for legal reforms in the area of religious freedom. In the negative side, we can mention that the CALR has been often ignored in practice. The conclusions of its studies of legal reforms have been almost always disregarded for one or other reason. Many important laws and regulations susceptible of having an impact on the lives of religious communities and their members – for instance, in the areas of education, abortion, marriage or economic cooperation – have been enacted without requesting the previous opinion of the CALR, with patent infringement of Article 8 LOLR. Moreover, the CALR has been too dependent on the director general competent on religious affairs in the Ministry of Justice, with two consequences. On the one hand, as the CALR is not functionally autonomous, the character – and interests – of the relevant director general have determined the actual extent of its work and contributions. Some directors have worked in close collaboration with the CALR and others simply have let it languish for months or years without convoking the plenary. On the other hand, being the directorate general competent on religious affairs a low-level directorate in the context of the ministerial structure, the CALR has inherited its lack of political leverage. Indeed, this has been one of the main causes of the scarce intervention of the CALR in legal initiatives promoted by other ministries with a potential impact on religious freedom. In sum, the CALR appears to many as an institution that was well conceived by the LOLR in 1980 and was called to play an interesting role in the protection of religious freedom, but has been in practice underestimated and underutilized.[377] The new regulations of the 2013 royal decree definitely endeavour to change this inertia. The experience of the last two years provides some reasons for optimism but it is still too soon to see if the redesigned CALR will have in Spain the impact and role foreseen by the LOLR in 1980.

377. For a detailed analysis of these points, together with proposals for the future, *see* the volume VV.AA., *Comisión Asesora de Libertad Religiosa*, cited in para. 291.

Part III. Legal Status of Religious Communities

Chapter 1. Formal Status of Religious Communities

297. The Constitution and the Organic Law on Religious Freedom guarantee the freedom of ideology, religion and worship for all individuals and communities, on equal conditions and without distinction. In practice all religious communities are equally free to worship, to gather in religious meetings, to train their ministers, to communicate or cooperate with other churches, to disseminate their doctrines in the way the choose – including proselytism and distribution of religious literature – and to organize their internal life, etc. However, their respective position vis-à-vis the state is not at all the same. The Spanish law on religious communities is based upon a multi-tier system and envisages several types of legal statuses for religious communities, with significant differences between them regarding especially two aspects: the instruments that religious communities have available for the effective protection of their freedom and the manifestations of state cooperation with religion. More precisely, we can distinguish *five categories* of religious communities from the perspective of their legal status. In the following paragraphs they are mentioned in descending order.

298. The first one is the *Catholic Church*, which is by far the major church in Spain – the vast majority of Spanish citizens are baptized in Catholicism and about 70% of the Spanish population identify themselves as Catholic according to the surveys of the National Institute of Statistics.[378] As a consequence of the legal personality of the Holy See in international law, there is a dual relationship of the Spanish state with the Catholic Church: one at an international level, which implies diplomatic relationships between Spain and the Vatican, with their respective embassies (called 'nunciatures' in the case of the Holy See); and other at a national level, with the official hierarchy of the Catholic Church in Spain, which has the Bishops Conference as the main interlocutor. This duality is reflected in the variety of bilateral or contractual legal instruments used to regulate the legal status of the Catholic Church in Spain. On the one hand, there is a Concordat, with all the characteristics of an international treaty, composed by an Agreement signed in 1976 and four Agreements signed in 1979.[379] On the other hand, the Concordat has been developed by so-called minor agreements between the government and the Spanish Bishops Conference, for instance in the areas

378. *See supra* , General Introduction, §2.
379. *See infra* , Part III, Ch. 5 §1.

of salaries of religion teachers in public schools,[380] or religious assistance in hospital and penitentiaries.[381] Other times the Concordat has been developed by unilateral state laws, previously negotiated by the government with the Bishops Conference, as occurred with the social security of the clergy,[382] or with the raise of the percentage of the income tax that taxpayers can donate to the Catholic Church.[383]

299. There are other manifestations of the special legal status of the Catholic Church. Among them we can mention the following. Canonical entities that constitute the official ecclesiastical structure, such as dioceses or parishes, are subject to specific and more beneficial rules with regard to their acquisition of civil legal personality; they are exempt from the need to register in the RER and their civil legal personality is recognized automatically, once their canonical legal personality is notified to the Ministry of Justice.[384] State cooperation with the teaching of Catholic religion in public schools is higher than in the case of the teaching of other religions;[385] and the same applies to state economic cooperation[386] and the recognition of civil legal effects to marriages celebrated in accordance with canon law.[387] The Catholic clergy and members of religious institutes are included in the national system of social security.[388] The Catholic Church has several representatives in the Advisory Commission on Religious Freedom in the Ministry of Justice, in a number slightly higher than the other religious communities with 'well-known roots'[389] (and in any event, the most significant issues of mutual interest or concern for the state and the Catholic Church are often negotiated directly by the Bishops Conference and the government, without intervention of the CALR). There is a system of permanent Catholic chaplaincies in the military, public hospitals and penitentiaries, paid with public funding – although this is normally conceived as a state action or service to facilitate the Catholics' fundamental right to religious freedom, rather than another expression of the privileged legal status of the Catholic Church as such.[390] The author is not suggesting that these expressions of the special legal status of the Catholic Church necessarily constitute an unjustified privilege and therefore a discrimination of other religious communities, and even less that Catholic bishops pressure the state to deny similar expressions of cooperation to other churches or religious communities, but it is important to be aware of these differences when analysing the implementation of the constitutional principle of equality in Spain.

300. The second category is constituted by those *religious communities that have signed a cooperation agreement with the state*, in application of Article 7 LOLR.

---

380. *See Orden* of 9 Apr. 1999 decreeing the publication of the *Convenio* of 26 Feb. 1999 *sobre el régimen económico-laboral de las personas que, no perteneciendo a los Cuerpos de Funcionarios Docentes, están encargadas de la enseñanza de la religión católica en los centros públicos de Educación Infantil, de Educación Primaria y de Educación Secundaria.*
381. *See infra*, para. 365.
382. *See infra*, para. 412.
383. *See infra*, para. 489.
384. *See supra*, para. 266.
385. *See infra*, Part IX, Ch. 1.
386. *See infra*, Part VIII, Ch. 1.
387. *See infra*, Part X, Ch. 1.
388. *See infra*, Part VI, Ch. 2.
389. *See supra*, Part II, Ch. 4 §3.
390. *See infra*, Part III, Ch. 6.

Until now the state has signed only three agreements, in 1992, all in the same date and with very similar provisions, with the Protestant Federation (FEREDE), the Jewish Federation (FCJE) and the Islamic Federation (CIE), respectively.[391] Since then, no government, either socialist or conservative, has made further attempts to negotiate cooperation agreements with other religious communities, and no official reason has been given to explain such reluctance. Apparently, it has been assumed that the degree of protection of religious freedom and state cooperation with religion is good enough and does not need to be perfected. This attitude has been criticized by scholars,[392] but no sign of change of this approach is visible for the time being.

301. The religious communities that are part of the three federations signatories of the 1992 Agreements benefit from similar advantages to those of the Catholic Church – although sometimes in a lesser degree – in areas such as religious instruction in public schools, tax benefits and economic cooperation, civil legal effects of religious ceremonies of marriage, and social security of religious ministers. However, there are not permanent services of religious assistance of Protestants, Jews and Muslims in public establishments similar to Catholic chaplaincies. Over the years the three federations have requested more state cooperation than what can be expected from the application of the common rules of the LOLR, but new developments have occurred only in the realm of penitentiaries.[393] There are currently five representatives of those federations among the members of the Advisory Commission on Religious Freedom in the Ministry of Justice (two Protestants, two Muslims and one Jew).[394]

302. The third category is constituted by the *religious communities that have been formally recognized as having 'well-known roots'* (*notorio arraigo*) by the Ministry of Justice, on account of their spreading and number of believers in Spain, *but do not have a cooperation agreement* with the state.[395] Four religious denominations are in this situation: the Church of Jesus Christ of Latter-Day Saints (Mormons), since 2003; Jehovah's Witnesses, since 2006; the Buddhist Federation, since 2007; and Christian Orthodoxy (with an Assembly of Orthodox Bishops of Spain and Portugal as interlocutor of the government), since 2010. These religious communities are in an awkward situation. In theory they have been acknowledged as religions with strong rooting in Spain, and therefore they meet the necessary requirements to reach a cooperation agreement with the state under Article 7 LOLR. Nevertheless, no government has had political will to negotiate more agreements since 1992. And, as Article 7 LOLR does not grant automatically to religions with *notorio arraigo* any right to a cooperation agreement – it only opens that *possibility* to them, but the decision is entirely in the

---

391. *See infra* , Part III, Ch. 5 §2.
392. *See* , for instance, D. Llamazares, *Los acuerdos y el principio de igualdad: comparación con los acuerdos con la Iglesia católica y situación jurídica de las confesiones sin acuerdo*, in *Acuerdos del Estado español con confesiones religiosas minoritarias* 198–199 (V. Reyna & M.A. Félix eds, Marcial Pons 1996); J. Martínez-Torrón, *El estatuto jurídico de las minorías religiosas sin acuerdo de cooperación en España*, in *Constitución, leyes de libertad religiosa, acuerdos, Derecho común* 165–176 (P. Pardo Prieto ed., Servicio de Publicaciones de la Universidad de León 2010).
393. *See infra* , paras 366–368.
394. *See supra* , Part II, Ch. 4 §3.
395. *See infra* , para. 356.

hands of the government – they cannot legally request to start a negotiation aimed at obtaining a juridical status comparable to the federations signatory of the 1992 Agreements.

303. In the last years, being aware that no perspective of a formal agreement was foreseeable in the next future, these religious denominations have asked the government to grant them, via unilateral state legislation or regulations, some of the manifestations of state cooperation contained in 1992 Agreements. They requested, in particular, tax benefits, but also the recognition of civil effects to religious marriage, social security for religious ministers, and in some cases, the possibility of religious instruction in public schools. These claims are totally viable from a legal perspective but have been unsuccessful to date. The whole situation looks obviously discriminatory and has been often criticized with good reason. The lack of political will on the part of the government to negotiate an agreement cannot be considered 'reasonable and objective justification' in the sense that this notion has been understood by the Strasbourg jurisprudence. The fact is that, until now, the only clear legal consequences of the acknowledgement of *notorio arraigo* are the right of these religious denominations to have a representative as member of the CALR (Article 8 LOLR) – indeed each of them has a representative[396] – and, since the reform of Article 60 CC in 2015, the recognition of civil effects of their religious marriages. Apart from this, these religious communities have a legal status that is almost the same as the fourth category.

304. The fourth category is constituted by religious communities *registered in the Registry of Religious Entities*. Registration in the RER, per se, does not produce many substantial legal consequences. The most important of those consequences are that registered communities see their internal autonomy strengthened by the application of Article 6 LOLR,[397] enjoy a reinforced protection of their religious freedom by criminal law,[398] and their foreign religious ministers do not need a working permit to legally reside in Spain.[399] In theory, registered communities may obtain from the state the recognition of civil effects to religious marriages (Article 59 CC), or facilities to provide religious assistance and religious instruction in public institutions (Article 2.3 LOLR). However, the praxis to date has been to reserve those aspects to religious communities with a formal cooperation agreement or at least with recognition of well-known roots in Spain.

305. Finally, there is a fifth category of religious communities that are *not registered in the Registry of Religious Entities*, either because their application for registration was rejected or because they have not applied to register. Registered or not in other public registries, such as the Registry of Associations, they are free to practise their religion or worship, to disseminate their ideas, etc., just as the communities included in the RER. However, they do not have access to the instruments of state cooperation with religion. And, if they request from public authorities the application of specific protective measures envisaged by the law for collective religious freedom, they will have to provide evidence of their religious nature by means other than registration in the RER (which would be obviously the easiest way and also the one

396. *See ibid.*
397. *See infra*, Part III, Ch. 2.
398. *See infra*, Part VII, Ch. 8.
399. *See infra*, para. 411.

in principle foreseen by law).[400] To the author's knowledge, only a residual number of religions are in this fifth category.

400. *See supra*, para. 268.

Chapter 2. Autonomy of Religious Communities

306. The collective and institutional dimensions of religious freedom entail recognition of religious communities' autonomy. Article 2.2 LOLR guarantees to all religious communities some characteristic expressions of autonomy, such as the right to establish places of worship or meeting, to appoint and train their ministers, to propagate their faith, and to freely communicate with their own organizations or with other churches, inside the country as well as abroad. These manifestations of autonomy are also mentioned by the 1981 UN Declaration on the Elimination of All Forms of Intolerance and of Discrimination Based on Religion or Belief, an authoritative interpretive source of religious freedom in Spain;[401] and by the Human Dimension Commitments of OSCE, in which Spain is a participating state, especially as developed by the 1989 Vienna Concluding Document.[402]

307. Those rights are recognized to all religious communities without distinction and therefore also to non-registered communities – registration in the RER, let us remind it once again, is an option, not a legal obligation. At the same time, however, it is possible to perceive an implicit reference to registration in the use of the term 'religious' used by the LOLR, in the sense that, in principle, the entities deemed religious are those registered in the RER in accordance with Article 5 LOLR. Nevertheless, that implicit reference to the RER must be compatible with the non-mandatory character of registration, and therefore it should be understood just as evidence of the religious nature and aims of a group; with the consequence that, as evidence, it can be substituted by other means of proof, for it would be unacceptable to make a fundamental right dependent on compliance with a formal requisite. Alternative means of proof may not be particularly difficult for groups that never applied for registration in the RER – although it would certainly be unusual that a group that refuse to register seeks the specific protection of the LOLR – but could be more problematic for those groups whose registration in the RER has been rejected for lack of religious nature or aims. In any event, as indicated above, refusal of registration is highly improbable since the judgment of the Constitutional Court that, in 2001, interpreted in a very restrictive fashion the competence of public authorities to assess the religious nature and aims of applicant entities.[403]

308. Article 6.1 LOLR guarantees a *reinforced* autonomy for religious communities *registered* in the RER.[404] They have 'full autonomy' to establish their own organizational rules, internal regime and personnel regime. Their normative autonomy includes the possibility of enacting, for them and for their internal entities, 'clauses aimed at safeguarding their ethos and religious identity, as well as the due respect for their

401. *See* Art. 6 of the Declaration, which was proclaimed by General Assembly resolution 36/55 of 25 Nov. 1981.

402. *See* especially para. (16) of the 1989 Vienna Document, which is perhaps the most detailed OSCE document as far as religious autonomy is concerned. Its text is available in *OSCE Human Dimension Commitments, vol.1: Thematic Compilation* 119–120 (OSCE/ODIHR 2011).

403. *See supra* , paras 282–285.

404. *See* J. Otaduy, *Las cláusulas de salvaguarda de la identidad de las instituciones religiosas*, 27 *Ius Canonicum* 673–696 (1987).

beliefs, without prejudice to the respect for the rights and freedoms recognized by the Constitution and in particular freedom, equality and non-discrimination'. This provision has been in practice of particular significance for private religious schools, whose religious identity has been protected by the Spanish laws on education; and also for the determination of the legal status of teachers of Catholic religion in public schools, whose qualification depends on the judgment of ecclesiastical authorities.[405]

309. Although Article 6.1 LOLR indicates that its provisions are applicable to registered entities, it would be inappropriate, for the reasons mentioned above, to deny their application to non-registered entities that prove their religious nature and aims by means other than registration in the RER. Indeed, Article 6.2 LOLR – also dealing with religious autonomy – omits, just as Article 2.2 LOLR, all explicit reference to registration when recognizing the right of churches and religious communities to create associations, foundations and institutions for the fulfilment of their purposes, in accordance with the law.

310. The issues related to the legal personality of internal associations and foundations created by churches or religious communities are examined in the section dealing with the Registry of Religious Entities.[406]

405. *See* in more detail *infra*, Part IX.
406. *See supra*, Part II, Ch. 4 §2 IV.

Chapter 3. Places of Worship and Meeting

§1. A Broad Concept of Place of Worship

311. Article 2.2. LOLR explicitly recognizes that the collective dimension of religious freedom includes 'the right of churches, religious denominations and communities to establish places of worship or meeting for religious purposes'. Similar provisions are in the 1981 Declaration on the Elimination of All Forms of Intolerance and of Discrimination Based on Religion or Belief, and in the OSCE 1989 Vienna Concluding Document.[407] The ECtHR has also held that the right to have appropriate places of worship is an integral part of religious freedom.[408] It is commonly accepted that the concept of place of worship should be construed broadly, so that it includes cemeteries and places of meeting for religious purposes.

312. Spanish law considers the protection of places of worship as part of the legal status of religious communities, but does not define specifically this notion. It is therefore assumed that the concept of place of worship should be understood in the light of an implicit and flexible remission to the relevant religious concepts. This seems to be confirmed by the fact that, in addition to the general mention of places of worship and meeting by Article 2.2. LOLR, the Concordat and the state cooperation agreements with religious communities contain explicit references to places of worship. In this respect, it is worth noting that the term 'place of worship' has a polyvalent meaning and refers to a concept used by state law (and international law) rather than to a properly religious notion – this terminology is not normally used as such by any religion. Thus, for example, the equivalent expression in the canon law of the Catholic Church would be 'sacred place'; and other religions use more specific words, such as 'synagogue', 'mosque', 'church', 'temple', 'chapel', 'shrine' or alike.

313. Article I.5 of the Agreement on Juridical Affairs with the Holy See, when recognizing the inviolability of Catholic places of worship, implicitly remits to the ecclesiastical notion of sacred place, as defined by canon 1295 of the Code of Canon Law, which includes cemeteries: 'Sacred places are those which are designated for divine worship or for the burial of the faithful by a dedication or a blessing which the liturgical books prescribe for this purpose.'

314. Even a broader notion is adopted by the three Agreements signed in 1992 with the most significant religious minorities in Spain, which define the legal notion of places of worship for those communities. Thus, Article 2.1 of the Agreement with the Evangelical Federation provides that shall be deemed places of worship 'those buildings or premises devoted to the functions of worship and religious assistance in a permanent and exclusive manner', when this is so certified by the respective church with the approval of the Evangelical Federation. Article 2.1 of the Agreements with the Jewish and Islamic Federations contain similar provisions, but adding the function of 'religious training'. The Agreement with the Islamic Federation has further particular

407. Cf. Art. 6(a) of the Declaration and para. (16.4) of the Vienna Document.
408. Cf. *Manoussakis v. Greece*, 26 Sep. 1996.

nuances, as it replaces 'worship' by 'prayer', and 'permanent' by 'habitual'. The Agreements with the Jewish and Islamic Federations equate cemeteries with places of worship for all legal purposes, and recognize the rights of Jewish and Islamic communities to have their own private cemeteries, to have specific places reserved for them within municipal cemeteries, and to perform their own funeral rites.[409]

§2. The Inviolability of Places of Worship

315. The Concordat with the Catholic Church explicitly provides that 'the inviolability of places of worship is guaranteed in accordance to the law'.[410] This provision is replicated, almost literally, by the 1992 Agreements with the Evangelical, Jewish and Islamic Federations.[411] The Concordat also guarantees the inviolability of ecclesiastical archives and documents,[412] and a similar protection is granted to the archives of Islamic communities.[413]

316. The inviolability of sacred places – especially those of Christian churches – has a long-standing tradition in Spain, as in most European countries, and was understood in older times as full immunity from the secular jurisdiction. It is commonly agreed that this conception is no longer in force, but the Spanish law does not define explicitly the notion of inviolability with regard to places of worship.

317. By inference, we can affirm that the inviolability of places of worship includes the protection of privacy contained in Article 18 of the Constitution, and especially the guarantee that Article 18.2 CE applies to private domiciles: 'Domicile is inviolable. No entry and search in domicile shall be carried out without the consent of the occupant or a judicial warrant, except in flagrante delicto.'

318. In addition to this general concept of inviolability, criminal law provides for a specific protection of religious functions in places of worship. Thus, the inviolability of places of worship goes beyond the physical space or the material premises and extends to the religious activities – rites or meetings – performed in them. Several articles of the Criminal Code deal with issues relating to inviolability, within a section entitled 'Crimes against freedom of conscience, religious feelings and respect for the deceased'.

---

409. Cf. Art. 2.6 of the Agreement with the Jewish Federation and Art. 2.5 of the Agreement with the Islamic Federation. Cemeteries and burials are the competence of local and regional authorities, which in some places have developed the rules of the 1992 Agreements with the Jewish and Islamic communities, and normally have endeavoured to be as flexible as possible to make the religious rules on inhumation compatible with the administrative regulations aimed at the protection of public health. *See* M. Rodríguez Blanco, *Libertad religiosa y cementerios (primeras aproximaciones)*, in *La libertad religiosa y su regulación legal*, 824–846 (R. Navarro-Valls, J. Mantecón & J. Martínez-Torrón eds, Iustel 2009).

410. Article I.5 of the Agreement on Juridical Affairs.

411. *See* Art. 2.2 of each of the 1992 Agreements.

412. *See* Art. I.6 of the Agreement on Juridical Affairs.

413. *See* Art. 2.3 of the Agreement with the Islamic Federation. There is no equivalent provision in the Agreements with the Jewish and Evangelical Federations, most likely because those federations did not request it during the negotiation process.

319. Article 523 of the Criminal Code considers a crime the violent interference with ceremonies or services of religious communities registered in the RER, and punishes it with particular severity when it is committed in a place of worship:

Article 523 CP:

Those who obstruct, interrupt or disturb acts, functions, ceremonies or manifestations of religious communities registered in the [RER] with violence, threats, tumult, or other illegal facts, shall be punished with imprisonment from 6 months to 6 years if the fact was committed in a place devoted to worship, and fine from 4 to 6 months if it was committed in any other place.

320. Article 524 of the Criminal Code sanctions the crime of profanation in places of worship or in religious ceremonies. In order to harmonize this provision with Article 523, some scholars interpret the expression 'religious feelings protected by law' as an implicit reference to religious communities registered in the RER. Others, on the contrary, maintain that Article 524 is applicable to any religion, registered or not. The question is not very significant in practice, for the immense majority of religious communities existing in Spain are registered in the RER:

Article 524 CP:

Those who execute acts of profanation with offence to religious feelings protected by law, in temples, in places devoted to worship, or in religious ceremonies, shall be punished with imprisonment from 6 months to 1 year or fine from 12 to 24 months.

321. Article 526 of the Criminal Code extends the criminal law protection of the inviolability of places of worship to all kinds of burial places, religious or not – in practice this type of offences is often committed with anti-religious intentions:

Article 526 CP:

Those who, with lack of due respect for the memory of the deceased, violate sepulchres or graves, desecrate a corpse or its ashes, or, as an affront, destroy, alter or damage funeral urns, tombs, gravestones or ossuaries, shall be punished with imprisonment from 3 to 5 months or fine from 6 to 10 months.

§3. Places of Worship and Urban Planning

322. The Spanish laws on urban planning provide that use of land for religious purposes, and more precisely for the edification of places of worship, must be taken into account in the elaboration of city planning.[414] Plots reserved for public or social interest can be destined to religious uses.[415] In the region of Catalonia, a specific regional law on places of worship, enacted in 2009, provides that city planning must reserve plots qualified as of community services for new religious places of worship, in accordance with the needs and possibilities of the relevant town – which must be ascertained without any discrimination on religious grounds.[416] The practice of regions and towns is, of course, very diverse, but some of them have a well-established experience of permitting the utilization of plots of municipal property for building places of worship.[417] Very often this is done in favour of the Catholic Church, as a consequence of the overwhelming majority of Catholics in Spain, but it is becoming more and more usual to do it also in favour of other religions, especially Islam. In addition, as far as urban planning is respected, places of worship can be obviously built in private property. When regional laws foresee the participation of citizens – individuals and groups – in the elaboration of cities' general plans for urban development, the Supreme Court has held that negligence in the implementation of those clauses on the part of local authorities are sufficient ground for an action of nullity.[418]

323. To build a place of worship, it is necessary to obtain the appropriate municipal licence, as in any other types of building. In the past it has been debated if it is possible to legally require also a specific licence to open the place to the public, as in other buildings in which the attendance of a relatively numerous and diversified congregation is expected. Two decisions of the Supreme Court rejected that possibility long ago, considering that it would be an unjustified restriction of religious freedom. One of the decisions involved a Catholic private chapel,[419] and the other concerned a chapel of the 'Evangelical Church of Philadelphia' in Madrid.[420] Nevertheless, at a regional level, the Catalonian law of 2009 made it mandatory to obtain a specific municipal licence prior to the opening of a place of worship to the public. The declared purpose of such licence is guaranteeing that the premises have the adequate safety and health conditions, and also preventing that the use of the place could be a source of disturbance for others (for instance, because of lack of due noise isolation). According to the same Catalonian law, the requisites imposed to obtain the licence must be proportionate lest they impair the normal use of the religious facilities, and may not be stricter than the equivalent requisites imposed on other places open to the public.[421] In spite of how reasonable these provisions may be in the abstract, some scholars have

414. *See Ley* 38/1999, 5 Nov. 1999, *de ordenación de la edificación*, Art. 2.1.a).

415. *See Real Decreto* 2159/1978, 23 Jun. 1978, *por el que se aprueba el Reglamento de planeamiento para el desarrollo y aplicación de la Ley sobre régimen del suelo y ordenación urbana*, Arts 25.1.d) and 45.1.e).

416. *See Ley* 16/2009, 22 Jul. 2009, *de los centros de culto* (Generalitat de Catalunya), Art. 4. The administrative regulations for the development of this law are in the Decreto 94/2010, 20 Jul. 2010 (Generalitat de Catalunya).

417. *See* J.J. Guardia Hernández, *Libertad religiosa y urbanismo: estudio de los equipamientos de uso religioso en España* 69–75, 157–177 (Eunsa 2010).

418. *See* STS 2000/2016, 4 May 2016.

419. Cf. STS 4872/1988, 24 Jun. 1988.

420. Cf. STS 4895/1992, 18 Jun. 1992.

421. *See Ley* 16/2009 of the Generalitat of Catalonia, Arts 8–9.; and *Decreto* 94/2010 of the Generalitat of Catalonia, Arts 8–29.

warned about the risk that local authorities could use the issuing of these licences, in practice, as an instrument to discriminate those religious communities that are deemed more atypical or 'inconvenient'.[422] Other scholars maintain that the application of the common rules on licences for opening other places of public access would have been sufficient.[423]

324. At a national level, there is no specific comprehensive legislation that regulates the opening of places of worship.[424] There is, however, an additional provision introduced in a national law of 2013 on local governments with the aim of facilitating the opening of places of worship without having to wait for a municipal licence. This provision merely requires that religious communities must prove their legal personality before the competent local authorities with an ad hoc certification provided by the Registry of Religious Entities, which shall specify the location of the place of worship in question.[425] In principle, religious communities should be able to begin their worship activity once they have applied for the municipal licence and have provided – together with the above-mentioned certificate – a *declaración responsable*, i.e., a formal statement declaring that the place of worship complies with all applicable requisites established by local regulations.[426] Nevertheless, the practice of municipal governments is very diverse and it seems that some of them adopt a position similar to the rule of the 2009 Catalonian law, i.e., not to permit the opening of the place of worship until the licence has been issued. This proves something that is commonly agreed by legal scholars, namely that such a national law is much needed to avoid discrimination by guaranteeing a certain level of homogeneity in the legal treatment of this matter by local governments. One of the working groups of the Advisory Commission on Religious Freedom[427] is committed to the elaboration of a draft law on the subject, taking into account the case law of the ECtHR, as well as the actual practices of local governments, and in consultation with the most relevant religious denominations in Spain. The work is still in a very preliminary stage.

---

422. *See* M. Moreno Antón, *El tratamiento urbanístico de los lugares de culto: a propósito del Proyecto de Ley de Cataluña sobre centros de culto o de reunión con fines religiosos*, 17 Revista General de Derecho Canónico y Derecho Eclesiástico del Estado 43 (2008).

423. *See* J.J. Guardia Hernández, *La relación entre urbanismo y libertad religiosa en Cataluña: Llei 16/2009 dels centres de culte*, 101 Ius canonicum 322 (2011).

424. For a suggestive proposal for a regulation of places of worship, *see* S. Aznar García, *Reflexiones jurídicas en torno a una propuesta de regulación legal para los lugares de culto*, 38 Revista General de Derecho Canónico y Derecho Eclesiástico del Estado 1-33 (2015). In the same issue of that legal journal there are several interesting studies on the various questions raised by the regulation of places of worship at national and local level.

425. *See Ley* 27/2013, 27 Dec. 2013, *de racionalización y sostenibilidad de la Administración Local*, additional provision 17.

426. *See Ley* 30/1992, 26 Nov. 1992, *de Régimen Jurídico de las Administraciones Públicas y del Procedimiento Administrativo Común*, Art. 71 bis.

427. *See supra* , para. 294.

§4. Privileges Concerning Expropriation, Demolition, Immunity from Seizure and Taxes

325. The current Concordat with the Holy See provides that, in case of expropriation of Catholic places of worship, the competent ecclesiastical authorities must be heard beforehand.[428] A similar provision was included in the 1992 Agreements with the Evangelical, Jewish and Islamic Federations,[429] recognizing the right to a previous hearing to the representative bodies of the respective federation. In addition, an old administrative regulation of 1957, still in force and based on the provisions of the 1953 Concordat, is applicable to the Catholic Church; according to this regulation, the expropriation of Church's property requires that the competent ecclesiastical authority is given the right to a previous hearing and is communicated the amount of the compensation that has been fixed.[430]

326. Catholic, Evangelical, Jewish and Islamic places of worship may not be demolished without being previously deprived of their sacred or religious character, except in cases of emergency or danger.[431]

327. No similar provisions exist with regard to the places of worship of religious communities without cooperation agreement with the state. However, a sensible interpretation of Article 2 LOLR, which generally recognizes collective religious freedom and the right to have places of worship, should lead public authorities to treat all places devoted to religious worship with the due respect and deference. This entails taking into account the specific notion of places of worship – and the specific rules – of each religious community, which differs greatly from one community to another.

328. In cases of execution of judicial decisions, the Code of Civil Procedure provides that the property of all legally registered religious communities that is considered sacred, or is devoted to religious worship, cannot be seized.[432]

329. The Concordat and the state cooperation agreements grant specific tax benefits to some property of the relevant religious communities. One of these benefits is the exemption from property tax applied to Catholic, Evangelical, Jewish and Islamic places of worship – temples, chapels, mosques, synagogues and alike – as well as to their adjunct premises devoted to pastoral activities or spiritual assistance.[433]

---

428. *See* Art. I.5 of the Agreement on Juridical Affairs.
429. *See* Art. 2.3 of the Agreements with the Evangelical and Jewish Federations, and Art. 2.2 of the Agreement with the Islamic Federation.
430. *See* *Decreto* of 26 Apr. 1957, *por el que se aprueba el reglamento de la ley de expropiación forzosa*, Art. 23.
431. *See* Art. I.5 of the Agreement on Juridical Affairs; Art. 2.4 of the Agreements with the Evangelical and Jewish Federations; and Art. 2.2 of the Agreement with the Islamic Federation.
432. *See* *Ley* 1/2000, 7 Jan. 2000, *de Enjuiciamiento Civil*, Art. 606.3.
433. Cf. Art. IV.A.1 of the Agreement on Economic Affairs with the Holy See; and Art. 11.3.A).a) of the 1992 Agreements with the Evangelical, Jewish and Islamic Federations. *See infra*, paras 500 and 502.

Chapter 4. Fundamental Rights and Religious Communities

§1. The Protection of Fundamental Rights of Religious Communities

330. In addition to religious autonomy and other rights directly stemming from freedom of religion, religious communities are entitled to the exercise of all fundamental rights recognized by the Constitution and by international treaties to legal persons. The only exceptions are those rights that, by their own nature, apply only to individuals, such as, for instance, the right to life or the right to access to public office. Of particular significance for religious communities are the following fundamental rights.

331. Article 27.6 CE guarantees 'the *freedom to create educational centres*, with respect for constitutional principles', which is recognized to all individuals and legal persons. The exercise of this right is subject to the general conditions established by law – especially two organic laws of 1985 and 2006, respectively, and its regulations.[434] These legal conditions are common for all private schools, of religious or any other ethos.[435]

332. Article 20 CE guarantees *freedom of expression and information*, which is compatible with, and reinforces, the freedom to manifest one's religion through teaching recognized by Article 9 ECHR. According to Article 20 CE, this freedom includes, among other aspects, the right 'to freely manifest and disseminate thoughts, ideas and opinions orally, in writing or by any other means'; and the right 'to freely communicate or receive veracious information through any media'. No prior censorship can be imposed on the exercise of those rights. Religious communities are within the category of 'significant social and political groups' that shall have access to media owned or managed by public authorities – their access shall be guaranteed by law, 'with respect for the pluralism of society'.[436]

333. Article 21 CE recognizes the *freedom of peaceful assembly*, without previous authorization. This Article strengthens the freedom to manifest one's religion in community with others and protects the right to hold religious meetings, in private or in public. If religious meetings or demonstrations are held in the public square – i.e., in places freely accessible to the public – 'prior notification shall be given to the authorities', and they can only be prohibited 'on the basis of well-grounded reasons of public order, involving danger for persons or property'. In practice, most of the religious meetings held in the public square reflect traditional expressions of Catholic religiosity, such as, for instance, processions during the Holy Week, Corpus Christi, or in the feast of the local patron saint, which in many places attract a large part of the local population (and numerous visitors).

---

434. *Ley Orgánica* 8/1985, 3 Jul. 1985, *reguladora del derecho a la educación*; and *Ley Orgánica* 2/2006, 3 May 2006, *de educación*.
435. *See infra*, Part IX, Ch. 2.
436. *See infra*, Part XI, Ch. 2.

334. Article 22 CE recognizes *freedom of association*, which is a guarantee for the existence and activities of all religious denominations, registered or not in the Registry of Religious Entities in the Ministry of Justice.[437] The common prohibition of secret and paramilitary associations applies also to religious communities.

335. The *state is obliged to adopt an active role* in the guarantee of fundamental rights of religious communities, as a consequence of two factors. On the one hand, the general provision of Article 9.2 CE, which requires public authorities to set up the conditions to make 'real and effective' the freedom and equality of individuals and groups. And on the other hand, the constitutional principle of state cooperation with religion, according to which 'public authorities shall take into account the religious beliefs of Spanish society and shall maintain the consequent relationships of cooperation with the Catholic Church and the other denominations' (Article 16.3 CE).[438]

336. As all other legal (and natural) persons, religious communities have the 'right to obtain the effective protection of the judges and the courts' – with absolute respect for their right to defence – in the exercise of their legitimate interests (Article 24.1 CE). One of the expressions of this right is that religious communities are entitled to request the judicial protection of their fundamental rights by ordinary courts, 'according to a procedure based on the principles of preference and summariness', as well as by the Constitutional Court through a specific constitutional procedure – the appeal for protection or *recurso de amparo* (Article 53.2 CE). The procedural channels explained with reference to religious freedom are applicable to all other fundamental rights of religious communities.[439]

337. The fundamental rights of religious communities receive also a specific protection by penal law provisions that criminalize religious hate speech as well as slander and libel against religious groups (Article 510 of the Criminal Code).[440]

§2. The Protection of Fundamental Rights by Religious Communities

338. From a different perspective, *religious communities are obliged to respect*, in their activities and in their organization, *the fundamental rights of others*, which is one of the legitimate limitations on the exercise of religious freedom – collective as well as individual – according to Article 3.1 LOLR and Article 9.2 ECHR. This implies, for instance, that they may not incur abusive proselytism[441] or attempt to restrict the missionary activity of other churches in order to eliminate 'the competition'. In their proselytizing activity, religious communities are of course free to criticize other churches, but the use of hate or defamatory speech, as indicated in the previous paragraph, is punished by Article 510 of the Criminal Code.

437. *See supra*, Part II, Ch. 4 §1.
438. *See supra*, Part I, Ch. 3 §4.
439. *See supra*, Part II, Ch. 1 §3.
440. *See infra*, Part VII, Ch. 8.
441. The European Court of Human Rights, in two judgments in the 1990s, clarified what must be understood, respectively, by permissible or abusive proselytism: *Kokkinakis v. Greece*, 25 May 1993, and *Larissis et al. v. Greece*, 24 Feb. 1998.

339. The obligation of respect for fundamental rights also operates in the internal life of religious communities, and this implies excluding, for example, the use of violence or the manipulation of the will of their members in order to prevent them from abandoning the community. The Spanish courts judged a situation of this type some years ago, when the Catalan police help 'rescue' some members of a 'sect' on the alleged ground that they had suffered 'brainwashing'. The Court of Strasbourg, however, in its *Riera Blume* decision, reached the conclusion that Spanish public authorities have exceeded their legitimate powers and acted against the free will of the 'rescued' members of that community.[442]

340. The protection of fundamental rights of individuals inside the community is in a delicate balance with religious autonomy. Article 6.1 LOLR refers to it when providing that the autonomy of churches and religious communities, and the specific provisions or clauses they may establish to safeguard their identity or ethos, must be guaranteed 'without prejudice to the respect for the rights and freedoms recognized by the Constitution, and in particular freedom, equality and non-discrimination'. This statement, however, does not constitute a sufficiently clear criterion to face the diverse challenging issues that may emerge in cases of conflict between decisions adopted by a religious authority in defence of a religious ethos and decisions adopted by individuals that are members of that community – particularly if those individuals are linked with the church by a labour contract. In such cases the state and religious communities may have divergent views on the same issue. The state may maintain that respect for privacy rights of individuals is the paramount interest, while churches will likely hold the opposite opinion in order to preserve their doctrinal, organizational and disciplinary autonomy, and even their credibility in front of their faithful.

341. Sometimes it is not difficult to provide a solution to such conflicts, especially when their reach is definitely circumscribed within the boundaries of religious doctrine or discipline. Such is the case, for instance, of disputes about the acceptance or not of women to priesthood, about clergy's celibacy, or about the use of female headscarf in Islam. These are matters for internal debate within the respective religious community and the state must not interfere, for otherwise it would violate both its neutrality and the fundamental right to religious autonomy.[443] Other times, however, the answers are not so easy, as demonstrated by some decisions of the ECtHR in the last years, in relation to persons that incurred indiscipline or engaged in personal behaviour deemed gravely immoral by the religious institutions for which they worked.[444] In Spain, there have been some significant conflicts in this area, with regard to the withdrawal of the ecclesiastical permit to teach Catholic religion in public schools not out of lack of

---

442. *Riera Blume v. Spain*, 14 Oct. 1999. *See supra* , para. 122.

443. The prevalence of the community over the individual in cases of doctrinal disputes has been affirmed by the ECtHR, following a previous case law of the European Commission of Human Rights. In those conflicts, the Court has maintained that the freedom of individuals is guaranteed by their right to abandon their church or religious community. *See Holy Synod of the Bulgarian Orthodox Church (Metropolitan Inokentiy) and others* v. *Bulgaria*, 22 Jan. 2009; *Miroļubovs et others* v. *Latvia*, 15 Sep. 2009.

444. *See* especially *Obst v. Germany* and *Schüth v. Germany*, both of 23 Sep. 2010; and *Sindicatul Păstorul Cel Bun v. Romania*, 31 Jan. 2012 (chamber) and 9 Jul. 203 (Grand Chamber).

academic qualifications, but out of conduct that the Church considered immoral and scandalous.[445]

445. *See* in more detail *infra* , paras 416–421.

Chapter 5. Contractual Religious Freedom

§1. The Concordat with the Catholic Church

342. Concordats with the Catholic Church have a long-standing tradition in Spain, as a result of its political configuration as a confessional Catholic monarchy for five centuries. The Concordat signed in the time of General Franco's regime (1953) had been preceded by the Concordats of 1753 and 1851 (the Holy See considered the latter implicitly repealed by the anti-ecclesiastical provisions and policies of the Second Republic, which were in clear violation of the Concordat). The main concordats were often complemented by partial agreements on specific issues.

343. The substitution of the 1953 Concordat – which had been signed with a Catholic confessional state represented by a dictatorial regime – commenced in 1976, a few months after Franco's death. On 28 July 1976, the Spanish government and the Holy See signed an Agreement[446] in which they acknowledged 'the profound process of transformation that Spanish society has experienced in the last years' and formally declared their intention to proceed, by common agreement and 'as soon as possible', to the revision and modification of the 1953 Concordat. The preamble of the 1976 Agreement explicitly mentioned, as a basis for the revision process, the doctrine of the Second Vatican Council on the right to religious freedom and the principle of mutual autonomy and collaboration of church and state. The Agreement was implicitly envisioning that Spain would cease to be, in the next future, a Catholic confessional state.

344. In addition to signalling the beginning of the revision process of the 1953 Concordat, the 1976 Agreement included two specific provisions that abolished the main institutions that symbolized the close and privileged relation between church and state in Franco's time (such privileged relation and institutions, however, dated back to much older times in Spain). On the one hand, the Agreement eliminated the government's power of intervention in the appointment of bishops in Spanish dioceses. According to the 1953 Concordat,[447] to fill a vacant diocese the Pope would propose a tern of names out of a reduced list previously negotiated between the Spanish government and the Vatican nuncio; the head of state had the final decision on which of those three persons would be appointed as the new bishop. By contrast, Article I of the 1976 Agreement clearly stated that the appointment of bishops was of 'the exclusive competence of the Holy See' and provided that, when a new bishop was chosen, his name would be merely 'notified' to the Spanish government prior to his appointment, in case it wanted to express some political objection (which the Holy See was not bound to accept). The only exception was the appointment of the Vicar General for the Army (*Vicario General Castrense*), who continued to be appointed according to a

446. The Agreement was in force since 20 Aug. 1976.

447. The 1953 Concordat confirmed the formula adopted by a specific agreement signed by the Spanish government and the Holy See on 7 Jun. 1941, i.e., two years after the end of the civil war and the beginning of Franco's regime.

system similar to the one stipulated in 1953. On the other hand, the 1976 Agreement abolished the so-called *benefit of clergy*, an ancient privilege still present in the 1953 Concordat, according to which the criminal prosecution of a cleric or a religiously ordained person in Spanish courts could not be commenced without the explicit permit of the relevant bishop. Article II of the Agreement provided that, when criminal proceedings are initiated against a cleric or religious, civil authorities are obliged only to notify it to the relevant bishop. The same Article maintained the traditional protection of the 'clergy-communicant privilege', according to which priests or persons under religious vows shall not be required to testify on matters that they have known in the exercise of their religious ministry.

345. After the 1976 Agreement was ratified, a mixed church-state commission was constituted and began to work on the revision and modification of the 1953 Concordat. The commission's work took place in parallel with the political reforms occurring in Spain in those years and with the parliamentary works for the elaboration of the new Constitution. Two ideas, among others, guided the work of the members of the commission. First, the new concordat should be signed after the Constitution was promulgated, so that they were part of the new constitutional order. Second, it looked preferable to elaborate various specific agreements on concrete themes rather than a single text. The apparent reason was that, in case the political evolution in Spain led to substantial divergences of the government with respect to some of the new concordat provisions, or in case some of those provisions were deemed unconstitutional by the Constitutional Court in the future, it would not be necessary to denounce or renegotiate the entire concordat but just the precise agreement containing the provisions that created the problem.[448] The experience of these years, however, has demonstrated that the political tensions sometimes caused by certain provisions of the Concordat have never raised, in any government, a serious desire to denounce any of the Agreements. And the Constitutional Court, whenever it has had to deal with the Concordat, has never suggested, even by obiter dicta, than some of its provisions could be unconstitutional.[449]

346. On 3 January 1979 – i.e., a few days after the Constitution was in force – the Spanish government signed four thematic agreements with the Holy See,[450] which in toto form a concordat together with the 1976 Agreement. In reality they are distinct and independent parts of a single concordat, so that this name can be in rigour applied to them when taken as a whole.[451] Indeed, they were approved following the procedures established for international treaties, and are commonly regarded as having the nature of international treaties and being part of the international legal order. This factor distinguishes the 1979 Agreements with the Holy See from the cooperation agreements

448. On the new concordat *see*, generally, J. Fornés, *El nuevo sistema concordatario español (Los Acuerdos de 1976 y 1979)* (Eunsa 1980); J.M. Díaz Moreno, *Acuerdos Iglesia-Estado en España: notas marginales*, 54 Estudios Eclesiásticos 283–334 (1979). The latter author was a member of the commission that elaborated the text of the Concordat.

449. Cf., for instance, STC 38/2007, 15 Feb. 2007.

450. These Agreements are in force since 4 Dec. 1979.

451. According to the usual terminology of international relations, the term 'agreement' is utilized with regard to specific thematic covenants between a state and the Catholic church in areas of common interest, while 'concordat' is reserved for covenants between a state and the Holy See that contain a comprehensive regulation of their mutual relationship.

mentioned by Article 7 LOLR.[452] In contrast with its predecessor of 1953, the 1979 Concordat endeavours to reconcile the right to religious freedom and the non-confessional character of the Spanish state, as defined in the Constitution, with the constitutional principle of cooperation, with particular reference to what the Catholic Church understands to be its specific needs.

347. The four Agreements of 1979 deal, respectively, with legal affairs, educational and cultural affairs, economic affairs, and the Church and the military. In order to have a comprehensive view of the matters covered by the Concordat, it is worth describing briefly the content of the four Agreements. More detailed references to their provisions, and to their complementation by subsequent specific agreements or legislation, are made in the relevant sections of this monograph.

348. The *Agreement on Juridical Affairs* deal with:

- the Catholic Church's right to its autonomy and self-organization;
- the legal personality of ecclesiastical institutions and territorial units (dioceses, parishes, etc.) under civil law;
- the inviolability of places of worship and ecclesiastical registries and archives;
- the Holy See's freedom to publish any rule related to the Church's government and to communicate with the clergy and the faithful;
- the recognition of Sunday as a non-working day;
- the right to provide Catholic religious assistance to the citizens confined in public or private establishments such as penitentiaries, hospitals or orphanages;
- the Church's freedom to develop charitable work and institutions, as well as the state cooperation with them;
- the civil effects of canonical marriage.

349. The *Agreement on Economical Affairs* deals with:

- the Church's freedom to request and receive money or donations;
- the state's economic cooperation with the Catholic Church;
- tax exemptions and other benefits for ecclesiastical activities, property and institutions.

350. The *Agreement on Education and Cultural Affairs* deals with:

- the recognition of the parents' rights to ensure the moral and religious teaching of their children in school;
- the teaching of Catholic instruction in public schools and the designation and stipend of religion teachers;
- the Church's right to establish seminars, schools, universities and centres for the study of ecclesiastical sciences;
- the state's obligation to ensure that the religious feelings of Catholics are respected by public media;
- the cooperation between Church and state for the preservation of ecclesiastical heritage and for making it available to the public.

---

452. *See infra*, para. 355.

351. Finally, the *Agreement on Religious Assistance to the Army and Military Service of the Clergy and Members of Religious Orders* deals with:

- the structure and organization of Catholic religious assistance to people in the army (both professional and performing military service) through the Vicariate General for the Army, conceived as a personal diocese;
- the specific ways in which the clergy and members of religious orders must perform their military service, seeking the compatibility with their canonical status;
- the exemption of bishops from performing military service.

352. Since 1979, the Concordat has been modified in one occasion, through an atypical channel. On 22 December 2006, through an exchange of letters between the Spanish Ministry of Foreign Affairs and the Apostolic Nunciature in Spain, the Catholic Church renounced the exemption from paying VAT granted by the 1979 Agreement on Economic Affairs. This renouncement was done to accommodate the Spanish law to European Union law and in exchange for a raise in the percentage of income tax that citizens could voluntarily donate every year to the Catholic Church.[453]

353. Some of the Concordat provisions have been developed by other domestic agreements, either at a national level, normally between the government and the Bishops Conference, without the need of a parliamentary ratification; or at a regional level, between a regional government and the relevant diocesan bishops. These agreements are usually known as 'minor' agreements. At a national level, for instance, there have been agreements on the Catholic religious assistance in hospitals[454] and penitentiaries;[455] and on the salaries of religion teachers in public schools.[456] Some other Concordat provisions have been developed by unilateral state regulations that had been previously negotiated with the Bishops Conference, as, for instance, the royal decrees on the social security of the clergy and members of religious orders.[457]

---

453. *See* , for further details, *infra* , Part VIII, paras 489 and 499.
454. *See Acuerdo* of 24 Jul. 1985, *sobre asistencia religiosa católica en centros hospitalarios públicos*; and *Convenio* of 23 Apr. 1996, *sobre asistencia religiosa católica en los Centros hospitalarios del Instituto Nacional de Salud.*
455. *See Orden* of 24 Nov. 1993, *por la que se dispone la publicación del Acuerdo sobre la asistencia religiosa católica en los Establecimientos penitenciarios.*
456. *See Orden* of 9 Apr. 1999 decreeing the publication of the *Convenio* of 26 Feb. 1999 *sobre el régimen económico-laboral de las personas que, no perteneciendo a los Cuerpos de Funcionarios Docentes, están encargadas de la enseñanza de la religión católica en los centros públicos de Educación Infantil, de Educación Primaria y de Educación Secundaria.*
457. *See Real Decreto* 2398/1977, of 27 Aug. 1977, *por el que se regula la seguridad social del clero*; and *Real Decreto* 3325/1981, of 29 Dec. 1981, *por el que se incorpora al Régimen Especial de la Seguridad Social de los Trabajadores por Cuenta propia o Autónomos a los religiosos y religiosas de la Iglesia Católica.*

§2. Cooperation Agreements with Other Religious Communities

354. Article 7 LOLR created a new legal institution in Spain, the cooperation agreements between state and religious denominations,[458] inspired by the long-standing tradition of the concordats with the Catholic Church. In brief, the approach of the LOLR seems to have been based on the following consideration: if shortly after the Constitution the state had decided to continue the praxis of establishing concordat relations with the majority church in Spain, the principle of equality persuaded the legislator to create an analogous channel of cooperation with those other religious denominations that had remarkable social relevance. In taking this decision, the legislator also took into account the institution of the *intese*, created by the 1948 Republican Constitution of Italy.

355. The legal design of the cooperation agreements in Article 7 LOLR posed some important questions, theoretical as well as practical. From a theoretical perspective – with significant practical consequences – the key question is probably the one about the precise legal nature of the new institution, which had no precedents in the history of Spanish law. Clearly, these cooperation agreements could not be conceived as international treaties – this is a unique particularity of the concordats, derived from the international legal personality of the Holy See. But was the legislator creating a new source of law in Spain, an intermediate bilateral source between international treaties and unilateral state legislation? The vast majority of scholars has answered this question in the negative and holds that, from the formal perspective of sources of law, the cooperation agreements created by the LOLR must be considered as state legislation. Indeed, Article 7 LOLR requires that each of them must be approved by a parliamentary statute. However, most scholars also recognize that the parliament cannot modify the text of an agreement previously negotiated by the government and a religious denomination – the parliament can approve it or reject it in toto, but not alter the text submitted for legislative sanction. In other words, cooperation agreements are *formally unilateral state legislation* but their *material content is provided by a bilateral agreement*, which makes them an institution of hybrid nature.[459]

356. Article 7 LOLR posed also two important practical questions. One concerns the legal term used to define the main condition that religious denominations must meet to reach a cooperation agreement with the state. In addition to being registered in the RER, they must have acquired 'well-known roots' (*notorio arraigo*) in Spain by their extension and number of adherents. Being this term also without precedents in the Spanish legal system, it was logical to expect that, as this concept was applied in practice, the government would provide more precise criteria about the understanding of 'well-known roots'. However, the practical application of this concept over the years did not properly clarified its meaning, and the government retained a large margin of discretion to grant or refuse applications for recognition of well-known roots in Spain. Historical rooting, expansion in other countries, transparent organization and a substantial minimum – but imprecise – number of adherents in Spain were some of the criteria used in practice to decide on particular cases, but they have been utilized

458. *See supra*, para. 65.

459. *See*, for a detailed analysis of this issue, J. Martínez-Torrón, *Separatismo y cooperación en los acuerdos del Estado con las minorías religiosas* 95–116 (Comares 1994).

with vagueness in order not to limit the government's discretion. The only clear rule, until recently, was a practical one, namely that recognition of well-known roots had to be supported by an affirmative opinion of the Advisory Commission on Religious Freedom created by Article 8 LOLR in the Ministry of Justice.[460] A royal decree of 2015[461] has finally regulated the procedure and criteria for the recognition of 'well-known roots' to religious communities (and for their loss). The procedure begins with the application of a religious community registered in the RER and ends with a decision (affirmative or negative) of the Minister of Justice. The royal decree makes now mandatory that the CALR must be necessarily consulted on the matter, thus transforming into a rule what was just customary for all these years. Although the Advisory Commission's opinion is not binding for the Minister, in practice its view has always been respected and it would be unthinkable to recognize 'well-known roots' to a religious group against the CALR's opinion. With respect to the criteria for decision, the royal decree makes an interesting effort to clarify the requisites for the recognition of 'well-known roots' but at the end falls short of objectivity and still leaves broad discretion to the public authorities in this matter.[462] Some clearly objective requisites are: (a) the applicant community must have been registered in the RER for at least 30 years (or, alternatively, 15 years and prove its recognition abroad for more than 60 years); (b) the community must submit evidence of its presence in no less than 10 autonomous regions (in Spain there are 17 regions plus 2 autonomous cities, Ceuta and Melilla); and (c) the community must have at least 100 entries in the RER counting entities and places of worship. Nevertheless, on the less objective side are: (a) the applicant community must have a 'structure and representation' that is deemed 'appropriate and sufficient' to the purpose of the recognition of 'well-known roots'; and (b) it must provide proof of its 'active presence and participation in Spanish society'. It is still too soon to say, but it seems plausible that the objective quantitative conditions established by the 2015 Royal Decree will serve to discard applications that do not deserve serious consideration, and the less objective conditions will be used to give discretion to the CALR – and the Minister of Justice – to decide which applicant religious communities it is advisable to recognize.

357. The other important practical question raised by Article 7 LOLR was to what extent a religious denomination that has been recognized well-known roots was entitled to negotiate and sign a cooperation agreement with the state. Again, Article 7 LOLR is elusive in this point and defers the decision to the governments' discretion – 'The state…shall establish, when appropriate, cooperation agreements…' The decision to initiate the proceedings eventually leading to a cooperation agreement relies entirely on the political will of the government. Indeed, to date only three religions – Protestantism, Judaism and Islam – have been accepted as interlocutors in a negotiation process, despite the fact that, since 2003, four other religious denominations have been recognized well-known roots: the Church of Jesus Christ of Latter-Day Saints (Mormons), Jehovah's

460. *See* , on this consultative body, *infra* , Part II, Ch. 4 §3.

461. *Real Decreto* 593/2015, 3 Jul. 2015, *por el que se regula la declaración de notorio arraigo de las confesiones religiosas en España.*

462. *See ibid.*, Art. 3. For an analysis of this royal decree, *see* A. López-Sidro, *El notorio arraigo de las confesiones religiosas en España a partir del Real Decreto que regula su declaración*, 55 Ius Canonicum 821–833 (2015).

Witnesses, the Spanish Buddhist Federation and a consortium of Christian Orthodox Churches. As things now stand, since 1992 no government has expressed a minimum interest in starting the negotiation of a cooperation agreement with them; on the contrary, their claims in that regard have been continuously overlooked or rejected.

358. Only once has been Article 7 LOLR put into practice until now, when the government signed three cooperation agreements, respectively, with the Evangelical, Jewish and Islamic Federations in April 1992 and the parliament approved them by statute in November of the same year.[463] The negotiations began in 1981 thanks to the impulse of the Evangelical and Jewish communities, but followed a slow pace until the late 1980s. This allowed the incorporation of the Islamic Federation to the negotiation process in 1989 – Muslim communities had more problems to organize themselves in a single federation that could act as interlocutor with the government.[464] The issues addressed by the 1992 Agreements are inspired by the Concordat experience. Moreover, the content of the three Agreements is very similar, for the government was determined to grant the same level and essentially the same expressions of cooperation for the three religions. There are only minor differences between them, mostly related to specific religious terminology or to aspects of state cooperation that the Evangelical Federation explicitly renounced – as, for instance, cooperation regarding religious dietary rules or cultural heritage.

359. In order to have a comprehensive view of the matters covered by the three 1992 Agreements it is worth describing briefly the main aspects of their content. More detailed references to their provisions are made in the relevant sections of this monograph:

- the control of the respective federations over the religious communities that may integrate into them in the future;
- the protection of places of worship;
- the legal status of ministers of worship, rabbis and imams;
- the civil effects of religious marriage;
- religious assistance in the military, hospitals and penitentiaries;
- religious instruction in public schools;
- economic state cooperation through tax benefits;
- the protection of sabbath rest (or collective prayer) and religious festivities;
- state cooperation with respect to religious heritage (the Evangelical Federation renounced this aspect of the Agreements, considering that it did not possess any religious heritage in Spain);
- the protection of Kosher and Halal, and of the dietary rules of Jews and Muslims.

360. In the last two decades, the three federations have addressed the government asking for a development of diverse aspects of the 1992 Agreements, with varying degrees of success. Their claims refer above all to religious assistance in public

463. The three agreements were signed on 28 Apr. 1992, and approved, respectively, by the Laws 24/1992, 25/1992 and 26/1992, all of them promulgated on 10 Nov. 1992.

464. *See* , for the history of the negotiations and the different drafts produced, A. Fernández-Coronado, *Estado y confesiones religiosas: un nuevo modelo de relación (los pactos con las confesiones: leyes 24, 25 y 26 de 1992)* (Civitas 1995); J. Martínez-Torrón, *Separatismo y cooperación*, 129–135.

institutions, state economic cooperation and religious instruction in public schools. So far, there are two main aspects of the 1992 Agreements that have been developed by other agreements, or by unilateral state regulations previously negotiated with the respective religious federation: religious assistance in penitentiaries,[465] and the conditions for the appointment and salaries of religion teachers in public schools (with the Evangelical and Islamic Federation).[466]

465. *Real Decreto* 710/2006, 9 Jun. 2006, *de desarrollo de los Acuerdos de Cooperación firmados por el Estado con la Federación de Entidades Religiosas Evangélicas de España, la Federación de Comunidades Judías de España y la Comisión Islámica de España, en el ámbito de la asistencia religiosa penitenciaria*; and *Convenio de colaboración del estado con la comisión islámica de España para la financiación de los gastos que ocasione el desarrollo de la asistencia religiosa en los establecimientos penitenciarios de competencia estatal*, of 24 Oct. 2007.
466. *Convenio sobre designación y régimen económico de las personas encargadas de la enseñanza religiosa evangélica, en los centros docentes públicos de educación primaria y secundaria*, published by *Resolución* of 23 Apr. 1996; and *Convenio sobre designación y régimen económico de las personas encargadas de la enseñanza religiosa islámica, en los centros docentes públicos de educación primaria y secundaria*, published by *Resolución* of 23 Apr. 1996.

Chapter 6. Religious Assistance in Public Institutions

361. As indicated above,[467] Article 2.1.b) LOLR guarantees every person's right to 'receive religious assistance of his own denomination'. In normal conditions, every person can obtain spiritual care on his own initiative and by his own means, but in certain circumstances the state active cooperation is necessary to ensure the exercise of this right. This is the case of people confined in places under the responsibility of public authorities, where they do not enjoy free movement for various reasons. In such circumstances, Article 2.3 LOLR provides for a specific state action:

> [t]o ensure the real and effective application of these rights, public authorities shall adopt the necessary measures to facilitate religious assistance in hospitals, penitentiaries, public, military and charitable establishments, and other establishment under the public authorities' aegis.

362. The state's intervention to guarantee religious assistance in the military, penitentiaries and hospitals is conceived by Spanish law as indirect, rather than direct, cooperation with religious communities. Its main purpose is not to grant a particular status or privileges to well-established churches but to facilitate individuals the actual exercise of their right to religious assistance – it they so wish – in places where they are under the responsibility of public authorities and it is difficult, or even impossible, to procure spiritual assistance by themselves. In practice, the implementation of Article 2.3 LOLR is bound to lead to a dialogue and cooperation with the main religious communities. With the rest of denominations it should be enough to ensure that, upon request of the interested person, ministers of worship can have free access to the relevant military establishment, penitentiary or hospital; or, when appropriate, to grant military personnel permission to attend a place of religious worship or meeting.

363. Religious assistance in the military, public hospitals and penitentiaries is a matter that in Spain is regulated both by bilateral norms – i.e., by agreements between state and religions – and by state unilateral laws.

364. Within the 1979 Concordat system, there is a specific Agreement between the Spanish state and the Holy See on Religious Assistance to the Armed Forces and Military Service of the Clergy and Members of Religious Orders. This Agreement sanctions the arrangement of Catholic religious assistance in the military, which is organized around a specific ecclesiastical structure – the Military Vicariate (*Vicariato Castrense*) – consisting in a system of stable chaplaincies. The ecclesiastical personnel of those chaplaincies, following an old tradition, were *organically* integrated within the military ranks. The system was challenged before the Constitutional Court, which in 1982, without a specific pronouncement on the issue of the *organic integration* of chaplains in the military structure, sustained the constitutionality of a system aimed at guaranteeing the right of Catholic members of the military to receive spiritual assistance.[468] A few years later, in 1990, the government approved – after consultation with the Catholic Church – a general regulation on the Service of Religious Assistance

467. *See supra* , Part II, para. 120.
468. Cf. STC 24/1982.

to the Armed Forces,[469] which in theory was of general application to all religious denominations but in reality had in mind only the Catholic chaplaincies. Since then, chaplains ceased to be within the military ranks and passed to have a 'relation of professional services' with the army. This relation can be permanent or non-permanent, but chaplains are in both cases paid by the state and are under the spiritual authority of the Military Archbishop (*Arzobispo Castrense*, formerly called General Military Vicar or *Vicario General Castrense*). The regulations of the different branches of the army contain further rules with respect to religious assistance and religious worship in military establishments – again, these rules are generally applicable to all religions but in practice keep mostly in mind the specific needs of Catholic citizens.[470] The aim of these regulations is to facilitate as much as possible religious practices for the military personnel, within the framework of the due discipline and order in the army.

365. Catholic religious assistance in penitentiaries and public hospitals is not regulated by the Concordat but by agreements between the government and the Bishops Conference (private hospitals, which are often managed by Catholic religious orders or have a Catholic ethos, abide by their own rules). These norms have preserved the traditional systems of Catholic assistance and have adapted them to the requirements of a non-confessional state. The service of Catholic religious assistance in the hospitals of the public health system is governed by two agreements of 1985 and 1986, respectively.[471] In every hospital, the service – available upon request of the patients or their relatives – consists of chaplains, chapels and offices, which must include, if possible, an appropriate place where the chaplain can spend the night. The precise number of chaplains depends on the size of each hospital, and they are paid with public funding. Another agreement between the government and the Bishops Conference, of 1993,[472] contains the legal regime of a similar service of religious Catholic assistance in penitentiaries – likewise supported financially by the state. It is also applicable the general Regulation of Penitentiaries, which does not add anything significant to the regulations of the agreement.[473]

366. The three 1992 Agreements with the Evangelical, Jewish and Islamic Federations contain specific provisions on religious assistance, which design a system very different from the one in force for the Catholic Church. This seems based on the fact that the number of adherents of those religions is much lower and would not justify the creation of stable services similar to Catholic chaplaincies. In essence, the 1992 Agreements structure a system that pivots on two elements. On the one hand, religious

469. *Real Decreto* 1145/1990, 7 Sep. 1990, *por el que se crea el Servicio de Asistencia Religiosa en las Fuerzas Armadas y se dictan normas sobre su funcionamiento.*

470. *See Reales Ordenanzas del Ejército de Tierra*, approved by the *Real Decreto* 2945/1983, 9 Nov. 1983, Arts 234–244, *Reales Ordenanzas de la Armada*, approved by the *Real Decreto* 1024/1984, 23 May 1984, Arts 432–442; *Reales Ordenanzas del Ejercito del Aire*, approved by the *Real Decreto* 494/1984, 22 Feb. 1984, Arts 291–299.

471. *Acuerdo sobre asistencia religiosa católica en centros hospitalarios*, 24 Jul. 1985; and *Convenio sobre asistencia religiosa católica en los centros hospitalarios del Instituto Nacional de Salud*, 23 Apr. 1986.

472. *Orden* of 24 Nov. 1993, *por la que se dispone la publicación del Acuerdo sobre la asistencia religiosa católica en los establecimientos penitenciarios.*

473. *Real Decreto* 190/1996, 9 Feb. 1996, *por el que se aprueba el Reglamento Penitenciario. See* especially Arts 11, 226 and 230.

ministers have *free access* to public facilities to provide spiritual care, upon request of persons interested in receiving such care. And on the other hand, in the case of the military, officers shall enjoy *free leave*, when appropriate and possible, to comply with their religious obligations. Thus, Article 8 of the Agreements guarantees the right of members of the military – Protestant, Jewish or Muslim, respectively – to receive spiritual care from the ministers, rabbis or imams appointed by the respective federations. Jewish and Muslim officers shall also be given leave of absence to attend religious services when it is feasible within the functioning of their respective regiments. Article 9 of the Agreements establishes a similar system of free access of religious ministers to penitentiaries and public hospitals (for obvious reasons, leave of absence is not foreseen by this article); free access is not restricted to any particular time frame but must respect the internal rules of the relevant centre. In both articles, there are specific provisions to guarantee the compliance with funerary rites in the case of Jews and Muslims.

367. In view of the aforementioned data, it is probably fair to affirm that the legal regime of religious assistance in the military, in penitentiaries and in public hospitals designed by the 1992 Agreements do not create particular advantages for Protestants, Jews or Muslims. There is almost nothing in Articles 8–9 of those Agreements that were not already, explicitly or implicitly, in the LOLR and in other state regulations that are generally applicable to any individual belonging to any religious denomination.[474] Even more, from a certain perspective the 1992 Agreements seem to limit, rather than enlarge, the right to religious assistance of Protestants, Jews and Muslims in public institutions, for they do not have complete free choice of the persons providing spiritual care – they are supposed to choose among the ministers appointed by the respective religious federation and authorized by the competent public authorities. In 2006, a royal decree developed this aspect of the 1992 Agreements with regard to penitentiaries.[475] This regulation provides that the appointment of ministers by the relevant religious federation and the subsequent authorization by the competent public authorities shall take place on a stable basis. Both have annual character and are renewed automatically every year, save explicit revocation. Certainly, this variation introduced in the system facilitates the free access of religious ministers to penitentiaries in practice, but at the same time it constitutes a further limitation on the inmates' free choice of ministers. It seems that security reasons played a role in the new regulation, which makes easier for the government to control the *reliability* of religious leaders with access to prisons.

368. Another difference between the legal regime of Catholic and non-Catholic religious assistance in public facilities concerns the use of *public funding*. As mentioned above, the salaries of Catholic chaplains are paid by the state. Almost no provision for payment of other religious ministers is contained in state laws and regulations. The 1992 Agreements with the Evangelical and Jewish Federations (Article 9) explicitly indicate that the relevant religious communities shall take care of the expenses stemming

474. Cf. the general regulations of the different branches of the army, as well as the general regulation of penitentiaries, cited *supra* , in paras 364–365.

475. *Real Decreto* 710/2006, 9 Jun. 2006, *de desarrollo de los Acuerdos de Cooperación firmados por el Estado con la Federación de entidades Religiosas Evangélicas de España, la Federación de Comunidades Judías de España y la Comisión Islámica de España, en el ámbito de la asistencia religiosa penitenciaria.*

from spiritual assistance. Instead, the parallel Article 9 of the Agreement with the Islamic Federation remits to further agreements in this matter. In application of that article, in 2007 the government and the Islamic Federation agreed that, in the case of penitentiaries, a limited amount of public funding could be paid to the personnel in charge of religious assistance to Muslim inmates.[476]

476. *Convenio de colaboración del Estado con la Comisión Islámica de España para la financiación de los gastos que ocasione el desarrollo de la asistencia religiosa en los establecimientos penitenciarios de competencia estatal*, 24 Oct. 2007.

Part IV. International, Transnational, Regional Effects on Religious Communities

Chapter 1. International Law Effects on Religious Communities

369. International treaties, in addition to involving the international responsibility of the state, are sources of law in Spain.[477] Therefore, international conventions on human rights, once signed and ratified by the Spanish state, are applicable sources of law on issues relating to religious freedom, both in their individual and collective dimensions. Moreover, according to Article 10.2 of the Constitution, international conventions on human rights, as well as the Universal Declaration of Human Rights, are mandatory points of reference for the interpretation of the constitutional provisions on fundamental rights and freedoms. They are, therefore, a necessary reference for the interpretation of the freedom of ideology, religion and worship protected by Article 16 CE.

370. Spain is a Member State of all international institutions with relevance on religious freedom – the most significant of them are the United Nations, the Council of Europe and the Organization for the Security and Cooperation in Europe. Spain is also a signatory to the main international instruments for the protection of human rights. Among the UN instruments, the following have a particular significance for the protection of religious freedom:

- The International Covenant on Civil and Political Rights (1966), whose Article 18 guarantees freedom of thought, conscience and religion. Spain has recognized the competence of the Human Rights Committee to examine individual communications for alleged violation of rights recognized by the Covenant.
- The International Covenant on Economic, Social and Cultural Rights (1966), whose Article 13.3 guarantees the parents' right to ensure the religious and moral education of their children in conformity with their convictions. Spain has recognized the competence of the Committee on Economic, Social and Cultural Rights to examine individual complaints.
- The Convention on the Rights of the Child (1989), which prohibits the discrimination of children on religious grounds (Article 2), and recognizes the children's right to freedom of thought, conscience and religion, as well as the parents' right to

477. Cf. Art. 96 CE.

provide guidance to their children in the exercise of this freedom in a manner consistent with the evolving capacities of the child (Article 14).

- The Declaration on the Elimination of All Forms of Intolerance and of Discrimination Based on Religion or Belief (1981), which is normally regarded as an authoritative source notwithstanding its non-binding nature.

371. As an OSCE Participating state, Spain accepts the human dimension commitments, which contain detailed provisions with regard to the consequences of the guarantee of religious freedom, both from an individual and collective perspective. Among the different human dimension documents, the 1989 Vienna document is probably the most significant and specific.[478]

372. In practice, the most important of international instruments of human rights for the protection of religious freedom in Spain is the ECHR (1950, amended by successive protocols), elaborated within the Council of Europe. Article 9 ECHR guarantees freedom of thought, conscience and religion; Article 14 ECHR prohibits discrimination on religious grounds; and Article 2 of the First Protocol to the ECHR protects the parents' right to ensure that the education and teaching of their children will be in conformity with their own religious or philosophical convictions (Article 2). The significance of the ECHR does not derive only from its text but also, and above all, from the fact that it is interpreted and applied by the ECtHR, with seat in Strasbourg, which has jurisdiction over all Member States of the Council of Europe and can adjudicate on individual applications alleging violations of the rights and freedoms included in the Convention. With respect to issues relating to religious freedom, Spain has been a respondent state in some applications, and three times the Court actually found a violation of the Convention. The most significant cases have been the following.

373. In 1986, the European Commission of Human Rights (no longer existing[479]) rejected the application filed by an elected member of the autonomous regional parliament of Galicia, who refused to take the oath or pledge of allegiance that was mandatory to take possession of his parliamentary seat. He alleged, among other grounds, his freedom of thought, conscience and religion, guaranteed by Article 9 ECHR. The Commission declared the application inadmissible as manifestly ill-founded,[480] on the basis of the limitation clauses of Article 9.2 ECHR. The Commission held that, on the ground of public order, the Spanish law could legitimately interfere with the freedom of the applicant by requiring an oath or pledge of allegiance to the Constitution, which was merely a symbolic act by which an elected member of the legislature accepted that only legal means might be used to modify the constitutional order.

374. In 1992, in the case of *Iglesia Bautista El Salvador*, the European Commission declared also inadmissible, as manifestly ill-founded, the application of a small Baptist church that claimed to be victim of discriminatory treatment because it had been refused exemptions from property taxes on places of worship similar to those granted

478. These documents can be found in: http://www.osce.org/odihr/76902 (accessed 9 Dec. 2017).
479. The Commission disappeared when Protocol Nr. 11 to the Convention came into force in November 1998. Until then, it filtered – through inadmissibility decisions – the applications that could be sent to the Court to be judged on the merits.
480. Decision on the admissibility of Appl. Nr. 11321/85, 6 Oct. 1986.

to the Catholic Church in the 1979 Concordat.[481] The Commission held that Article 9 ECHR, as such, could not be invoked to claim a specific tax status different from other taxpayers. In addition, the Commission remarked that the tax benefits of Catholic places of worship were granted by an agreement with the state, and that such agreements, according to Article 7 LOLR, were available to other religious communities with strong roots in Spain. In the Commission's view, such specific legal basis constituted an objective and reasonable justification for the difference in legal treatment, because the applicant church neither had concluded an agreement with the state nor had sought to do so. It must be noted that this application was filed – and decided – before the signature and approval of the 1992 Agreement between the state and the Evangelical Federation (FEREDE), which explicitly provides for such tax exemptions; the applicant church is member of FEREDE.

375. A similar application was declared inadmissible as manifestly ill-founded in 2001, this time by the European Court, in the case of *Alujer Fernández and Caballero García*.[482] The applicants were two members of a Baptist Church that claimed their right to the same tax assignment system recognized to the Catholic Church. According to this system, which was foreseen by the Concordat and implemented by a state law in 1987,[483] all taxpayers are given every year the opportunity to allocate a small percentage of their income tax to be paid to the Catholic Church instead of to the state general budget. The reasoning of the Court was very similar to the case mentioned in the precedent paragraph, and focused on the interpretation of the equality principle and on the lack of implications of Article 9 with regard to tax benefits. In addition, the ECtHR noted that the applicants acted in a purely individual capacity and not as representatives of their Church. Indeed, the decision makes clear that neither their Church nor the Evangelical Federation, which had already a cooperation agreement since 1992, had asked the government to be beneficiaries of the tax assignment system applicable to the Catholic Church.

376. Another issue relating to the application of the principle of equality was judged by the ECtHR in *Manzanas Martín*, in 2012.[484] The applicant was a retired full-time Evangelical pastor that had been refused his right to a retirement pension on the ground that he had not paid his social security contributions for the minimum required time of fifteen years. On the one hand, the applicant argued that Protestant ministers were not allowed to integrate into the social security system until 1999,[485] notwithstanding that a royal decree of 1977 envisaged that possibility, while Catholic priests were integrated since 1978. And on the other hand, he complained that he had not been given the opportunity to contribute the sums corresponding to the missing annuities in order to complete the minimum period required by law to be entitled to a retirement pension (he missed about 65% of the legally required time), while such possibility was open to Catholic secularized priests and religious. The European Court

481. *Iglesia Bautista El Salvador and Ortega Moratilla v. Spain*, decision on the admissibility of Appl. Nr. 17522/90, 11 Jan. 1992.
482. *Alujer Fernández and Caballero García v. Spain*, decision on the admissibility of Appl. Nr. 53072/99, 14 Jun. 2001. The case was declared inadmissible by a chamber of seven judges.
483. *See infra*, Part VIII, Ch. 1
484. *Manzanas Martín v. Spain*, 3 Apr. 2012.
485. *See infra*, para. 413.

noted the enormous delay – more than twenty years of difference – that it took to the government to apply to Protestant ministers the same system of social security applied to Catholic priests, but the Court considered that it could be justifiable, in the light of the state margin of appreciation, by the Spanish policies of cooperation agreements with religious communities. Instead, the Court accepted the applicant's second argument and held that the legal disparity between Evangelical pastors and secularized Catholic priests was based solely on a difference of religion, and therefore was discriminatory.

377. On a totally different topic, in 1999, in the *Riera Blume* case,[486] the ECtHR faced a situation of suspected abuse or 'brainwashing' of individuals by a religious movement that public authorities considered to be a 'sect'. The applicants were adult members of an organization called *Centro Esotérico de Investigaciones* (Esoteric Centre of Research). Following the issuance of a judicial order, the applicants' homes were searched, and the applicants themselves were subsequently confined in a nearby hotel against their will for 'deprogramming'. The confinement of the applicants, however, was not supported by any judicial order and was carried out by a private 'anti-sect' association with the consent of the applicants' families and a limited cooperation of the Catalan police. The Court avoided pronouncing any opinion under Article 9 ECHR and decided in favour of the applicants under Article 5.1 ECHR (right to liberty and security).

378. In 2012 and 2014, the European Court dealt with a complex case concerning the system of religious instruction in Spanish public schools: *Fernández Martínez.*[487] The applicant was a former Catholic priest that had worked as teacher of Catholic religion in public schools following his abandonment of priesthood and subsequent civil marriage. Six years after his first contract as religion teacher, the Holy See granted his canonical secularization and dispensation from celibacy, and the diocesan bishop decided not to renew his annual proposal as religion teacher, which is an indispensable legal requisite for being hired as religion teacher,[488] with the consequence that the applicant was dismissed from his position at a public school. The reason alleged by the bishop was that the Vatican's decree of secularization explicitly indicated that former priests should not be allowed to teach Catholic religion in public schools, unless the relevant bishop thought otherwise and there was no danger of scandal. In this case, the bishop perceived that there was risk of scandal, not only because of the former condition of priest of the applicant but also, and above all, because of his active and public involvement in a 'movement pro optional celibacy' of priests. The European Court held that, in these circumstances, the autonomy of the Catholic Church to freely decide who is appropriate to teach religion on its behalf must prevail over the applicant's right to privacy and family life (Article 8 ECHR), and remarked that state religious

486. *Riera Blume v. Spain*, 14 Oct. 1999.
487. *Fernández Martínez v. Spain*, 15 May 2012 (Chamber) and 12 Jun. 2014 (Grand Chamber).
488. Cf. Agreement on Education and Cultural Affairs between Spain and the Holy See, Arts III and IV. The status of religion teachers will be explained in more detail, *infra* , in Part IX, Ch. 1 §1.

neutrality prevents from interfering with an ecclesiastical decision adopted on religious and moral grounds.[489]

379. So far, the last case against Spain decided by the ECtHR in respect of an issue concerning religion, even indirectly, is *Sociedad Anónima del Ucieza*, in 2014, regarding the ownership of ecclesiastical property.[490] The conflict was raised by the fact that a bishop registered as ecclesiastical property an old abandoned church that was within the land acquired, sixteen years before, by an agricultural company. The Spanish courts rejected all claims made by the company to recover what it understood to be an unjustified deprivation of part of its property. It is not necessary to enter here into the intricate circumstances of the case and the technicalities of Spanish law on real property. It suffices to say that the European Court decided in favour of the applicant company not in the light of Article 9 ECHR but in the light of Article 6.1 (right to a fair and public hearing) and Article 1 of the First Protocol to the Convention (protection of property). In any event, some scholars have remarked that cases like this reveal the type of problems that the mechanism of registration applicable to ecclesiastical property may originate.[491]

489. This has been one of the most complex cases regarding religious autonomy before the ECtHR. The case is analysed in detail by Ian Leigh and Javier Martínez-Torrón in their respective chapters in *When Human Rights Clash at the European Court of Human Rights: Conflict or Harmony?* 192–241 (Stijn Smet & Eva Brems eds, Oxford U. Press 2017).

490. *Sociedad Anónima del Ucieza v. Spain*, 4 Nov. 2014.

491. *See* M. Moreno Antón, *Luces y sombras en el acceso de los bienes eclesiásticos al Registro de la Propiedad*, 38 Revista General de Derecho Canónico y Derecho Eclesiástico del Estado 1–42 (2015).

Chapter 2. Transnational Law Effects on Religious Communities

380. Spain is a member country of the European Union since 1986. A Declaration on the status of churches and non-confessional organizations was annexed to the Treaty of Amsterdam, amending the Treaty on the European Union in 1997, providing that the EU 'respects and does not prejudice the status under national law of churches and religious associations or communities in the Member States'. A similar provision follows with reference to 'philosophical and non-confessional organizations'. The consequence is that EU law shall not interfere with the system of relations between state and religion in Spain, unless there is some violation of fundamental rights recognized by the EU Charter.

381. The CFREU (2000, adapted in 2007) is legally binding in Spain.[492] Article 10 CFREU protects both individual and collective religious freedom, in terms almost identical to Article 9 ECHR and adding the guarantee of the right to conscientious objection in its diverse manifestations:[493]

Article 10 CFREU – Freedom of thought, conscience and religion:

1. Everyone has the right to freedom of thought, conscience and religion. This right includes freedom to change religion or belief and freedom, either alone or in community with others and in public or in private, to manifest religion or belief, in worship, teaching, practice and observance.
2. The right to conscientious objection is recognised, in accordance with the national laws governing the exercise of this right.

382. Article 14.3 CFREU, in the context of the right to education, guarantees two rights of significance for religious communities. One is 'the freedom to found educational establishments with due respect for democratic principles'. The other is 'the right of parents to ensure the education and teaching of their children in conformity with their religious, philosophical and pedagogical convictions'. In both cases, they shall be guaranteed 'in accordance with the national laws governing the exercise of such freedom and right'. Interestingly, the second clause of Article 14.3 CFREU, which is clearly inspired by Article 2 of the First Protocol to the ECHR, adds the adjective 'pedagogical' in connection with the parents' rights over their children education – the ECHR only considers religious and philosophical convictions. The broad meaning of such term has raised some controversy, especially with respect to the possible recognition of a right to homeschooling, which is so far rejected by the Spanish Constitutional Court.[494]

383. Another relevant provision of the CFREU is Article 21, which prohibits discrimination on any ground, including specifically religion or belief. Prior to the

---

492. *See* Art. 6.1 of the Consolidated Version of the Treaty on European Union.
493. *See supra* , with regard to the recognition of the right to conscientious objection, para. 161.
494. *See* M.J. Valero, *Homeschooling en España, supra* , note 202.

Charter, the Treaty of Amsterdam, in 1997, provided that the Council might take 'appropriate action to combat discrimination based on sex, racial, or ethnic origin, religion or belief, disability, age or sexual orientation'.[495] One of the results of this provision has been the Council Directive 2000/78/EC, of 27 November 2000, establishing a general framework for equal treatment in employment and occupation. The purpose of this Directive was to lay down a general framework for combating discrimination on the grounds of religion or belief, among others. The 2000 Directive was aimed at the elimination not only of direct discrimination, but also of indirect discrimination, which was defined with the following words:

> indirect discrimination shall be taken to occur where an apparently neutral provision, criterion or practice would put persons having a particular religion or belief … at a particular disadvantage compared with other persons unless … that provision, criterion or practice is objectively justified by a legitimate aim and the means of achieving that aim are appropriate and necessary.[496]

384. The main legislative instrument for the implementation of the 2000 Directive in Spain has been a law of 2003, which contains a specific chapter on measures for equality treatment.[497] With regard to religious discrimination, this law basically repeats the content of the Directive 2000/78/EC. Most efforts for the implementation of the Directive, especially apropos of indirect discrimination, have focused on sex, sexual orientation and disabilities.

495. Article 13 of the consolidated version of the Treaty on European Union after the Treaty of Amsterdam.
496. Article 2.2(b) of the Directive 2000/78/EC.
497. *Ley* 62/2003, de 30 Dec. 2003, *de medidas fiscales, administrativas y del orden social. See* Arts 27–43.

Chapter 3. Regional Law Effects on Religious Communities

385. According to Article 53.1 CE, the rights and freedoms recognized by the Constitution can only be regulated by statutory law. And, according to 81.1 CE, in the case of fundamental rights – as the freedom of ideology, religion and worship guaranteed by Article 16 CE – their regulation and development is reserved to organic laws, which are the competence of the national parliament (*Cortes*) and require the positive vote of the absolute majority of members of the Congress. This means that regional legislatures (*parlamentos autonómicos*) are not competent to legislate on religious freedom; or, for example, to establish their own independent registries for religious entities, as far as this type of registry is conceived as an instrument to recognize legal personality to religious communities and, therefore, to regulate their exercise of religious freedom.

386. The foregoing, however, does not prevent regional governments from taking actions to facilitate the exercise of religious freedom by churches and religious communities within their legitimate competences, in compliance with the constitutional mandate of cooperation with religion (Article 16.3 CE), which concerns all public authorities and not only the national government or legislature. Indeed, some regions (*comunidades autónomas*) have developed a variety of policies to that purpose, including agreements or coordinated actions for the preservation of religious heritage, especially in the case of the Catholic Church.

387. In addition, the region of Catalonia, with the same aim of facilitating the exercise of religious freedom, as well as the dialogue between the regional government and religious communities, has created a specific Directorate General on Religious Affairs (*Direcció General d'Afers Religiosos*), which is currently in the Department of Government and Public Administrations (*Governació i Administracions Públiques*) of the regional government. The Catalan government also signed, in 2010, an agreement with the Ministry of Justice in which the central and regional governments accept a compromise of mutual collaboration in the management of the Registry of Religious Entities with respect to those religious communities that have their domicile in Catalonia.[498]

388. Local governments are not competent to regulate religious freedom, or to impose limitations on its exercise. This was the main reason why the Supreme Court annulled in 2013 a municipal ordinance of the city of Lérida prohibiting the use of burka or full veil in public facilities.[499] Nevertheless, municipal governments possess legitimate competences on issues that have an influence on the life of religious communities, such as cemeteries and urban planning; these competences are partly shared with the regional government. Thus, the Catalan Parliament, in the exercise of its legitimate competences on urban planning, enacted in 2009 a law on places of worship, followed by more detailed administrative regulations.[500]

---

498. VCP/3751/2010, of 16 Nov. 2010, *per la qual es dóna publicitat al Conveni de col·laboració de 22 de setembre de 2010 establert entre l'Administració general de l'Estat i l'Administració de la Generalitat de Catalunya en matèria d'afers religiosos.*

499. *See supra*, para. 212.

500. *See supra*, Part III, Ch. 3.

Part V. Religion and Politics

Chapter 1. Religion Influence in Politics

389. Being Spain a country of ancient Catholic tradition, the influence of the Catholic Church and institutions in social life is enormous – from the many religious symbols that can be seen everywhere to the presence and activity of Catholic organizations in public life. However, there are no specific positions reserved for Catholic bishops or other religious leaders either in parliament or in regional legislatures. With the logical exception of the Advisory Commission on Religious Freedom,[501] there are not religious representatives appointed as such for state bodies.

390. Catholic bishops do not endeavour to intervene directly in strictly political issues of secular nature, but they often address the general public to express publicly and clearly what they consider to be the right doctrine with regard to questions of moral consequence. To a large extent, their public discourse places great emphasis on the preservation of Spanish Catholic identity, both formally and substantially. Individual Spanish bishops or the Bishops Conference often speak out against governmental or legislative actions deemed to be detrimental for public morals. In the recent past, the most important cases have been some measures adopted by a socialist government, in particular the legal reforms on family law in 2005 (above all, the legalization of same-sex marriages, and the simplification and facilitation of divorce proceedings[502]), the liberalization of the right to abortion in 2010,[503] and the introduction of a compulsory school subject called 'education for citizenship', which touched upon sensitive moral issues and was deemed to pave the way for moral indoctrination in public schools.[504] In all those cases, Spanish bishops have expressed plainly their views in formal pronouncements and have spread them widely through the media and the web pages of the Bishops Conference. In addition, they also try to stimulate Catholic citizens to take an active part in changing those laws. For example, Spanish bishops explicitly fostered conscientious objection to 'education for citizenship';[505] and, in the case of

501. *See supra*, Part II, Ch. 4 §3.
502. Operated, respectively, by the *Ley* 13/2005, 1 Jul. 2005, *por la que se modifica el Código Civil en materia de derecho a contraer matrimonio*, and by the *Ley* 15/2005, 8 Jul. 2005, *por la que se modifican el Código Civil y la Ley de Enjuiciamiento Civil en materia de separación y divorcio*.
503. Operated by the *Ley Orgánica* 2/2010, 3 Mar. 2010, *de salud sexual y reproductiva y de la interrupción voluntaria del embarazo*.
504. *See supra*, Part II, Ch. 2 §8 IV.
505. *See ibid.*

family law reforms, promoted a huge demonstration in Madrid in defence of the traditional concept of family, which continued for some years in the form of an open-air multitudinous mass (the Mass of Families) in a public square in Madrid, celebrated at the end of December.[506] In recent years, the economic crisis has been another recurrent theme in the public discourse of Spanish bishops, who have often urged Catholics to act in solidarity with people in need.

391. With the same aim of reminding Catholic moral doctrines vis-à-vis specific issues, the Bishops Conference normally makes some pronouncements before general elections. They never make any explicit reference, positive or negative, to political parties but they mention moral questions that Catholics must take into account when deciding their vote; these questions can easily be linked to the programmes of the relevant political parties. The main topics mentioned in those public statements are: the protection of the right to life, family policies, social and distributive justice, the guarantee of parents' rights over the moral education of their children, violence and terrorism. The Bishops Conference has made similar pronouncements before other political consultations of significance – for instance, the 2005 referendum on the European Constitution – and with the occasion of other events with political impact, including relevant decisions adopted by the Constitutional Court or by the ECtHR.[507] In recent years, the political crisis generated by pro-independence movements in Catalonia has divided Spanish bishops. Some Catalan bishops, and an uncertain number of Catalan members of the clergy and religious orders, have declared themselves in favour of the independence of Catalonia. Although the majority of the rest of Spanish bishops are against the separation of Catalonia, the Bishops Conference has taken no official stance on this issue and has just insisted that it is necessary to respect democratic rules and institutions as well as to engage in a dialogue between opposite political positions.[508] After the unilateral (and failed) declaration of independence of the Catalan government in October 2017, the President of the Bishops Conference publicly expressed his support to the defence of the constitutional order.[509]

392. Religious leaders of the main minorities speak out much more rarely. They normally avoid making public pronouncements similar to those of the Catholic bishops, even when they share the same moral views, and tend to intervene only apropos of issues that concern them directly. This has been the case, for example, of the use of hijab in public schools[510] or the prohibition of full veil in municipal facilities,[511] which have led representatives of Islamic communities to publicly defend the Muslim women's right to wear the garments of their choice. In 2005, in the first anniversary of the jihadist

506. In 2014, the new archbishop of Madrid moved the mass to the inside of the Cathedral of Madrid and gave it a more local air.
507. For example, the Constitutional Court's judgment on the constitutionality of same-sex marriages (STC 198/2012), or the ECtHR's judgment *Sindicatul Păstorul Cel Bun v. Rumania*, 31 Jan. 2012. For a consultation of the documents of the Spanish Bishops Conference, *see* http://www.conferenciaepiscopal.es/base-documental/ (accessed 9 Dec. 2017).
508. http://www.conferenciaepiscopal.es/declaracion-la-comision-permanente-ante-la-situacion-cataluna/ (accessed 9 Dec. 2017).
509. *See* http://www.conferenciaepiscopal.es/cardenal-blazquez-reitera-apoyo-al-orden-constitucional/ (accessed 9 Dec. 2017)
510. *See supra* , Part II, Ch. 2 §9 I.
511. *See supra* , Part II, Ch. 2 §9 II.

terrorist bombing of 11 March 2004 in Madrid, the Secretary General of the Islamic Commission of Spain published a fatwa against Bin Laden and Al Qaeda, in very strong terms, declaring out of Islam all those who misuse the sharia to commit and justify terrorist attacks.[512] In recent years, with the occasion of various terrorist attacks by self-proclaimed Islamist organizations, it has been frequent that Islamic communities and leaders make public statements condemning such attacks and claiming that Islam is a religion of peace.[513]

393. In Spain there are no religious political parties. In the early years of the political transition to democracy after General Franco's death, there was a small Christian Democratic Party based on Christian values, which was soon absorbed (1978) by a more powerful party (*Unión de Centro Democrático*), which won the first general elections. Most people of Christian-Democrat ideas are now militant in the Popular Party, one of the two most powerful parties in Spain, which does not have religious affiliation but claims to be based on – among other values – 'the Christian humanism of Western tradition'. More clear and explicit used to be the Christian-Democrat inspiration of a regional Catalan party, *Unió Democràtica de Catalunya*, which, in coalition with other Catalan party (*Convergència Democràtica de Catalunya*), had representation both in the regional and national legislatures; the coalition broke in 2015, and two years later, as a consequence of electoral setbacks, the party decided to dissolve. No other religion has inspired a political party in Spain. At a national level, it is commonly assumed that the relationships of Catholic bishops are normally better with the Popular Party than with the Socialist Party.

394. Spanish politicians and public officials rarely disclose or speak about their beliefs and do not use a political discourse based explicitly on religious ideas. Sometimes, politicians have been permitted to abandon disciplined voting in parliament – which is a common rule in the functioning of Spanish political parties – or to publicly oppose to government or party policies on religious or moral grounds. This has been the case, for example, of some socialist politicians with respect to abortion, and of some conservative politicians with respect to same-sex marriage.

395. Although Spain is no longer a Catholic state, the Spanish monarchy and the royal family do not conceal or dissimulate their traditional links with the Catholic Church. All married members of the royal family have celebrated a Catholic canonical marriage (in the case of the King, also a Christian Orthodox marriage, authorized by Pope John XXIII, because Queen Sofia was a Greek Orthodox before converting to Catholicism with the occasion of her wedding). Religious Christian symbols are frequently visible in the royal palaces and offices. In the King's formal Christmas address, which is broadcast by TV and radio to the entire country in the evening of every 24 December, a traditional Christmas crèche can be clearly seen in the King's office. These facts are commonly accepted and have been only occasionally criticized by left-wing politicians of republican orientation.

512. *See* the text of the fatwa in: http://www.webislam.com/noticias/43520-la_comision_islamica_de_espana_emite una fatua condenando_el_terrorismo_y_al_gru.html (accessed 9 Dec. 2017).

513. *See* , for instance, http://comisionislamicadeespana.org and https://www.webislam.com (both accessed 9 Dec. 2017).

Chapter 2. Political Influence in Religion

396. In Spain, the government does not control the life religious communities or, more generally, the religious lives of citizens. In the Ministry of Justice, there is a department with specific competence to deal with religious juridical persons and, in general, with competence on religious freedom issues: the Vice-Directorate General of Relations with Religious Communities, which is part of the Directorate General of International Legal Cooperation and Relations with Religious Communities.[514] In former governments, and for many years until 2010, this department had the rank of Directorate General and carried a name that was indicative of a different – and broader – understanding of its functions: Directorate General on Religious Affairs. Its function, however, is not to control religion in Spain but to facilitate and organize the relationships of cooperation between the government and religious communities, in application of Article 16.3 CE, as well to take the appropriate measures for a better protection of religious freedom of individuals and groups.

397. Article 14 CE (principle of non-discrimination) and Article 16.2 CE (prohibition of coercion on individuals to declare about their religion or belief) are supposed to act as a shield against hypothetical interferences from the state. In addition, Article 6 LOLR specifically guarantees the autonomy of religious communities with respect to their internal affairs. This includes their self-organization and they appointment of their leaders and ministers.

398. There are some partial exceptions in the case of the Catholic Church. As explained above,[515] the old privilege of the Spanish King to intervene in the appointment of bishops was abolished by the 1976 Agreement with the Holy See, and since then this matter is of 'the exclusive competence of the Holy See'. However, the Catholic Church is obliged to notify the government the name of a newly elected bishop prior to his appointment, in case the government wants to express some political objection (which the Holy See is not bound to accept). Moreover, the appointment of the Vicar General for the Army (*Vicario General Castrense*) continues to be appointed according to a system similar to the one stipulated in 1941 and 1953 – the Spanish government and the Vatican nuncio, by common agreement, propose a tern of names, authorized by the Holy See, out of which the King will choose one and propose him to the Pope for appointment. These rules tend to be justified by historical reasons, as well as by the special social and legal position of the Catholic Church in Spain. In practice, the selection of Vicar General is done by the Catholic Church with full independence.

399. No similar state intervention exists with respect to other religious communities. The government, however, has indirectly intervened once in the organization of religious minorities in Spain. After the promulgation of the LOLR in 1980, when the main minority religious communities took the initiative to begin the negotiations of cooperation agreements with the state – in particular Protestants, Jews and, later, Muslims – the government made very clear to them that it would only negotiate with one interlocutor of the respective religion, i.e., one Protestant interlocutor, one Jewish interlocutor and

514. *See* the Directorate General's site in: http://www.mjusticia.gob.es/cs/Satellite/es/1215197982464/Estructura_P/1215198297241/Detalle.html (accessed 25 Nov. 2017).

515. *See supra* , para. 344.

one Islamic interlocutor. This forced the relevant communities to organize in their respective federations. These three federations were formed for the exclusive purpose of the dialogue with the government, before and after the Agreements. Nevertheless, their representatives have acknowledged that, in the long run, the existence and functioning of the federations has had an influence on the internal life of those religious communities – a positive influence, in their opinion, for it has contributed to create stronger links of collaboration between independent religious communities.

400. There are some administrative controls that are conceived as instruments to facilitate legal certainty in important issues rather than aimed at conditioning or limiting the life and freedom of religious communities. This is the case, for example, of the state controls prior and subsequent to the celebration of religious marriages, established in the relevant cooperation agreements, and in Article 60 CC, as a requisite for their civil effects.[516] It is the case also of the Registry of Religious Entities, which is the mechanism through which the state recognizes the legal personality of churches and religious denominations – and which in fact, since a judgment of the Constitutional Court in 2001, does not scrutinize in practice the religious nature of entities applying for registration.[517]

401. As explained below in more detail,[518] the Spanish state provides direct and indirect funding to religious communities, but the system is designed to make it compatible with churches' autonomy, free from state interference. In the case of the Catholic Church this is patent, for tax benefits are clearly stated in the Concordat and in legislation, and the state direct funding relies exclusively on the explicit will of taxpayers when they fill in the income tax form every year. In other words, the government does not have discretion to vary its economic support to the Catholic Church depending on the latter's affinity or lack of affinity with governmental political action or initiatives. Something similar occurs with regard to the tax benefits granted to the religious federations that were signatory of the 1992 Agreements (Protestants, Jews and Muslims), but in this case the direct financing they receive is more dependent on the government's discretion. In 2004, the government created a public foundation (*Pluralismo y Convivencia*), with the main purpose of providing funding to the Evangelical, Jewish and Islamic Federations. As this is a government-controlled foundation, it has been sometimes argued that it could hinder in practice the freedom of those religious communities to express publicly their disagreements with the government apropos of controversial political or legislative measures of moral significance.

---

516. *See infra* , Part X, Ch. 1.
517. *See supra* , Part II, Ch. 4 §2.
518. *See infra* , Part VIII.

Chapter 3. Interaction Between Religion and State on a Political and Legal Level

402. The Advisory Commission on Religious Freedom (CALR), created by the 1980 LOLR, is the main body in which interaction between government and religious communities is supposed to occur. As explained above,[519] this commission is competent to study and give opinions on all legislative and governmental initiatives relating to religious freedom, and one-third of its members are representatives of the main religions existing in the country – those with recognized 'well-known roots' or *notorio arraigo.* Nevertheless, the negotiation of the most important measures affecting the interests of the Catholic Church have often taken place out of the CALR, as, for example, the new conditions for state economic support, or the rules concerning the details of teaching Catholic religion in public schools. For religious minorities, instead, the CALR is a useful forum to manifest their needs and proposals to the government, without prejudice to their respective efforts for parallel bilateral negotiations.

403. In accordance with the international legal personality of the Holy See, the Spanish state and the Vatican have diplomatic relationships. There is a papal nuncio in Madrid, as well as a Spanish ambassador to the Holy See, in Rome. In the numerous times that, since the election of John Paul II, the Pope has visited Spain, he has been received not only as a spiritual leader but also with the honours befitting a head of state.

404. There are diverse expressions of the interaction between Catholic religion and state in public life. The following are just some examples. When public official takes office, he is given the choice between pledging allegiance to the Constitution by oath on the Bible and the crucifix or by promise 'on his conscience and honour'.[520] Many Catholic religious holidays are considered also civil labour holidays at a national, a regional, or a local level – e.g., Christmas, Epiphany, Good Friday, Saint James (patron saint of Spain), the Assumption of the Virgin and Saint Joseph. It is considered normal, in some places, the tradition of a protocolary presence of public authorities, as well as army or police units, in public solemn manifestations of Catholic worship, such as religious processions in Corpus Christi day or during the Holy Week. The Constitutional Court has found nothing unconstitutional in these customary practices, as far that no public official is obliged to take part in religious ceremonies against his will.[521]

405. Although more reduced, there is also interaction between state and other religions. For instance, the public foundation *Pluralismo y Convivencia* has been disseminating, in the last years, a calendar with indication of the festivities of the most important religious communities existing in Spain, including not only Christian (Catholic, Protestant and Orthodox), Jewish and Islamic holidays, but also Mormon, Jehovah's Witnesses and Buddhist holidays. Since 2004, Spain commemorates the Holocaust Remembrance Day in January; on that date, there are various public

---

519. *See supra* , Part II, Ch. 4 §3.
520. *See supra* , Part II, Ch. 2 §11 I.
521. *See supra* , para. 96.

commemorations in Spanish cities, in national and regional legislatures – with particular solemnity in Madrid – with the presence of representatives of the Jewish communities together with high public officials.

406. Religious leaders or ministers are not subject to any disqualification to stand for elections or to become public officials. No religious leader is appointed as such for a position in state bodies, with the exception, for obvious reasons, of the Advisory Commission on Religious Freedom.

Part VI. Labour Law Within Religious Communities

Chapter 1. Scope of Application of Labour Law

407. Religious communities are considered a specific type of entities by Spanish law. Insofar as they are actually committed to religious activities they are not considered enterprises or companies. As a consequence, the tendency is to exclude from the common rules of labour law the relationships that take place inside a religious community to the extent that they refer to its spiritual mission and to its religious ministers. In those cases, out of respect for religious autonomy, it is assumed that the relationship is governed by the internal rules of each religious community, which vary greatly from one community to another. Instead, labour law is applied to religious communities when they act as employers and hire the services of other people for non-religious activities. In any event, the Spanish law endeavours to guarantee the welfare rights of both religious ministers and employees.

Chapter 2. Religious Ministers and Labour Law

408. The type of relationship between a religious minister and his respective religious community varies depending on each community. In Spanish law, it is normally accepted that this relationship is out of the boundaries of state labour law and governed by the internal rules of the relevant religious denomination. Neither ministers are deemed employees, nor religious communities are deemed employers. This is the position of the Spanish courts with particular reference to those activities of religious ministers that are part of their religious compromises and mission, such as worship or spiritual assistance.[522] The Constitutional Court has taken a similar stance with regard to the activities performed by members of religious orders in service of their respective communities, confirming the precedent case law of labour courts.[523]

409. An analogous notion applies to the relationship of religious ministers with public or private institutions when they perform the spiritual activities corresponding to their ministry – for instance, religious assistance and worship in prisons or hospitals, which, in the case of public institutions, are regulated by specific agreements between the state and religious denominations.[524] The understanding is that the nature of the service is spiritual and the application of labour law would be inadequate. The Spanish Constitutional Court has excluded from the scope of labour law even the relationship between a member of a Catholic religious order or congregation and a school run by her institution, even though that person worked as ordinary teacher and performed educational tasks comparable to those performed by her lay colleagues in the same school. According to the Court, all the activity done by the religious was permeated by and had to be seen in the light of her religious compromise and vows; she was not just doing a job for the school, she was complying with the religious mission assigned by her superiors, and indeed her religious condition was the very reason why she performed those teaching tasks at the school.[525]

410. Naturally, when the work of religious ministers is not directly related to their religious status and mission – for instance, a history teacher at a public school or at a university – their relationship with the relevant institution is governed by common labour law.

411. Religious ministers, as well as professed member of religious orders, of foreign citizenship are exempted from the obligation to obtain a working permit to the purpose of their legal residence in Spain, as far as they meet the following requirements: (a) they must belong to a religious community duly registered in the Registry of Religious Entities; (b) their activities in Spain must be strictly of religious nature; and (c) their respective religious communities must take care of their maintenance. This

522. *See* STS 3946/2001, 14 May 2001, FJ 3.
523. *See* STC 63/1994, FJ 4.
524. *See supra* , Part III, Ch. 6.
525. *See* STC 63/1994, FJ 4.

exemption does not apply to seminarists, persons in period of training to become ministers, or members of religious orders who are not professed yet.[526]

412. Since the late 1970s, the tendency in Spanish law is to include religious ministers in the social security system in order to guarantee their welfare rights in case of health problems or old age. The social security benefits of the Catholic clergy are not regulated by the Concordat. In 1977, the Catholic clergy were integrated into the social security system under conditions equivalent to those of employees (*trabajadores por cuenta ajena*).[527] Taking into account the ordinary circumstances of Catholic priests, certain welfare rights were excluded, among them the unemployment benefits and the extension of welfare benefits to the family; the latter exclusion, however, was eliminated in 2007 in view of the circumstances of Greek-Latin priests and situations of family placement, but exclusion of benefits for maternity and paternity remains, as well as social security protection in case of temporal inability to work.[528] The relevant diocese must assume the social security obligations of the employer. In 1981, members of Catholic religious orders were also integrated into the social security system as self-employed persons (*trabajadores autónomos o por cuenta propia*).[529] In 1998, the government produced two regulations to make possible that all secularized Catholic priests and religious persons had access to retirement pensions; to that purpose their years of religious service were computed as years of employment and payment of social security quotas; if they did not reach the minimum required number of fifteen years, they were given the opportunity to contribute the missing annuities in order to be entitled to receive a retirement pension.[530]

413. The 1992 Agreements with the Evangelical, Jewish and Islamic Federations (Article 5) provided that the religious ministers of those communities should be integrated into the social security system as employees (*trabajadores por cuenta ajena*), and that the relevant religious community should assume the obligations of employers. The Agreement with the Jewish Federation specifically indicated that the social security status of rabbis would be the same as the status of the Catholic clergy, and that their social security protection would extend to their families. The provisions of the 1992 Agreements have been implemented for Evangelical and Muslim ministers, in 1999

526. *See* Article 41.1.h) *Ley Orgánica* 4/2000, 11 Jan. 2000, *sobre derechos y libertades de los extranjeros en España y su integración social*, modified by *Ley Orgánica* 2/2009, and Article 117.h) *Real Decreto* 557/2011, 20 Apr. 2011.

527. *See Real Decreto* 2398/1977, 27 Aug. 1977, *por el que se regula la Seguridad Social del Clero*.

528. *See Real Decreto* 1613/2007, 7 Dec. 2007, *por el que se modifica el Real Decreto 2398/1977, de 27 de agosto, por el que se regula la Seguridad Social del Clero*

529. *See Real Decreto* 3325/1981, 29 Dec. 1981, *por el que se incorpora al Régimen Especial de la Seguridad Social de los Trabajadores por Cuenta propia o Autónomos a los religiosos y religiosas de la Iglesia Católica.*

530. *See Real Decreto* 487/1998, 27 Mar. 1998, *sobre reconocimiento, como cotizados a la Seguridad Social, de periodos de actividad sacerdotal o religiosa de los sacerdotes y religiosos o religiosas de la Iglesia Católica secularizados*, complemented by *Real Decreto* 2665/1998, 11 Dec. 1998.

and 2006, respectively.[531] Unemployment benefits are excluded from their social security protection, but not maternity and paternity benefits. In 2012, a judgment of the European Court of Strasbourg held that an Evangelical minister had the same rights as those recognized by the law to Catholic secularized priests and religious persons in order to complete the annuities necessary to reach the minimum number of years legally required to receive a retirement pension.[532] In application of this judgment of the ECtHR, in 2015 the Spanish government modified the regulation of 1999 with a new royal decree,[533] which the Supreme Court has partly declared null and void as discriminatory because it did not completely equalize the Social Security rights of Evangelical ministers vis-à-vis former Catholic priests – the latter were permitted to contribute to complete the maximum possible number of years while the former could only complete the minimum number of annuities.[534]

414. Beyond the cooperation agreements system, the government has provided for the integration of religious ministers into the social security system in the case of Jehovah's Witnesses and Russian Orthodox priests, in conditions similar to the Catholic priests, i.e., they are considered employees (*trabajadores por cuenta ajena*), and benefits in situations of unemployment, maternity and temporary inability to work are specifically excluded. The social security obligations of employers are assumed, respectively, by the Church of Jehovah's Witnesses and by the Moscow Patriarchate.[535]

531. *See Real Decreto* 369/1999, 5 Mar. 1999, *sobre términos y condiciones de inclusión en el Régimen General de la Seguridad Social de los Ministros de Culto de las Iglesias pertenecientes a la Federación de Entidades Religiosas Evangélicas de España*; and *Real Decreto* 176/2006, 10 Feb. 2006, *sobre términos y condiciones de inclusión en el Régimen General de la Seguridad Social de los dirigentes religiosos e imames de las comunidades integradas en la Comisión Islámica de España*. No such implementation has taken place with respect to the social security of rabbis. It seems that, at least in some communities, rabbis are hired by the respective community with an ordinary labour contract and the community pays their social security accordingly.

532. *Manzanas Martin v. Spain*, 3 Apr. 2012. *See supra*, para. 377.

533. *See Real Decreto* 839/2015, 21 Sep. 2015, which modifies the RD 369/1999.

534. *See* STS 3988/2017, 13 Nov. 2017.

535. *See Real Decreto* 1614/2007, 7 Dec. 2007, *por el que se regulan los términos y las condiciones de inclusión en el Régimen General de la Seguridad Social de los miembros de la Orden religiosa de los Testigos de Jehová en España*; and *Real Decreto* 822/2005, 8 Jul. 2005, *por el que se regulan los términos y las condiciones de inclusión en el Régimen General de la Seguridad Social de los clérigos de la Iglesia Ortodoxa Rusa del Patriarcado de Moscú en España*.

Chapter 3. Other Church Employees and Labour Law

415. Leaving aside religious ministers or members of religious orders, the relationship between churches and their employees is subject to the ordinary rules of labour law, including the prohibition of discrimination contained in the Statute of Workers and in the EU Council Directive 2000/78 EC.[536] The same applies to the employees of institutions run or explicitly inspired by religious communities, such as hospitals or schools. It should be taken into account, however, that the labour relationship in these cases is nuanced by the employees' duty of loyalty and respect for the religious rules or ethos of the relevant community or institution, protected by Article 6 LOLR. With regard in particular to private religious schools, funded or not with public money, Spanish laws on education have always recognized their right to have their own ethos, which must be accepted by the teachers and other staff, as well as by the students and the students' parents.[537]

416. The most frequent conflicts between churches and employees have arisen apropos of the situation of religion teachers in public schools, and in particular teachers of Catholic religion. As explained below in more detail,[538] the Concordat provides that Catholic religion must be offered, as an elective subject, in all public schools and shall be taught by teachers authorized by the competent diocesan bishop. These teachers are hired and paid by the state, and not by the Catholic Church. Therefore, there is not a labour relationship between religion teacher and the Church, for teachers are employees of a public educational centre. However, diocesan bishops are competent to propose every year the persons appropriate for teaching Catholic religion. Thus, the ecclesiastical decision on the teachers' qualification determines if they can remain or not in their position. Once granted, the proposal of teachers are automatically renewed every year – as well as their annual labour contracts with the state – but the bishop can remove a teacher that he considers is no longer adequate for that task. To fully understand the bishops' position, it is important to keep in mind that religion teachers in public schools are supposed to teach religious doctrines on behalf of the Catholic Church, fulfilling an ecclesiastical mission; they provide a confessional religious instruction and do not teach courses based on a neutral or purely academic approach to religion.

417. Occasional problems have arisen when some persons have been deprived from their ecclesiastical permission to teach religion not because of lack of pedagogical capabilities but because their behaviour out of school was known to infringe serious moral principles of the Catholic Church or to act against the interests of the Church. The relevant bishops, in those cases, considered that such a contradiction between the example of life they offered and the doctrines they taught at school necessarily had an impact on the efficacy of religious instruction, in addition to constituting a scandal. Consequently, the bishops withdrew their authorization to teach religion, as a way to protect the credibility of the Church as well as the rights of the parents that chose that school subject for their children.

---

536. *See supra*, paras 222–224 and 227.
537. *See*, in more detail, *infra*, Part IX, Ch. 2.
538. *See infra*, Part IX, Ch. 1 §1

418. Some cases of this type have reached the Constitutional Court. The first of them, decided in 2007, was raised by a divorced woman who cohabited with a man.[539] On this basis, the bishop removed her from the persons proposed for the next academic year to teach Catholic religion, which she had taught for ten years in various public schools. The Court decided in favour of the Church's autonomy and held that ecclesiastical authorities were free to judge when a person was or was not appropriate to teach Catholic religion on behalf of the Catholic Church in a public school. Such judgment, in the Court's view, could be based not only on the teacher's pedagogical skills, or on the doctrine actually explained in class, but could also take into account the teacher's personal circumstances of moral relevance, considering that teaching religion goes beyond the mere communication of knowledge and implies transmitting a faith that must be somehow evinced by a personal testimony of life. Nevertheless, the Court added that, existing a labour contract between the religion teacher and a public institution, the ecclesiastical autonomy was not complete or free from control by the state jurisdiction. On the contrary, according to the Court, as the constitutional rights of the employee were at stake, state courts could – and must – scrutinize if the reasons that justified the bishop's decision were of religious nature or not. In the present case, the Court concluded that the bishop had acted on the basis of religious and moral reasons, and the state could not supervise or interfere with the ecclesiastical judgment, for otherwise it would infringe on religious autonomy and violate the principle of state religious neutrality.

419. Other Constitutional Court's decisions of 2007 resolved eleven 'questions of unconstitutionality' (*cuestiones de inconstitucionalidad*)[540] with an analogous reasoning, always asserting the autonomy of ecclesiastical authorities to judge freely on the qualification of religion teachers. All those questions had been addressed by the same court – the Superior Court of Justice of Canarias – challenging some articles of the Concordat and some provisions of a general act on education of 1990 that implemented the Concordat. At the origin of those questions was the withdrawal of the ecclesiastical permission to teach religion from persons that had been actively involved in protests, strikes and demonstrations against policies on religion teachers.[541]

420. Also in 2007, and again with a similar rationale, the Constitutional Court rejected the appeal of another religion teacher that was no longer proposed by his bishop because of a conduct considered contrary to the doctrine and interests of the Catholic Church.[542] In this case, the plaintiff was a former priest who had worked as teacher of Catholic religion in public schools – with the bishop's authorization – following his abandonment of priesthood and subsequent civil marriage. Six years after he began to teach religion, the Holy See conceded his canonical secularization and dispensation from celibacy. Following the Vatican's decree, the diocesan bishop

539. STC 38/2007.

540. A question of unconstitutionality is different from an 'appeal for protection' or *recurso de amparo* (*see supra* , para. 137); the Constitutional Court intervenes not to resolve an appeal filed by a plaintiff but upon request of an ordinary court that, having found a legal provision or a public action unconstitutional in the course of a judicial process under its jurisdiction, remits the question to the Constitutional Court for consideration.

541. *See* STC 80/2007 to 90/2007, all of them of the same date, 19 Apr. 2007.

542. STC 128/2007.

decided that the plaintiff should no longer be proposed as religion teacher, with the consequence that he was dismissed from his position at a public school. The reason alleged by the bishop was that the decree of secularization explicitly indicated that former priests should not be allowed to teach Catholic religion in public schools, unless the relevant bishop thought otherwise and there was no danger of scandal. In this case, the bishop could not ignore that there was risk of scandal, because of the ex-priest's active and public involvement in a 'movement pro optional celibacy' of Catholic clergy. The European Court of Strasbourg confirmed in 2012 and 2014[543] the Constitutional Court's judgment, holding that, in those circumstances, the autonomy of the Catholic Church to freely decide who is appropriate to teach its doctrines on its behalf prevails over the applicant's right to privacy and family life (Article 8 ECHR). The European Court also remarked that interfering with an ecclesiastical decision adopted on religious and moral grounds was incompatible with the necessary state neutrality on issues concerning the internal autonomy of religious communities.

421. In 2011, the Constitutional Court decided another case of withdrawal of ecclesiastical permit from a religion teacher on moral grounds relating to her private life.[544] Interestingly, the Court affirmed the same principles stated in the 2007 judgments but reached the opposite conclusion notwithstanding that the facts were very similar. The plaintiff was a woman that was removed from the list of persons qualified to teach religion because she had contracted civil marriage with a divorced person, who was also a Catholic (civil divorce is not recognized by the Catholic Church as a valid mechanism of dissolution of a religious marriage; under Roman canon law, Catholics bound by a canonical marriage may not legitimately marry a third person unless they obtain a declaration of nullity from an ecclesiastical court or a dissolution of marriage from the Pope in case of an unconsummated union). The Constitutional Court accepted that the bishop has acted on religious grounds, but counterbalanced religious autonomy with the constitutional right of the dismissed teacher – in particular her right to the 'free development of personality' (Article 10.1 CE), her right to marriage (Article 32 CE), and her right to the 'respect for private and family life' (Article 8 ECHR). The Court concluded that it would be discriminatory to make the plaintiff choose between keeping her job or exercising her fundamental rights, and therefore the latter should prevail over the religious freedom of ecclesiastical authorities to decide which persons are appropriate to teach religion in public schools on behalf of the Catholic Church. This decision of the Constitutional Court has raised some criticism among scholars[545] because, among other reasons, it emphasizes the significance of the labour situation of the plaintiff and ignores the constitutional basis of the current system of teaching Catholic religion in public schools, namely the principle of state cooperation with religion (Article 16.3 CE) and the parents' right to ensure for their children a religious and moral education in accordance with their convictions (Article 27.3 CE). From that

543. *Fernández Martínez v. Spain*, 15 May 2012 and (GC) 12 Jun. 2014. *See supra* , para. 378. The European Court took an identical approach in a subsequent judgment, *Travaš v. Croatia*, 4 Oct. 2016.

544. STC 51/2011.

545. *See* , for instance, M. Gas Aixendri, *La declaración canónica de idoneidad para la enseñanza de la religión católica y su control jurisdiccional por parte del Estado*, 29 Revista General de Derecho Canónico y Derecho Eclesiástico del Estado 1–17 (2012).

perspective, it seems contradictory to permit a person to teach a religious doctrine *on behalf of a church* that has explicitly disqualified her from that task. Nevertheless, in 2016, the Supreme Court, after making clear that the no renovation of the annual contract of a religion teacher should be equalled to a dismissal, declared null and void the dismissal of another female teacher in a similar situation (contracting civil marriage with a divorced man).[546] Ignoring the crucial aspect that teachers of Catholic religion in public schools perform a strictly religious function regulate by the Code of Canon Law and other ecclesiastical rules, the Court treated the case as an ordinary labour contract and held that the fundamental rights of the teacher have been violated because the bishop did not provide sufficient motivation for his decision to remove the plaintiff from the list of eligible religion teachers.[547]

546. *See* STS 876/2016, 20 Oct. 2016.
547. For an extensive analysis of the diverse legal interests that converge in this type of cases, *see* I. Leigh and J. Martínez-Torrón, *supra* , note 489.

Part VII. Religious Communities and Protections of the Individual

Chapter 1. Protection of Privacy

422. The autonomy rights of religious communities comprise the protection of their right to handle their own internal affairs free from state or other external interferences, including the *confidentiality of their communications and files*. With regard to the Catholic Church, the inviolability of ecclesiastical archives is explicitly recognized in broad terms by Article I.6 of the Agreement on Juridical Affairs between Spain and the Holy See:

> The state respects and protects the inviolability of archives, registrics and other documents that belong to the Spanish Bishops Conference, to episcopal offices, to the offices of high superiors of religious orders and congregations, to parishes and to other ecclesiastical institutions or entities.

Article 2.3 of the 1992 Agreement with the Islamic Federation uses a similar language to guarantee the inviolability of archives and documents of the Spanish Islamic Commission (*Comisión Islámica de España*) and of the Muslim communities that are a part thereof. No such provision exists in the 1992 Agreements with the Jewish and Evangelical Federations, but Article 6 LOLR (religious autonomy) should be interpreted as implicitly guaranteeing the same inviolability to all registered religious denominations.

423. Article 16.2 of the Constitution protects the right of individuals to keep their religion or belief private – 'Nobody shall be obliged to declare about his ideology, religion or beliefs.' This constitutional provision must be understood in the Spanish historical context, often characterized by religious (or anti-religious) discrimination and sometimes persecution. Articles 16.2 CE is consistent with the Strasbourg case law, which considers incompatible with the ECHR any rule or practice that forces citizens, directly or indirectly, to reveal their religion or belief.[548] The Spanish praxis has understood this protection of individual religious privacy as prohibiting the elaboration of a religious census. This is the reason why there are not official statistics about religious affiliation in Spain. The only available data are those obtained through the information given by the religious communities – perhaps not always precise – and

548. *See* J. Martínez-Torrón, *Manifestations of Religion or Belief in the Case Law of the European Court of Human Rights*, 12 Religion and Human Rights 117–118 (2017).

through the monthly surveys performed by the Centre of Sociological Research (which also have an undetermined error rate).[549]

424. Tensions may occasionally emerge between individuals' right to privacy and their membership of or their relationship with a religious community. Two concrete issues in this regard have been taken to the Spanish courts in the last years. One is the claim of some people who, alleging their freedom of religious choice and their right to privacy, asserted their right to oblige their former church to recognize formally their withdrawal or apostasy. The other is the situation of religion teachers in public schools who, on the ground of behaviour regarding their private and family life that was deemed gravely immoral, were deprived from the ecclesiastical authorization to teach Catholic religion on behalf of the Church. The latter issue is analysed in other pages of this monograph.[550]

425. The issue of apostasy was raised in Spain, in the mid-2000s, by persons that, having formally abandoned their Catholic faith, required ecclesiastical authorities to completely remove or 'cancel' their data from baptism registries,[551] alleging their rights under the data protection laws.[552] To some extent, this was an organized initiative, nurtured by some political and ideological movements, in which several hundred people participated. The response from the competent ecclesiastical authorities – diocesan bishops – was unanimously negative in all cases, based on three concurring grounds. First, the Catholic Church's right to its religious autonomy includes the inviolability of ecclesiastical archives, as specifically recognized by the Concordat.[553] Second, ecclesiastical registries of baptism cannot be considered 'personal data filing systems' either from the perspective of Spanish law[554] or from the perspective of European Union law,[555] for they are not 'structured sets of personal data which are accessible according to specific criteria'. And third, the entries about the baptism of people do not properly constitute personal data but just records of historical facts that, in themselves, do not convey information on the current belief or religious choices of baptized persons; from the Catholic Church's perspective, baptism is like a new birth to supernatural life and, therefore, a person's request to erase the record of baptism is as groundless as a request to erase his civil record of birth.

426. The complex administrative and judicial itinerary of the aforementioned claims includes some resolutions of the Spanish Agency for Data Protection (*Agencia*

549. *See supra* , paras 12–17.
550. *See supra* , paras 416–421.
551. *See* M. Gas Aixendri, *Apostasía y libertad religiosa: conceptualización jurídica del abandono confesional* (Comares 2012); B. González Moreno, *El derecho fundamental a la protección de datos personales: su contenido y límites respecto al bautismo y la apostasía*, and F. Pérez-Madrid, *Protección de datos personales y apostasía*, both in 19 Revista General de Derecho Canónico y Derecho Eclesiástico del Estado (2009); J. Otaduy, *Iglesia católica y Ley española de protección de datos: falsos conflictos*, 48 Ius Canonicum 117–140 (2008).
552. The basic law on this matter is the Organic Law on the Protection of Personal Data (*Ley Orgánica* 15/1999, 13 Dec. 1999, *de protección de datos de carácter personal*).
553. *See* Art. I.6 of the 1979 Agreement on Juridical Affairs.
554. *See Ley Orgánica* 15/1999, Art. 3.b).
555. *See* Directive 95/46/EC of the European Parliament and of the Council of 24 Oct. 1995 on the protection of individuals with regard to the processing of personal data and on the free movement of such data, especially Art. 2.c).

Española de Protección de Datos) ordering to the relevant bishop to add a 'side annotation' on the baptism entry stating that the baptized person 'had exercised his right to the cancellation' of his entry. These resolutions were confirmed by the National Court (*Audiencia Nacional*) in 2007,[556] but were subsequently revoked by the Supreme Court in 2008.[557] The Supreme Court based its decision on the fact that the ecclesiastical registries of baptism could not be considered 'personal data filing systems' (*ficheros*) under the current legislation. The reason is that they are a mere 'accumulation of [personal data] that makes difficult their search, access or identification, for they are not organized either alphabetically or by date of birth, but only by date of baptism, so that it is absolutely necessary to know the parish in which the christening was performed; in addition, [baptism data] are not accessible to any other person different from the baptized, and no third party can request a baptism certificate'.[558] The Court, having decided in favour of the ecclesiastical authorities, did not consider necessary to analyse the issue from the perspectives of religious autonomy and the inviolability of ecclesiastical archives guaranteed by the Concordat, thus leaving unresolved two very important legal questions in dispute.

556. *See* SAN 4111/2007 and other similar decisions of the same date.
557. *See* STS 4646/2008, 19 Sep. 2008. Many other similar judgments have followed.
558. *Ibid.*, FJ 4.

Chapter 2. Freedom to Marry

427. Article 32 of the Constitution recognizes the right to marry:

Article 32 CE:

1. Men and women have the right to contract marriage with full legal equality.
2. The law shall regulate the forms of marriage, the age and legal capacity to contract marriage, the rights and duties of spouses, the causes for separation and dissolution as well as their effects.

428. The Civil Code, after its reform in 1981,[559] grants individuals free choice between celebrating their marriage in civil form or in any of the religious forms recognized by state law.[560] If the marriage takes place abroad, or if it is celebrated between foreign citizens, other religious forms may be acceptable in accordance with the law of the place of celebration or with the personal law of the parties.[561] As explained below in more detail,[562] until 2015 there were *four religious forms of marriage recognized with civil effects*, in application of cooperation agreements with the state: Catholic, Evangelical, Jewish and Islamic.[563] After its modification in 2015, Article 60 of the Civil Code grants civil effects also to the religious forms of marriage of those religious communities that have obtained a recognition of well-known roots in Spain (*notorio arraigo*); so far, well-known roots have been recognized to the Mormon Church, Jehovah's Witnesses, Buddhists and Orthodox Churches.[564] People who have contracted a valid religious marriage in any of those forms do not need to celebrate an additional civil ceremony to have their marriage recognized by the state law – they only need to register their marriage in the Civil Registry.

429. Religious communities are free to apply their own rules on marriage and therefore have discretion to accept or reject candidates to the celebration of a religious marriage. They are not obliged to consent to the religious marriage of persons that comply with the civil requirements of marriage but not with the relevant religious requirements, which are normally more demanding. For example, religious communities are not compelled to accept the religious celebration of a same-sex marriage – valid in Spanish civil law since 2005[565] – if this is against their internal rules on marriage; neither are they required to accept the celebration of a projected marriage against which there is a religious impediment that does not exist in civil law.

559. The reform was operated by the *Ley* 30/1981, 7 Jul. 1981.
560. Cf. Arts 49 and 59–60 CC.
561. Cf. Arts 49–50 CC.
562. *See infra*, Part X, Ch. 1.
563. *See*, respectively, Art. VI of the Agreement on Juridical Affairs between Spain and the Holy See; and Art. 7 of the 1992 Agreements with the Evangelical, Jewish and Islamic Federations.
564. *See supra*, paras 302-303.
565. Cf. *Ley* 13/2005, 1 Jul. 2005, *por la que se modifica el Código Civil en materia de derecho a contraer matrimonio.*

430. Spouses bound by a religious marriage with civil effects and wishing to terminate their marital relationship for the purposes of civil law can freely choose to go to state courts to ask for the separation, nullity or dissolution of their marriage.[566] In that case, the civil courts shall apply the provisions of the Civil Code and follow the ordinary rules of civil procedure. The spouses may choose to go instead to the relevant religious jurisdiction but only the decisions of the Catholic jurisdiction will be recognized civil effects, through a specific procedure of execution (*exequatur*), in accordance with the provisions of the Concordat and the Civil Code.[567] The nullity or dissolution of religious marriages other than Catholic can be decreed by the respective religious jurisdiction but those decisions shall not have civil effects; they will be relevant only for conscience purposes, or as a necessary condition required by the relevant religious law to celebrate a new marriage; the parties must go to the state courts if they want that to have their marriage terminated under Spanish civil law.

431. As civil and religious jurisdictions have reciprocal autonomy and apply their own legal rules, neither of them is conditioned by the other's marriage law. Thus, just as the state jurisdiction is not bound to recognize civil effects to the decisions of religious jurisdictions – save for the Catholic courts under certain circumstances – religious communities are not bound to recognize the effects of a civil dissolution or nullity. For instance, people who celebrated a Catholic or Jewish marriage and obtained a civil divorce from their spouse can be – and normally will be – required to obtain, respectively, an ecclesiastical judgment of nullity or a repudiation in conformity with Jewish law before they are permitted to contract a new religious marriage with a third person.

566. Cf. Arts 73, 81 and 85 CC.

567. *See infra*, Part X, Ch. 1 §2

Chapter 3. Freedom of Expression

432. The fundamental right to freedom of expression is guaranteed to all individuals, irrespective of their situation vis-à-vis a given religious community. Free expression includes the right of individuals and groups to freely criticize the doctrines of a religion or the acts of members or authorities of a religious community. In addition to the sanctions specifically provided by the Criminal Code apropos of anti-religious offensive speech,[568] freedom of expression with respect to religious communities is subject to the common limitations on this fundamental right established in Spanish law – which include criminal law penalties for hate speech.[569]

433. Members of a religious community are also free to express their disagreement with the official doctrines or with the policies adopted by the hierarchy of their church. However, religious communities' autonomy implies their right to sanction or expel those of their members that use a speech deemed unacceptable. The state law does not recognize any right to remain within a religious community in a position of heterodoxy.[570]

434. In some cases, religions teachers' expressions of criticism against ecclesiastical authorities or discipline has led the relevant bishop to stop proposing them as persons qualified to teach Catholic religion in public schools. In those cases, the Constitutional Court has maintained that religious autonomy should prevail and held that bishops acted within their legitimate competences.[571]

568. *See infra* , para. 482. *See* , on this issue, F. Pérez-Madrid, *Conflictos entre libertad religiosa y libertad de expresión en el nuevo código penal*, in, *La libertad religiosa y de conciencia ante la justicia constitucional* 761–763 (J. Martínez-Torrón ed., Comares 1998).

569. *See infra* , paras 483–484.

570. *See supra* , para. 113.

571. *See supra* , paras 419–420.

Chapter 4. Due Process Norms and Religious Groups

435. Religious communities, as well as their ministers and other members, are subject to the same state laws than the rest of the citizens and to the state jurisdiction. In former times, Article XVI of the 1953 Concordat, signed in the times of Franco's regime, had confirmed the traditional 'benefit of clergy' (*privilegium fori*). According to this privilege, holding a criminal trial against a priest or a religious person required the prior authorization of the relevant diocesan bishop; in addition, the high clergy could not be brought before a state court – criminal or civil – without the ad hoc licence of the Holy See. The 1976 Agreement between Spain and the Holy See abolished that article of the old Concordat and provided that Catholic clergy and members of religious orders could be brought to state courts as accused in a criminal procedure as any other citizen. The sole condition imposed by the 1976 Agreement was to notify it to their ecclesiastical ordinary (the Holy See, if the accused was a bishop).[572]

436. Religious autonomy protects the right of religious communities to manage their own internal affairs. This includes the application of their respective legal systems or statutes through the relevant procedures. As far as they refer to exclusively religious issues, decisions adopted by religious jurisdictions cannot be appealed to civil jurisdiction and the state cannot interfere with religious procedures and impose its own concept and criteria of due process. Instead, the state may, and must, intervene when they involve rights or legal interests protected by state laws. This was, for instance, the situation in the *Pellegrini* case,[573] decided by the ECtHR in 2001, related to the civil effects recognized by Italian law to an ecclesiastical summary declaration of nullity of a canonical marriage. In its judgment, the European Court considered that the applicant had not been granted adequate opportunity to be heard and present her case before the ecclesiastical jurisdiction; and, as the civil recognition of the matrimonial nullity declared by the ecclesiastical judgment had a significant impact on the economic maintenance that the applicant should receive from her husband, the ECtHR held that that such civil recognition of an ecclesiastical decision taken without due respect for the adversarial principle constituted a violation of Article 6.1 ECHR (right to a fair trial, which embraces the right to a fair hearing by a court).[574]

437. As explained below in more detail,[575] judgments of Catholic ecclesiastical courts declaring a canonical marriage null and void, as well as pontifical dissolutions of unconsummated marriages, are recognized civil effects in Spain under the condition that a state court declares them 'in conformity with the state law'. This control of conformity includes the verification that the ecclesiastical decision was rendered following a procedure that duly guaranteed the parties' right of defence. Such scrutiny of ecclesiastical decisions by the civil courts is not deemed a state interference in

572. *See supra*, para. 344.
573. *Pellegrini v. Italy*, 20 Jul. 2001.
574. The issue of religious autonomy and its relationship with the right to a fair trial has been revisited by the ECtHR in two recent judgments adopted by a divided Court: *Károly Nagy v. Hungary*, 1 Dec. 2015 (Chamber) and 14 Sep. 2017 (Grand Chamber). The case involved the disciplinary suspension of a pastor by a reformed church.
575. *See infra*, paras 551–555.

religious autonomy, for its purpose is not to supervise the ecclesiastical jurisdiction per se but rather to examine whether ecclesiastical judgments comply with some minimum guarantees derived from the adversarial principle. Otherwise, the civil execution of an ecclesiastical decision could cause an unjustified harm to legitimate legal interests of the other party. No similar scrutiny exists with regard to the decisions of other religious jurisdictions – as the rabbinical or cadi's jurisdictions – for they are not recognized civil effects in Spanish law and therefore their consequences remain in the internal life of the relevant religious community.

Chapter 5. Professional Secrecy

438. Many religious communities have a specific protection of the confidentiality of the relationships and communications between their faithful and their ministers.[576] The latter are specially obliged to keep those communications secret, sometimes under severe spiritual penalties. In the Catholic Church, this obligation is particularly strict when priests receive communications in the context of the sacrament of penance. Thus, canon 983.1 the Code of Canon Law provides: 'The sacramental seal is inviolable; therefore it is absolutely forbidden for a confessor to betray in any way a penitent in words or in any manner and for any reason.' Such obligation of secrecy binds also other people – e.g., interpreters – that have knowledge of sins of sacramental confession for whatever reason (canon 983.2). It is also forbidden to make use of the information received in confession to the detriment of the penitent or for external governance (canon 984). The Code of Canon Law imposes grave sanctions on those who betray the secrecy of penance, including the excommunication *latæ sententiæ*[577] of priests that directly violate the sacramental seal (canon 1388).

439. Information disclosed in the context of religious confidentiality is considered by many legal systems privileged communication, with the consequence that religious ministers are exonerated from any legal obligation to reveal such information even in criminal trials. In Spain, the protection of the clergy-communicant privilege operates on different levels: constitutional, legal, and contractual. Various articles of the Constitution protect this privilege implicitly, in particular Article 16 (religious freedom), Article 18 (right to privacy and to the secret of communications), and Article 24 (right not to testify out of professional secrecy). The Code of Criminal Procedure (*Ley de Enjuiciamiento Criminal*) explicitly protects the confidentiality of religious communications by excusing religious ministers from the obligation to report crimes they have known through that channel (Article 263). The same Code exempts from the obligation to testify in criminal trials 'ecclesiastics and ministers of dissident religions, with regard to facts that have been revealed to them in the exercise of functions of their religious ministry' (Article 417.1).[578] With varying terminology, a similar exemption is guaranteed by the Concordat to Catholic priests and members of religious orders,[579] and by the 1992 cooperation agreements to Evangelical, Jewish and Islamic religious ministers.[580] The exemption contained in these agreements has a more general scope and is not circumscribed to the sphere of criminal procedure. The protection of confidentiality extends not only to the sacrament of penance but also to the exercise of religious ministry or assistance in general.

576. For an extensive study of this issue, *see* R. Palomino, *Derecho a la intimidad y religión: la protección jurídica del secreto religioso* (Comares 1999).

577. In Catholic canon law, *latæ sententiæ* penalties are those imposed automatically on offenders by the mere authority of the law, without the need of a judicial sentence.

578. The peculiar terminology of this article (ministers of *dissident* religions) dates back to the nineteenth century.

579. *See* Art. II.3 of the 1976 Agreement on the renouncement to the presentation of bishops and the benefit of clergy between Spain and the Holy See (*see supra* , paras 343–344).

580. *See* Art. 3.2 of the 1992 Agreements with the Evangelical, Jewish and Islamic Federations.

440. In addition to safeguarding the privacy of religious communications, Spanish law sanctions its violation by religious ministers. In this respect, Article 199.2 of the Criminal Code, which punishes the violation of professional secrecy in general, is applicable to religious ministers:

> Professionals that, with breach of their obligation of secrecy and confidentiality, disclose the secrets of other person shall be punished with the penalty of imprisonment from 1 to 4 years, fine from 12 to 24 months, and specific disqualification from that profession for a period from 2 to 6 years.

441. The case law in these matters is very scarce, probably because the protection of the clergy-communicant privilege is well established in Spanish law. In the few reported cases, the Spanish courts have definitely protected this privilege[581] and understood it in an extensive fashion, so that it covers, in the case of Catholic priests, information revealed to them out of the sacrament of penance and in the broader context of spiritual assistance.[582]

581. *See* STS 7201/1990, 11 Oct. 1990.
582. *See* admissibility decision (*auto*) of the Juzgado de Instrucción Nr. 4, Bergara (Guipúzcoa), of 30 Nov. 1999 (unpublished).

Chapter 6. Medical Deontology

442. The main issues concerning the deontology of medical and in general healthcare professions in Spanish law are conscientious objections to abortion, to the dispensation of some pharmacological products, and to undergo certain medical treatments. Being cases of conscientious objection, they should be examined mainly from the perspective of individual moral choices protected by freedom of conscience. Membership of a religious community, however, maybe of significance in order to provide evidence of the sincerity of the conscience claim. This is the case, for instance, of the opposition of Jehovah's Witnesses to blood transfusions, or of the Catholics' rejection of abortion.

§1. Conscientious Objection to Abortion

443. Conscientious objection to abortion has been an issue in Spain since abortion became partly decriminalized in 1985. Since then abortion can be performed in a public hospital (or in a private hospital) in the circumstances established by law, thus raising the question whether the healthcare personnel is legally obliged to cooperate in that procedure.

444. In 1983, an organic law modifying the Criminal Code was approved by the Spanish parliament. It decriminalized abortion in three circumstances: when pregnancy was a consequence of rape, when the foetus would be predictably born with severe malformations and when the continuation of pregnancy would result in serious danger for the mother's life or health. The law did not contain any specific clause protecting the conscientious objection of physicians and other healthcare personnel to take part in this type of procedures. This was one of the reasons alleged in the 'ex ante' appeal of constitutionality filed by some congressmen, which suspended the application of the law.[583] As indicated above,[584] the Constitutional Court held that such omission was not sufficient ground to declare the statute unconstitutional and recognized the right to conscientious objection in very broad terms, emphasizing at the same time that 'the life of the *nasciturus* is not only protected by the Constitution but it also materializes a central value of the constitutional order'.[585] The law was finally passed and entered into force in 1985.[586]

445. In the years that followed the 1985 law, the Spanish courts – of different jurisdictional levels – have had to adjudicate on a variety of conflicts related to the exercise of conscientious objection to abortion by physicians, midwives or nurses. The most noteworthy of these conflicts referred to: the disciplinary measures taken by a hospital director against a gynaecologist for refusing to continue, while he was

583. The 'ex ante' appeal of constitutionality (*recurso previo de inconstitucionalidad*), which could be presented before a law came into force and suspended the application of the law until the Constitutional Court decided on it, no longer exists in Spain; it was abolished in 1985.

584. *See supra*, para. 166.

585. STC 53/1985, FJ 9.

586. *See Ley Orgánica* 9/1985, 5 Jul. 1985.

on call, an abortion procedure initiated by other colleagues; the refusal of nurses to participate in anaesthetics or other procedures used during abortion; the transfer of healthcare personnel to other hospital services different from gynaecology, which they claimed to be discriminatory and vindictive. The case law of Spanish courts has not been uniform, although it has been, in its largest part, favourable to the objectors' claims.[587]

446. In 2010, a new statute changed substantially the legal regulation of abortion in Spain.[588] If the 1985 law conceived abortion as a conduct that was decriminalized under certain conditions, the 2010 law adopts a perspective focused on the performance of abortion as a 'health service' included in the services provided free of charge by the National Health System, which can be requested by pregnant women once they have reached the age of 16 years. No particular cause is now needed to request an abortion within the first fourteen weeks of pregnancy. In addition, the law permits abortion within the first twenty-two weeks of pregnancy in case of danger for the mother's life or health or risk of severe anomalies in the foetus. No time limit is required to perform an abortion if the anomalies observed in the foetus are 'incompatible with life' or if the foetus suffers from 'an extremely grave and incurable illness'.[589]

447. Article 19.2 of the 2010 law introduced a conscience clause, which was inserted in the draft during the process of introduction of amendments in Congress:

> Healthcare professionals directly involved in the voluntary interruption of pregnancy shall have the right to exercise conscientious objection provided that access to and the functional quality of the service cannot be impaired by the exercise of conscientious objection. The refusal or opposition to perform an intervention of interruption of pregnancy on conscience grounds is always an individual decision of the healthcare personnel directly involved in the performance of the voluntary interruption of pregnancy, which must be expressed in advance and in writing. In any event, healthcare professionals shall dispense appropriate treatment and medical attention to women that need it before and after they have undergone an intervention of interruption of pregnancy.

448. The conscience clause of the 2010 law on abortion has raised criticisms for various reasons. On the one hand, there is the fact that it is circumscribed to healthcare personnel 'directly involved' in abortion, especially taking into account that, in the first fourteen weeks, no medical cause is needed to request an abortion and it is difficult, therefore, to conceive it in rigour as a 'medical service'. On the other hand, the law requires that conscientious objection must be declared in advance and in writing; this has led to the creation of registries of objectors in some regions, which has raised the suspicion of stigmatization – and potential discrimination – of the registered personnel. From the perspective of freedom of conscience, this clause is apparently aimed at restricting the rights of conscientious objectors rather than at

587. *See* , for further details and references, R. Navarro-Valls & J. Martínez-Torrón, *Conflictos entre conciencia y ley*, 150–154.

588. *Ley Orgánica* 2/2010, 3 Mar. 2010, *de salud sexual y reproductiva y de la interrupción voluntaria del embarazo.*

589. *See ibid.*, Arts 13–15.

guaranteeing them; indeed, the clause was inserted into Article 19, whose title is 'measures to guarantee the performance [of abortion] by health services'. Certainly, the dictum of the law contrasts with the doctrine established by the Constitutional Court in 1985, as well as with the deontological codes of the Spanish associations of physicians and nurses, respectively.

449. From an institutional perspective, another controversial aspect of the 2010 law is the provision that imposes the inclusion of compulsory teaching about 'sex and reproductive health' in general, and about the practice of abortion in particular, in the curricula of medical and healthcare studies (Article 8). An equivalent and adapted teaching is also ordered for the entire educational system (Article 9). These provisions immediately generated the opposition of some private universities and some associations of schools with a Catholic ethos.

450. In 2014, the Constitutional Court decided an appeal of inconstitutionality (*recurso de inconstitucionalidad*) filed by more than fifty members of Parliament against a regional law of Navarra that created a registry of conscientious objectors.[590] The Court sustained the constitutionality of the law, whose declared aim was to clarify who among the medical personnel of Navarra were objectors in order to facilitate the organization of public hospitals and ensure that pregnant women wishing an abortion could have it performed. For the Court, the law was a proportionate limitation on the procedural, not the substantial, aspects of freedom of conscience, especially considering that the law guaranteed the confidentiality of the data given by the people who would register as objectors. One of the judges wrote a strong dissenting opinion noting that the experience of the time in which the law had been in force demonstrated that it had a powerful dissuasive impact on conscientious objection in that part of Spain – prior to the law there was a massive objection among health professionals, and four years after registry was created only a gynaecologist had registered as objector. This, in the dissenting judge's opinion, revealed that the fear of discrimination was real and that the effect of the law went beyond the mere procedure and touched on the very substance of freedom of conscience.

§2. Conscientious Objections of Pharmacists

451. Conscientious objections of pharmacists is often aimed at guaranteeing their right not to dispense contraceptive products – those that prevent the fertilization of the ovule or the development of the fertilized ovule. Their conscientious scruples not necessarily are grounded on religious beliefs. Sometimes they are based on pure deontological grounds, as has occurred in the case of levonorgestrel (also known as the 'morning-after pill'), for this chemical, which apparently may have important side effects, can be legally bought in some parts of Spain without prescription, or obtained for free, even by minors.

452. As pharmacists are deemed to provide as a public service, the question arises whether they are legally obliged to sell those products in their pharmacies even

590. STC 151/2014. For a critical comment, *see* R. Navarro-Valls, *Una ocasión perdida. Comentario a la STC de 23 de septiembre de 2014, sobre registro de objetores de conciencia al aborto*, 36 Revista General de Derecho Canónico y Derecho Eclesiástico del Estado 1–7 (2014).

in the case of a serious conflict of conscience. In this regard, he Spanish deontological code of pharmacists of 2001 (*Código de Ética farmacéutica y deontología de la profesión farmacéutica*) guarantees their right to freedom of conscience, indicating that 'the personal responsibility and freedom of pharmacists make them entitled to exercise their right to conscientious objection with respect for the patient's freedom and right to life and health' (Article 28).

453. The pharmacists' right to conscientious objection has been recognized, in general terms, by the laws on the organization of pharmacies enacted by some regional legislatures, such as Galicia, La Rioja or Castilla-La Mancha.[591] These laws provide also that public authorities are obliged to adopt the appropriate measures to ensure that the exercise of conscientious objection will not endanger the health of citizens. Some scholars have remarked that the term 'health' must be interpreted in its proper meaning, without confusing it with the mere legitimate desire to acquire a legal chemical substance; and that the protection of citizens' health must be reconciled with the ad hoc protection of pharmacists' freedom of conscience, with the consequence that it would be inadequate to force a pharmacist to sell a product that can be easily bought elsewhere.[592]

454. Two judicial decisions have incidentally recognized the pharmacists' right to conscientious objection in the particular case of post-coital contraceptives – one of the Supreme Court in 2005[593] and other of the Superior Court of Andalusia in 2007,[594] the latter with explicit reference to Article 28 of the pharmacists' ethical code. In 2015, the Constitutional Court adjudicated on the appeal for protection (*recurso de amparo*) of a pharmacist of a big city (Seville) that refused to store and sell in his pharmacy levonorgestrel as well as condoms, in contravention of the regional laws of Andalusia.[595] He was fined for that reason following a routine inspection performed by a public official. The Court recognized the right to conscientious objection against selling levonorgestrel taking into account that this chemical may have abortive effects. The Court's reasoning was that, if its previous case law had unequivocally recognized the right to object to abortion on moral grounds (in 1985),[596] the pharmacist's infraction of Andalusian laws was a legitimate consequence of the exercise of his freedom of conscience, especially in the case of a city as Seville, where pharmacies are abundant and easily accessible, so that the rights of no potential buyers were actual harmed. However, the Court did not recognize a similar right to conscientious objection with regard to contraceptive products, and even refused to enter into the merits of the

591. *See Comunidad Autónoma de Galicia*, Art. 6 of *Ley* 5/1999, 21 May 1999, *de ordenación farmacéutica*; *Comunidad Autónoma de La Rioja*, Art. 5.10 of *Ley* 8/1998, 16 Jun. 1998, *de ordenación farmacéutica*; *Comunidad Autónoma de Castilla-La Mancha*, Art. 17 of *Ley* 5/2005, 27 Jun. 2005, *de ordenación del servicio farmacéutico*.

592. *See* , for instance, A. González-Varas, *La objeción de conciencia del farmacéutico en la jurisprudencia y su regulación legal en España*, 15 Revista General de Derecho Canónico y Derecho Eclesiástico del Estado 1–18 (2007); A. del Moral García, *Objeción de conciencia y vida humana dependiente*, 4 Anuario Jurídico Villanueva 93–130 (2010).

593. Cf. STS 2505/2005, FJ 5.

594. Cf. STSJ Andalucía 1/2007, FJ 5.

595. STC 145/2015.

596. *See supra* , para. 444.

plaintiff's claim – it merely declared, without further explanation, that 'it does not raise any conflict of conscience of constitutional significance'.[597]

§3. Conscientious Objection to Medical Treatments

455. Conscientious objection to medical treatment is a particularly delicate issue, for the protection of the right to life is often at stake. In addition, it entails the opposition of two different and opposing consciences: on the one hand, the conscience of the objector; and on the other hand, the conscience of the healthcare professional, who normally is inclined to make any possible effort to save the patient's life, considering it a paramount deontological duty.

456. Conscientious objection to medical treatment has usually a religious origin; there are other reasons why people reject medical care, but rejections on specifically moral grounds have almost always an identifiable religious cause. According to some religious beliefs, it is immoral to undergo some medical treatments or procedures. The most well-known cases are Jehovah's Witnesses, which interpret certain passages of the Bible as drastically prohibiting blood transfusions, and Christian Science, which trusts prayer as the principal healing method and consider that conventional medical care is illicit.

I. The Law on the Patient's Autonomy

457. In Spain, there is no specific legislation on conscientious objection to medical treatment but some provisions of the 2002 law on the patient's autonomy[598] are applicable to this type of situations. The law pivots around the widely recognized principle that no medical procedure can be performed without the patient's informed consent (Article 8). There are, however, two exceptions in which physicians can act without the patient's – or anyone else's – consent (Article 9.2). One is the existence of 'danger for the public health', as in epidemics. The other is the 'immediate and grave risk for the physical or psychological integrity of the patient', when 'it is not possible to obtain his authorization'; in this circumstance, physicians can take the appropriate clinical decisions but must, if possible, 'consult' with the patient's family or relatives.

458. In three other situations, the consent of legal representatives can substitute for the patient's consent (Article 9.3): (a) when the patient has been declared legally incompetent; (b) when the patient is unable to adopt autonomous decisions or to understand his state of health; (c) when the patient is a non emancipated minor, less than 16 years, who cannot comprehend the seriousness of the medical intervention;

597. *See* , for a critical analysis of this judgment's rationale, J. Martínez-Torrón, *La objeción de conciencia farmacéutica en la reciente jurisprudencia constitucional española: otra oportunidad perdida*, 39 Revista General de Derecho Canónico y Derecho Eclesiástico del Estado 1–29 (2015).

598. *Ley* 41/2002, 14 Nov. 2002, *básica reguladora de la autonomía del paciente y de derechos y obligaciones en materia de información y documentación clínica.*

in the latter case, however, if he has reached the age of 12, his opinion must be heard by his legal representative before consenting to the medical procedure in question.

459. The cases judged by the Spanish courts have always been related to the conscientious objection of Jehovah's Witnesses to blood transfusions, from diverse perspectives.

II. Objection to Medical Treatment of Adults

460. One of the issues in which it is possible to observe an evolution of the Spanish case law is the judge's power to authorize a blood transfusion explicitly rejected by a conscious adult of sound mind, aware that his refusal put his life in danger. In 1983, the Supreme Court exempted from criminal responsibility the judge that authorized a forceful transfusion to a woman – she and her husband, both Jehovah's Witnesses had repeatedly refused the procedure, and they later sued the judge accusing him of a crime against religious freedom. The Court not only declared that the judge had acted correctly when he deemed that the patient's life was preponderant; it added that, had the judge not given his authorization, he could have then incurred criminal responsibility.[599] The Constitutional Court ratified the Supreme Court's decision, arguing that the protection of health is one of the legitimate limitations on religious freedom.[600]

461. Some scholars have criticized these judicial decisions, noting that in their background there seems to be a wrong perception of Jehovah's Witnesses objection to blood transfusions as equivalent to suicidal intentions.[601] In later decisions, the Constitutional Court has adopted an approach more favourable to the respect for individuals' choices that can put their lives in danger. The turning point in this direction were two judgments of 1990 related to a very different issue, such as hunger strikes commenced by members of a terrorist group while in prison. The Court justified the coercive feeding and medical treatment of the inmates to save their lives because of the public authorities' specific responsibility to preserve the life and health of people under their custody. But it added that medical assistance could be illegitimate if forced on a person that has assumed the risk of death by a voluntary decision that is of his sole concern.[602] This position of the Constitutional Court has influenced subsequent decisions of Spanish courts, which have been since then reluctant to justify or permit the imposition of blood transfusions on adult Jehovah's Witnesses against their will.[603]

599. ATS of 22 Dec. 1983. There is a similar precedent, ATS of 14 Mar. 1979.

600. ATC 369/1984.

601. *See* R. Navarro-Valls & J. Martínez-Torrón, *Conflictos entre conciencia y ley*, 219, as well as other authors there cited.

602. Cf. STC 137/1990, FJ 5, and STC 120/1990, FJ 7.

603. *See* , for instance, ATSJ Madrid, 23 Dec. 1992; AAP Las Palmas (*Sección 2ª*) 143/1999, 7 Sep. 1999, ARP 1999/2584; AAP Vizcaya (*Sección 6ª*) 291/2001, 6 Jul. 2001, ARP 2001/749; AAP Guipúzcoa (*Sección 2ª*) 2053/2005, 18 Mar. 2005, JUR 2005/196739.

III. Objection to Medical Treatment of Minors

462. When patients that must undergo medical treatment are minors, the response of the Spanish courts, in harmony with the dominant trends in comparative law, has been the opposite. Irrespective of how extreme the parents' opposition may be, the courts always grant the authorization requested by the medical team when, according to their professional opinion, the transfusion is indispensable to prevent a serious danger for the life or health of the minor. As the Supreme Court held in 1978, the interest in preserving the minor's right to life takes priority over parental authority.[604] In any event, in 2012, the General Public Prosecutor's office published a circular with clear and specific criteria to follow in those cases. In principle, in cases of serious danger for minors' health or life, if their parents or legal representatives do not agree to the treatment, the physicians in charge must obtain judicial authorization but are allowed to intervene on their own initiative in emergency situations. This rule applies also to mature minors (16–17 years old).[605]

463. While the power of judges in these cases is not debated, the parents' religious objection to have their children submitted to a blood transfusion, even in emergency situations, have raised other more controversial questions, in and out of Spain. One of the questions is the relevance of parents' religion when a court decides on which of them is more adequate to be awarded the custody of the children. This was precisely the situation in the *Hoffmann* case, decided by the ECtHR in 1993. The European Court – by a five-to-four decision – held that it was constitutive of religious discrimination to take into account the fact that the mother was Jehovah's Witness, for there were other ways to prevent and deal with the risks derived from a hypothetical need to perform blood transfusions in the children in the future.[606] In Spain, the Supreme Court had decided in 1980 in the opposite direction, i.e., indicating that it was logical to take into account the parents' beliefs among a variety of factors, as far as they could entail a possible future danger for the children.[607]

464. Notwithstanding this isolated decision of the Supreme Court, most often the Spanish courts – sometimes explicitly influenced by the *Hoffmann* case – have shown a clear tendency in the last two decades to reject that membership of Jehovah's Witnesses could be deemed a relevant factor to determine if a parent is qualified to be awarded the custody of the children. Any other position would be, according to Spanish

604. ATS of 26 Sep. 1978. A similar position inspires, for instance, AAP Huelva *(Sección 1ª)*, ARP 1995/1149, 6 Mar. 1995.

605. *Fiscalía General del Estado*, Circular 1/2012, 3 Oct. 2012, available in: http://www.congreso.es/docu/docum/ddocum/dosieres/sleg/legislatura_10/spl_78/pdfs/79.pdf (accessed 2 Dec. 2017)

606. *Hoffmann v. Austria*, 23 Jun. 1993. Ten years later the European Court decided, in the same way, the case *Palau Martinez v. France*, 16 Dec. 2003, which offered some similarities with *Hoffmann* (one of the spouses was Jehovah's Witness and her religion might have had some influence on the husband's decision to divorce). However, in *Palau Martinez* the issue of blood transfusions was raised neither before the national courts nor before the European Court. For a critique of the lack of nuances in the *Hoffmann* decision, *see* J. Martínez-Torrón, *A Critical Analysis of the Case Law of the European Court on Human Rights on Blood Transfusion and Religious Beliefs*, in *Welfare of the Child and Beliefs of the Parents: Blood Transfusion, Religious Education and Custody* 19–37 (A.C. Emilianides ed., U. Nicosia Press 2010).

607. *See* STS (Civil Chamber) of 27 Feb. 1980, RJ 1980/1012.

courts, an unjustified unequal treatment on the ground of religion, in violation of the freedom guaranteed by Article 16 CE.[608] Nevertheless, when the custody is awarded to the parent who is a Jehovah's Witness, some courts have specifically conditioned custody to certain prudential measures aimed at minimizing the risks for the children in the hypothesis they might need a blood transfusion in the future – for instance, imposing on the custodial parent the obligation to communicate to the other parent any circumstance that may affect the children's life or health.[609]

IV. Objection to Medical Treatment and Criminal Liability

465. Another crucial question is if the death of a minor for lack of appropriate medical treatment entails criminal liability on the part of the objector parents. In Spain, a significant case was decided by the Constitutional Court in 2002 after eight years of judicial battles.[610] The facts, rather unusual, were the following. In 1994, three days after an apparently unimportant bicycle accident, a 13-year-old boy had to be hospitalized because of a serious nasal haemorrhage, which was, with all likelihood, a symptom of a serious internal injury. Like his parents, the boy was a sincere believer and an active Jehovah's Witness. The medical team considered that a blood transfusion was necessary and, as his parents refused to consent, obtained a judicial authorization, which the parents did not resist or contest. The transfusion, however, could not be performed, because of the firm opposition and the agitation of the boy, who became terrified and discomposed by what he believed would be the transfusion's negative moral consequences; the physicians in charge discarded the possibility to perform the treatment under anaesthetics, both on medical and ethical grounds. In these circumstances, the parents were requested to try to persuade his son to accept the transfusion but they rejected such active cooperation on religious grounds. Neither the medical team of the hospital nor other physicians consulted by the parents considered that there were available and efficient alternative clinical procedures. Having arrived to an impasse, the parents obtained the boy's hospital discharge and took him home, despite his very weak condition. A new judicial order decreed that the boy had to be transferred again to the hospital and, like the first time, his parents did not resist or oppose. When the boy arrived to the hospital he was in a coma and, despite undergoing then a blood transfusion, died a few hours later as a result of a brain haemorrhage. The concrete illness that caused the haemorrhage could not be diagnosed but the medical team inferred that most likely it was a type of leukaemia that could have offered a 60%–80% of probabilities of cure if treated in time and supported with successive blood transfusions.

466. Criminal proceedings were initiated against the boy's parents, who were absolved in first instance in 1996. Nevertheless, the Supreme Court, understanding that the parents' religious motivation was not sufficient ground for excuse, overruled

608. *See* , for instance, among appeal decisions, SAP Almería (*Sección 2ª*) 194/1999, AC 1999/1365, 14 Jun. 1999; SAP Barcelona (*Sección 12ª*) 99/2006, JUR 2006\111352, 21 Feb. 2006; SAP Murcia (*Sección 4ª*) 242/2008, JUR 2008\363131, 26 Jun. 2008.

609. *See* , for example, SAP León, AC 1994/1124, 7 Jun. 1994; SAP Salamanca 502/1999, AC 1999/6511, 14 Jul. 1999.

610. STC 154/2002.

in 1997 and sentenced the parents to two and a half years of imprisonment as guilty of homicide, with the mitigating circumstances of 'blind stubbornness and state of passion' (*obcecación y estado pasional*). On 'appeal for protection' (*recurso de amparo*), the Constitutional Court declared the parents exempted from criminal liability.

467. Two main reasons moved the Constitutional Court to adjudicate in favour of the parents. First, the maturity of the boy, who personally and firmly rejected the medical procedure in exercise of his religious freedom and his right to physical integrity. Although it is doubtful that the degree of the boy's maturity permits to conclude that his free will should prevail over the will of his parents or exempt them from their parental responsibilities, his decision could be ignored neither by his parents nor by the courts. Second, the Constitutional Court affirmed that parental custodial duties do note deprive parents from their right to religious freedom, especially when, as in the present case, it was not their conduct what caused the boy's death. The parents did their best, at all times, to search for medical treatments compatible with their religious beliefs, and never obstructed the medical procedures authorized by the judge even though they considered them morally unacceptable. In these circumstances, the Court concluded that the parents could not be held criminally responsible for their son's death just because they refused to try to persuade the boy to accept a blood transfusion when they have taught him, for all of his life, it was prohibited by God. The Court also noted that the parents' conviction was even less fair taking into account that 'it was not proved that the parents' attempt to persuade their son would have been likely efficient'.[611]

468. The issue of the criminal liability of objectors to blood transfusions, out of the parent-child relationship, had been already judged by the Supreme Court in 1990 in another atypical case.[612] In this occasion, a woman, Jehovah's Witness, had undergone an emergency surgical intervention as a consequence of a severe haemorrhage caused by an episode of domestic violence – she had been stabbed by her husband. When the woman had just left the operating room and was, still unconscious, being submitted to haemo-therapy, a member of Jehovah's Witnesses entered the patient's room and took away violently the catheters, insisting that the transfusion had to be immediately interrupted because of the religious beliefs of the patient, who died shortly afterwards as a result. The Supreme Court sentenced that person as guilty of homicide, with the mitigating circumstance of 'blind stubbornness' (*obcecación*), considering that his religious beliefs were not ground for excuse, as he was the immediate cause of her death and was aware of the illegal nature of his behaviour.

V. Objection to Medical Treatment and Reimbursement of Hospital Expenses

469. Another interesting question is the existence or not of economic responsibility of the state if a Jehovah's Witness has sought, and successfully obtained, an alternative procedure to blood transfusions in a private hospital, when that alternative procedure had been previously denied by a public hospital. Is the state obliged to reimburse the

611. *Ibid.*, FJ 12.
612. *See* STS (*Sala de lo Penal*) of 27 Mar. 1990, RJ 1990/2626.

patient for the expenses incurred with the occasion of receiving in a private clinic a medical treatment that the Public Health System refused to apply?

470. The superior courts of justice of some regions have given an affirmative response to this question, noting that the plaintiffs' refusal of transfusions was not abusive or arbitrary, but consistently grounded on religious reasons. Therefore, according to these courts, denying the right to reimbursement would constitute religious discrimination, which would be even less acceptable if the requested alternative therapy was available in the public hospital, above all taking into account the insignificant amount that those reimbursements implied in the context of the enormous expenses of the Public Health System. However, the equivalent courts of other regions have adopted the opposite position.[613] And, more importantly, the Supreme Court and the Constitutional Court have followed the latter orientation.

471. The Supreme Court, in several decisions aimed at unifying the case law of the superior courts of different regions, has rejected the argument of indirect discrimination in these cases, emphasizing that religious freedom implies the right to refuse the medical treatment recommended by a hospital but does not grant individuals the right to receive medical assistance in accordance with the tenets of a particular religion.[614]

472. The Constitutional Court has taken a similar stance in 1996,[615] remarking that the state is not obliged to actively provide services to guarantee that believers can comply with their religious duties. The Court affirmed that 'Article 14 of the Constitution [principle of equality] recognizes the right not to be discriminated but not the hypothetical right to impose or demand differential treatment'.[616] This is a curious doctrine, indeed, especially if we consider that four years later the ECtHR declared just the opposite.[617] It is therefore not surprising that one of the judges of the Constitutional Court wrote a dissenting opinion reminding that Article 9.2 CE provides that public authorities must facilitate the appropriate conditions to make fundamental freedoms 'real and effective', which is especially applicable when the exercise of religious freedom does not contradict the *lex artis* of medicine, as proven by the fact that a private clinic could offer an alternative medical procedure that was compatible with the patient's religious beliefs.

613. For a detailed mention of the case law on this issue, *see* M. Cebriá García, *Objeciones de conciencia a intervenciones médicas. Doctrina y jurisprudencia* 92 et seq. (Thomson-Aranzadi 2005); R. Navarro-Valls & J. Martínez-Torrón, *Conflictos entre conciencia y ley*, 227–231.

614. *See* STS (*Sala de lo Social*) of 14 Apr. 1993, RJ 1993/3338; STS (*Sala de lo Social*) de 3 May 1994, RJ 1994\5353; STS of 25 Jul. 2009 (*Sala de lo Social*), RJ 2009/5045. In the same direction, at the regional level, *see* STSJ Catalonia 227/2016, 19 Jan. 2016.

615. *See* STC 166/1996. For a critical comment on this decision, *see* A. Castro, *Asistencia sanitaria y libertad religiosa, un supuesto: la denegación de reintegro de gastos médicos a los testigos de Jehová*, in VV.AA., *Estudios jurídicos en homenaje al Profesor Vidal Guitarte* 211–220 (Diputació de Castelló 1999).

616. *Ibid.*, FJ 5.

617. *See Thlimmenos v. Greece*, 6 Apr. 2000, cited *supra* , in para. 79.

Chapter 7. Non-discrimination

473. The Spanish Constitution (Article 14) and the ECHR (Article 14) guarantee the principle of equality and the right to non-discrimination. The European Council Directive 2000/78/EC[618] and Article 17.1 of the Statute of Workers[619] (*Estatuto de los Trabajadores*) have applied those notions to the specific area of labour relationships, prohibiting direct as well as indirect discrimination. The autonomy of religious communities to manage their own affairs is susceptible of raising issues in relation to those non-discrimination provisions of European and Spanish law, especially when there is a conflict between the particular ethos of a religious institution and a particular behaviour of their employees. The latter may make personal choices that are in principle protected by fundamental rights (freedom of ideology, right to privacy, etc.) but have at the same time a negative moral significance from the perspective of the relevant religious doctrine.

474. It is not always easy to reach the appropriate balance between religious communities' right to autonomy and individuals' right to non-discrimination, as demonstrated by the various judgments rendered by the ECtHR on such disputes,[620] as well as by the case law of the Spanish Constitutional Court – mentioned in other part of this monograph[621] – about the withdrawal of the ecclesiastical permit to teach Catholic religion in public schools from people engaging in personal behaviour deemed profoundly immoral by the relevant bishop.

475. In any event, it is clear that sanctions adopted by a church against those of its members that contradict its official doctrine or infringe its discipline do not constitute discrimination if those sanctions have only religious significance, even if they entail the loss of administrative positions within the church. There is a relatively well-established Strasbourg case law affirming that in such cases religious autonomy must prevail and individuals' religious freedom is sufficiently protected by their right to change religion.[622]

476. It is equally clear that the concept and criteria of non-discrimination elaborated by state and European laws are not applicable to the internal laws of religious communities that define the rights and duties of their members vis-à-vis the institution, or the conditions required to occupy positions of responsibility within the community, as far as their effects remain within the realm of the internal organization of the relevant community and do not impinge on individuals' rights in the secular sphere. Consequently,

618. Council Directive 2000/78/EC, of 27 Nov. 2000, establishing a general framework for equal treatment in employment and occupation.

619. *Real Decreto Legislativo* 1/1995, 24 Mar. 1995, *por el que se aprueba el texto refundido de la Ley del Estatuto de los Trabajadores*.

620. *See*, e.g., *Obst v. Germany* and *Schüth v. Germany*, both of 23 Sep. 2010; *Siebenhaar v. Germany*, 3 Feb. 2011; *Sindicatul Păstorul Cel Bun v. Rumania*, 31 Jan. 2012.

621. *See supra*, paras 416–421.

622. *See supra*, para. 113. However, the strong division of the Court in the two judgments on *Károly Nagy v. Hungary*, 1 Dec. 2015 (Chamber) and 14 Sep. 2017 (Grand Chamber), exemplifies that such cases may offer many complexities. The case involved the disciplinary suspension of a pastor by a reformed church.

the state – bound by the constitutional principle of neutrality on religious issues[623] – must abstain from interfering in the internal rules and life of internal communities in such cases, no matter how contrasting they may be with state or international law categories. For instance, the state lacks legitimacy to enforce its own notions of non-discrimination on strictly religious issues such as the rules of some churches or religious communities that exclude women from priesthood or religious ministry, require celibacy for priests, or impose that religious marriage can be celebrated only with a person of the same religion.

623. *See supra* , Part I, Ch. 3 §3.

Chapter 8. Penal Law and Religion

477. In Spain, there is a tradition of protecting religion by penal law. Spain being a Catholic confessional state for centuries, such protection was understood typically as referred to the Catholic religion. Things changed when the 1978 Constitution abandoned Catholicism as the state religion. In the years that followed, the Spanish criminal laws were modified to adapt the old legal provisions containing a specific protection of the Catholic Church to the new constitutional principles informing the relations between state and religion. These modifications included the decriminalization of acts aimed at 'eroding' the Catholic Church as the official religion of the state; and, later, the elimination of the crime of blasphemy as well as the protection of all religions on equal terms.[624] Taking into account the new legal context, in the mid-1980s the Constitutional Court sustained the constitutionality of the protection of religious freedom through criminal law, considering that such protection was conceived not to privilege a particular religion or church but to create the adequate conditions in which all persons can actually exercise their fundamental freedoms.[625]

478. The Criminal Code in force, enacted in 1995, has preserved the idea of protecting religious freedom by penal law. Indeed, it has a *specific section*, composed by Articles 522–526 CP, on 'crimes against freedom of conscience, religious feelings and respect for the deceased' (within the chapter devoted to crimes related to the exercise of fundamental rights and public freedoms). Article 522 CP adopts the perspective of *individual religious freedom*, while the other articles of that section take the perspective of *collective religious freedom*. In practice these articles are very rarely applied by the courts.

479. Article 522 CP sanctions different types of violent or coercive conducts that interfere with the religious life and choices of *individuals*, all of them punishable with a moderate pecuniary penalty (which can be substituted by custodial penalties in case of lack of payment). In particular, violence or coercion to prevent a person from practising his religion; to force a person to practise acts of worship or to reveal his beliefs; and to oblige a person to change his religion. It is commonly understood that the latter aspect implies the punishment of abusive proselytism, which must be understood in the light of the *Kokkinakis* case decided by the ECtHR – i.e., 'improper proselytism' that involves 'pressure on people in distress or need; … violence or brainwashing':[626]

Article 522 CP:

624. *See* M. López Alarcón, *Tutela penal de la libertad religiosa*, in *Derecho Eclesiástico del Estado Español* 117 (J. Ferrer Ortiz ed., 6th ed., Eunsa 2007). On the subject of the protection of religious freedom by criminal law in Spain, *see* generally J. Ferreiro, *Protección jurídico-penal de la religión* (servicio de publicaciones de la Universidad de La Coruña 1998); I. Martín Sánchez, *El derecho a la libre formación dela conciencia y su tutela penal* (Tirant lo Blanch 2000).

625. *See* ATC 271/1984 and ATC 180/1986.

626. *Kokkinakis v. Greece*, 25 May 1993, para. 48.

Shall incur a penalty of fine from four to ten months:

1. Those who, by violence, intimidation, force or any other illegitimate coercion, prevent one or more members of a religious denomination from practicing the acts proper to the beliefs they profess, or from attending those acts.
2. Those who, by the same means, force other person or persons to practice or attend acts of worship or rites, to perform acts revealing that they profess or do not profess a religion, or to change the religion they profess.

480. Out of the specific section mentioned in paragraph 478, other articles of the Criminal Code have an influence on the protection of individual religious freedom. More precisely:

- *Article 314 CP* punishes 'those who cause serious labour discrimination against a person on the ground of his ideology, religion or beliefs ... '. Penalty: imprisonment from six months to two years, or fine from twelve to twenty-four months.
- *Article 511 CP* punishes 'people in charge of a public service when they refuse to provide that service to a person entitled to it, on the ground of his ideology, religion or beliefs ... '; or when the same facts are committed 'against an association, foundation, society or corporation, or against their members, on the ground of their ideology, religion or beliefs ... '. Penalty: imprisonment from six months to two years and fine from twelve to twenty-four months, and specific disqualification from public service or office, for a period of time between one and three years.
- *Article 512 CP* punishes 'people that, in the exercise of their profession or business, refuse to provide a service to a person entitled to it, on the ground of his ideology, religion or beliefs ... '. Penalty: specific disqualification from their profession, occupation, business or commerce, for a period of time between one and four years.
- *Article 612.2 CP* punishes those who take occasion of an armed conflict to 'exercise violence on healthcare or religious personnel ... '. Penalty: imprisonment from three to seven years, in addition to the sanctions that should be imposed as a result of the harm caused.

481. From the perspective of *collective religious freedom*, as mentioned above apropos of the inviolability of places of worship,[627] three other articles of the section of the Criminal Code mentioned in paragraph 478 protect religious communities against violent interference in ceremonies or services (Article 523), profanation in places of worship or religious ceremonies (Article 524), and violation of graves or desecration of corpses (Article 526).

482. Moreover, some articles of the Criminal Code criminalize some types of offensive speech considered particularly serious. Article 525 CP punishes public scornful offences against the beliefs of any religion and public vexation of believers or non-believers. This article has been sometimes criticized as opening too broad a door to unjustified limitations on freedom of expression, through the repression of

627. *See supra* , paras 318–321.

what the ECtHR has named, with imprecise wording, 'gratuitous offences' to religious feelings.[628] In practice, this article is rarely applied:

Article 525 CP:

1. Shall incur a penalty of fine from eight to twelve months those who, to offend the feelings of members of a religious denomination, make public scorn of their dogmas, beliefs, rites or ceremonies orally, in writing or through any kind of document, or vex publicly the people that profess or practice those beliefs.
2. Shall incur the same penalties those who make public scorn, orally or in writing, of people that do not profess any religion or belief.

483. More reasonable and widely accepted in Europe is the criminalization of hate speech operated by Article 510 CP, which was modified in 2015[629] following the indications of an EU framework decision of 2008.[630] Article 510 is now much larger and more complex – and perhaps also less clear on the whole – than it was prior to its reform, and includes the crime of negationism, in particular the public negation, gross trivialization or praise of crimes of genocide. For the purposes of this monograph it suffices to say that, according to Article 510, hate speech is conceived as the public encouragement, promotion, or incitement to hatred, hostility, discrimination or violence against a group, or its individual members, defined by certain identitarian characteristics. Ideology, religion and belief are included among those characteristics, together with others such as ethnicity, race, national origin or sex. Explicit mention is made of aiding and abetting in the commission of crimes of hate speech. Hate speech, cooperation with hate speech and negationism (Article 510.1) are punished with imprisonment from 1 to 4 years and with fine from 6 to 12 months. Lower sanctions are foreseen for less serious crimes that do not properly constitute hate speech but are connected with it (Article 510.2), namely the use of abusive language against the dignity of people that involves humiliation, contempt or discredit; and the praise or justification of crimes of hate speech (imprisonment from 6 months to 2 years, and fine from 6 to 12 months). In all cases, Article 510.5 imposes also a penalty of disqualification for educational professions for a period between 3 and 10 years on top of the imprisonment time, depending on the gravity and circumstances of the crime. According to Article 510.6, the court that imposes a sentence shall also order the destruction of all means and materials used for the dissemination of the message that caused the conviction. Curiously, the current text of Article 510 has eliminated the reference to the falsity of the content of the message or information that was present in the prior version. Falsity should now be taken into account, when appropriate, from the perspective of the crime of defamation (*injuria*, Article 208 CP), which considers only the damage to the dignity

628. *See* J. Martínez-Torrón, *Freedom of Expression versus Freedom of Religion in the European Court of human Rights*, in *Censorial Sensitivities: Free Speech and Religion in a Fundamentalist World* 233–269 (A. Sajó ed., Eleven Intl. Publg. 2007).
629. By the Organic Law 1/2015, 30 Mar. 2015.
630. EU Council Framework Decision 2008/913/JHA, 20 Nov. 2008, on combating certain forms and expressions of racism and xenophobia by means of criminal law.

and reputation of a person, without any reference to religion, belief or any other of the circumstances mentioned by Article 510 CP.

This is the text of the beginning of Article 510 CP:

1. Shall be punishable with imprisonment from 1 to 4 years and with fine from 6 to 12 months:

   a. Those who publicly encourage, promote or incite, directly or indirectly, to hatred, hostility, discrimination, or violence against a group, a part of a group, against a person because of his belonging to a group, on racist or anti-Semitic grounds, or on other grounds concerning a person's ideology, religion, beliefs, family situation, ethnicity, race, nation, national origin, sex, sexual orientation or identity, as well as on grounds of gender, illness or disability.

484. The reform of the Penal Code in 2015 has included a new Article 510 bis, which foresees the possibility of criminal responsibility of legal persons for the crimes described in Article 510, and imposes a penalty of fine from two to five years. In the same line, Article 515.4 CP declares illegal and punishable the associations that 'encourage, promote or incite, directly or indirectly, to discrimination, hatred or violence against persons, groups or associations on grounds relating to their ideology, religion or beliefs, the belonging of their members or some of them to an ethnic group, race or nation, or their sex, sexual orientation, family situation, illness or disability'. Beyond the use of offensive, defamatory or hate speech, the Criminal Code also sanctions other activities aimed at causing harm to religious groups. Article 170 CP regulates the offence of making threats against religious groups, among others. Articles 607 and 607 bis CP, respectively, apply genocide and crimes against humanity specifically to religious groups, among others, and punish them with severe penalties.

485. The application of the foregoing articles by Spanish courts is not frequent – partly because of lack of prosecution – and has not been always consistent. In general it is possible to say that the courts use Article 510 CP less easily in the case of anti-religious hate speech than in other types of similar language. Thus, the courts normally do not have problems with sentencing anti-Semitic hate speech[631] but are more reluctant to do the same if the speech is directed against Catholics or the Catholic Church, even when the language in question would have been definitely sanctioned if used against other groups of people, such as women, homosexuals or persons of a certain race.[632] Such reluctance is even clearer in the case of contemptuous expressions against the

631. *See* , for instance, *Sentencia* of the *Juzgado de lo Penal* nº 1 of Pamplona 273/2016, 11 Oct. 2016.

632. *See* , for instance, AAP Madrid 73/2013, 24 Jan. 2013, concerning an anarchist campaign of anti-Catholic posters with images such as a burning church, a bishop in the gallows or a contour of the Pope within a rifle telescopic sight and the motto *totus muertos* (meaning 'all dead').

Catholic Church (Article 525 CP).[633] The position of the courts is more open to sentencing in cases of physical activities that go beyond mere expression and interfere violently with religious ceremonies or incur profanation of religious places (Articles 523 and 524 CP).[634]

---

633. *See* , for example, the AAP Madrid cited in the precedent note, and the inadmissibility decisión (*auto*) of the *Juzgado de Instrucción* nº 18 of Valencia, 23 Jun. 2016, rec. nº 1084/2016, concerning the publicación of a poster with the image of two famous advocations of the Holy Virgin kissing each other in a lesbian attitude.
634. *See* , for example, SAP Balearic Islands 102/2016, 13 Oct. 2016 (confirmed by STS 835/2017 (Criminal Section), 19 Dec. 2017); and SAP Albacete 10/2014, 22 Jan. 2014; in both cases the punished actions were against ceremonies in Catholic churches. In the opposite direction we have a the SAP Madrid 14311/2016, 16 Dec. 2016, which absolved a well-known political figure who had profaned a Catholic chapel in a public university; interestingly, the court elaborated its own 'secular' notion of profanation instead of following the case law of the Supreme Court, which has held that this concept should be understood in the light of the relevant religion (*see* STS 688/1993 (Criminal Section), 25 Mar. 1993, FJ 4).

Part VIII. Church Financing

486. One of the manifestations of the constitutional principle of state cooperation with religion (Article 16.3 CE)[635] consists in providing economic support to religious communities, *directly* through the supply of public funding or *indirectly* through tax benefits. With one form or another, most European countries contribute to the financing of religious communities, on the implicit understanding that it is a way of facilitating the citizens' exercise of religious freedom and strengthening the positive role that religion often plays in society.

487. In Spain, economic support of religion has been channelled exclusively, so far, through state cooperation agreements with religious communities.[636] Therefore, other communities registered in the Registry of Religious Entities that have not reached a cooperation agreement are excluded from these economic benefits, even in the case of religious communities that, having been recognized 'well-known roots' in accordance with Article 7 LOLR, would be in theory entitled to negotiate such a cooperation agreement with the government.[637]

635. *See supra*, Part I, Ch. 3 §4.
636. *See El sostenimiento económico de la Iglesia Católica en España. Nuevo modelo* (J. Otaduy & D. Zalbidea eds, Eunsa 2008); A. Torres Gutiérrez, *Aspectos legales de la financiación de las confesiones religiosas minoritarias en España y los Acuerdos de 1992*, 44 Revista General de Derecho Canónico y Derecho Eclesiástico del Estado 1–59 (2017).
637. *See supra*, Part I, Ch. 2 §3.

Chapter 1. Direct Financing of Religious Communities

§1. Direct Financing of the Catholic Church

488. The Catholic Church has received economic aid from the Spanish state since the state's massive confiscation of Church properties that took place in the mid nineteenth century, especially between 1834 and 1855, through the process historically known as *desamortización*, or confiscation of mortmain property.[638] Indeed, the state's financial aid was conceived as a sort of compensation for that deprivation of property. The forms of economic cooperation with the Catholic Church have varied over the last century and a half.[639] Until the 1979 Concordat, the system usually adopted was the so-called *provision for worship and clergy* (*dotación de culto y clero*), consisting in allocating part of the state budget directly for the maintenance of the Catholic Church. This system was convenient from the perspective of a state with Catholicism as its official religion. Naturally, no other religion received economic aid – they were not recognized religious freedom then, and therefore it was even less conceivable that they could obtain financing from the government.

489. The 1979 Agreement on Economic Affairs between Spain and the Holy See made an important change in the financing of the Catholic Church, which should be implemented gradually.[640] Article II of the Agreement, after declaring that the state would cooperate with the Catholic Church to make viable its economic maintenance, introduced the system called *tax assignment* (*asignación tributaria*), which permits taxpayers to voluntarily allocate a percentage of their income tax to be paid every year to the Catholic Church. Initially, when the new system began to be implemented in 1988,[641] the percentage that taxpayers could allocate was 0.5239%. Over the years, such percentage proved insufficient to provide the Catholic Church with approximately the same funding received under the old system. As a consequence, the state had to reserve a budget item every year to complement the money received by the Church through the new system.[642] In 2006, the Spanish government and the Catholic Church agreed to raise that percentage to 0.7% on a permanent basis, with the compromise that thereafter the Church would receive no more funding through budgetary provisions. In the same agreement, the Church renounced the exemption from paying VAT, which

638. On the issue of *desamortización, see* F. Tomás y Valiente, *El marco político de la desamortización en España* (Ariel 1989).
639. *See* J.R. González Armendia, *Sistemas históricos de dotación del Estado español a la Iglesia española: siglos XIX–XX* (Servicio de Publicaciones de la Universidad Pontificia de Salamanca 1990).
640. *See* I. Martín Sánchez, *Marco normativo general. Interpretación del Acuerdo sobre Asuntos Económicos*, in *El sostenimiento económico* 15–42, cit. *supra* , note 636.
641. *See Ley* 33/1987, 23 Dec. 1987, *de Presupuestos Generales del Estado para 1988,* additional provision 5.
642. The possibility of such complement was envisaged by the Concordat as a transitory solution, which was supposed to last no longer than three years. In practice, however, political inertia made it last nineteen years.

was established by the Concordat, in order to accommodate European Union law requirements; and accepted to elaborate an annual explanatory report on the use of the funding received from the state. This agreement, which modified a particular aspect of the Concordat, did not follow the procedures established for international treaties, but was formalized by a mere 'exchange of letters' between the Spanish Foreign Ministry and the Apostolic Nunciature in Spain.[643] The agreement was implemented by the 2006 law that approved the state budget for 2007.[644]

490. Under the current law,[645] taxpayers may express their will to allocate 0.7% of their income tax to the Catholic Church by checking off the appropriate box when filling out every year the relevant forms for the Spanish Internal Revenue Service (*Agencia Tributaria*). The resultant money is administered by the Spanish Bishops Conference attending to the needs of each diocese. In addition, taxpayers can choose to allocate an identical percentage of their income tax to 'activities of social interest', and in that case the resultant money is distributed by the government among NGOs. These are voluntary options for taxpayers; they can check off the two available boxes, any of them, or none of them, at their discretion.

491. In Article II.5 of the 1979 Agreement on Economic Affairs, the Catholic Church explicitly declared its intention to reach its complete self-financing in the future. When such goal is achieved – the same article continued – the Catholic Church and the Spanish state should agree on 'other areas and forms of economic collaboration' to substitute the current system of state funding. In retrospect, this provision of the Agreement seems too optimistic. After more than three decades, the goal of self-financing seems to be very far away from the actual possibilities of the Catholic Church. Indeed, the above-mentioned exchange of letters[646] seems to confirm that both the Spanish state and the Catholic Church accept the present form of direct economic cooperation for an indefinite time. Moreover, religious minorities, which began by insisting on their self-financing and by requesting only tax benefits from the state, are currently aspiring to the same economic cooperation granted to the Catholic Church.

§2. Direct Financing of Other Religious Communities

492. The tax assignment system is not available to any other religious community in Spain, not even to the federations that signed the cooperation agreements of 1992. It seems that the Evangelical and Jewish Federations rejected such possibility when

643. *Intercambio de Notas entre la Nunciatura Apostólica en España y el Ministerio de Asuntos Exteriores y Cooperación, referidas a los acuerdos sobre asignación tributaria a favor de la Iglesia Católica*, 22 Dec. 2006. The text of this exchange of letters has not been officially published, but its text is available in: http://www.unav.es/ima/legislacion_prueba/eclesiastica/2006/6.html (accessed 17 Nov. 2017).
644. *Ley 42/2006*, 28 Dec. 2006, *de Presupuestos Generales del Estado para 2007*, additional provision 18.
645. *See* S. Meseguer Velasco, *A propósito de la reforma del sistema de asignación tributaria: hacia el sostenimiento económico de las confesiones*", 22 Revista General de Derecho Canónico y Derecho Eclesiástico del Estado 1–24 (2010).
646. *See supra*, para. 489.

the government offered it during negotiations, and declared its preference for a complete economic autonomy – as a way to guarantee their independence of the government – based exclusively upon tax benefits that could facilitate their self-financing. The Islamic Federation was apparently in favour of the tax assignment system but, as they joined the negotiation process at a later stage, they had to accept the same channels of economic cooperation agreed by the Evangelical and Jewish Federations, because the government was determined not to distinguish between the three federations in this respect.[647]

493. Since the early 2000s, however, there has been a clear change in the attitude of the Evangelical, Jewish and Islamic Federations. Alleging the constitutional principle of equality, they have been repeatedly requesting, for years, some sort of direct state financing, preferably the same tax assignment system applied to the Catholic Church. Other religious communities with recognized 'well-known roots' (*notorio arraigo*)[648] have made similar requests. No matter which party was in power, the government has been adamant so far and has rejected all these claims, especially because of the reluctance of the Finance Ministry. Such unequal treatment was, however, declared compatible with the ECHR by the ECtHR in 2001.[649] The Supreme Court of Spain held a similar position in 2016, on the basis of an interpretation of the right of petition, in response to an appeal of the Evangelical Federation, which has requested being granted the same possibility as the Catholic Church.[650] The Evangelical Federation announced to appeal to the Constitutional Court and, if necessary, to the Strasbourg Court, which might perhaps change the position taken 2001 in view of its judgment on the case of the Hungarian Mennonite Church in 2014.[651] In the meantime, in January 2017, the Ministry of Justice declared its intention to extend the tax assignment system to the religious communities signatories of the 1992 agreements as well as to those that have been recognized well-known roots in Spain.[652]

494. Although for the moment left out from the tax assignment system, the three federations which are signatories of the 1992 cooperation agreements receive direct funding from the Spanish state through a public foundation, whose origins date back to 2004. That year, while waiting for better times to introduce the appropriate changes in tax laws to permit the equalization with the system applied to the Catholic Church, the newly elected government, following a proposal of the Ministry of Justice, decided to create a public foundation named 'Pluralism and Coexistence' (*Pluralismo y Convivencia*).[653] The main purpose of this foundation was to provide direct state financial support to the Protestant, Jewish, and Islamic Federations through the funding

647. *See Los acuerdos con las confesiones minoritarias. Diez años de vigencia* 152–153, 192–194, 213 (J. Mantecón ed., Ministerio de Justicia 2003).

648. *See supra* , para. 302.

649. Cf. *Alujer Fernández and Caballero García v. Spain*, decision on the admissibility of Appl. Nr. 53072/99, 14 Jun. 2001. *See supra* , para. 375.

650. *See* STS 5475/2016, 14 Dec. 2016.

651. *Magyar Keresztény Mennonita Egyház and others v. Hungary*, 8 Apr. 2014.

652. *See* , e.g., Diario *El Mundo*, 3 Jan. 2017: http://www.elmundo.es/sociedad/2017/01/03/586b975aca474156128b460e.html (accessed 9 Dec. 2017).

653. The decision to create the Foundation *Pluralismo y Convivencia* was adopted by the Council of Ministers on 15 Oct. 2004. The foundation was constituted by the Ministry of Justice on 25 Jan. 2005, and registered via the Order ECI/935/2005, 8 Mar. 2005.

of activities relating to education, culture, or social integration – not, at least in theory, strictly religious or worship activities.[654] Like many other forms of state cooperation with religion, the state funding channelled through this public foundation applies only to those three religious communities but not to the rest of religious minorities without cooperation agreement, not even to those with recognized well-known roots. The creation of the Foundation *Pluralismo y Convivencia* has been criticized by some scholars, noting that, curiously enough, this way of providing economic aid to major religious minorities in Spain shows some similarities to the old system of budgetary provision (*dotación presupuestaria*) for the Catholic Church, succinctly described above,[655] and underlining that such a system is not the most adequate instrument from the perspective of the constitutional principles of neutrality and equality. Among other drawbacks of this foundation, it has been also remarked that, being a public foundation, it is susceptible of being controlled by political criteria; and, as religious communities do not have institutional representation within the governing bodies of the foundation, decisions about the distribution of funding may be conditioned by criteria of political interest.[656]

---

654. To find official information about this foundation, *see* : http://www.pluralismoyconvivencia.es (accessed 5 Dec. 2017).
655. *See supra* , para. 488.
656. For a critical analysis of this foundation in the context of the diverse systems of state aid to religion in Spain, *see* C. Garcimartín, *Direct Financing of Religious Denominations in Spain*, 48 J. Church & St. 189–196 (2005).

Chapter 2. Indirect Financing of Religious Communities

495. Both the Concordat and the 1992 Agreements grant specific tax benefits to the Catholic Church and to the Evangelical, Jewish and Islamic Federations, in very similar terms. No such benefits are granted to other religious communities, not even to those with recognized well-known roots in Spain, in spite of the many requests they have made to that purpose. The Spanish Constitutional Court[657] and the ECtHR, with reasoning certainly not very persuasive, have denied that such a differential legal treatment is constitutive of discrimination on religious grounds.[658] Nevertheless, equality in this area is, in the view of many scholars, one of the aspects in which Spanish law on religion should be perfected, for the justification of tax exemptions to religious communities should pertain primarily to the religious nature of the group and its activities, rather than to history, bilateral institutional relationships, or social influence.[659] Significantly, this area of the Spanish law on religion has been characterized by a notorious immobilism for more than twenty-five years.

496. Although only the above-mentioned religious communities are per se granted tax benefits, all foundations or other institutions of whatever religious inspiration, if they meet the appropriate legal requirements, may be eligible for tax benefits generally granted by the state to non-profit organizations irrespective of their religious or non-religious nature. This is, therefore, a possibility open to every religious community to obtain indirect state financing while (and if) the system is not reformed.

§1. Non-taxation and Tax Exemptions

497. Articles III–IV of the 1979 Agreement on Economic Affairs between Spain and the Holy See, and Article 11.1-3 of the 1992 Agreements with the Evangelical, Jewish and Islamic Federations enumerate the cases of non-taxable activities and tax exemptions.[660] They have been developed by different state laws. Some of these tax benefits are common to all non-profit institutions and activities under current state laws. In this respect, both the Concordat and the 1992 Agreements foresee that the relevant religious communities, and their internal entities created for religious or charitable purposes, shall have the same tax benefits established by law for non-profit activities. Laws on non-profit entities typically make the appropriate references to

657. Cf. ATC 480/1989, 2 Oct. 1989.

658. Cf. *Iglesia Bautista El Salvador and Ortega Moratilla v. Spain*, decision on the admissibility of Appl. Nr. 17522/90, 11 Jan. 1992. *See supra*, para. 375.

659. *See*, among others, R. Rodríguez Chacón, *El factor religioso ante el tribunal constitucional* 99–101 (Servicio de Publicaciones de la Facultad de Derecho de la Universidad Complutense 1992). *See also* J. Martínez-Torrón, *Freedom of Religion in the Case-Law of the Spanish Constitutional Court*, Brigham Young U. L. Rev. 734–736 (2001).

660. *See Aspectos del régimen económico y patrimonial de las confesiones religiosas* (A.C. Álvarez Cortina & M. Rodríguez Blanco eds, Comares 2008).

religious communities. The most important law in this respect is the Law 49/2002.[661] In the case of tax exemptions, the Law 49/2002 extends to the Catholic Church and to the religious communities signatory of the 1992 Agreements the same exemptions granted to non-profit entities.[662] An identical rule applies to the relevant religious foundations constituted by those religious communities, as long as they provide certification of their registration in the RER.[663]

498. It is considered non-taxable the *money raised by public collection or given as charity or alms* to the Catholic Church, as well as to Evangelical, Jewish and Islamic communities. Also non-taxable are the teaching activities for the education and training of religious ministers and leaders, in seminaries, faculties or ecclesiastical universities; and the publication and distribution of religious bulletins or documents for the use of the faithful when it is given free of charge.

499. The 1979 Concordat considered non-taxable by VAT the acquisition of *objects of worship. Transmission of real property* to the Catholic Church was also exempt from paying VAT. However, as mentioned above,[664] the Catholic Church renounced these tax benefits in 2006 in exchange for a raise in the percentage of the income tax that citizens can voluntarily allocate to the Church. This permitted to adapt Spanish law to European Union law, which does not envisage VAT exemptions in those cases. Nevertheless, such renunciation of a privilege contained in the Concordat – which has a nature analogous to an international treaty – was conceived by the Catholic Church as neither unconditional nor necessarily perpetual. On the contrary, the Holy See explicitly declared its intention to keep such renunciation effective as long as the current system of tax assignment is in force.[665]

500. The entities that compose the official structure of the Catholic Church (Holy See, Bishops Conference, dioceses, parishes and other territorial structures), as well as religious orders and institutes of consecrated life, are exempted from the payment of *real property taxes* with respect to: places of worship and their annexes devoted to pastoral activity; residences of bishops and priests with pastoral activity; diocesan and parochial offices; seminars for the training of priests and religious, and the parts of ecclesiastical universities devoted to teaching ecclesiastical disciplines; buildings devoted to residence or conventual life of religious orders or institutes of consecrated life. A similar exemption applies to the municipal *tax on the increase of value of urban land.*[666]

---

661. *Ley* 49/2002, 23 Dec. 2002, *de régimen fiscal de las entidades sin fines lucrativos y de los incentivos fiscales al mecenazgo*.
662. Articles 2–3 of the *Ley* 49/2002 specify the legal requirements to be considered a non-profit entity.
663. Cf. *ibid., disposiciones adicionales 8ª 9ª*. Cf. also the regulations of that law, contained in the *Real Decreto* 1270/2003, 10 Oct. 2003, *por el que se aprueba el Reglamento para la aplicación del régimen fiscal de las entidades sin fines lucrativos y de los incentivos fiscales al mecenazgo* (additional provision).
664. *See supra*, para. 489.
665. *See* Nr. 3 of the exchange of letters cited in para. 489.
666. Cf. Art. 105 of the *Real Decreto Legislativo* 2/2004, 5 Mar. 2004, *por el que se aprueba el texto refundido de la Ley Reguladora de las Haciendas Locales*. *See also* STS 4952/2000, 16 Jun. 2000.

501. The same entities of the Catholic Church are also exempted from paying other taxes. In particular: *corporate taxes*, with respect to revenues that proceed, directly or indirectly, from activities that constitute the specific purpose of the ecclesiastical entity in question (benefits from economic exploitations or from property whose use is lent to third parties are excluded from this exemption);[667] *taxes on inheritance*, *gifts*, *transfers of real property* and *documented legal acts*, as far as the acquired property, goods or rights are destined to worship, apostolate, charity or the maintenance of clergy; the municipal *tax on buildings, installations and infrastructural works*.[668] With regard to the latter tax, a judgment of 2017 of the Court of Justice of the European Union held that tax exemptions for works done in a building property of a religious congregation but not devoted to religious activities might infringe the prohibition of Article 107.1 TFEU (prohibition of state aids that may distort economic competition) in case the activities in question are of economic nature.[669]

502. Similar exemptions apply to the religious communities integrated into the Evangelical, Jewish and Islamic communities. In addition to a slightly varying terminology, one of the few differences between the 1992 Agreements and the Concordat is that Article 11 of the respective agreements specify that, in order to benefit from the exemption from real property taxes, the residences of religious ministers must be an annex to places of worship; and the seminars or centres for the training or religious ministers or leaders must be exclusively devoted to that purpose.

503. Salaries, stipends or other payments received by religious ministers for the exercise of their functions – including those of chaplains in hospitals, penitentiaries or the military – are not subject to any privileged tax status, and therefore they abide by the common rules applicable to the income tax. The same criterion applies to taxes or fees charged by the state, regions or municipalities for specific services provided to religious communities.

§2. TAX-DEDUCTIBLE DONATIONS

504. The 1979 Concordat and the 1992 Agreements contain provisions envisaging that tax benefits established by law for non-profit institutions and activities would be applied to the Catholic Church and to Evangelical, Jewish and Islamic communities, as well as to their respective internal entities created for religious, educational (non-

667. Cf. Arts 9 and 121 of the *Real Decreto Legislativo* 4/2004, 5 Mar. 2004, *por el que se aprueba el texto refundido de la Ley del Impuesto de Sociedades.*

668. Cf. *Orden* of the Finance Ministry, 5 Jun. 2001.

669. *Congregación de Escuelas Pías Provincia Betania v. Ayuntamiento de Getafe* (Grand Chamber), C-74-16, 27 Jun. 2017, ECLI:EU:C:2017:496. In application of that judgment, an administrative court of first instance denied the exemption requested by the religious congregation (*Juzgado de lo Contencioso-Administrativo* No. 4 of Madrid, Sentencia 1/2018, 8 Jan. 2018). *See* M. Cebriá, *La exención en el ICIO de la Iglesia Católica en el Estado español y la prohibición de ayudas de Estado del derecho de la Unión Europea*, 45 Revista General de Derecho Canónico y Derecho Eclesiástico del Estado 1–21 (2017).

profit), healthcare or social assistance purposes. These provisions mention specifically tax deductions for donations to those institutions and remit to future ad hoc legislation.[670]

505. These rules of the agreements were implemented by the Law 49/2002, which also provided that, to be eligible for these tax benefits, the internal entities of those religious communities must obtain from the tax authorities (*Agencia Tributaria*) the relevant certification of non-profit aims. According to this law, donations to those religious communities and institutions are tax-deductible in the same terms as donations to non-profit institutions.[671] The 2002 law established some percentages of the sums donated that could be deducted from the amount payable for their income tax in the case of individuals (*impuesto sobre la renta de las personas físicas*) and from the amount payable for corporate taxes in the case of corporations (*impuesto de sociedades*). Such percentages applied not only to donations in monies but also to other forms of donation, such as real property or chattels, constitution of usufructs, or works of art.[672] A law of 2014[673] has raised the percentages of tax-deductible donations. Currently, individuals can deduct from their income tax 75% of the first 150 € of their donations plus 30% of the excess; and, in order to stimulate loyalty in donations, the deductible percentage of the excess is raised to 35% when the taxpayer has been contributing to the same religious community or non-profit organization for three consecutive years. Corporations can deduct 35% of the sums donated, which increases to 40% if they have been contributing to the same community or organization for three consecutive years. The total amount of such deductions, in both cases, cannot be higher than 10% of the taxable income.

§3. Other Economic Contributions

506. In addition to tax benefits, the state finances other specific religious activities. As explained in other part of this monograph,[674] Catholic religious assistance in public institutions such as military establishments, hospitals and penitentiaries is organized around permanent chaplaincies sustained with public funding. To a lesser extent, Islamic personnel in charge of religious assistance in penitentiaries are paid by the state as well. The state pays also the salaries of Catholic religion teachers in public schools and provides an economic compensation for the teaching hours of Evangelical and Islamic religion.[675] Religious schools, under the same conditions as any other private school, can be partly subsidized by the state if they comply with certain legal requirements and reach an agreement with the relevant regional educational authority.[676]

670. *See* Arts IV.2 and V of the 1979 Agreement on Economic Affairs between Spain and the Holy See; and Art. 11 of the 1992 Agreements with the Evangelical, Jewish and Islamic Federations.
671. Cf. *Ley* 49/2002, additional provision 9. Cf. also the additional provision of the *Real Decreto* 1270/2003.
672. *See* Arts 18–20 of the *Ley* 49/2002, 23 Dec. 2002, *de régimen fiscal de las entidades sin fines lucrativos y de los incentivos fiscales al mecenazgo*.
673. *Ley* 27/2014, 27 Nov. 2014, *del Impuesto de Sociedades*. Cf. its Fifth Final Provision.
674. *See supra*, Part III, Ch. 6.
675. *See* para. 527.
676. *See* para. 535.

These economic contributions, however, are normally perceived as payment for specific services aimed at facilitating the citizens' fundamental right to freedom of religion, or for contributing to education as a public service in the case of private schools, rather than indirect ways to finance religious communities strictly speaking.

507. As mentioned in other part of this monograph,[677] there is also state cooperation with religious communities, especially with the Catholic Church, in the area of historic and cultural heritage of religious origin. Again, this is normally understood as mutual collaboration in an area of common interest rather than state funding of the church strictly speaking.

---

677. *See infra*, Part XI, Ch. 1.

Part IX. Education

508. The area of education may be sometimes a source of conflicts between the educational project of the state and the freedom of conscience of the students or their parents, as we have seen in a different section of this monograph.[678] More frequently, however, education is an area of public activity in which the state cooperates with the citizens' exercise of religious freedom, especially in two ways: by facilitating religious education in public schools, and by funding private schools with a religious ethos. These expressions of state support are of course expressions of cooperation with religious communities – which indeed usually welcome such support – and as such they are grounded in the principle of cooperation established by Article 16.3 CE. However, they are also ways to implement, on the one hand, the parents' rights over the religious and moral orientation of their children's education;[679] and on the other hand, the freedom of teaching, which is an autonomous constitutional right in addition to being an integral part of religious freedom.[680]

---

678. *See supra*, Part II, Ch. 2 §8.
679. These rights are guaranteed by Art. 27.3 CE and Art. 2 of the Protocol to the ECHR.
680. *See* Art. 27.1 CE and Art. 9.1 ECHR.

Chapter 1. Religious Education in Public and Private Schools

509. In Spain, there is religious teaching in schools as a part of the ordinary curriculum, always as an elective subject. The way this teaching is organized varies when we compare Catholic religious instruction with religious instruction of other denominations. Although there is a trend towards a certain gradual convergence on the normative level, the very different social demand of Catholic and other religious teachings makes it unrealistic to equalize their respective situations on a factual level.[681]

510. In both cases, *two main features* are characteristic of religious education in Spanish schools. In the first place, it is a subject of free choice. Religious communities may provide religious instruction in public schools only upon the request of the students or their parents or legal representatives, and therefore confessional religious instruction cannot be enforced as mandatory courses. In the second place, not all religious denominations are entitled to provide religious teaching in public schools, but only those with which the state has concluded a cooperation agreement – i.e., the Catholic Church, and the communities integrated into the Evangelical, Jewish and Islamic Federations.

511. It must be noted that, so far, religious education in Spain has always been conceived as *confessional education*, i.e., as instruction in a specific religion, taught by members of that particular religion and under the supervision of institutions representing it. Such religious instruction is normally aimed not only at providing information about religious tenets and doctrines but also at transmitting a given faith and values. It is, by definition, neither neutral nor objective, although it can – and should – be carried out in accordance with the appropriate academic standards and methodology. Neutral teaching about religion has never been introduced effectively as a school subject, elective or mandatory, in the Spanish educational system.[682]

681. The statistics of religious instruction for the academic year 2014–2015, provided by the Ministry of Education, can be found in: http://www.mecd.gob.es/dms/mecd/servicios-al-ciudadano-mecd/estadisticas/educacion/indicadores-publicaciones-sintesis/cifras-educacion-espana/2014-15/e4-pdf.pdf (accessed 5 Dec. 2017). According to the 2016 *Annual report on the status of religious freedom in Spain*, published by the Ministry of Justice, 41–44, there were 25,660 teachers and more than 3.5 million students of Catholic religion courses. Evangelical education was provided by approximately 240 teachers to 16,000 students in 800 schools. No data are given about students of Islamic religion courses, which were taught by 55 teachers, the vast majority of them distributed among Andalusia (22), Ceuta (14) and Melilla (10). No other religious instruction is currently provided in public schools.

682. *See infra*, paras 529–530.

§1. Teaching of Catholic Religion

I. The Normative Framework

512. The teaching of Catholic religion in schools is based on the Concordat provisions and, more precisely, in Articles I–VII of the 1979 Agreement on Education and Cultural Issues between Spain and the Holy See. The regulation of religious instruction in this Agreement was not only aimed at protecting the right of the Catholic Church to disseminate its doctrines, as part of its constitutional right to religious freedom, but was also the result of three intertwined elements. First, Article 27.3 CE, which recognizes the parents' right to guarantee that their children will receive religious and moral instruction in accordance with their beliefs. Second, Article 16.3 CE, which establishes the principle of state cooperation with religious denominations according to 'the beliefs of Spanish society'. And third, the deeply rooted Spanish tradition of providing and financing Catholic religious education in public schools.

513. The *basic rules of the Concordat* with respect to Catholic religious instruction, and their implementation by state legislation, have been declared in conformity with the Constitution on various occasions by the Constitutional Court[683] and by the Supreme Court.[684] They can be summarized as follows:

- *Catholic religious instruction has to be included in the school curricula* of all pre-university educational levels, from primary education to high school. The same rule applies to university schools for teacher training. The Concordat does not distinguish between public and private schools. This raises a significant theoretical question: to what extent private schools can be subject to the same obligation to offer Catholic instruction as public schools. In practice, the Concordat's lack of distinction between types of schools does not create particular problems, for most private schools are based on a Catholic ethos and are often run by ecclesiastical institutions. Private schools without a specific religious ethos do not normally have difficulties in offering courses on Catholic religion. There are few private schools based on religious non-Catholic ethos, and they are not usually attended by children of parents that require Catholic religious instruction. In any event, in case of actual conflict, they could probably argue their right to have their own religious ethos respected[685] in order to refuse the obligation to offer Catholic instruction, especially if they do not receive public funding.
- Courses on Catholic doctrine must be offered as *elective subjects*[686] and shall never be mandatory for students. They, or their parents, must explicitly request those courses. The school authorities must ensure that students' choice in favour

683. *See infra*, paras 519–523.
684. *See*, for instance, STS 6999/2008, 10 Dec. 2008.
685. *See infra*, para. 536.
686. Some regional laws have been annulled for not specifying that all schools were obliged to offer Catholic religion courses as electives for students. *See* STSJ Balearic Islands 84/2016, 9 Feb. 2016.

of Catholic instruction does not produce negative or discriminatory effects with regard to their school activity.

- Courses of Catholic religion must be offered *in conditions equivalent to the rest of fundamental courses*. This provision, according to the case law of the Constitutional Court, includes a proportionate assignment of credits to the subject of Catholic religion.[687]
- *Teachers of Catholic religion* are appointed by the competent state authorities among the persons *proposed by the bishop* of the diocese where the school is located. The ecclesiastical hierarchy is also the only competent authority to define the contents of religious instruction and to approve the relevant textbooks. The curricula of the courses of Catholic religion for the different educational levels have been defined by the Bishops Conference.[688]

514. According to a decision taken in 2007 by the Plenary Assembly of the Bishops Conference, people who want to be proposed as religion teachers by a diocesan bishop to the relevant state education authority need to meet two requirements, which combine the autonomy of each bishop to judge the moral qualification of candidates with a uniform academic profile applicable to all Spanish dioceses.[689] In the first place, the candidate must have obtained an 'ecclesiastical certification of academic competence' (DECA, *declaración eclesiástica de competencia académica*), which is granted by the Episcopal Commission of Teaching and Catechesis of the Bishops Conference after completing a specific academic training. In the second place, it is necessary to obtain an 'ecclesiastical certification of adequacy' (DEI, *declaración eclesiástica de idoneidad*), granted by the bishop of the diocese within which the candidate intends to teach religion. In accordance with the Code of Canon Law,[690] the second certification is based upon 'considerations of religious and moral nature', and 'entails right doctrine and testimony of Christian life'. It can be revoked any time by the bishop if he thinks that the candidate no longer meets the necessary requisites, and it is not valid for other dioceses. The requirement of DEI was introduced likely as a consequence of the judicial litigation brought up by persons who were removed from the diocesan list of religion teachers because of a personal behaviour that was deemed immoral from a Catholic perspective, rather than because of lack of academic qualifications – these cases are explained in other part of this monograph.[691] Apparently, the Bishops Conference thought that, in order to prevent further litigation along those lines, it would be useful to state more clearly the academic and moral requisites to be proposed as religion teacher, as well as to indicate the revocability of such proposals when some teachers lose, in their bishop's opinion, their moral qualification to teach Catholic doctrine.

515. To fully understand the Spanish bishops' position, it is important to keep in mind that, from the perspective of canon law, religion teachers fulfil an ecclesiastical function, for which they need a *missio canonica*, and are supposed to teach religious

687. Cf. STC 187/1991 and STC 155/1997. *See infra*, paras 520–521.
688. Those curricula are available in: http://www.conferenciaepiscopal.org/curriculo-de-religion/ (accessed 6 Dec. 2017).
689. *See*: http://www.conferenciaepiscopal.org/requisitos-deca/ (accessed 6 Dec. 2017).
690. Cf. Code of Canon Law, canons 804–805.
691. *See supra*, paras 416–421.

doctrines representing the Catholic Church, in exercise of the Church's teaching function (*munus docendi*). Indeed, the position of the Spanish Bishops Conference is consistent with the provisions of the 1983 Code of Canon Law of the Roman Catholic Church, which specifically assigns to diocesan bishops the duty to ensure that 'those who are designated teachers of religious instruction in schools … are outstanding in correct doctrine, the witness of a Christian life, and teaching skill'.[692]

516. In order to reconcile the stability of teachers with the ecclesiastical autonomy and competences, the 2006 Organic Law on Education[693] provides that proposals for *religion teachers* are for a one-year term, and are automatically renewed every year, unless the relevant bishop decides to remove a teacher that is no longer considered appropriate for that function.[694] Although religion teachers are proposed by the ecclesiastical hierarchy, they are appointed, hired and paid by the state. Religion teachers may be public servants with tenure in the realm of education (*funcionarios docentes*) that have been proposed by the competent ecclesiastical authority. In such case, their salaries and working conditions are determined by their public servant status; being in charge of Catholic religion is just a specification of their teaching assignments. If they are not public servants, they must sign a labour contract with the relevant educational authority at a regional level (state competences on education are highly decentralized in Spain).[695] Their labour contract is open-ended and can be full-time or part-time, depending on the teaching needs. Teachers of Catholic religion can teach other subjects different from religion at the same school, provided that they possess the necessary academic requirements. If they are not professional teachers with tenure they receive the same salary as interim teachers of other subjects, adapted to the number of teaching hours per week.[696] Teachers who only teach religion are not eligible for the position of school director. In practice, teachers of Catholic religion are not only clergymen and there is a high percentage of lay people, men and women.

517. There is a high social demand of Catholic instruction in school, although the figures tend to decline slowly over the years. According to the statistics published by the Bishops Conference, during the academic year 2016–2017, combining the figures of all educational levels in public and private schools, around 63% of the students in Spanish schools have chosen courses on Catholic religion. However, the numbers decrease as the students' age increase. The percentage of students that choose classes of Catholic instruction is much higher in elementary and primary education

692. Code of Canon Law, canon 804.2. On the issue of Catholic education generally, as part of the Church's teaching function, *see* canons 793–806 of the Code.
693. *See Ley Orgánica* 2/2006, 3 May 2006, *de Educación*, additional provision 3.
694. On their own motion, state authorities could decide not to renew the contracts of religion teachers only on the ground or 'serious academic or disciplinary reasons' (cf. Order of the Ministry of Education, 11 Oct. 1982, para. 3).
695. The labour relationship of religion teachers is regulated by the *Real Decreto* 696/2007, 1 Jun. 2007, *por el que se regula la relación laboral de los profesores de religión*.
696. The economic conditions of religion teachers with a labour contract are determined by an agreement between the government and the Bishops Conference. *See Orden* of 9 Apr. 1999 decreeing the publication of the *Convenio* of 26 Feb. 1999 *sobre el régimen económico-laboral de las personas que, no perteneciendo a los Cuerpos de Funcionarios Docentes, están encargadas de la enseñanza de la religión católica en los centros públicos de Educación Infantil, de Educación Primaria y de Educación Secundaria*.

than in secondary education, especially in public schools and in private non-ecclesiastical schools.[697]

518. According to a 2013 organic law on education,[698] during primary and secondary education all students must choose necessarily either a religion course (Catholic or other) or an alternative subject, which is called 'social and civic values' in primary education and 'ethical values' in secondary education. The system changes in the two years of the Baccalaureate – those that immediately precede university education – in which religion is just one of the many elective courses offered to students on equal conditions.

II. The Case Law of the Constitutional Court

A. Courses on Catholic Religion

519. There are two important cases adjudicated by the Constitutional Court in relation to the status of courses on Catholic religion in the school for teacher training at the Autonomous University of Madrid (*Universidad Autónoma de Madrid*). The two cases involved the refusal of the governing bodies of the university to comply with Concordat provisions.

520. In the first decision, in 1991,[699] the Constitutional Court sustained the enforceability of Concordat provisions that oblige all schools for teacher training to include Catholic instruction in the school's curriculum as an elective subject, overruling the University authorities' decision not to offer such courses. The Court held that the stipulations of the Concordat, an international treaty legitimately signed by the government and approved by the legislature, limited the university's autonomy and were legally binding for the Autonomous University's authorities. Moreover, the Court declared that this policy was consistent with Article 27.3 of the Constitution, which recognizes the right of parents to ensure that their children receive religious and moral instruction according to their beliefs. For the Court, it was reasonable that the school responsible for training future teachers gave to those interested in teaching Catholic religion courses the chance to receive the appropriate education.

521. In the other case, decided in 1997,[700] the Court ruled again in favour of the Catholic Church. After being compelled by the Constitutional Court to comply with the ecclesiastical demands to offer Catholic instruction in the curriculum for the school for teacher training, the Autonomous University of Madrid had assigned a very low number of credits to that course. The Constitutional Court held that, while a university had discretion to specify the number of credits awarded for its Catholic religious courses, the Concordat necessarily obliged the institution to keeping those credits in

697. The annual statistics since 1996 can be found in: http://www.conferenciaepiscopal.es/alumnos-que-reciben-formacion-religiosa-y-moral-catolica/ (accessed 5 Dec. 2017). The Bishops Conference figures are substantially coincident with the more comprehensive, but not so updated, figures provided by the Ministry of Education (*see* the source *supra* , in para. 509).

698. *Ley Orgánica* 8/2013, 9 Dec. 2013, *para la mejora de la calidad educativa.*

699. STC 187/1991.

700. STC 155/1997.

fair proportion with other 'fundamental courses'. After examination of the Autonomous University's curriculum, the Court concluded that assigning only four credits to Catholic religion courses was clearly disproportionate in relation to the number of credits assigned to other fundamental courses, such as plastic arts and music, which were worth eighteen and twenty-four credits, respectively.

B. Religion Teachers

522. It should be noted that, for the Constitutional Court, the rule that public schools must offer courses on Catholic religion 'in the same conditions as other fundamental courses' does not mean that religion teachers must be treated the same as teachers of other subjects in all respects. Indeed, religion teachers receive different legal treatment in two ways. First, they are paid the same salary as interim teachers, which is lower than the salary paid to ordinary permanent teachers. Second, they are not eligible for the position of school director. Both differences have been declared legitimate by the Constitutional Court on the ground that the appointment of religion teachers is not permanent and depends on the renovation of their proposal – at least tacitly – every year by ecclesiastical authorities. This fact justifies both placing them on the same economic level as interim teachers and disqualifying them from serving as school directors, which are elected for a three-year term.[701]

523. The Constitutional Court has also ruled, on various occasions, on the conflicts arisen by the ecclesiastical removal of religion teachers on the ground of behaviour against Catholic moral rules, or because they were involved in public protests against ecclesiastical policies. Those cases are mentioned in other section of this monograph.[702]

§2. Teaching of Religious Doctrines Other than Catholic

524. While the 1979 Concordat with the Holy See provided for Catholic religious instruction in public schools, no legislative provision was made for the denominational teaching of other religious doctrines in the years that immediately followed the 1978 Constitution. The natural interpretation of the constitutional principle of equality, however, favoured the extension of the system designed for the Catholic Church – with the necessary adaptations – to other religious communities. Some of them, therefore, initiated immediately successful negotiations with the government in order to have their doctrines offered as an optional subject in public schools.

525. Nevertheless, the 1990 Organic Law of General Regulation of the Educational System provided that confessional religious instruction had to be regulated by cooperation agreements between the state and religious denominations.[703] This, in fact, restricted the offer of religious instruction in public schools to those churches that had concluded

701. *See* ATC 1155/1987 (salaries of religion teachers), and STC 47/1990 (religion teachers are not eligible for the position of school director).

702. *See supra*, paras 416–421.

703. *See Ley Orgánica* 1/1990, 3 Oct. 1990, *de Ordenación General del Sistema Educativo*, additional provision 2.

an agreement with the state. As at that time only the Catholic Church was in that position – the Spanish state and the Holy See had signed in 1979 the Agreement on Education and Cultural Affairs, which is part of the Concordat – the practical consequence was that religious teaching other than Catholic was excluded from the schools curricula.[704] The legislative reservation of confessional religious instruction for religious communities with cooperation agreement has continued in all legal reforms on education to date.

526. In 1992, the Spanish legislator approved the cooperation agreements with the Evangelical, Jewish and Islamic Federations, respectively. In the three agreements, Article 10 regulates specifically religious education. Its basic rules are the following:

- Confessional teaching of Evangelical, Jewish or Islamic religion is guaranteed in all pre-university educational levels, *upon request of the students or their parents*, in public schools and in private schools supported with public funds (*centros privados concertados*). In the latter, however, such religious teaching is conditioned to the fact that it is not in conflict with the school's ethos – as may be the case in some Catholic schools, for example. Schools are obliged to facilitate the appropriate classrooms.
- In contrast with the criterion applied to the teaching of Catholic religion, *public schools are not generally obliged to offer* the option of courses on Evangelical, Jewish or Islamic religion unless there is an explicit application by some students or their parents. This rule is based on practical reasons stemming from the number of students that presumably may request religious education other than Catholic.
- As in the case of Catholic religious instruction, *religion teachers shall be proposed by the relevant religious federation.* Defining the content of religious education and choosing the adequate textbooks is also a competence of the religious federations.

527. Article 10 of the 1992 Agreements was developed in 1996 for Evangelical and Islamic teaching, by two agreements between the respective federations and the government.[705] These agreements are aimed at two objectives. First, they endeavour to guarantee that all students requesting Evangelical or Islamic instruction can actually have it, irrespective of their number. Second, they provide for state financing of religious instruction, which was not mentioned by the 1992 Agreements. By virtue of the 1996 Agreements, the government accepts to pay teachers of Evangelical and Islamic religion

704. This fact produced some paradoxes. For instance, the Mormon Church was the first church – after the Catholic Church – to have teaching of its religious doctrine included in the curricula of public schools, but it was not accepted as a member of the Evangelical Federation that signed a cooperation agreement with the state in 1992, and consequently its doctrines have been no longer taught in Spanish public schools after 1990.

705. *See Resolución* of 23 Apr. 1996, of the Vice-Secretary (of the Ministry of the Presidency), ordering the publication of the *Acuerdo* of the Council of Ministers of 1 Mar. 1996, and the *Convenio sobre designación y régimen económico de las personas encargadas de la enseñanza religiosa evangélica, en los centros docentes públicos de educación primaria y secundaria*; and *Resolución* of 23 Apr. 1996, of the Vice-Secretary (of the Ministry of the Presidency), ordering the publication of the *Acuerdo* of the Council of Ministers of 1 Mar. 1996, and the *Convenio sobre designación y régimen económico de las personas encargadas de la enseñanza religiosa islámica, en los centros docentes públicos de educación primaria y secundaria.*

in the same conditions as teachers of Catholic religion – i.e., as interim teachers and depending on their effective teaching hours – when those courses have been requested by a minimum of ten students. In order to reach that minimum number, it is possible to gather students from different ages in the same school.[706]

528. In practice, the system of Evangelical and Islamic religious teaching does not work as efficiently as Catholic religious teaching, for two main reasons. One is the difficulty to reach the minimum number of ten students in the same school. The other – especially in the case of Islamic communities – is the difficulty to reach a consensus about the appropriate persons to teach religion and about their academic or theological qualifications. The places in which teaching of Islamic religion in public schools probably functions better are the extra-peninsular cities of Ceuta and Melilla, which have a high percentage of Muslim population and in which the Spanish government, together with local civil authorities, worked hard to obtain the agreement of local Islamic communities. Andalusia is the only other region with a noticeable number of Islamic religion teachers.[707] In an effort to facilitate the implementation of legal provisions on Islamic education and its standardization, the government has published in 2016 the official syllabi of Islamic instruction for the different school levels.[708] Both the Evangelical Federation and the Islamic Federation – and also the Catholic Church – complain that often students do not receive sufficient information from public schools about the possibilities they have to choose religious instruction; and that sometimes the school authorities do not have the necessary knowledge about the laws governing this area of education.[709]

§3. The Possibility of Neutral Teaching on Religions and Beliefs

529. The 2002 Organic Law on the Quality of Education[710] designed an innovative and plural system of religious education, aimed at reconciling the provisions contained in the Concordat and the 1992 cooperation agreements with the recommendations of the Parliamentary Assembly of the Council of Europe, which had encouraged the inclusion of comparative teaching of religion in school curricula as a way to foster

706. It seems that the Jewish Federation did not express a specific interest in joining that system in 1996, probably because they thought they could not reach that minimum number of students in a school.

707. *See* the numbers *supra* , note 681. To better understand those figures in context, one should take into account that the estimated population of Andalusia is 8.4 million, while Ceuta and Melilla have about 85,000 each.

708. *Resolución* of 14 Mar. 2016, of the *Dirección General de Evaluación y Cooperación Territorial, por la que se publica el currículo de la enseñanza de Religión Islámica de la Educación Infantil*, and *Resolución* of 14 Mar. 2016, of the *Dirección General de Evaluación y Cooperación Territorial, por la que se publican los currículos de la materia de Religión Islámica en Educación Secundaria Obligatoria y Bachillerato*.

709. *See* 2016 *Annual report on the status of religious freedom in Spain*, published by the Ministry of Justice, 41–48.

710. *Ley Orgánica* 10/2002, 23 Dec. 2002, *de Calidad de la Educación*.

tolerance.[711] The new system comprised two alternative ways of teaching religion, at the students' (or their parents') choice.[712] One was the teaching that had traditionally existed in Spain, i.e., the confessional or denominational teaching of religion, which implied instruction in the tenets and values of a certain religion. The other was a pluralistic and non-denominational teaching of religion, i.e., a neutral approach to religious education – or, rather, education *about* religion. The former would be in charge of teachers that were authorized and proposed by those religious communities that had a cooperation agreement with the state, while the latter would be in charge or teachers appointed by the state on strictly academic qualifications according to the common rules applicable to the selection of teachers. Technically, religious teaching was conceived as one *mandatory* subject in the school curriculum – religious instruction – with two possible alternatives – confessional or neutral. Students or their parents could freely choose one of the two ways of religious education, but they necessarily had to choose one of them.

530. This system was never applied. In March 2004, the party in power lost the elections, and the new socialist government suspended the application of the law shortly afterwards, a few months before the scheduled implementation of the new system of religious education. Two years later, a new law on education was enacted, and it returned to the preexisting system. Since then, the school curriculum includes only denominational teaching of religion as an elective subject, in accordance with the system described above in this chapter. In the area of moral values, the efforts of that government focused on a new mandatory subject, 'education for citizenship', which created a strong contrary reaction on the part of the Catholic bishops and thousands of families.[713] This subject was eliminated in a subsequent educational reform and replaced by the obligatory cross-disciplinary teaching of 'civic and constitutional education' – which is supposed to leave out the most controversial aspects of the prior 'education for citizenship' – as well as by the teaching of 'social and civic values' or 'ethical values', which is offered as a necessary alternative to confessional religion courses in primary and secondary education.[714]

---

711. *See* especially the Recommendation 1396 (1999), on Religion and Democracy; and Recommendation 1202 (1993), on Religious Tolerance in a Democratic Society, recommended. There is a subsequent recommendation of the Parliamentary Assembly specifically on this subject: Recommendation 1720 (2005). In the same line, there is an interesting and detailed document elaborated by the OSCE/ODIHR Advisory Council of Experts on Freedom of Religion or Belief, the *Toledo Guiding Principles on Teaching about Religions and Beliefs in Public Schools* (ODIHR: Warsaw, 2007).

712. *See* , for further details on this project, M.E. Olmos Ortega, *Sociedad, Cultura y Religión: asignatura de doble configuración*, 3 Revista General de Derecho Canónico y Derecho Eclesiástico del Estado 1–16 (2003); and R. Palomino, *El área de conocimiento 'Sociedad, Cultura y Religión': algunos aspectos relacionados con la libertad religiosa y de creencias*, 10 Revista General de Derecho Canónico y Derecho Eclesiástico del Estado 1–27 (2003).

713. *See supra* , Part II, Ch. 2 §8 IV.

714. *See supra* , para. 518.

§4. Religious Symbols in Public Schools

531. In some public schools in Spain, there are Catholic religious symbols, normally crucifixes, in visible places such as classrooms or common areas. This usually occurs in older centres, where they have been kept out of respect for tradition. The display of these religious symbols has not been understood normally with any aim of proselytism or indoctrination, but rather as a way of expressing respect for the history and cultural identity of the educational institution. There have been occasional claims against these symbols on the part of students' parents with atheistic beliefs who demanded their removal. The reason asserted in these claims was not religious indoctrination but the constitutional principle of state neutrality about religion (*laicidad*) and the alleged parents' right not to have their children exposed to religious symbols with which they profoundly disagreed. The most important case is mentioned in other section of this monograph.[715]

715. *See supra*, paras 214–215. Other cases that were not resolved by judicial decision are mentioned in S. Cañamares, *Las manifestaciones externas de religiosidad en el ordenamiento jurídico español: el empleo de simbología religiosa*, in *El ejercicio de la libertad religiosa en España: cuestiones disputadas* 177 (A. de la Hera, R. Palomino & A. Motilla eds, Ministerio de Justicia 2003); and G. Moreno Botella, *Libertad religiosa y neutralidad escolar. A propósito del crucifijo y de otros símbolos de carácter confesional*, 58 Revista Española de Derecho Canónico 207 (2001).

Chapter 2. Religious Schools

532. According to Article 27 of the Constitution, the state has the responsibility of guaranteeing the citizens' right to education and organizing the educational system in the country. The Constitution defines the aim of education as 'the full development of human personality, with respect for democratic principles and for fundamental rights and freedoms' (Article 27.2 CE). The right to education is conceived as a right of every citizen that, among other things, makes them entitled to receive elementary education free of charge – elementary education is compulsory. State responsibility and competences vis-à-vis the educational system do not imply that all schools have to be owned or run by the state. On the contrary, as freedom of teaching is also recognized to all citizens, individuals as well as legal persons have the right to establish educational centres, with respect for constitutional principles (Article 27.1 and 27.6 CE). Naturally, this right must be exercised within the legal framework designed by the state to guarantee the quality and efficiency of the educational system.

533. Over the last three decades, many important statutes have been enacted in Spain to regulate or modify the main coordinates of the educational system (indeed, many scholars opine that there have been *too many* statutes, for this is a matter that requires stability and social consensus). The most significant laws are: the Organic Law on the Right to Education (1985); the Organic Law of General Regulation of the Educational System (1990); the Organic Law on the Quality of Education (2002), a substantial part of which was never put into practice, for its application was suspended by the new government that came to power in April 2004; the Organic Law on Education (2006), which was designed to replace the statutes of 1990 and 2002, and modified some articles of the statute of 1985; and the Organic Law on the improvement of quality in education (2013), which modifies important aspects of the 2006 law.[716]

534. Schools in Spain may be public or private. The former are managed by the state – more precisely by the educational regional authorities – and are supposed to be ideologically neutral; they neither have nor may have a specific religious or denominational orientation. The latter are owned and managed by individuals or institutions, and may have a specific religious or philosophical orientation if they so wish. Provided that they comply with the legal requirements aimed at guaranteeing the quality of education, schools of any educational level – including universities – can be founded by private initiative or associations. This rule, naturally, applies also to religious communities.

535. Private schools may be partly subsidized by the state when they offer tuition-free teaching and satisfy regular schooling necessities in the area.[717] In order to benefit from public funding, a school must conclude an economic agreement (*concierto*) with the educational authority of its region. Normally these agreements are signed for a term of several years with the possibility of a renewal. Preferential

716. *Ley Orgánica* 8/1985, 3 Jul. 1985, *reguladora del Derecho a la Educación*; *Ley Orgánica* 1/1990, 3 Oct. 1990, *de Ordenación General del Sistema Educativo*; *Ley Orgánica* 10/2002, 23 Dec. 2002, *de Calidad de la Educación*; *Ley Orgánica* 2/2006, 3 May 2006, *de Educación*; and *Ley Orgánica* 8/2013, 9 Dec. 2013, *para la mejora de la calidad educativa.*

717. *See* Arts 116–117 of the *Ley Orgánica* 2/2006, 3 May 2006, *de Educación.*

access to economic agreements is given to schools that cater for economically disadvantaged children, develop educational experiments of pedagogical interest or operate as cooperatives. Regional authorities have some latitude to define the criteria for these *conciertos* or economic agreements with private schools, but it is illegal to deny such possibility to single-sex schools when they comply with the anti-discrimination criteria approved by UNESCO and there is no evidence of discrimination on the ground of sex.[718] In exchange for public funding, private schools accept to submit to a large part of the legal criteria and rules applicable to public schools. Thus, they must permit a participation of the school community at large (including teachers and students' parents) in the government of the school in terms similar to public schools[719] – but without detriment to the school ethos. In addition, subsidized private schools may not request from the students' families any economic contribution for gratuitous education, or to impose in practice 'voluntary' donations to foundations that support the school.[720] The 2006 Organic Law on Education provides for a relative assimilation of the expenses of subsidized private schools to those of public schools.[721] Reality, however, is different. When comparing the figures of state expenditure – publicly available – in public and private schools, the conclusion is that the mean cost per pupil for the state budget in subsidized private schools is approximately half the mean cost per pupil in public schools.

536. Subsidized or not by the state, private schools are entitled to define their own ethos – the so-called *carácter propio* or *ideario* – that define their aims and functional characteristics. In addition to pedagogical aspects, the school ethos may include moral aspects, of religious nature or not. In any event, the school ethos must respect the students', teachers' and parents' rights as recognized by the Constitution and other laws. The school ethos must be available to all current and potential members of the school community. By completing the registration process, students accept to respect the school ethos.[722]

537. In the admission process of new pupils, subsidized private schools may not discriminate applicants on religious or other grounds,[723] while non-subsidized schools are free to use religious criteria to select their students. Pupils of all schools have the right to the respect for their freedom of conscience as well as for their religious and moral convictions.[724] Moreover, the law prescribes, with specific reference to subsidized private schools, that teaching shall be carried out 'with full respect for freedom of conscience' and that 'all confessional practices shall be voluntary'.[725] As

718. *See* Art. 84.3 of the 2006 Organic Law on Education and modified by the 2013 Organic Law on the improvement of quality in education, both cited in note 716. This interpretation was confirmed by the Supreme Court by STS 749/2017, 4 May 2017.
719. *See ibid.*, Art. 119.
720. *See ibid.*, Art. 88.
721. *See ibid.*, Art. 118.
722. *See ibid.*, Art. 115.
723. *See ibid.*, Art. 84.3.
724. *See* Art. 6.3.e) of the *Ley Orgánica* 8/1985, 3 Jul. 1985, *reguladora del Derecho a la Educación*, as modified by the *Ley Orgánica* 2/2006, 3 May 2006, *de Educación*, final provision 1.
725. *See* Art. 52 of the *Ley Orgánica* 8/1985, 3 Jul. 1985, *reguladora del Derecho a la Educación*.

a consequence, out of respect for the school ethos, pupils might be requested to attend religion classes but may never be obliged to participate in religious rites or ceremonies.

538. Approximately two-thirds of pre-university students in Spain attend public schools and one-third study in private schools.[726] About 80% of private schools receive state funding through economic agreements or *conciertos* with the relevant regional authorities. Owned or not by ecclesiastical institutions with legal personality under canon law, the vast majority of private school in Spain have an ethos inspired in Catholic doctrine and morals, which often pervades the entire school curriculum. Sometimes, subsidized private schools require their pupils to take classes of Catholic religion but never compel them to participate in religious practices. Often, however, they attempt to accommodate the religious views of their pupils without disruption to the school ethos, especially when students were sent to that school not by their own choice but because they could not obtain a place in a public school nearby. The praxis of non-subsidized private schools is not uniform. Some of them follow practices similar to those of subsidized schools, and some others tend to apply stricter religious criteria.

726. Statistical detailed information may be found in the Internet pages of the Ministry of Education: http://www.mecd.gob.es/servicios-al-ciudadano-mecd/estadisticas/educacion/no-universitaria.html (accessed 5 Dec. 2017).

Part X. Matrimonial and Family Law

Chapter 1. Legal Position of Religious Marriage

§1. The Right to a Religious Marriage

539. For many people, marriage is a divine institution that requires a religious ceremony. It is the religious bond what matters to them rather than the civil bond created by state laws. Legal systems deal in different ways with this dual perspective of marriage, religious and civil. In Spain, the legal history of religious marriage reflects the pendular movement between state Catholic confessionality and anti-Catholic policies that characterized Spanish political history until the 1978 Constitution.[727]

540. Thus, because Catholicism has been the official religion in Spain, almost without interruption, since 1492 to 1978, there is a long-standing tradition of recognizing full civil effects to marriages celebrated in accordance with the rules of Roman Catholic canon law. Only in two ephemeral periods of Spanish history has state legislation discontinued the recognition of canon law marriage. In both occasions, with different connotations, the relevant laws had some anti-religious nuance. One was in 1870, when the first law establishing civil marriage was passed in Spain. That law adopted the system usually known as 'obligatory civil marriage', i.e., it provided that civil marriage was the only marriage accepted as valid vis-à-vis the state; interestingly, the civil marriage introduced by the 1870 law was indissoluble and conceived as a replica of canon law marriage. The law was abrogated in 1875, and since then both civil and canonical marriages were recognized by the state, according to the so-called system of 'subsidiary civil marriage', which would be later adopted by the Civil Code promulgated in 1889. Under this system, canonical marriage prevailed over civil marriage. All Catholic citizens – i.e., the immense majority of citizens – were obliged by civil law to contract canonical marriage unless they made a formal statement declaring that they no longer professed Catholic religion. In addition, canon law marriage and the decisions of ecclesiastical jurisdiction were granted full civil effects; state laws recognized the exclusive competence of ecclesiastical courts on issues related to the validity and separation of canonical marriages. The second period began in 1932, six months after the Republican Constitution of 1931 was enacted. Civil

727. For a clear account of the history of the interaction between religious and civil marriage in Spain, *see* M. López Alarcón & R. Navarro-Valls, *Derecho matrimonial canónico y concordado* 39–53 (7th ed., Tecnos 2010).

marriage – this time susceptible of dissolution by divorce – was again imposed as the only marriage recognized by state laws. This law was repealed in 1938 – the civil war was still in progress – by the first government of General Franco and Spanish law returned to the precedent system of subsidiary civil marriage.

541. The attitude of the 1978 Constitution and subsequent legislation on marriage echoes the constitutional change of perspective about religion and religious freedom. Article 32 CE,[728] instead of imposing civil marriage as mandatory, referred to an unspecified plurality of forms of marriage that should be later regulated by legislation. Thus, the Constitution, in addition to implicitly preserving the tradition of recognizing the civil effects of canonical marriage, envisaged its extension to other religious marriages. That is, instead of returning to the model of obligatory civil marriage adopted in 1870 and 1932, the Constitution implicitly transformed the precedent system of dual marriage (canonical and civil) into a pluralist system (civil marriage plus various types of religious marriages). This constitutional approach to marriage was confirmed by different laws in the ensuing years. Currently, Spain has a pluralist matrimonial system whose main characteristics can be described as follows.

542. Everybody has the right to marry in accordance to the religious ceremony of his choice. Article 2 LOLR explicitly indicates that freedom of religion comprises every person's right 'to celebrate his matrimonial rites', whatever his religion is. No civil ceremony, before or after the matrimonial rite, is required by law. However, under the LOLR the right to a religious marriage does not include per se the right to the recognition of civil effects of that marriage.

543. According to the Civil Code (Article 59), as a general rule a religious marriage produces civil effects only when that specific form of religious marriage has been explicitly recognized by the state, either by an agreement with the relevant religious community or by state unilateral legislation. There are two exceptions: marriages celebrated abroad by Spanish citizens in a religious form accepted by the law of the land (Article 49 CC); and marriages celebrated in Spain by two foreign citizens in a religious form recognized by the personal law of any of them (Article 50 CC).

544. Until 2015, Spanish civil law recognized civil effects to religious marriages only by agreement, in particular to Catholic, Evangelical, Jewish and Islamic marriages, through the 1979 Concordat and the 1992 Agreements with the major religious minorities. For twenty-three years no recognition of other religious marriages was operated by unilateral state legislation, despite the repeated requests of religious communities with 'well-known roots' that do not have a reasonable prospect of signing a cooperation agreement with the state in the next future.[729] The situation changed when the 2015 Law on Non-Contentious Judicial Proceedings modified Article 60 of the Civil Code, which now explicitly accepts the civil effects of marriages celebrated according to the form of those religious communities with recognized 'well-known roots' (*notorio arraigo*)[730] – currently the Mormon Church, Jehovah's Witnesses, Buddhists and the Orthodox Church.

728. *See supra*, para. 53.
729. *See supra*, paras 302–303.
730. See *Ley* 15/2015, 2 Jul. 2015, *de Jurisdicción Voluntaria.*

545. The legal position of Catholic marriage under Spanish civil law is superior to the other recognized religious marriages, in accordance with the international obligations assumed by the state in the 1979 Concordat, which are a consequence of the stronger social rooting of the Catholic Church in Spain and of the well-established historical influence of canonical marriage in the Spanish legal concept of marriage (as in all Western countries). The most significant difference is that Spanish law recognizes civil effects to some decisions of ecclesiastical jurisdiction on the issue of the termination of marriage. It has been argued that, together with the long-standing tradition of civil effects of ecclesiastical jurisdiction in Spain – as in Italy or Portugal – the main reason for this differential treatment is the 'reliability' of ecclesiastical jurisdiction before the state. Unlike other religious matrimonial systems, Roman canon law offers a unified and hierarchically structured jurisdiction, with an ancient, consistent and well-known body of jurisprudence and case law.[731] During the negotiations of the 1992 Agreements, the Jewish and Islamic communities expressed to the government – unsuccessfully – their interest in having some sort of recognition for the decisions of their religious courts. After 1992 these claims, to the author's knowledge, have not been reiterated.

§2. The Civil Effects of Catholic Marriages

546. The basic rules about the position of canon law marriage vis-à-vis Spanish law are in the Concordat, more precisely in Article VI of the 1979 Agreement on Juridical Affairs, which guarantees the civil effects of canonical marriages, subject to their registration in the Civil Registry, as well as the recognition of the most significant decisions of ecclesiastical jurisdiction on the termination of marriage, after a summary proceeding before state courts:

Article VI of the Agreement on Juridical Affairs:

1. The state recognizes the civil effects of marriages celebrated in accordance with the norms of canon law.
   Canonical marriages produce civil effects since the moment of their celebration. For the full recognition of those effects registration in the Civil Registry is necessary. For such registration it is only required to provide an ecclesiastical certificate or marriage.
2. The contracting parties, in accordance with canon law provisions, may go to the ecclesiastical courts to request a declaration of nullity of their marriage, and may also ask for a pontifical dissolution of a valid and unconsummated marriage. Upon request of any of the parties, such ecclesiastical decisions shall be granted civil effects if they are declared in conformity with state law by a decision adopted by the competent civil court.

731. *See* J. Martínez-Torrón, *Concordato, cooperación e igualdad. La cooperación del Estado español con las confesiones religiosas a la luz del vigente sistema de acuerdos con la Iglesia católica*, 4 Revista General de Derecho Canónico y Derecho Eclesiástico del Estado 6–10 (2004).

547. The Concordat rules were developed, and also nuanced, by the Civil Code after its reform in 1981.[732] With regard to the celebration of marriage, two articles of the Civil Code are particularly important. Article 59 CC refers indiscriminately to religious forms of marriage, while Article 60 CC distinguishes canonical marriage from other religious marriages:

Article 59 CC:

Matrimonial consent can be expressed in the form of a registered religious denomination [in the Registry of Religious Entities], in the terms agreed with the state or, in the absence of such agreement, authorized by unilateral state laws.

Article 60 CC:

1. Marriages celebrated in accordance with the norms of canon law or in any of the religious forms mentioned in the cooperation agreements between state and religious communities shall have civil effects.
2. Civil effects shall be also recognized to marriages celebrated in the religious form of those churches, religious denominations or communities, or federations thereof, which, once registered in the Registry of Religious Entities, had obtained official recognition of well-known roots in Spain.

   ...
3. The full recognition of the civil effects of marriages celebrated in a religious form is subject to the provisions of next chapter [dealing with registration of marriage in the Civil Registry].

548. The text of Article 60 CC singles out canonical marriage among all other religious marriages and suggests that it constitutes an exception from the general rule that accords civil effects to religious marriages merely as forms of celebration (such specific distinction of canon law marriage already existed prior to the modification of Article 60 CC in 2015).[733] However, the wording of Article 60 CC was – and is – sufficiently ambiguous to raise doubts about its intended meaning and reach. Indeed, immediately after the 1981 reform, scholars discussed if this article actually contained a *substantial* or only a *formal* recognition of canonical marriage.[734] Certainly, the nominal differentiation of canonical marriage, together with the expression 'in accordance with the norms of canon law', which had an unequivocal meaning in Spanish legal tradition, seemed to imply a substantial recognition of canonical marriage. The consequence of it would be that Article 60 CC recognized civil effects to *all canon law rules* on marriage and not only to those rules dealing specifically with the religious

---

732. *See* *Ley* 30/1081, 7 Jul. 1981, *por la que se modifica la regulación del matrimonio en el Código Civil y se determina el procedimiento a seguir en las causas de nulidad, separación y divorcio.*
733. *See* *supra*, para. 544.
734. For an account of that scholarly debate, *see* M. López Alarcón & R. Navarro-Valls, *Derecho matrimonial canónico y concordado*, 463–472.

form or ceremony of celebration. Beyond theoretical disputes, the practical solutions adopted by other articles of the Civil Code, in conjunction with the case law of Spanish courts, have clarified that the Spanish matrimonial system is hybrid, not always consistent, and with many intricacies whose detailed analysis exceeds the purpose of this monograph.[735] In essence, it could be described as a system that establishes the predominance of civil marriage but makes it compatible with a partial substantial recognition of Roman canonical marriage, and with a formal recognition of other religious marriages. The basic rules that determine the civil effects of canonical marriage in Spain are, in summary, the following.

549. Canonical marriages are granted *civil effects in Spanish law since the moment of their celebration*, subject to their *registration in the Civil Registry*. Being the Concordat an international treaty with a foreign state (the Holy See), this rule has extraterritorial validity; i.e., a canonical marriage celebrated abroad by Spanish citizens will have civil effects irrespective of the fact that canonical marriages are recognized or not by the civil law of the country where the marriage was celebrated. No civil certificate or authorization prior to the ecclesiastical celebration is required. To register a marriage in the Civil Registry, it is sufficient to provide the relevant ecclesiastical certificate that the spouses receive after the religious celebration. Although the spouses can register their marriage by themselves, the Concordat provides that registration shall be in any event requested by the pastor of the parish where the wedding took place within five days after the ceremony.[736]

550. Article 63.2 CC, however, establishes some restrictions on the registration process. In particular, *registration shall be refused* when the data contained in the ecclesiastical certification, or the information already existing in the Civil Registry, reveal that a particular marriage does not comply with the necessary civil law requirements. This constitutes a definite limitation on the substantial recognition of canonical marriage. In principle, according to Article 60 CC all marriages validly celebrated under canon law should be recognized; but, according to Article 63.2 CC, only those canonical marriages that also meet the civil law requisites can be registered. In other words, to be accepted in the Civil Registry, canonical marriages must be free not only from the legal impediments established by the Code of Canon Law but also from those established by the Civil Code. In practice, if we analyze in parallel the legal impediments to marriage in both codes, these are the situations in which canonical marriages could encounter problems at the time of their civil registration:

- Marriages of non-emancipated minors that can be validly celebrated in accordance with canon law – under Spanish civil law the minimum age for marriage is 18 years, but under Roman canon law it is 16 years for men and 14 years for women.[737] This situation – which is certainly unusual in Spain – can be avoided if the relevant contracting party becomes emancipated. In Spanish law, legal emancipation can

735. *See ibid.*, 473–499, for a relatively detailed analysis and further bibliographical references.
736. *See* final protocol with respect to Art. VI of the 1979 Agreement on Juridical Affairs between Spain and the Holy See.
737. Cf. Art. 46 CC and canon 1083 of the Code of Canon Law, respectively.

be granted, after a minor reaches the age of 16, by the persons that have parental authority and also, under certain circumstances, by a court.[738]

- Canonical marriages celebrated by a Catholic who has a prior civil marriage with a third party. As Roman canon law does not recognize the civil marriage of a Catholic as valid,[739] this circumstance does not constitute a canonical impediment to marry.[740] Nonetheless, from the civil perspective, permitting the civil registration of a new canonical marriage with a different person would be equivalent to recognizing bigamy. This situation can be avoided by obtaining the divorce of the first civil marriage.
- Canonical marriages celebrated with ecclesiastical, but not civil, dispensation of a canon law impediment that is also an impediment under civil law. There are three possible cases of coincident impediments:[741] (a) impediment of consanguinity in the third degree of the collateral line (e.g., marriage between uncle and niece); (b) impediment of crime by mutual cooperation (i.e., the marriage between persons sentenced as authors or accomplices of the intentional homicide of the spouse of either of them); (c) impediment of adoption, in the direct line or in the second degree of the collateral line (i.e., marriage between adopter and adoptee, or between siblings by adoption). The first case is avoidable by obtaining the appropriate civil dispensation by a judge. The second case is very unlikely, for the ecclesiastical impediment of crime is very rarely dispensed in practice; in any event the civil impediment is dispensable by a judge. The third case is the most problematic one, for the impediment of adoption can be dispensed under canon law but Spanish civil law does not foresee its dispensation and besides considers adoption irrevocable.[742] In that case, therefore, a canonical marriage could not be recognized in Spain; it is not, however, a frequent situation.

551. Two modalities of termination of marriage under Roman canon law are recognized by Spanish civil law. One is the *declaration of nullity of a marriage* by an ecclesiastical court. Declarations of nullity do not break the matrimonial bond strictly speaking; they contain a pronouncement that a marriage has been null and void since the beginning and therefore declare that a matrimonial bond never existed. A declaration of nullity is possible only on these grounds: insufficient or inexistent matrimonial consent of the parties, existence of a legal impediment at the time of marriage, or defective form of celebration.[743] The other modality is the *dissolution of a valid but unconsummated marriag*e, decreed by the Roman Pontiff. In the Catholic Church, there is no divorce or any other ordinary way to dissolve a marriage (apart from the death of one of the spouses). However, canon law has accepted for centuries that the Pope has the extraordinary power to dissolve marriages in exceptional circumstances,

738. *See* Arts 314–324 CC.
739. Cf. canon 1117 of the Code of Canon Law.
740. However, canon 1071.1.2 of the Code of Canon Law requires a specific authorization of the bishop in this type of cases, although not as a condition for the validity.
741. Cf. Arts 46–47 CC; and canons 1090, 1091 and 1094 of the Code of Canon Law.
742. Cf. Art. 180 CC.
743. The legal grounds for the nullity of canonical marriage – by lack of legal capacity, consent or due form – are regulated in canons 1073–1117 of the Code of Canon Law.

which include cases of no consummation, i.e., lack of completed coitus between the spouses after contracting marriage.[744] Both the Concordat and the Civil Code provide that these two types of ecclesiastical decisions shall have civil effects under two conditions: (a) the civil effects must be requested by at least one of the parties; and (b) the ecclesiastical resolution must be declared 'in conformity with the state law' (*ajustadas al derecho del Estado*) by a competent civil court.

552. After its reform in 1981, Article 80 CC introduced an important nuance to those conditions that was to some extent an add-on to the Concordat. Article 80 provided specific guidance for the declaration of 'conformity with the state law' by indicating that it had to be adopted by the competent civil court in accordance with the criteria set up by Article 954 of the Code of Civil Procedure (*Ley de Enjuiciamiento Civil*) that was then in force. The reference caused some perplexity among scholars, because Article 954 enumerated four conditions for the exequatur of foreign courts' judgments coming from a state that did not have a treaty of judicial cooperation with Spain. Compliance with those conditions determined if Spanish courts could grant the exequatur – if any of those conditions was not met, the execution of the foreign judgment would be rejected. The interpretation of that provision as applied to ecclesiastical decisions on marriage generated lively scholarly debates, as well as a case law of the Supreme Court that was not always consistent, especially with regard to two of the four conditions mentioned by Article 954: that the judgment had not been rendered in default (*rebeldía*), and that the legal effect pursued with the exequatur was licit in Spain.[745] The situation changed in 2015, when the Law on International Legal Cooperation on Civil Proceedings abrogated Article 954 of the old procedural code.[746] Now, the reference of Article 80 CC must be understood as redirected to Articles 44–49 of the Law on International Legal Cooperation, which has simplified things in this area. The 2015 Law departs from the premise that all foreign judgments shall be granted exequatur unless there is a ground for refusal under Article 46. Applying that article to the particular case of ecclesiastical jurisdiction, we can conclude that all decisions of nullity or dissolution of marriages mentioned by the Concordat must be recognized in conformity with the state law and hence executable, except in the following cases:[747]

– If the ecclesiastical decision has been rendered with 'manifest violation of the parties' rights of defence'. In the particular case of default judgments (*rebeldía*), the law presumes that this occurs if the defendant was not duly served (Article

744. Dissolution of canonical marriage, in extraordinary situations, is regulated in canons 1141–1150 of the Code of Canon Law.

745. For a more detailed analysis of these conditions, and the appropriate bibliographical and case law references, *see* M. López Alarcón & R. Navarro-Valls, *Derecho matrimonial canónico y concordado*, 491–497.

746. Article 80 CC remitted to Art. 954 of the old Code of Civil Procedure, which was replaced by a new procedural code in 2000. Article 954, however, was left in force by the new code and has only recently been abolished by the 2015 Law on International Legal Cooperation on Civil Proceedings (*Ley* 29/2015, 30 Jul. 2015, *de cooperación jurídica internacional en materia civil*).

747. *See* R. Navarro-Valls & S. Cañamares Arribas, *El momento crítico de los matrimonios religiosos*, in *Tratado de Derecho de la Familia* 964–968 (M. Yzquierdo & M. Cuena eds, 2nd ed., Thomson-Aranzadi 2017).

46.1.b). As a consequence, if one of the parties was voluntarily absent from the ecclesiastical process, he cannot allege that circumstance to have the other party's application for civil recognition rejected.

- If the ecclesiastical decision is irreconcilable with a judgment rendered by Spanish courts, or with a judgment previously rendered by other state's court that can be recognized in Spain (Article 46.1.d-e). Such will be the situation, for instance, if one of the parties to the ecclesiastical process applies for the civil recognition of a pontifical dissolution of a marriage that has already been dissolved or declared null and void by a civil court.
- In case of lis pendens, i.e., when there is a parallel procedure still ongoing in Spain, with the same matter and between the same parties, which has commenced prior to the ecclesiastical procedure (Article 46.1.f).

553. The competent civil courts for these declarations of conformity with the state law are family courts or first instance courts. If the application for execution has been filed by only one of the parties to the ecclesiastical process, the civil court must give the other party the opportunity to be heard in this procedure, and that party may express his opposition. The court, however, has full discretion to decide if the reasons alleged by that party are sufficient or not to halt the execution.[748] It is important to note that, according to Article 48 of the Law on International Legal Cooperation, it is explicitly forbidden to Spanish courts to engage in a review of the merits of the judgment whose exequatur is requested.

554. The recognition of the civil effects of ecclesiastical decisions declaring the nullity or decreeing the dissolution of canonical marriages does not imply any reservation of jurisdiction in favour of ecclesiastical courts, as occurred in older times.[749] Since 1981, the Civil Code is very clear in affirming the competence of civil courts and the applicability of civil rules to the separation, nullity of divorce to all marriages, irrespective of their form of celebration – civil or religious.[750] Therefore, the parties to a canonical marriage have a choice between two jurisdictions. They may have their marriage terminated by a civil court – which applies the Civil Code provisions – or they may prefer having their marriage declared null and void by an ecclesiastical court (or, if unconsummated, dissolved by the Pope) and applying later for the civil execution of the ecclesiastical decision.

555. The Spanish matrimonial system has had an impact on the EU law on the recognition and enforcement of judgments in matrimonial matters. In application of the Council Regulation (EC) No. 2201/2003, ecclesiastical decisions on the nullity or dissolution of canonical marriages, once declared in conformity with the state law and executed by Spanish civil courts, shall be recognized with civil effects in any Member State of the European Union as if they were decisions of nullity or divorce rendered

748. *See* Art. 778 of the 2000 Code of Civil Procedure. This Article has changed the prior system and enlarged the court's discretion to decide the right way to proceed. Under the additional provision 2 of the *Ley* 30/1081 that reformed the Civil Code, the mere opposition of the other party obliged the court to discontinue the procedure, which in practice was equivalent to reject the application for the execution of the ecclesiastical decision.

749. *See supra* , para. 540.

750. *See* Arts 73, 81 and 85 CC.

by Spanish civil courts. Such recognition is obliged under European Union law also for states whose matrimonial systems do not recognize the ecclesiastical jurisdiction on marriage or even the canonical form of celebration of marriages.[751]

§3. The Civil Effects of Religious Marriages Other than Catholic

556. The recognition of civil effects to other religious marriages generates less complex problems, for it is exclusively a *formal* recognition. The only religious rules accepted by the state law are those relating to the form of celebration of marriage – with some additional civil requirements, especially important for Islamic marriages. Article 7 of the 1992 Agreements with Protestantism, Judaism and Islam implemented for the first time the provisions of Article 59 CC,[752] in terms almost identical for the three federations signatory of the agreements (however, the wording of Article 7 of the Agreement with the Islamic Federation is obscure in some points, and indeed required a subsequent interpretation by the Ministry of Justice).[753] In 2015 the Law on Non-Contentious Judicial Proceedings[754] modified Article 60 CC and extended the same system of civil recognition to the religious marriage of those religious communities with well-known roots in Spain – to date Mormons, Jehovah's Witnesses, Buddhists and the Orthodox Church.[755] Other provisions of the same law (which modified Article 7 of the 1992 Agreements, and some articles of the 2011 Law on the Civil Registry[756]) had also an impact on this area.[757] In summary, the rules that govern the recognition of civil effects of religious marriages other than Catholic are the following.

557. Spanish law currently recognizes civil effects to religious marriages celebrated in Evangelical, Jewish, Islamic, Mormon, Jehovah's Witness, Buddhist and Orthodox form, as far as they comply with *three requisites*:

---

751. *See* Art. 63 of the Council Regulation (EC) No. 2201/2003, of 27 Nov. 2003, concerning jurisdiction and the recognition and enforcement of judgments in matrimonial matters and the matters of parental responsibility. The same rule applies to Portugal, Italy and Malta, whose concordats also accept the civil effects of ecclesiastical decisions. For a detailed analysis of this issue, *see* R. Rodríguez Chacón, *Sentencias matrimoniales canónicas y Unión Europea*, 7 Revista General de Derecho Canónico y Derecho Eclesiástico del Estado 1–33 (2005).

752. *See supra*, para. 547.

753. Such authoritative interpretation was done, in particular, by the Directorate General in charge of Civil Registries. *See Instrucción* of 10 Feb. 1993, of the *Dirección General de los Registros y del Notariado, sobre la inscripción en el Registro Civil de determinados matrimonios celebrados en forma religiosa*.

754. *Ley* 15/2015, 2 Jul. 2015, *de Jurisdicción Voluntaria.*

755. *See supra*, para. 544.

756. *Ley* 20/2011, 21 Jul. 2011, *del Registro Civil.*

757. Of some significance is also a 2016 Order of the Ministry of Justice regarding the registration of religious marriages (*Orden* JUS/577/2016, 19 Apr. 2016, *sobre inscripción en el Registro Civil de determinados matrimonios celebrados en forma religiosa y aprobación del modelo de certificado de capacidad matrimonial y de celebración de matrimonio religioso*).

- The parties must express their consent in the presence of a *religious minister* of the relevant religious community and at least *two other witnesses of full age*. This requisite is particularly significant for Islamic marriages, whose religious rules do not require the presence of an imam as a condition of validity of the celebration of marriage.
- Except in the case of Islamic marriages, the contracting parties, prior to the celebration, must apply for and obtain a *certificate of matrimonial capacity* from the Civil Registry. This certificate shall be granted if the parties meet the requisites generally established by the Civil Code for the validity of marriage. The certificate can be used for six months, and the parties must deliver it to the religious minister in charge of the celebration. In the case of Islamic marriages, such certificate is not mandatory – although is highly recommended[758] – but, if obtained, is also valid for six months. This different treatment of civil matrimonial certificates for Islamic marriages seems to be motivated by the Islamic Federation's claims to the recognition of the polygamy at the time of the negotiation of its cooperation agreement with the state. The government rejected such claims, on the ground that polygamy was incompatible with the Spanish notion of public order, but accepted that the parties were not obliged to obtain their civil certificate of matrimonial capacity before the religious celebration of marriage. Thus, the Spanish government implicitly opened the door to polygamous marriages celebrated in accordance with Islamic law, although these marriages will lack civil effects, for they cannot be registered in the Civil Registry.[759]
- Religious ministers in charge of the celebration are responsible for *registering religious marriages in the Civil Registry*. They must send to the Civil Registry, within five days after the ceremony, the appropriate religious certification, together with his accreditation as a minister with competence to celebrate a religious marriage. The parties to the marriage must receive also a certification of their religious marriage and a copy of this certification must be kept in the archives of the relevant religious community. In the case of Muslims that celebrated their marriage without a civil certificate of matrimonial capacity, the official in charge of the Civil Registry shall have to check not only that the religious certificate meets the formal requirements for registration but also that the parties had legal capacity for a valid marriage in accordance with the provisions of the Civil Code.[760]

558. It is commonly accepted, since long, that the recognition of civil effects to Evangelical, Jewish and Islamic marriages has no extraterritorial application because, in contrast to the Concordat, the 1992 Agreements do not have the juridical nature of international treaties (they are formally state legislation from the perspective of the Spanish system of sources of law[761]), and also because the relevant religious federations only cover the range of national territory. Therefore, since 1993 the Ministry of Justice

758. *See* the *Instrucción* cited in note 753, para. IV.

759. For a critique to that approach, which in practice could be detrimental for Muslim women, *see* J. Martínez-Torrón, *La igualdad de sexos en el sistema acordado de relaciones entre Estado español y confesiones religiosas*, 10-11 Æqualitas 66–67 (2002).

760. *See* para. IV of the *Instrucción* of 1993 mentioned in note 753.

761. *See supra*, para. 355.

made clear that marriages celebrated by Spanish citizens abroad in any of those three religious forms could not be recognized by civil law unless those forms were accepted as valid by the law of the land.[762] A fortiori, the same rule must be applied to the civil effects of any other religious form of marriage accepted by virtue of Article 60 the Civil Code as modified in 2015.

559. The civil jurisdiction is competent to adjudicate on the separation, nullity or dissolution of all religious marriages, applying the general rules of the Civil Code on marriage.[763] The decisions of religious jurisdictions other than Catholic on the termination of marriage (or on any other issue relating to their respective religious marriages) are not recognized civil effects by Spanish law – although they might have some indirect effects through mediation, as indicated in the next chapter.

762. *See* para. II of the *Instrucción* of 1993 mentioned in note 753.
763. *See* Arts 73, 81 and 85 CC.

Chapter 2. Legal Position of Religious Family Law

560. Apart from the civil recognition of religious marriage, according to what has been explained in the previous chapter, Spanish law does not recognize, per se, civil effects to any provision of religious family law or to the decisions of the relevant religious jurisdiction. Legal relationships between persons bound by a religious marriage, parent-child relationships, and inheritance rights derived from family relationships, are therefore subject to the ordinary rules of Spanish civil law.

561. Nevertheless, in the context of marriage relationships, religious family law may have civil effects indirectly, through the matrimonial agreements (*capitulaciones matrimoniales*) that the contracting parties may voluntary enter into before or after marrying.[764] These agreements must be solemnized, as a condition of validity, by an authenticated document before a notary public, and abide by the general norms on contract. They often take place before the celebration of marriage and usually refer to the economic regime of marriage, which under the Spanish law can be freely decided by the contracting parties (by default it is community property). Matrimonial agreements may also extend to other issues as, for example, the religious upbringing of the offspring. However, if there is a later disagreement on aspects related to the children's education or welfare, prior agreements that are the consequence of a religious legal provision may be appealed to the civil jurisdiction. In any event, the civil efficacy of religious family law through matrimonial agreements is restricted by Article 1328 CC, which declares null and void 'any stipulation contrary to the law or accepted principles of morality, or limiting the equal rights of each spouse'.

562. The most significant aspects of parent-child relationships are regulated by Spanish civil law and do not leave room for the application of religious legal provisions, which, being at stake the rights of minors, cannot prevail over civil law provisions aimed at the protection of those rights. Something similar occurs with regard to inheritance rights. Religious law provisions can only be effective through their explicit acceptation by the testator, within the margin left by civil law to his discretion. It must be taken into account that Spanish law on succession, following the Roman law pattern, impose strict limitations on the testator's freedom to decide on the future destination of his properties.

563. Decisions of religious jurisdictions on family issues cannot acquire civil effects through arbitration, which under Spanish law is possible only with regard to 'conflicts about matters of free disposal in accordance to the law'.[765] Family law provisions, save for questions relating to the determination of the economic regime of marriage, are not disposable by the parties. However, nothing prevents the parties from submitting, by mutual consent, the issues concerning the termination of their marriage to a religious jurisdiction – not only with regard to the termination of the marriage as such, but also to the economic consequences thereof or questions connected with the custody and future care of the children. In any event, with the exception of the recognition of Catholic ecclesiastical decisions mentioned in the previous chapter, the judgments adopted by religious courts shall not have civil effects either as judicial

764. Matrimonial agreements (*capitulaciones matrimoniales*) are regulated in Arts 1325–1335 CC.
765. Article 1 of the *Ley* 60/2003, 23 Dec. 2003, *de Arbitraje*.

decisions or as arbitration awards. In such cases, religious courts could be considered as mediators from the perspective of Spanish law. Their decisions may have civil effects only if incorporated in the divorce agreement that the parties may reach and later submit to the civil judge for approval. And even in that case, the civil judge is not bound by the parties' agreement when he observes that it is 'harmful for the children or seriously prejudicial for one of the spouses'.[766]

766. Article 90 CC.

Part XI. Religion and Culture

Chapter 1. Religion and Art

564. The Constitution (Article 46) provides that 'public authorities shall guarantee the preservation and shall foster the enrichment of historical, cultural and artistic heritage of the peoples of Spain ... irrespective of its legal regime and ownership'. This obligation of the state, therefore, extends to *heritage of religious origin and ownership*, which in Spain is *almost entirely Catholic*. Articles 148–149 CE distribute this public responsibility between central and regional authorities.

565. As religious cultural heritage is often destined to worship, evangelization or other religious purposes, protection of religious freedom requires that in its preservation the state *harmonize its cultural value with its religious value* for the Catholic Church. This may sometimes raise difficult questions, as in a case decided by the Supreme Court in 2009, in relation to some works done in the cathedral of the city of Avila.[767] The diocese, after obtaining the appropriate administrative licences, carried out some remodelling works in the main chapel, with the aim of adapting its old structure to the norms of the Second Vatican Council and facilitating that the largest possible number of faithful could duly attend liturgical ceremonies and keep the altar in sight. Upon request of the Royal Academy of History, which argued that the remodelling could endanger the conservation of some old gravestones, the superior regional court ordered that the chapel be returned to its original condition. The Supreme Court confirmed the judgment with a reasoning that tried to reach a balance between the cultural and the religious values present in the cathedral. After examination of the expert evidence, the Court reached the conclusion that there were technical choices that permitted to make compatible the conservation of the endangered gravestones with the adaptation of the main chapel to the religious purposes legitimately pursued by the diocese; and in such situation, the regional court was right in ordering the removal of the remodelling works already realized. Had there been a situation of incompatibility of interests, the Supreme Court added, the liturgical use of a religious building would have prevailed over its secular use (understood as the citizens' right to contemplate the original funerary monuments).

767. STS 528/2009, 10 Feb. 2009. *See* , for a comment on this decision, S. Meseguer, *Hacia una nueva comprensión de la regulación estatal del patrimonio cultural eclesiástico*, 29 Revista General de Derecho Canónico y Derecho Eclesiástico del Estado 8–10 (2012).

566. Like the Constitution, the 1985 Law on Spanish Historical Heritage,[768] inspired by the intention to maintain and develop the Spanish heritage so that it can be known and enjoyed by the present and future generations, refers indiscriminately to movable and immovable property of cultural value, irrespective of its ownership or original purpose. This Law, however, contains a provision that addresses the specific situation of movables of particular value owned by ecclesiastical institutions – in particular, movables declared of 'cultural interest' and those others included in the General Inventory. According to Article 28.1 of the Law, such movable property neither can be transferred nor its use can be given to individuals or mercantile societies; it can only be transferred to the state, to entities of public law (such as universities or museums, for instance) or to other ecclesiastical institutions.

567. The Concordat with the Catholic Church refers to ecclesiastical heritage, in terms of mutual collaboration between Church and state, in the 1979 Agreement on Education and Cultural Affairs. After emphasizing in the preamble that ecclesiastical heritage constitutes an essential part of the national legacy, the Agreement (Article XV, first paragraph) embodies the compromise of mutual cooperation that must dominate the activity of church and state in this area:

> The Church reiterates its intention to continue placing its historical, artistic and documentary heritage at the service of society, and shall agree with the state the basis to make effective the common interest and collaboration of both parties, with the aim or preserving, making known and cataloguing the cultural heritage in possession of the Church, as well as facilitating its contemplation and study, achieving its better conservation and preventing all kinds of losses within the framework of Article 46 of the Constitution.

568. The first paragraph of Article XV has been sometimes criticized for its too general approach, as well as for the fact that it mentions specifically only the cultural side of ecclesiastical heritage but not its religious value, purposes and inspiration. In any event, the second paragraph of the same article envisaged the constitution, within a year, of a mixed church-state commission. That commission was created in 1980 and elaborated a legal framework for the joint activity of church and state in this area. The guidelines that defined such framework were, in summary, the following: the preferential religious use of ecclesiastical heritage must be respected; the religious use of ecclesiastical heritage must be harmonized with activities of scientific and artistic study; ecclesiastical heritage must be widely available for public visits but without detriment to its religious use and scientific study; and ecclesiastical heritage, as far as possible, shall be exhibited in their original location. These guidelines are supposed to be applied to all types of ecclesiastical heritage or historical, cultural and artistic value, including movable and immovable property, archives and documents, libraries and archaeological sites.

569. A large part of the church-state cooperation in the area of ecclesiastical heritage has taken place at a regional level (*comunidades autónomas*). Regional

768. *Ley* 16/1985, 25 Jun. 1985, *del Patrimonio Histórico Español*. This law was later developed by the *Real Decreto* 111/1986, 10 Jan. 1986, *de desarrollo parcial de la Ley 16/1985, de 25 de junio, del Patrimonio Histórico Español*, modified by the *Real Decreto* 64/1994, 21 Jan. 1994.

legislation and regulations are many and diverse but some common features are identifiable. First, the reference to future specific agreements. Second, the constitution of mixed commissions with members that represent regional authorities and the Catholic Church; these commissions are conceived as consultative bodies with limited decision-making power. Third, the interest in harmonizing the religious and the cultural aspects of ecclesiastical heritage. And fourth, the interest in fostering the collaboration with local authorities.[769]

570. Article 13 of the 1992 Agreements with the Jewish and Islamic communities also refer to the collaboration between state and the relevant federation in order to preserve, catalogue and make available to society Jewish and Islamic heritage, respectively, of historical, artistic and cultural value. This reference must be understood broadly, i.e., to heritage of Jewish and Islamic origin and nature, not necessarily ownership, for the largest part of the heritage that was originally Jewish or Islamic has become secularized or has passed to the Catholic Church in the course of time. As in the Concordat, it seems surprising that Article 13 of the Agreements only mentions the cultural value of Jewish and Islamic heritage but not its religious signification. It is interesting to note that no parallel article exists in the Agreement with the Evangelical Federation; the reason is that this federation declined it considering that there was not sufficient Protestant historical heritage in Spain to justify it. The 1992 Agreements with the Jewish and Islamic Federations did not envisage the creation of ad hoc mixed commissions. In contrast to the Spanish experience on Catholic ecclesiastical heritage, Article 13 of the 1992 Agreements has had virtually no further development.

571. Historical, artistic or cultural heritage of religious origin and ownership attracts many visitors all over Spain and is – directly and indirectly – a large source of income for the country within the tourism sector. This includes not only religious buildings but also many other artistic expressions, such as paintings, sculptures, codices, liturgical ornaments, music and religious celebrations (e.g., the Catholic processions during the Holy Week, above all in southern Spain and Castile). Festivals of religious music are more and more popular in Spanish cities. Christian music is naturally the main focus, but the music of traditional religious minorities is gradually gaining attention from the public. There is, for instance, an annual festival of Sephardic music held in Cordoba since 2001.

---

769. *See* , for instance, *Ley* 10/1998, 9 Jul. 1998, *de Patrimonio Histórico de la Comunidad de Madrid*; *Ley* 3/1999, 10 Mar. 1999, *del Patrimonio Cultural Aragonés*; *Ley* 4/1999, 15 Mar. 1999, *de Patrimonio Histórico de Canarias*; *Ley* 27/1999, 29 Mar. 1999, *de Patrimonio Histórico y Cultural de Extremadura*; *Ley* 7/2004, 18 Oct. 2004, *de Patrimonio Cultural, Histórico y Artístico de La Rioja*. For a complete guide of the laws and agreements on ecclesiastical heritage, *see* I. Aldanondo & C. Corral, *Nuevo código del patrimonio cultural de la Iglesia* (2nd ed., Edice 2013).

Chapter 2. Religion and Media

572. As explained in other part of this monograph, the Criminal Code imposes some limitations on freedom of expression for the protection of religious feelings as well as with the intention to eradicate hate speech.[770] Those limitations are conceived as means to protect religious and ideological pluralism by fostering religious tolerance and respect.

573. In line with those provisions, Article XIV of the 1979 Agreement on Education and Cultural Affairs between Spain and the Holy See provides: 'Safeguarding the principles of religious freedom and freedom of expression, the state shall ensure that the feelings of Catholics are respected in state-owned media, and shall establish the appropriate agreements with the Bishops Conference on this issue.' No subsequent agreement has been actually signed with the Bishops Conference in application of this provision of the Concordat. The 1992 Agreements with the Evangelical, Jewish and Islamic Federations contain no equivalent article.

574. Nevertheless, both the provisions of the Criminal Code and the Concordat provision are very seldom applied. Religion and religious communities are often in the media and not necessarily depicted in objective or merely informative terms. Frequently, information about religion is biased and based on an emotional view rather than on factual data. Strong criticism of religion or religions is not an exception, especially in privately owned media. When referred to Christianity, such critical language not rarely becomes blasphemous. Islam is often implicitly or subliminally associated with terrorism, violence or women's discrimination. Now and then, there are sensationalist campaigns or prejudiced information about atypical minority religions, usually qualified, indiscriminately, as 'sects'.

575. From a different perspective, the media provide some occasions for state cooperation with religion, in line with Article 16.3 CE. Spanish law and praxis grants religious communities right to access to state-owned media – radio and television, for there are not state-owned journals in Spain. Article 20.3 CE recognizes such right to access, in very general terms, for all 'significant' social and political groups, and not only for religious communities:

> Article 20.3 CE:
>
> The law shall regulate the organization and parliamentary control of the media that are under the authority of the state or of any other public entity, and shall guarantee the right to access to those media for significant social and political groups, with respect for the pluralism of society and for the various languages of Spain.

576. Article 28 of the 2006 Law on State-owned Radio and Television[771] applies those constitutional guidelines to the particular case of state radio and television

770. *See supra* , paras 482–484.
771. *Ley* 17/2006, 5 Jun. 2006, *de la radio y la televisión de titularidad estatal.*

(RTVE), also in general terms that replicate the language of Article 20.3 CE and envisage two possible ways of access to RTVE: one 'through the participation of significant social and political groups, as sources and channels of information and opinion, in RTVE programmes considered as a whole'; and the other 'through specific programmes in radio and television'. The same Article 28 emphasizes the need to guarantee, in RTVE programmes, 'the expression of the social, ideological, political and cultural plurality of Spanish society'. For the development of these principles, Article 28 remits to future ad hoc decisions to be adopted by the board of directors of RTVE. The development of this article has been very precise with respect to political parties, in particular concerning the time they will be assigned in programmes during electoral campaigns, but has remained very vague with reference to religious groups.

577. For instance, there is no specific definition of the concept 'significant group' as applied to religious communities. This term is often understood as applicable, at least, to all those communities that have been recognized 'well-known roots' (*notorio arraigo*) under Article 7.1 LOLR.[772] In practice, however, religious programmes have been granted in RTVE only to the Catholic Church and, with less time and programmes assigned, to the three religious federations signatory of the 1992 Agreements.[773] Thus, the practical recognition of Spanish religious pluralism from the perspective of state cooperation is restricted, once again, to those religious communities that have concluded a formal cooperation agreement with the state. The situation is rather similar in the norms that regulate the media owned and managed by the regions or *comunidades autónomas*, whose respective laws are also comparable to the law on RTVE in this aspect.[774]

578. While the Protestant, Jewish and Islamic Federations have a weekly programme each in RTVE (television and radio), the Catholic Church has several weekly programmes. They include the broadcast of the holy mass on Sundays. In addition, the big Catholic festivities in Christmas and the Holy Week have traditionally received a special treatment, which includes the broadcast of pontifical masses and other religious services from the Vatican.

579. The Catholic Bishops Conference has its own news agency[775] and controls several media, in the areas of radio, television and written press.[776] Of particular influence is its radio station COPE, which in the last years steadily ranks second in radio audience share in Spain. The Evangelical and Jewish Federations control one radio station each, with low audience share. In Spain, there is no prohibition or restriction of religious programming in radio and television. The only limitations on religious

772. *See supra*, paras 302 and 356–357.
773. The religious programmes in RTVE can be found in the relevant Internet pages: http://www.rtve.es/alacarta/programas/tve/religiosos/1/ (accessed 8 Dec. 2017) and http://www.rtve.es/alacarta/programas/rne/religiosos/1/ (accessed 8 Dec. 2017). *See also* http://www.conferenciaepiscopal.es/departamento-de-radio-y-tv/ (accessed 8 Dec. 2017).
774. *See* for further details and references J. Rossell, *El derecho de acceso de las minorías religiosas a los medios públicos de comunicación*, in *Medios de comunicación y pluralismo religioso* 127–150 (Consejo del Audiovisual de Cataluña 2010).
775. *See* http://www.agenciasic.es (accessed 8 Dec. 2017).
776. *See* http://www.conferenciaepiscopal.es/medios-comunicacion-participa-la-cee/ (accessed 15 Dec. 2017).

broadcasting are indirect, derived from the administrative general regulations of media using radio and television waves, which is a state-regulated and not a free market.

580. As in many Western countries, extraordinary events in the Catholic Church, such as the election of a new Pope, attract a great social attention and receive a wide coverage by public and private media – radio, television and written press.

Chapter 3. Religion and Civil Society

581. Being Spain a country of ancient Catholic tradition, social life is full of multifarious Christian symbols. The presence of the history of the Catholic religion in Spain is continuous and overwhelming. In addition to very visible Catholic temples even in small town or villages, representations of the crucifix, the Holy Virgin or many saints can be found everywhere and anywhere, in streets, public buildings, schools, roads, mountains, etc. Names of advocations of Jesus Christ, the Virgin or saints are given to towns, streets, schools, hospitals, etc. Usually all Spanish towns, and many public institutions (universities and their faculties, professional associations, etc.), have their own patron saint and celebrate publicly his or her festivity. Spain, as a nation, has a patron saint, Saint James, whose festivity (25 July) is a non-working day in several regions (it used to be a national public holiday until recently). Most often, newborn children are named in accordance with the Christian tradition. In some periods of the year, especially during the Holy Week and Christmas, and in specific festive days – such as Corpus Christi – religious processions, ceremonies and celebrations are held all over Spain, with the participation – sometimes very active – of the majority of the population.

582. Save for the few cases mentioned in other section of this monograph,[777] this visible and symbolic presence of Catholicism is commonly accepted as a normal part of Spanish social life, also by non-Christians or by people of atheistic or agnostic beliefs. To a lesser extent, there are also remnants of the historical presence of Islam and Judaism, more visible in southern Spain. For the rest, Spanish society is very secularized. Many people recognized themselves as Catholics[778] but live without a feeling of dependence on the Catholic Church's authorities and, leaving aside the acceptance – and sometimes veneration – of religious symbols, without strict compliance with religious rules, either moral or ritual.

583. Catholic institutions and their activities are deeply embedded in many and diverse aspects of Spanish social life. Indeed, numerous initiatives of the civil society have direct or indirect Catholic inspiration, especially in the areas of education, healthcare and charities. There are ecclesiastical orders or congregations that have traditionally focused their activity on these areas. Some associations that have worship as their main purpose, as fraternities constituted for the veneration of and the dissemination of the devotion to a sacred image in a temple (*hermandades* or *cofradías*), have a dimension of service to the community, for instance through pro bono work for disadvantaged people. A high number of NGOs are inspired by Catholic ideas and some of them are in close connection with the Catholic Church's authorities – Caritas is the best example, and is likely the most appreciated NGO in Spain. These NGOs can apply for the subsidies that the government distributes with the money collected through the 0.7% of income tax that taxpayers can destine to 'activities of social interest'.[779] There is normally a high social appreciation of the social work done by these institutions.

777. *See supra*, Part II, Ch. 2 §9 IV.
778. *See supra*, paras 12–14.
779. *See supra*, para. 490.

Chapter 4. Religion and Public Debate

584. Religion and issues of religious or moral consequence are frequent topics in public debate, in the political sphere as well as in the media. This area is permeated by a broad understanding of free speech. It is normally accepted that the public have the right to express their opinions on such issues and, correspondingly, religious leaders have the right to express their views on secular issues that they consider morally significant, including political questions or governmental initiatives. There are few exceptions to such common understanding of freedom of expression. Occasionally, there are some politicians – not many – that, while freely speaking about what religions should do or not do with regard to their internal lives, harshly criticize religious leaders when they speak about questions that, according to these politicians, are 'strictly secular' and therefore should be allegedly out of the reach of religious leadership. LGTB organizations have at times denounced Catholic bishops or pastors for their sermons on sexual morals, which they considered homophobic.[780]

585. A large part of the public debate about religion in Spain focuses on two topics: the presence and influence of Catholic religion and symbols in social life; and the visibility and alleged dangers of Islam. Citizens with deep religious and moral convictions participate frequently and intensively in public debate but normally without explicit reference to their religious identity or to religious arguments. Most of them adopt clear positions on issues of moral or religious significance using arguments rooted in secular reason.

586. Spanish Catholic bishops, individually or collectively through statements by the Bishops Conference, often intervene to remind the official doctrine of the Catholic Church or to provide doctrinal guidance to Catholic citizens apropos of issues or moral consequence in which there is not a univocal position of the Church. For instance, the Bishops Conference usually makes public statements before a general election. In the past, Spanish bishops have also spoken up strongly against the legalization of same-sex marriages in 2005, against the profile of a new mandatory school subject called 'education for citizenship' introduced in 2006, or against the liberalization of abortion in 2010.[781]

587. Minority religions' leaders tend to intervene much less in public debate, at least directly, except for issues that affect them directly, as has occurred especially with respect to some issues of interest for Muslims.[782] Among minority religions, Islam tends to play a more active role in public debate through some Internet sites.[783] These sites tend to focus almost exclusively on information and opinions directly relating to Islam but sometimes address other questions of broader moral relevance. The Jewish

---

780. *See* , for instance, *Auto* of 12 Jul. 2012 of the *Juzgado de Instrucción* nº 6 of Alcalá de Henares (diligencias previas nº 1368/12), confirmed in May 2014 by the *Audiencia Provincial* of Madrid, which declared inadmissible the legal suit brought against the bishop of Alcalá de Henares, accusing him of homophobia because of a sermon on Good Friday.
781. *See supra* the appropriate references in paras 390–391.
782. *See supra* , para. 392.
783. *See* , for instance, Webislam: http://www.webislam.com (accessed 8 Dec. 2017).

Federation is very active in denouncing and disseminating information about anti-Semitism.[784]

588. New religious movements, often called 'sects' by the general public, was a more or less popular subject in public debate and raised social concern years ago, but now it emerges only occasionally, when the media spread particularly shocking information about dramatic events in which some of these groups appear involved. It is likely a sign that Spanish society has got a better understanding of the meaning of religious pluralism.

784. *See* http://observatorioantisemitismo.fcje.org (accessed 8 Dec. 2017).

Selected Bibliography

§1. Specialized Journals

Anuario de Derecho Eclesiástico del Estado. Cuenca: Instituto para el Estudio de la Libertad Religiosa. Published since 1985 (in print).

Derecho y Religión. Madrid: Instituto Metodológico de Derecho Eclesiástico del Estado: Published since 2006 (in print and online).

Ius Canonicum. Pamplona: Instituto Martín de Azpilcueta, Universidad de Navarra. Published since 1961 (in print and on line).

Laicidad y Libertades: escritos jurídicos. Madrid: Asociación Derecho, Laicidad y Libertades. Published since 2000 (in print).

Revista Española de Derecho Canónico. (Salamanca: Universidad Pontificia de Salamanca. Published since 1946 (in print and online).

Revista General de Derecho Canónico y Derecho Eclesiástico del Estado. Madrid: Iustel <www.iustel.com>. Published since 2003 (online).

§2. Treatises, Textbooks and Other Comprehensive books

Ferrer Ortiz, J. (ed.). *Derecho Eclesiástico del Estado español.* 6th edn. Pamplona: Eunsa, 2007.

González del Valle, J.M. *Derecho Eclesiástico español.* 6th edn. Madrid: Civitas, 2005.

Ibán, I.C., A. Motilla & L. Prieto. *Manual de Derecho Eclesiástico.* 2nd edn. Madrid: Trotta, 2016.

Jusdado, M.A. (ed.). *Derecho Eclesiástico del Estado.* 2nd edn. Madrid: Colex, 2012.

Llamazares Fernández, D. (with the collaboration of Llamazares Calzadilla, M.C.). *Derecho de la libertad de conciencia.* 4th edn. Madrid: Civitas, 2011.

López Alarcón, M. & R. Navarro-Valls. *Curso de derecho matrimonial canónico y concordado.* 7th edn. Madrid: Tecnos, 2010.

Martí Sánchez, J. M. *La religión ante la ley. Manual de Derecho Eclesiástico.* Madrid: Digital Reasons, 2015.

Martín, M.M., Salido, M. & Vázquez García-Peñuela, J.M. *Derecho y Religión. Lecciones introductorias de derecho eclesiástico español.* 2nd edn. Granada: Comares, 2017.

Martín Sánchez, I. *Curso de Derecho Eclesiástico del Estado.* Valencia: Tirant lo Blanch, 1997.

Martínez-Torrón, J. *Religión, derecho y sociedad. Antiguos y nuevos planteamientos en el derecho eclesiástico del Estado.* Granada: Comares, 1999.

Navarro-Valls, R. & J. Martínez-Torrón (eds). *Base de conocimiento jurídico: Derecho Eclesiástico del Estado.* Madrid: Iustel <www.iustel.com>.

Navarro-Valls, R., J. Mantecón & J. Martínez-Torrón (eds). *La libertad religiosa y su regulación legal. La Ley Orgánica de Libertad Religiosa.* Madrid: Iustel, 2009.

Palomino Lozano, R. *Manual Breve de Derecho Eclesiástico del Estado.* 5th edn. Madrid: Universidad Complutense, 2017 (available in: http://eprints.ucm.es/40703/1/2017%20MBDEE%20%281%29.pdf)

Rodríguez Blanco, M. *Derecho y religión: nociones de derecho eclesiástico del Estado.* Madrid: Civitas, 2013.

Rodríguez García, J.A. *Derecho Eclesiástico del Estado: Unidades didácticas.* Madrid: Tecnos, 2015.

Souto, J.A. *El derecho de libertad de creencias.* Madrid: Marcial Pons, 2011.

Suárez Pertierra, G., Souto Galván, E., Ciáurriz Labiano, M.J., Regueiro García, M.T., Rodríguez Moya, A., Ariza Robles, A., Pérez Álvarez, S. & Pelayo Olmedo, D. *Derecho Eclesiástico del Estado.* 2nd edn. Valencia: Tirant Lo Blanch, 2016.

VV.AA. *Tratado de Derecho eclesiástico.* Pamplona: Eunsa, 1994.

§3. Monographic Books and Essays

Alberca de Castro, J.A. *Régimen jurídico del ministro de culto en España y Francia.* Granada: Comares, 1999.

Aldanondo, I. 'El Registro de Entidades religiosas'. *Anuario de Derecho Eclesiástico del Estado* 7 (1991): 13–48.

Aldanondo, I. 'El patrimonio cultural de las confesiones religiosas'. *Revista Catalana de Dret públic* 33 (2006): 149–179.

Aldanondo, I. & C. Corral. *Nuevo código del patrimonio cultural de la Iglesia.* 2nd edn. Madrid: Edice, 2017.

Alenda Salinas, M. *El Registro de Entidades Religiosas. La praxis administrativa tras la STC 46/2001.* Madrid: Iustel, 2009.

Selected Bibliography

Álvarez Cortina, A.C. & M. Rodríguez Blanco (eds). *La libertad religiosa en España. XXV años de vigencia de la Ley Orgánica 7/1980, de 5 de julio (comentarios a su articulado).* Granada: Comares, 2006.

Amorós, J.J. *La libertad religiosa en la Constitución española de 1978.* Madrid: Tecnos, 1984.

Areces Piñol, M.T. *El principio de laicidad en las jurisprudencias española y francesa.* Lleida: Edicions de la Universitat de Lleida, 2003.

Areces Piñol, M.T. 'Derecho a objetar en el ámbito educativo: educación para la ciudadanía. Resoluciones judiciales'. *Anuario de Derecho Eclesiástico del Estado* 25 (2009): 343–347.

Areces Piñol, M.T. *La prohibición del burka en Europa y en España.* Madrid: Dykinson, 2014.

Asensio Sánchez, M.A. *La patria potestad y la libertad de conciencia del menor. El interés del menor a la libre formación de su conciencia.* Madrid: Tecnos, 2006.

Beneyto Berenguer, R. *Régimen tributario de los bienes culturales de titularidad eclesiástica.* Valencia: Edicep, 2011.

Blanco, M. *Libertad religiosa, laicidad y cooperación en el derecho eclesiástico. Perspectiva actual del derecho pacticio español.* Granada: Comares, 2008.

Blanco, M. *La primera ley española de libertad religiosa: génesis de la Ley de 1967.* Pamplona: Eunsa, 1999.

Bonet Navarro, J. 'La celebración de festividades religiosas en los Acuerdos de cooperación de 1992'. *Revista Española de Derecho Canónico* 52 (1995): 293–306.

Borrero Arias, J. 'Fundamentos constitucionales del hecho religioso (a propósito de una publicación reciente). *Anuario de Derecho Eclesiástico del Estado* 28 (2012): 805–829.

Bravo, F. *La asistencia religiosa en las Fuerzas Armadas, derecho del militar creyente.* Salamaca: Universidad Pontificia de Salamanca, 2012.

Briones Martínez, I. 'La enseñanza religiosa evangélica en el ordenamiento jurídico español'. In *La enseñanza religiosa evangélica en la Comunidad Autónoma de Madrid*, edited by G. Moreno Botella & I. Martín Sánchez. Madrid: Colex, 2009, 53–82.

Briones Martínez, I. *El factor religioso y las autonomías.* Granada: Comares, 2011.

Bueno Salinas, S. 'Confesiones y entes confesionales en el derecho español'. *Anuario de Derecho Eclesiástico del Estado* 4 (1988): 107–134.

Bueno Salinas, S. & M.J. Gutiérrez del Moral. *Proselitismo religioso y derecho.* Granada: Comares, 2002.

Calvo Álvarez, J. *Los principios del derecho eclesiástico español en las sentencias del Tribunal Constitucional.* Pamplona: Navarra Gráfica Ediciones, 1999.

Camarero, V. *El velo integral y su respuesta en democracias europeas.* Valencia: Tirant Lo Blanch, 2012.

Cañamares Arribas, S. *El matrimonio canónico en la jurisprudencia civil* (Pamplona: Thomson-Aranzadi, 2003.

Cañamares Arribas, S. *Libertad religiosa, simbología y laicidad del Estado.* Pamplona: Thomson-Aranzadi, 2005.

Cañamares Arribas, S. 'Religious Symbols in Spain: A Legal Perspective'. *Ecclesiastical Law Journal* 11 (2009): 181–193.

Cañamares Arribas, S. 'Religious Freedom and Freedom of Expression in Spain'. *Religion & Human Rights* 9 (2014): 209–226.

Cañivano, M.A. *Las normas religiosas en el derecho español. La eficacia civil de los ordenamiento jurídicos de las confesiones religiosas (católica, musulmana, judía y protestante).* Barcelona: Bosch, 2005.

Capseta, J. *La cláusula de conciencia periodística.* Madrid: McGraw-Hill, 1998.

Castro Jover, A. 'Libertad religiosa y descanso semanal'. *Anuario de Derecho Eclesiástico del Estado* 6 (1990): 299–312.

Castro Jover, A. 'Asistencia sanitaria y libertad religiosa, un supuesto: la denegación de reintegro de gastos médicos a los testigos de Jehová'. In *Estudios jurídicos en homenaje al Profesor Vidal Guitarte*, edited by VV.AA. Castellón: Diputació de Castelló, 1999, 211–220.

Castro Jover, A. (ed.). *El derecho de la libertad de conciencia en la praxis jurisprudencial.* Pamplona: Universidad Pública de Navarra, 2005.

Catalá, S. *El derecho a la personalidad jurídica de las entidades religiosas.* Cuenca: Universidad de Castilla-La Mancha, 2004.

Cebriá García, M. *Objeciones de conciencia a intervenciones médicas. Doctrina y jurisprudencia.* Pamplona: Thomson-Aranzadi, 2005.

Cebriá García, M. 'La exención en el ICIO de la Iglesia Católica en el Estado español y la prohibición de ayudas de Estado del derecho de la Unión Europea', *Revista General de Derecho Canónico y Derecho Eclesiástico del Estado* 45 (2017): 1–21.

Ciáurriz, M.J. *La libertad religiosa en el derecho español. La Ley Orgánica de Libertad Religiosa.* Madrid: Tecnos, 1984.

Ciáurriz, M.J. 'La situación jurídica de las comunidades islámicas en España'. In *Los musulmanes en España. Libertad religiosa e identidad,* edited by A. Motilla. Madrid: Trotta, 2004, 23–64.

Combalía, Z. 'Inmigración y matrimonio en España'. In *Cuestiones actuales de derecho canónico y eclesiástico en el XXV aniversario de los acuerdos con la Santa Sede y XX aniversario de vigencia del CIC,* edited by R. Rodríguez Chacón & L. Ruano Espina. Salamanca: Universidad Pontificia de Salamanca, 2005, 283–302.

Selected Bibliography

Combalía, Z. *La contratación del profesorado de religion en la escuela pública.* Valencia: Tirant Lo Blanch, 2013.

Cubero Truyo, A. & R.J. Sanz Gómez. 'La declaración del IRPF como cauce de financiación de la Iglesia Católica (asignación voluntaria del 0,7 por 100 de la cuota íntegra)'. *Crónica Tributaria* 136 (2010): 85–102.

Cubillas Recio, L.M. 'Los acuerdos de cooperación y las demás técnicas de conexión interordenamientos'. In *Constitución, leyes de libertad religiosa, acuerdos, derecho común,* edited by VV.AA. León: Universidad de León, 2010, 101–142.

Cuenca Toribio, J.M. *Relaciones Iglesia-Estado en la España contemporánea (1833-1985).* 2nd edn. Madrid: Alhambra, 1989.

Díaz Moreno, J.M. 'Acuerdos Iglesia-Estado en España: notas marginales'. *Estudios Eclesiásticos* 54 (1979): 283–334.

Domingo, R. & Martínez-Torrón, J. (eds). *Great Christian Jurists in Spanish History.* Cambridge: Cambridge University Press, forthcoming in 2018.

Domingo Gutiérrez, M. 'La objeción de conciencia al aborto: evolución jurisprudencial'. *Revista General de Derecho Canónico y Derecho Eclesiástico del Estado* 23 (2010): 1–28.

Escrivá Ivars, J. 'La enseñanza de la 'religión y moral católicas' en el sistema educativo español'. *Anuario de Derecho Eclesiástico del Estado* 4 (1988): 205–240.

Escudero, J.A. *Estudios sobre la Inquisición.* Madrid: Marcial Pons, 2005.

Félix Ballesta, M.A. *Relaciones Iglesia-Estado en la España de 1919 a 1923, según el Archivo Secreto Vaticano.* Madrid: Dykinson, 2005.

Ferrari, S. (ed.). *Routledge Handbook on Law and Religion.* Abingdon: Routledge, 2015.

Ferrer Ortiz, J. 'Los principios constitucionales del derecho eclesiástico como sistema'. In *Las relaciones entre la Iglesia y el Estado: estudios en memoria del Profesor Pedro Lombardía,* edited by VV.AA. Madrid: Edersa, 1989, 309–322.

Ferreiro, J. *Protección jurídico-penal de la religión.* Coruña: servicio de publicaciones de la Universidad de La Coruña, 1998.

Ferreiro, J. *Relaciones Iglesia-Estado en la Segunda República Española.* Barcelona: Atelier, 2005.

Fornés, J. *El nuevo sistema concordatario español (Los Acuerdos de 1976 y 1979).* Pamplona: Eunsa, 1980.

García Gárate, A. 'Posición de los tribunales eclesiásticos en el ordenamiento español'. *Anuario de Derecho Eclesiástico del Estado* 4 (1988), 173–205.

García García, R. *La Comisión Asesora de Libertad Religiosa.* Madrid: Edisofer, 2003.

García García, R. (ed.). *La libertad religiosa en las comunidades autónomas. Veinticinco años de su regulación jurídica.* Barcelona: Institut d'Estudis Autonòmics, 2008.

García Oliva, J. 'Religious Freedom in Transition: Spain'. *Religion, State and Society* 36 (2008): 269–281.

García Oliva, J. 'The Controversy Surrounding the Teaching of Denominational Religion in Spain'. In *Law, Religious Freedoms and Education in Europe*, edited by M. Hunter-Henin. Aldershot: Ashgate, 2012, 183–205.

García-Pardo, D. *El sistema de acuerdos con las confesiones minoritarias en España e Italia.* Madrid: Centro de Estudios Políticos y Constitucionales, 1999.

García Villoslada, R. (ed.). *Historia de la Iglesia en España.* Madrid: BAC, 1979–1982.

Garcimartín, C. 'La laicidad de las Cortes Constituyentes de 1978'. *Ius Canonicum* 36 (1996): 539–594.

Garcimartín, C. *La personalidad jurídica civil de los entes eclesiásticos en el derecho español.* Barcelona: Cedex, 2000.

Garcimartín, C. 'Direct Financing of the Religious Denominations in Spain'. *Journal of Church and State* 48 (2006): 175–196.

Gas Aixendri, M. 'La declaración canónica de idoneidad para la enseñanza de la religión católica y su control jurisdiccional por parte del Estado'. *Revista General de Derecho Canónico y Derecho Eclesiástico del Estado* 29 (2012): 1–17.

Gas Aixendri, M. *Apostasía y libertad religiosa. Conceptualización jurídica del abandono confessional.* Granada: Comares, 2013.

González Armendia, J.R. *Sistemas históricos de dotación del Estado español a la Iglesia española: siglos XIX–XX.* Salamanca: Servicio de Publicaciones de la Universidad Pontificia de Salamanca, 1990.

González Moreno, B. *Estado de cultura, derechos culturales y libertad religiosa.* Madrid: Civitas, 2003.

González Moreno, B. 'El derecho fundamental a la protección de datos personales: su contenido y límites respecto al bautismo y la apostasía. *Revista General de Derecho Canónico y Derecho Eclesiástico del Estado* 19 (2009): 1–42.

González Sánchez, M. *Los ministros de culto en el ordenamiento jurídico español.* Madrid: Centro de Estudios Políticos y Constitucionales, 2003.

González-Varas, A. *Derecho y conciencia en las profesiones sanitarias.* Madrid: Dykinson, 2009.

González-Varas, A. 'Moral and Religious Teaching in Spanish Schools'. *Education Law Journal* 10 (2009): 271–279.

González-Varas, A. 'La educación para la ciudadanía: entre la objeción de conciencia y recursos contencioso-administrativos'. *Anuario de Derechos Humanos* 10 (2009): 331–388.

Selected Bibliography

Guardia Hernández, J.J. *Libertad religiosa y urbanismo: estudio de los equipamientos de uso religioso en España.* Pamplona: Eunsa, 2010.

Gutiérrez del Moral, M.J. & M.A. Cañivano. *El Estado frente a la libertad de religión: jurisprudencia constitucional española y del Tribunal Europeo de Derechos Humanos.* Barcelona: Atelier, 2002.

Gutiérrez del Moral, M.J. & S. Bueno Salinas. *Proselitismo religioso y derecho.* Granada: Comares, 2002.

de la Hera, A. *El regalismo borbónico en su proyección indiana.* Pamplona: Eunsa, 1963.

de la Hera, A. 'Actitud del Franquismo ante la Iglesia'. In *Iglesia Católica y regímenes autoritarios y democráticos*, edited by I.C. Ibán. Madrid: Edersa, 1987, 43–70.

de la Hera, A., R. Palomino & A. Motilla (eds). *El ejercicio de la libertad religiosa en España: cuestiones disputadas.* Madrid: Ministerio de Justicia, 2003.

Herrera Ceballos, E. *El Registro de Entidades Religiosas. Estudio global y sistemático.* Pamplona: Eunsa, 2012.

Jiménez-Aybar, I. *El Islam en España: aspectos institucionales de su estatuto jurídico.* Pamplona: Navarra Gráfica Ediciones, 2004.

Landete Casas, J. & J. Bonet Navarro. 'Aportaciones desde el Derecho Eclesiástico al concepto constitucional de orden público'. *Revista General de Derecho Canónico y Derecho Eclesiástico del Estado* 9 (2005): 1–16.

Llamazares, D. *Educación para la ciudadanía democrática y objeción de conciencia.* Madrid: Dykinson, 2008.

Lombardía, P. 'Actitud de la Iglesia ante el franquismo'. In *Iglesia Católica y regímenes autoritarios y democráticos*, edited by I.C. Ibán. Madrid: Edersa, 1987, 81–102.

López Alarcón, M. 'La función calificadora en el Registro de Entidades Religiosas'. *Anuario de Derecho Eclesiástico del Estado* 14 (1998): 459.

López Alarcón, M. 'La superación de la "cuestión religiosa" como tema clave de la transición: su expresión jurídica'.*Anales de Derecho* 23 (2005): 303–314.

López-Sidro, A. 'Las entidades religiosas como empleadoras de los profesores de religión en el proyecto de Ley Orgánica de Educación'. *Revista General de Derecho Canónico y Derecho Eclesiástico del Estado* 10 (2006): 1–21.

López-Sidro, A. 'La objeción de conciencia a la educación para la ciudadanía ante los Tribunales Superiores de Justicia'. *Revista General de Derecho Canónico y Derecho Eclesiástico del Estado* 17 (2008): 1–26.

López-Sidro, A. 'La objeción de conciencia de los jueces a los matrimonios entre personas del mismo sexo en la doctrina del Tribunal Supremo'. *Revista General de Derecho Canónico y Derecho Eclesiástico del Estado* 21 (2009): 1–18.

López-Sidro, A. 'El notorio arraigo de las confesiones religiosas en España a partir del Real Decreto que regula su declaración'. *Ius Canonicum* 55 (2015): 821–833.

Mantecón Sancho, J. (ed.). *Los acuerdos con las confesiones minoritarias. Diez años de vigencia.* Madrid: Ministerio de Justicia, 2003.

Mantecón Sancho, J. 'Islam in Spain'. In *The Legal Treatment of Islamic Minorities in Europe*, edited by R. Aluffi & G. Zincone. Leuven: Peeters, 2004, 213–231.

Mantecón Sancho, J. *El derecho fundamental de libertad religiosa: Textos, comentarios y bibliografía.* Pamplona: Eunsa, 1996.

Martí Sánchez, J.M., D. García-Pardo & S. Catalá. *El matrimonio religioso en el derecho español.* Albacete: Popular Libros, 2003.

Martí Sánchez, J.M. 'Balance de la libertad religiosa en España (situación de la mayoría católica)'. *Revista General de Derecho Canónico y Derecho Eclesiástico del Estado* 27 (2011): 1–34.

Martí Gilabert, F. *Política religiosa de la Segunda República española.* Pamplona: Eunsa, 1998.

Martín, M.M. *Las fundaciones religiosas en el derecho español.* Almería: Servicio de Publicaciones de la Universidad de Almería, 1995.

Martín Sánchez, I. *El derecho a la libre formación dela conciencia y su tutela penal.* Valencia: Tirant lo Blanch, 2000.

Martín Sánchez, I. *La recepción por el Tribunal Constitucional español de la jurisprudencia sobre el Convenio Europeo de Derechos Humanos respecto de las libertades de conciencia, religiosa y de enseñanza.* Granada: Comares, 2002.

Martín Sánchez, I. & M. González Sánchez (eds). *Los judíos en España: cuestiones del Acuerdo de cooperación con la FCJE de 1992.* Madrid: Delta, 2010.

Martín Sánchez, I. & J. Navarro Floria (eds). *La libertad religiosa en España y Argentina.* Madrid: Fundación Universitaria Española, 2006.

Martínez-Torrón, J. *Separatismo y cooperación en los acuerdos del Estado con las minorías religiosas.* Granada: Comares, 1994.

Martínez-Torrón, J. (ed.). *La libertad religiosa y de conciencia ante la justicia constitucional.* Granada: Comares, 1998.

Martínez-Torrón, J. *Religión, derecho y sociedad. Antiguos y nuevos planteamientos en el derecho eclesiástico del Estado.* Granada: Comares, 1999.

Martínez-Torrón, J. 'Derecho de asociación y confesiones religiosas en la Constitución de 1931'. *Cuestiones Constitucionales* 3 (2000): 91–120.

Martínez-Torrón, J. 'Freedom of Religion in the Case-Law of the Spanish Constitutional Court'. *Brigham Young University Law Review* (2001): 711–754.

Selected Bibliography

Martínez-Torrón, J. 'Concordato, cooperación e igualdad. La cooperación del Estado español con las confesiones religiosas a la luz del vigente sistema de acuerdos con la Iglesia católica'. *Revista General de Derecho Canónico y Derecho Eclesiástico del Estado* 4 (2004): 1–22.

Martínez-Torrón, J. 'School and Religion in Spain'. *Journal of Church and State* 47 (2005): 133–150.

Martínez-Torrón, J. 'Religious Freedom and Democratic Change in Spain'. *Brigham Young University Law Review* (2006): 777–809.

Martínez-Torrón, J. 'Institutional Religious Symbols, State Neutrality and Protection of Minorities in Europe'. *Law & Justice* 171 (2013): 21–51.

Martínez-Torrón, J. & Cañamares, S. (eds). *Tensiones entre libertad de expresión y libertad religiosa.* Valencia: Tirant Lo Blanch, 2014.

Martínez-Torrón, J. & Meseguer, S. 'The Atheist Bus Campaign and the Uncertain Future of Organized Atheism in Spain'. In *The Atheist Bus Campaign: Global Manifestations and Responses*, edited by S. Tomlins & S.C. Bullivant. Leiden: Brill, 2016, 286–310.

de Meer, F. *La cuestión religiosa en las Cortes Constituyentes de la II República española.* Pamplona: Eunsa, 1975.

Meseguer, S. 'El principio de cooperación y las donaciones a las confesiones religiosas'. *Revista Española de Derecho Canónico* 69 (2012): 757–779.

Meseguer, S. 'Hacia una nueva comprensión de la regulación estatal del patrimonio cultural eclesiástico'. *Revista General de Derecho Canónico y Derecho Eclesiástico del Estado* 29 (2012): 1–26.

Meseguer, S. *El sistema de financiación de la Iglesia Católica a Través de las exenciones fiscales.* Madrid: Universidad Complutense, 2000.

Meseguer, S., Cañamares, S. & Domingo, M. (eds), *Fuerzas armadas y factor religioso.* Cizur Menor: Aranzadi, 2015.

Meyerson, M.D. & E.D. English (eds). *Christians, Muslims, and Jews in Medieval and Early Modern Spain: Interaction and Cultural Change.* Notre Dame, Ind.: University of Notre Dame Press, 1999.

Minteguía, I. *Sentimientos religiosos, moral pública y libertad artística en la Constitución española de 1978.* Madrid: Dykinson, 2006.

del Moral García, A. 'Objeción de conciencia y vida humana dependiente'. *Anuario Jurídico Villanueva* 4 (2010): 93–130.

Morán García, G. 'The Spanish System on Church and State'. *Brigham Young University Law Review* (1995): 535–553.

Moreno Antón, M. 'El tratamiento urbanístico de los lugares de culto: a propósito del Proyecto de Ley de Cataluña sobre centros de culto o de reunión con fines religiosos'. *Revista General de Derecho Canónico y Derecho Eclesiástico del Estado* 17 (2008): 1–44.

Moreno Antón, M. *Multiculturalidad y libertad religiosa del menor de edad.* Madrid: Fundación Universitaria Española, 2007.

Moreno Botella, G. 'Libertad religiosa y neutralidad escolar. A propósito del crucifijo y de otros símbolos de carácter confesional'. *Revista Española de Derecho Canónico* 58 (2001): 173–218.

Moreno Botella, G. 'Autonomía de la Iglesia, profesorado de religión y constitucionalidad del Acuerdo sobre enseñanza de 3 de enero de 1979. A propósito de la STC 38/2007 de 15 de febrero'. *Revista General de Derecho Canónico y Derecho Eclesiástico del Estado* 14 (2007): 1–42.

Motilla, A. *El concepto de confesión religiosa en el derecho español.* Madrid: Centro de Estudios Políticos y Constitucionales, 1999.

Motilla, A. (ed.). *Los musulmanes en España. Libertad religiosa e identidad.* Madrid: Trotta, 2004.

Navarro-Valls, R. 'La enseñanza del derecho canónico en la jurisprudencia española'. *Anuario de Derecho Eclesiástico del Estado* 1 (1985): 49–92.

Navarro-Valls, R. 'La objeción de conciencia al aborto: derecho comparado y derecho español'. *Anuario de Derecho Eclesiástico del Estado* 2 (1986): 257–310.

Navarro-Valls, R. 'La objeción de conciencia a los matrimonios entre personas del mismo sexo'. *Revista General de Derecho Canónico y Derecho Eclesiástico del Estado* 9 (2005): 1–27.

Navarro-Valls, R. & J. Martínez-Torrón. *Conflictos entre conciencia y ley. Las objeciones de conciencia.* 2nd edn. Madrid: Iustel, 2012.

Olmos Ortega, M.E. 'La instrucción de la Conferencia Episcopal Española sobre la inscripción de asociaciones y fundaciones de la Iglesia Católica en el Registro de Entidades Religiosas. Texto y comentario'. *Revista Española de Derecho Canónico* 148 (2000): 213–226.

Olmos Ortega, M.E. 'Sociedad, Cultura y Religión: asignatura de doble configuración'. *Revista General de Derecho Canónico y Derecho Eclesiástico del Estado* 3 (2003): 1–16.

Olmos Ortega, M.E. 'El principio de cooperación entre los poderes públicos y las entidades religiosas'. In *Presente y futuro de la Constitución española de 1978,* edited by VV.AA. Valencia: Tirant lo Blanch, 2005, 595–610.

Orlandis, J. *La Iglesia en la España visigótica y medieval.* Eunsa: Pamplona, 1976.

Otaduy, J. 'Las cláusulas de salvaguarda de la identidad de las instituciones religiosas'. *Ius Canonicum* 27 (1987): 673–696.

Otaduy, J. 'Iglesia católica y Ley española de protección de datos: falsos conflictos'. *Ius Canonicum* 48 (2008): 117–140.

Palomino, R. *Derecho a la intimidad y religión: la protección jurídica del secreto religioso.* Granada: Comares, 1999.

Selected Bibliography

Palomino, R. 'El Acuerdo entre el Reino de España y la Santa Sede sobre asuntos de interés común en Tierra Santa. Una perspectiva histórico-jurídica, diez años después'. *Revista General de Derecho Canónico y Derecho Eclesiástico del Estado* 2 (2003): 1–50.

Palomino, R. 'El área de conocimiento "Sociedad, Cultura y Religión": algunos aspectos relacionados con la libertad religiosa y de creencias'. *Revista General de Derecho Canónico y Derecho Eclesiástico del Estado* 10 (2006): 1–27.

Palomino, R. *Religión y derecho comparado.* Madrid: Iustel, 2007.

Palomino, R. *Neutralidad del Estado y espacio público.* Cizur Menor: Aranzadi, 2014.

Prieto Álvarez, T. *Libertad religiosa y espacios públicos. Laicidad, pluralismo, símbolos.* Pamplona: Thomson-Civitas, 2010.

Payne, S.G. *Spanish Catholicism: An Historical Overview.* Madison: University of Wisconsin Press, 1984.

Pérez-Madrid, F. *Inmigración y libertad religiosa. Un estudio desde la Ley de Extranjería.* Madrid: Thomson-Civitas, 2004.

Pérez-Madrid, F. 'Protección de datos personales y apostasía'. *Revista General de Derecho Canónico y Derecho Eclesiástico del Estado* 19 (2009): 1–31.

Pérez-Madrid, F. 'Conflictos entre libertad religiosa y libertad de expresión en el nuevo código penal'. In *La libertad religiosa y de conciencia ante la justicia constitucional*, edited by J. Martínez-Torrón. Granada: Comares, 1998, 761–763.

Ramírez Navalón, R.M. (ed.). *Régimen económico y patrimonial de las confesiones religiosas.* Valencia: Tirant lo Blanch, 2010.

Reyna, V. & M.A. Félix Ballesta (eds). *Acuerdos del Estado español con confesiones religiosas minoritarias.* Barcelona: Marcial Pons, 1996.

Roca, M.J. 'La neutralidad del Estado: fundamento doctrinal y actual delimitación en la jurisprudencia'. *Revista Española de Derecho Constitucional* 16 (1996): 251–272.

Rodrigo Lara, B. *Minoría de edad y libertad de conciencia.* Madrid: Servicio de Publicaciones de la Facultad de Derecho de la Universidad Complutense, 2005.

Rodríguez Blanco, M. *Libertad religiosa y confesiones. El régimen jurídico de los lugares de culto.* Madrid: Centro de Estudios Políticos y Constitucionales, 2000.

Rodríguez Blanco, M. *Los convenios entre las administraciones públicas y las confesiones religiosas.* Pamplona: Navarra Gráfica Ediciones, 2003.

Rodríguez Blanco, M., *Régimen jurídico de cementerios y sepulturas.* Granada: Comares, 2015.

Rodríguez Chacón, R. *El factor religioso ante el Tribunal Constitucional.* Madrid: Servicio de Publicaciones de la Facultad de Derecho de la Universidad Complutense, 1992.

Rodríguez Chacón, R. 'Sentencias matrimoniales canónicas y Unión Europea'. *Revista General de Derecho Canónico y Derecho Eclesiástico del Estado* 7 (2005): 1–33.

Rodríguez García, J.A. *El control de los medios de comunicación.* Madrid: Dykinson, 1998.

Rodríguez Moya, A. 'Evolución y vigencia del principio de cooperación entre el Estado y las confesiones religiosas'. In *Derecho canónico en tiempos de cambio*, edited by J. Otaduy. Madrid: Dykinson, 2011, 109–124.

Rossell, J. 'Religious Denominations and the Media in Spain'. In *The Portrayal of Religion in Europe: The Media and the Arts*', edited by N. Doe. Leuven: Peeters, 2004, 231–258.

Rossell, J. 'El derecho de acceso de las minorías religiosas a los medios públicos de comunicación'. In VV.AA., *Medios de comunicación y pluralismo religioso.* Barcelona: Consejo del Audiovisual de Cataluña, 2010, 127–150.

Ruano Espina, L. *Derecho e Islam en España. Ius Canonicum* 53 (2003): 465–543.

Ruano Espina, L. *Régimen jurídico registral de los bienes de las confesiones religiosas y su tratamiento jurisprudencial.* Pamplona: Aranzadi, 2005.

Ruano Espina, L. 'Objeción de conciencia a la Educación para la Ciudadanía'. *Revista General de Derecho Canónico y Derecho Eclesiástico del Estado* 17 (2008): 1–61.

Ruano Espina, L. 'Las sentencias del Tribunal Supremo de 11 febrero 2009 sobre objeción de conciencia a EpC'. *Revista General de Derecho Canónico y Derecho Eclesiástico del Estado* 20 (2009): 1–60.

Sánchez-Lasheras, M. *Las negociaciones concordatarias y la transición política española (1972-1976). El Acuerdo de 28 de julio de 1976.* Granada: Comares, 2012.

Seglers, A. 'Religious Education in the Spanish School System'. *Journal of Church and State* 46 (2004): 561–573.

Seglers, A. *Libertad religiosa y Estado autonómico.* Granada: Comares, 2005.

Sieira, S. *La objeción de conciencia sanitaria.* Madrid: Dykinson, 2000.

Tarodo, S. 'Los recientes convenios de colaboración entre la Generalitat de Catalunya y algunas confesiones minoritarias'. *Laicidad y libertades: escritos jurídicos* 5 (2005): 353–388.

Tirapu, D. 'Notas sobre la posición jurídica de la Iglesia católica y las Confesiones en el Derecho español'. In *Las relaciones entre la Iglesia y el Estado. Estudios en memoria del profesor Pedro Lombardía*, edited by VV.AA. Madrid: Edersa, 1989, 391–402.

Tirapu, D. & J.M. Vázquez García-Peñuela. *La incapacidad sucesoria del confesor en el artículo 752 del Código Civil.* Granada: Comares, 1996.

Selected Bibliography

Tirapu, D. & J. Mantecón. 'La enseñanza de la religión en el sistema educativo público'. *Revista de la Facultad de Derecho de la Universidad de Granada* 17–20 (1989–1992): 128–144.

Tomás y Valiente, F. *El marco político de la desamortización en España.* Barcelona: Ariel, 1989.

Torres Gutiérrez, A. *Régimen fiscal de las confesiones religiosas en España.* Madrid: Colex, 2001.

Tusell, J. '*El impacto del Concilio Vaticano II en la política y en la sociedad española'*. In *El posconcilio en España*, edited by J.M. Laboa. Madrid: Encuentro, 1988, 377–390.

Valero, M.J. 'Homeschooling en España. Una reflexión acerca del artículo 27.3 de la Constitución y del derecho de los padres a elegir la educación de sus hijos'. *Revista General de Derecho Canónico y Derecho Eclesiástico del Estado* 28 (2012): 1–32.

Vega Gutiérrez, A.M. 'Balance del nuevo sistema de financiación de la Iglesia Católica en España'. In *El sostenimiento económico de la Iglesia Católica en España: nuevo modelo*, edited by J. Otaduy & D. Zalbidea. Pamplona: Eunsa, 2008, 173–188.

Vega Gutiérrez, A.M., et al. (eds). *Protección del patrimonio cultural de interés religioso* Granada: Comares, 2012.

Viladrich, P.J. 'Los principios informadores del Derecho eclesiástico español'. In *Derecho eclesiástico del estado español*, 1st edn. edited by VV.AA. Pamplona: Eunsa, 1980, 211–317.

Viladrich, P.J. 'Ateísmo y libertad religiosa en la Constitución española'. *Ius Canonicum* 22 (1982): 31–86.

VV.AA. *Comisión Asesora de Libertad Religiosa: realidad y futuro.* Madrid: Ministerio de Justicia, 2009, 69–121.

Index

The numbers here refer to paragraph numbers.

Abortion, 166, 176, 296, 390, 394, 442–450, 586.
Advisory Commission on Religious Freedom, 66, 73, 269, 278, 291–296, 299, 301, 303, 324, 356, 389, 402, 406
Agreements with religious denominations (for the Catholic Church, *see also Concordat*), 17, 53, 65–66, 70–73, 81, 88, 90–91, 100, 106, 119, 133–134, 171, 180, 182–183, 224–228, 269–272, 275, 277, 287–289, 295, 300–304, 312–315, 325–329, 346, 354–360, 363–368, 374–376, 386–387, 398–401, 409, 413–414, 422, 428, 435, 439, 487, 492, 494–497, 502, 504–506, 510, 525–529, 543–545, 556–558, 570, 573, 577
America, 2, 25–27, 31–35
Apostasy, 114, 424–425
Archives, 315, 422, 425–426, 568
Army, 46, 68, 73, 98, 132, 168, 170–175, 344, 351, 364–368, 398, 404
Associations, 37, 60, 64, 259, 266–267, 271, 274–275, 286–290, 305, 309–310, 380, 480, 483–484, 534, 583
Atheism, 12, 111, 214, 258–259, 531, 582

Baptism, 15, 114, 298, 425–426
Baptists, 100, 375–376
Benefit of clergy, 43, 344, 435
Bishop, 19, 27, 35–36, 40–41, 43, 69, 292, 302, 344, 351, 353, 364, 378–379, 389–393, 398, 416–421, 425–426, 434–435, 474, 500, 513–516, 530, 584–586
Bishops Conference, 192, 266, 290, 298–299, 353, 365, 390–391, 422, 490, 500, 513–518, 573, 579, 585
Blasphemy, 477
Buddhism, 17, 292, 302, 357, 405
Burka, 206, 208–212, 388

Catholic Church, Catholic institutions, Catholics, 12–43, 46–48, 65, 67–70, 72–73, 81, 85–86, 90, 95–99, 114, 116, 118–119, 125, 171, 188, 190, 203, 215, 220, 240, 266, 272, 274–275, 277, 287–290, 292, 298–299, 301, 308, 312–313, 315, 322–329, 333, 335, 341–354, 364–368, 374–378, 386, 389–395, 398, 401–405, 409, 412–414, 416–422, 424–426, 428, 430–431, 434–442, 449, 474, 477, 485, 488–491, 493–501, 504, 506, 509–528, 530–531, 538–540, 544–555, 563–571, 573, 577–583, 585–586
Catholic Monarchs, 25
Cemeteries, 119, 311, 313–314, 321, 388, 481
Chaplaincies, 98, 299, 301, 364–368, 503, 506
Charitable institutions, charities, 16, 35, 60, 65, 69, 73, 88, 120, 290, 348, 361, 497–498, 501, 583
Charter of Fundamental Rights of the European Union, 74, 102, 150, 161, 179, 380–383
Children, 14–15, 51, 102, 123, 148–153, 179–180, 184–199, 215, 217, 350, 370–372, 382, 391, 417, 421, 462–468, 508, 509–538, 561–563, 581
Children of God, 152, 186
Christmas, 15, 216, 395, 404, 578, 581
Church of Jesus Christ of Latter-Day Saints, 17, 292, 302, 357, 405, 526
Civil disobedience, 155
Civil service, *see public service*

Index

Clergy, 16, 37, 43, 68–69, 72, 171, 240, 298–299, 341, 344, 348, 351, 353, 364, 408–414, 420, 435, 438–441, 488, 501, 517,
Clergy-communicant privilege, 72, 344, 438–441
Coercion, 60, 93, 96, 107, 109, 111–112, 115, 141, 221, 254, 319, 339, 391, 397, 479–480, 483–484, 574
Concordat, 35, 40, 42–43, 53, 65, 67–70, 72, 90, 97, 106, 171, 266, 289, 295, 298, 312, 315, 325, 329, 342–355, 358, 364–365, 374–375, 401, 412, 416, 419, 425–426, 430, 435, 439, 488–489, 495–505, 512–513, 519–521, 524–525, 529, 544–552, 558, 567, 570, 573–574
Confessional state, confessionality, 34, 40, 46, 48, 82, 86, 116, 342–343, 477, 539
Confidentiality, 422–424, 438–441
Conscientious objection, 50, 52, 102, 123, 126, 130, 137, 150, 154–251, 381, 390, 442–472
Cooperation of the state with religion, 17, 35, 37, 46–47, 53, 63, 65–66, 69–73, 75, 78, 80–81, 85–91, 94, 100, 119, 120–121, 131–134, 182, 225, 228, 256–260, 265–272, 275, 280, 287, 294–305, 327, 329, 335, 342–362, 376–377, 386, 396, 399–400, 414, 421, 428, 439, 486–508, 510, 512, 525–526, 529, 544, 567–570, 575, 577
Criminal law, 73, 98, 136, 140–141, 257, 268, 304, 318–321, 337–338, 432, 477–485, 572, 574
Criminal liability, 147–148, 152, 185–186, 247, 279, 344, 435, 439–440, 460, 465–468
Crucifix, 215, 217, 404, 531, 581
Custody, 60, 123, 149–153, 461, 463–464, 563

Data protection, 114, 422–426
Dietary rules, 131–134, 358–359
Discrimination, *see equality*
Divorce, 14, 151–153, 390, 418, 421, 431, 463, 540, 550–551, 554–555, 563
Donation, 298, 349, 352, 504–505, 535
Due process, 435–437

Ecclesiastical jurisdiction, *see religious jurisdiction*
Education, 35, 50–51, 60, 68, 73, 88, 102–103, 112, 123, 148, 150, 153, 179–205, 215, 217, 295, 308, 331, 350, 370, 372, 382, 390–391, 409, 415–421, 449, 494, 498, 504, 506, 508–538, 561, 567, 573, 583, 585
Elections, 8, 245–247, 391, 393, 406, 585
Employer, employees, *see labour relations*
Equality, 6, 21, 24, 47–48, 53, 59–60, 64–66, 70–71, 73, 75, 78–82, 84–85, 88–89, 95, 98, 100, 105–106, 109, 116, 119, 124–126, 141, 153, 155, 162, 191, 211–212, 222–224, 227, 232, 238, 259, 267, 297, 303, 308, 322, 324, 335, 340, 354, 370, 372, 375–377, 383–384, 415, 421, 423, 427, 445, 463–464, 469–475, 477, 480, 483–484, 493–495, 509, 513, 524, 537, 561, 574
Expropriation, 325
European Convention on Human Rights, 6, 44, 49, 51, 61, 76, 102–103, 113, 122, 128, 139, 143–148, 150, 180, 194, 196, 215, 239, 252–255, 260, 332, 338, 372–379, 473, 420–421, 436, 493
European Union, 74, 102, 150, 161, 179, 222–223, 227, 352, 380–384, 489, 499, 555
Evangelical, 17, 27–28, 30, 33, 36, 72–73, 81, 90, 98, 106, 119, 171, 180–182, 224–226, 272, 274, 277, 289, 292, 300–301, 314–315, 324–329, 357–360, 366–368, 375–379, 399, 401, 405, 413, 422, 428, 439, 492–498, 502, 504, 506, 510, 526–528, 544, 556–559, 570, 573, 578–579

Family, 179, 185, 193, 377, 390–391, 412, 420–421, 424, 457, 483–484, 539–563
Financing, 78, 299, 365, 368, 401, 486-507, 512-513, 527, 535-538, 583
Forum internum, 93, 108, 194
Foundations, 64, 259, 266, 271, 274-275, 286-290, 309-310, 480, 496-497, 535

Index

Foundation *Pluralismo y Convivencia*, 401, 405, 494
Franco, 39–43, 46, 55, 67, 342–344, 393, 435, 540
Freedom of assembly, 50, 333
Freedom of association, 50, 143, 334
Freedom of religion, ideology or belief, 21, 37–38, 41–42, 46–47, 54–74, 75–80, 83–86, 93–98, 101–296, 297, 299–300, 304–306, 308, 311, 318, 324, 327, 330–333, 338, 343, 346, 369–374, 381–382, 385–388, 396, 400–402, 421, 424, 473, 475, 477–486, 488, 506–507, 512, 541–542, 565, 573
Freedom of conscience, 37, 73, 77, 79, 102–103, 118, 126–132, 141, 151, 154–251, 318, 370–374, 381, 404, 430, 442–472, 478, 508, 537
Freedom of expression, 50, 115, 148, 332, 432–434, 482–484, 572–580
Fundamental rights, 6, 41, 49, 51, 54–55, 60, 61, 74, 104, 135–138, 143–144, 147, 168, 211–213, 238, 253, 330–341, 369, 380, 385, 421, 432, 473, 478, 532

Hate speech, 337–338, 432, 483–484, 572
Health, 61, 103, 119, 132, 143–144, 148, 153, 166, 173, 176–178, 193, 260–263, 324, 365, 411, 442–472, 480, 504, 583
Heritage, 4, 350, 358–359, 386, 564–571
Heterodoxy, 113, 255, 433
Hijab, 201, 203–204, 206–207
Holy days, *see religious festivities*
Holy *See*, 40–43, 53, 67–69, 106, 294, 298, 313, 325, 342–353, 355, 364, 378, 398, 403, 420, 422, 435, 489, 497, 499–500, 512, 524, 565, 573, 578
Holy Virgin, 96, 118, 220–221, 404, 581
Holy Week, 15, 96, 118, 220, 333, 404, 571, 578, 581
Homeschooling, 184–186
Hospitals, 35, 60, 69, 73, 120–121, 148, 176, 298–299, 348, 353, 359, 361–368, 409, 415, 443, 445, 465–472, 503, 506, 581

Immigrants, 2, 3, 17, 280
Indoctrination, 78, 112, 123, 190–199, 390, 531
Inquisition, 28–31
International Covenant on Civil and Political Rights, 49, 103, 128, 370
International Covenant on Economic, Social and Cultural Rights, 103, 370
International law and standards, 6, 32, 38, 44, 49, 68, 70, 74, 76–77, 103–105, 128, 143–144, 179, 191, 199, 253, 268, 294, 298, 330, 346, 355, 369–379, 403, 476, 489, 499, 520, 545, 549, 558
Intolerance, 21, 30, 40–41, 191, 218
Inviolability, 313, 315–321, 348, 422, 425–426, 438, 481
Islam, 4, 13, 15, 17, 20–26, 28, 40, 72–73, 81, 90, 98, 106, 119, 133, 171, 180–183, 200–212, 224–226, 232, 272, 277, 289, 292, 299–301, 314–315, 323, 325–329, 341, 357–360, 366–368, 392, 399, 401, 405, 413, 422, 428, 439, 492–498, 502, 504–506, 510, 526–528, 544–545, 556–559, 570, 573–574, 578, 582, 587

Jehovah's Witnesses, 17, 79, 147–148, 151, 153, 240, 246–247, 264, 292, 302, 357, 405, 414, 442, 456, 459–472
Jewish, 17, 22–26, 33, 40, 72–73, 81, 98, 106, 119, 134, 171, 180–183, 213, 224–228, 272, 277, 289, 292, 300–301, 314–315, 325–326, 329, 358–359, 366–368, 399, 401, 405, 413, 422, 428, 431, 439, 492–498, 502, 504, 510, 526, 544–545, 556–559, 570–571, 573, 578–579, 587
Judicial protection of religious freedom, 62, 135–139, 336
Jury, 240–244

Labour relations, 10, 59, 119, 136, 148, 212, 222–232, 340–341, 383, 404, 407–421, 473–474, 480, 517
Legal personality, 51, 63, 71, 254, 256, 265–290, 298–299, 330–331, 348, 355, 385, 400, 403, 532, 538
Limitations on religious freedom, 47, 61–62, 103, 108, 142–148, 168, 205, 211–212,

239, 247, 260–262, 267, 338, 374, 388, 460, 579

Marriage, 14, 50, 53, 73, 80, 98–99, 116, 119, 248–251, 269, 295, 299, 301, 303–304, 348, 359, 378, 390, 394–395, 400, 420–421, 427–431, 436–437, 476, 539–563, 585
Media, 332, 350, 390, 572–580, 584, 588
Medical treatment, 151, 178, 455–472
Middle Ages, 18–24
Military, 50, 52, 60, 68–69, 79, 96, 98, 118, 120–121, 133, 137, 165, 167–175, 220, 237, 299, 351, 359, 361–368, 503, 506
Military service, 50, 52, 79, 137, 165, 167–175, 351
Ministry of Justice, 9, 63, 65–66, 71, 116, 173, 266, 268–269, 273, 278, 280, 290–292, 294–295, 299, 301–302, 334, 356, 387, 396, 494, 550, 556
Minorities, 2, 15, 53, 81, 162, 191, 240, 287, 294, 314, 392, 399, 402, 491, 494, 544, 571, 574, 587
Minors, 13, 60, 112, 123, 147, 149–153, 179–180, 189–199, 217, 451, 458, 461, 462–468, 550, 562–563
Morals, 16, 61, 103, 112, 143–144, 148, 198, 252, 260–264, 281–283, 390, 538
Mormon Church, *see Church of Jesus Christ of Latter-Day Saints*
Muslims, *see Islam*

National-Catholicism, 40
Neutral laws, 126, 130, 154, 159, 162, 200
Neutrality of the state (on religious matters), 47, 75, 78, 82–86, 89, 94–99, 118, 188, 197, 201, 214–221, 284, 341, 378, 418, 420, 476, 494, 531
Niqab, 206, 208–212, 388
Non-profit, 65, 73, 88, 100, 259, 496–497, 504–505
Notorio arraigo, see well-known roots
Nunciature, 298, 344, 352, 398, 403, 489

Oath, 233–239, 373, 404
Ombudsman (*Defensor del Pueblo*), 137, 172
Orthodox Churches, 17, 274, 292, 302, 357, 395, 405, 414
OSCE, 105, 306, 311, 370–371

Parents, 14–15, 51, 102–103, 112, 123, 147, 149–153, 179–199, 203, 215, 350, 370, 372, 382, 391, 415, 417, 421, 462–468, 508, 510, 512–513, 520, 526, 529, 531, 535–536, 560–563
Penitentiaries, 60, 69, 73, 120–121, 132–134, 298–299, 301, 348, 353, 359–368, 503, 506
Pharmacist, 177, 451–454
Places of worship, 60, 119, 256, 306, 311–329, 348, 359, 375, 388, 481, 500–502
Photograph, 206–207
Political parties, 45, 238, 391–394, 576
Polling station, 245–247
Pope, 28, 30, 37, 344, 395, 398, 403, 421, 437, 546, 551–552, 554, 578, 580
Privacy, 317, 340, 378, 420–426, 438–441, 473
Profanation, 320–321, 481
Property, 36, 37, 290, 322, 325–329, 333, 349, 375, 488, 499–502, 505, 566, 568
Proselytism, 30, 122, 153, 256, 297, 338, 479, 531
Protestant, *see Evangelical*
Public order, 47, 61, 103, 108, 142–144, 204, 211, 239, 247, 252, 260–264, 283, 333, 373, 552, 557
Public service, public office, 59, 79, 116, 119, 124, 177, 183, 207, 233–251, 330, 394, 404–406, 452, 480, 507, 517

Ramadan, 133, 225–226
Regalism, 35–36
Registry of Religious Entities, 63–65, 71–72, 257, 261–262, 265–271, 270, 273–290, 294, 299, 304–305, 307–309, 319–320, 334, 356, 387, 400, 487, 497, 547
Religion teachers, 97, 298, 308, 350, 353, 360, 378, 409, 416–421, 424, 434, 506, 513–517, 522–523, 526–527, 529
Religious assistance, 60, 68–69, 72–73, 98, 120–121, 290, 296, 298, 301, 304, 314,

329, 348, 351, 353, 359–368, 408–409, 438–441, 506
Religious autonomy, 64, 69, 72, 84–85, 89, 97, 113–114, 123, 255–256, 259, 267–268, 304, 306–310, 330, 340–341, 343, 348, 378, 397, 401, 407, 418–422, 425–426, 431, 433–434, 436–437, 473–476, 514–516
Religious education, 51, 60, 102–103, 150, 331, 350, 370, 372, 382, 391, 417–421, 509–530
Religious feelings, 73, 141, 318, 320, 350, 478, 482, 572–573
Religious festivities, 15, 60, 119, 181–183, 224–228, 359, 405, 571, 578, 581
Religious jurisdiction, 98, 430–431, 435–437, 540, 545–546, 552–555, 559–563
Religious ministers, 60, 171, 256, 290, 292, 297, 301, 303, 306, 351, 359, 362–368, 377, 397, 406–415, 435, 438–441, 498, 500, 502–503, 557
Religious symbols, 96, 200–221, 389, 392, 395, 531, 581–582
Romans, 4, 18–19

Sabbath rest, 72, 88, 119, 148, 180–183, 225–231, 359
Safety, 61, 103, 143–144, 216, 220, 252, 262, 324
School, 37, 60, 73, 80, 97, 99, 112, 118, 123, 131, 133, 152, 179–205, 215–216, 269, 290, 298–299, 301, 303, 308, 331, 341, 350, 353, 359–360, 378, 390, 392, 402, 409–410, 415–421, 424, 434, 449, 474, 506–538, 581, 585
Scientology, 264, 282, 285
Second Republic, 34, 37–39, 48, 342, 354, 540
Sects, 122, 152–153, 263, 283, 339, 378
Security, 37, 122, 206, 211, 367
Seventh-Day Adventist Church, 148, 181, 225–226, 229–231
Social security, 298–299, 301, 303, 353, 376, 411–414

Taxes
Tax assignment system, 100, 298, 352, 375, 489–490, 492–493, 499
Tax benefits, 37, 65, 73, 100, 267, 301, 303, 329, 349, 359, 374–375, 401, 486, 491–505, 583

Unequal treatment, *see discrimination*
Unification Church, 261–264, 282–283
Universal Declaration of Human Rights, 6, 77, 103, 128, 179, 283, 369
Urban planning, 322–324, 388

Vatican, *see Holy See*
Violence, *see coercion*
Visigoths, 4, 19–20, 22
Visitation rights, 153

Well-known roots, 65–66, 71, 90, 269–270, 292, 295, 299, 356–357, 402, 487, 494–494, 544, 577
Women, 53, 206–212, 341, 392, 427, 446–447, 476, 516, 550, 557, 574
Worship, 37, 40, 47–48, 59–61, 69, 101–103, 108, 111, 117–119, 127, 142, 224, 252–258, 281, 289–290, 297, 305–306, 311–329, 348, 359, 362, 364, 374, 381, 388, 404, 408–409, 479, 481, 499–502, 565, 583

www.ingramcontent.com/pod-product-compliance
Ingram Content Group UK Ltd.
Pitfield, Milton Keynes, MK11 3LW, UK
UKHW020136290926
15471UKWH00003B/528